DR ALHASAN KUNSA CEEASY
BADIBOU FOLKLORE

BY

DR. ALHASAN SISAWO CEESAY, MD

© 2014 by Dr. Alhasan Sisawo Ceesay, MD
All rights reserved. No part from this book may be reproduced in any form without written permission from the publisher, except by a reviewer who may quote passages in a review to be printed in a newspaper or magazine.

FIRST PRINTING

PUBLISH KUNSA.COM

ISBN 978-1-910117-16-3

INSCRIBE TO

My parents, wife and children, Teachers, Friends, Friends of Manding Charitable Trust, Colchester, UK and Alpena, Michigan, USA; and the downtrodden

Education and hard work are key to success.
DR. Alhasan S. Ceesay, MD

PREFACE AND ACKNOWLEDGMENT

Our will is that phenomenal force within us that is never deflected by challenge coming our way. We frequently hear opponents saying, "Put your purse where your mouth is." This is a grudging way of goring our will to spate or vacillates.

Hence, this work is about way a simple but penniless human being fought against the odds and mountains of inhuman laws at many crossroads of his life. It portrays struggle to be above treacherous waves while clamoring to bring rewarding health service to Gambian villagers.

Being most of the time jobless and penniless made it all look like an Alice in wonderland fairy tale adventure. The turbulent waves commenced in 1953 when I made up my mind to become part of the solution to rural Gambia's health service delivery shortage.

Even though young I was fully aware that no one could serve our people better other than indigenous Gambians. This belief propelled me into similar trip or experience Simbad the sailor or Marco Polo went through.

Most of the trials and tribulation I encountered have already been revealed in previous works of mine. Brace yourself and take heart to read about life of Dr. Alhasan S. Ceesay aka Dr. Alhasan Kunsa Ceesay before you.

Allow me express profound gratitude and many thanks to the numerous friends and my family who stood by me through thick and thin of this sojourn to bring health delivery service golden flees to the door steps of the villager.

Last but not the least, I am equally indebted and profoundly grateful to the Friends of Manding Medical Centre at Colchester, Uk and Alpena, Michigan, USA; the Diocese of Michigan who believed in my dreams of a modern medical service for the villagers. I wish all my friends were like them. God bless their hearts. Finally, many more thanks to my wife aaand children for persevering with me through this audius jouney to bring medical aid to villagers. I write to raise funds for building of the hospital at the Manding Medical centre Njawara, lower Badibou, NR, the Gambia, West Africa. Purchasing this book or donating cash or kind would help boost our goal for the people. I hope you will be inspired to join our effort to bring jmuch needed healthcare serffvice to villagers, especially children who frequently die rfrom malaria and childhood diseas from lack of facilities and or trained personnel. Proceeds from the work go to support Manding Medical Centre at Njawara Village, Gambia and provision of Scholarships for medicine and agriculture.

Dr. Alhasan Sisawo Ceesay MD

A MIRACLE BIRTH

In any human family the arrival of a new baby is rejoicing. My twin partner and I were born in wee hours of February 1946 at Njawara village, Lower Badbou District, North Division, the Gambia, West Africa. Mystery shrouding my birth was that the elderly villager assisting in the birth declared me a stillbirth and I was dumped at the back of the hut to be buried the following morning.

Legend has it that I cried so loud by dawn that, Binta Ceesay, my elder sister, came to my rescue and took me back indoors to be reunited with mum.

The incident was treated a hush, hush matter as most came to believe that I rose from the dead. Rather I believe that my being poorly covered, additionally that because of mosquitoes having a banqueting feast of me and fact of the cold air reaching my lungs made me let go my first fighting blows or struggle for dear life and my survival.

Yes, my life had been introduced to plasmodium Malaria, one of the most killer diseases of the developing countries at my very first day. From that day to today life has been an uphill battle in which I have to fight hard not only for survival but to have things happen for me.

My torturous life has an ancient pedigree which started with loss of my twin brother from treacherous measles followed by divorce our parents went through.

The divorce left me an orphan for mum moved back to her home village Njaba Kunda and remarried a year later. Dad in his unforgiving anger at mum hated the sight of his sibling with her. So he sort of banished my elder brother, Dudou Ceesay, to a madrasa at Ker Cherno in Nuimi, the Gambia.

My sister Binta Ceesay married under duress to one Sambujang Dibba of Salikenye village and they moved to the capital Bathurst, now Banjul. I stayed with a bitter father that pulled out all the stunts of spite upon me.

Dudou spent twenty one years at the Ker cherno in a semi slave-like life because father would not let him visit. It would take the intervention of friends and the Madrasa before Dudou was allowed back home in Njawara.

As for me I was given to cherno Ebrahima Jallow from Labe region of Guinea Conakry but stay most of the year as our guest. I became his Almudo in 1952 and together we the almudo travel bare feet to Senegal and neighbouring countries.

As small as I was I was made to carry heave load of either box of slates or bags on my head to any of our destinations. After one year of this travelling slavery with no education or future in sight with the bully boys madarasa subjecting me to constant harashment caused me to run back to Njaba Kunda to join mum.

This phase of my life lasted very short. While at Njaba Kunda in 1952 I was subjected to further harassment and relegated to being orphan by other wives of mum's new husband. These made it so hard I took chance and walked from Njaba kunda to Njawara, a distance of 12 km full of hyenas and leopards on the way. The intervening Dobo Forest was at the time lush and thick wooded harbouring giant snakes that swallow sheep and two year old cows.

I walked through thick canopy avoiding crawling insects and snake until reaching the village of Ker Ardo. At the out scats of which I ran into a Shepard who was alerted by barking dogs. He was a tall six footer Fulani Shepard called Jarga Wuri Bah, who stopped me and asks for my name, why I was walking in such dangerous bush that late and where was I heading.

Below is that conversation or call ker Ardo inquisition of Alhasan Kunsa Ceesay. The Shepard or inquisitor's name was Jarga Wuri Bah. It went thus:

Jarga: "Hey, young man. What is your name and were are you heading this late at night?

Alhasan; I am Alhasan Kunsa Ceesay and Sisawo Ceesay at Njawara is my dad. I no longer could stay with mum because of her co mates. They have been very bad toward my mum and I. I want to rejoin my dad at the next village.

Jarga: You must be very brave walking these dangerous paths alone. Are you aware of fact that hyenas and bad creatures like big pythons that could swallow you are abundant in Dobo Forest? Who allowed you to walk by yourself to Njawara?

Alhasan: Sir, please be not angry at me. No one ordered or allowed me to travel alone.

I was tired of ill treatment metered me by my step mothers and so I sneaked away and ran before being noticed; because no one cared about me. Please do not tell my father for he would return me to the madarasa in Guinea Conakry.

Jarga: Now feeling sorry for me said, "Do not worry. Let us thank God you reached this far not being feasted by hungry hyenas or snakes. I will take you to your Grandma Jainaba Sey and together with her sister Sallah Hanti Sey they will prevail upon your dad to let you stay in the compound.

Alhasan: Thank you! Thank you so much for understanding my predicament and for being so kind to help me out.

The fifty year old let a shy of relief and together we walked slowly with him holding my little hand to Njawara village. We reach at the crack of dawn and one could hear chickens 'natures' clock crowing all over the village.

At Grandma Jainaba's home Jarga knocked gingerly to avoid rattling them and forcing them think it was a burglar at the door. However and luckily, Jainaba's son Ismala also arrived from a hunting trip. He recognised the old man but wondered why he was holding my hand.

Ismail: "Blessing of the day is upon you. May I ask what your mission is and why this early at mother's door?"

Jarga pulled his hand in a friend gesture and greeted concerned Ismaila. He told him, "My mission is of peace and about your blood I found wondering in the Dobo forest almost serving as sacrificial lamb for beasts of Dodbo. He told the reason why such a venture and I agreed to bring him to your mother for her and your aunt Sallah sey to jointly talk to sisawo about way he is treating his children.

Ismaila in shock could not believe my bravery and was equally angry at my experience from adults. He called out for his mother to open the door and let us in. Once in side Grandma Jainaba Sey rushed to huge me and offered us some goat milk and food for breakfast.

After a lengthy chat and ritual of greeting my saviour, Jarga hit the nail while the Anvil was red hot. He urged that dad allow me stay at Njawara and not the sort of life things had been for me in the past years.

Grandma Jaiba and son Ismaila assured him that they will talk to dad and should he refuse then Grandma would have me stay at her home. This accomplished my Jarga Fulo left happy amidst many thanks from all of us.

One could sense the anger my history caused Grandma Jainaba. She despatched one of the helping hand to go fetch her sister Sallah Hanti Sey and prevail upon to come as quickly as possible to a meeting. In no time panicky Sallah Hanti Sey arrived breathless.

She thought her sister had bit the dust and that the messenger was being sensitive if not polite not to reveal the sad news of the day that early in the day to her. Undoubtedly she collapsed at the door and we dragged her inside.

Placed her in the bed and fanned her at the same giving warm sips of water to her. She revived and later joined the group to learn what actually brought her to the home of her sister what was immediately needed.

She ranted for a minute or two about her son's mistakes and promised that over her dead body would I leave Njawara again. Right there and then she took an oath to adopt me using God, Ismaila Sey and her mother as witness.

Right after Sallah Sey sent word to the deputy Imam of Njawara to by all means come to meet them at Jainaba Sey's compound. The gentleman, unable to squeeze reason of him being summand to the old Jainaba's, also reached wondering what might transpire.

Priests are only called in to pray to the departing, christenings and weddings aside their normal congregational duties. Hence he was certain the old lady had bid farewell to the village but he was surprised to find it otherwise. He wasted no time in summoning my father to the scene.

Father arrived very angry that my return to Njawara was causing him anguish and embarrasment before fellow villagers. He arrived to find a quarter of the village lined, like a funeral wake, up at Grandma Jainaba's gate. Some who dare to speak their mind gave him the best of thier minds he would not like to hear in a life time. Being the smart fellow he was.

He surprised all by first apologising for causing them leave their homes to attend to his mistakes. Using the word 'mistake' had an automatic calming effect and even brought some sort of instant support or empathy for him. He added, "Let me assure all and sunder that love I have for my children and family is immeasurable. It is as deep as the deepest great oceans of the world and wider than the universe.

I just wanted the best for them so that when I am no more they could stand on their own. Most of you aligned my decision to having divorced their mother but that is far from being case.

The world is on a move and this new generation will have to be strong on their feet in other to survive the challenges of knowledge and technological achievements man would have during their time.

So my aim was to give them knowledge and skill even though some may not agree at my method for their accomplishing lofty end." The muted crowd ruptured into an unexpected applause which rattled me. Knowing if dad worn this battle of the minds I might be exiled for good. However he went on to add at the end of the cherished applause; "Being that I will never hurt my children, especially my only surviving twin, causing everyone look at me in sympathy, be assured that he will henceforth stay here in Njawara and if his grand mothers choose to steal him from me they face no contest from me."

This said the crowd dispersed satisfied that I will never have to endanger my life because of unwarranted family mistakes. To prove his point father picked me and help me to his chest for a while to let me hear his pounding lion heart.

He has again worn dramatically even though I too had some victory on the side. My life being one of mystic trouble; would this be last or the beginning since the Jinni has now been let out of the bottle? Will my father keep his promise of not venting his anger about mother on me or my other sibling? Only what followed shed a light to that future.
For the next twelve months things went well between us to make me even regret having caused him trouble.
But brace up I was not one willing to turn into the regions' best farmer but all I wanted was to have Western style education and with it help my people move into or enjoy the modern day life. The tail will now lead into Senegal on wards for better perception of this life you are reading about.

Dr. Alhasan Ceesay and dad Mr. Sisawo Ceesay
Banjul, 1960

Chapter 2
THE RIGHT TO WESTERN EDUCATION

I was sent to a family friend in Senegal to start Madrasa schooling but knowing my build that lasted only for two years before my returning to Njawara and forcing my way to attend Kinte Kunda Primary School. I was not going to be left behind the modern day evolutionary trend of the new ways and Western Education or benefits it offers.

I wanted to be among the educated and with it help my people. I was determined to be educated come what may or despite any unforeseen obstacles. I was eager to acquire the tantalizing knowledge and challenging foreign language taught at Kinte Kunda Primary School.

Father and his peers frowned at western education for fear of their children being plunged or indoctrinated into an unknown culture and ways inimical to African traditions.

I started primary school January 1953. Mr. Louis Albert Bouvier, head teacher at Kinte Kunda was kind enough to take me in as a lodger at his resident. This opportunity helped greatly as we eventually gelled into the best friends on earth.

Our friendship did not in any affect the teach pupil understanding we had. My father was not pleased that I got myself entangled with a strange culture that is of no use to farming communities like the one at Njawara village.

However, after four years at Kinte Kunda Primary School, my father calmed and accepted that I continue my quest for more Western Education. I left Kinte Kunda School for Armitage High School in 1957. This was the country's only boarding school and it served the entire provinces of our country. It was and is still located at an island its Alumni doped Gambia's Alcatress.

At the island prisoners and students, in those days were under the rule of the principal of Armitage. It the iron fisted Mohamad Demba Sallah who served as prison committee chairman during my days at the school.

At times we wonder whether he knew what the difference was between the boarders and prisoners. Students lived under strict rules. We must attend classes as designated in lue of a medical excuse or be severely punished.

We have to attend mandatory daily prayers and to speak English from 7 am to 7 pm on weekdays or be given a symbol to wear until one can pass it to another caught speaking vernacular language.

Above all things one has to carry out assigned weekly dormitory chores before the start of assembly at 8.30 Am or else one is most likely to face the wrath of M. D. Sallah.

He was one person both teachers and student feared reverently. His word was gospel. Visit to the only settlement George Town was gained by permit or being designated one to the do the daily shopping for the various dormitories.

Saturdays where doped hygiene days because that was the time when dormitories and environment were inspected for cleanliness and proper maintenance. The best house of the week is given recognition and an award at the end of the term.

Very few of our teachers had degrees beyond the bachelor's level or then Yundum Teacher Training

College's certificate. Do not get me wrong. These were very good at their jobs and more so were equally dedicated to helping the student learn the core curriculum. One can never forget voluntary help Mr. Kekoto B. A. S. Manneh and Gabriel Goddard gave during our time at Armitage. We are highly appreciative of their dedication to teaching and kindness rendered us students.

I was a loner at Armitage because unlike the sons of chiefs attending the School I came from a humble village family and hardly get letters from my parents who could neither read nor were they able to write. The advantage of this state was that I did well in all my classes and left after completing five years of grueling life and growing up experience nowhere else provide after Armitage.

Armitage developed my will and sharpened my academic drive for excellence. Leaving a place as challenging and lively as Armitage was not easy. Departing senior pupils stamped or carved their names on trees or wet cement slabs and in books for other generations of students to know that they have scaled the rugged life of Armitage Secondary Boarding School in one pierce.

These name carvings served as footprints on the bark of trees for newcomers to take heart and be consoled that they too can and would survive Armitage with hard work and discipline as their guide.

One was not aware of how much the years had affected oneself until two days or a week before the final departure date. We did everything imaginable to have our names permanently displayed as testimonial to our having mastered and overcame the rigid life at the campus. Up to now, every reminder and news of progress about Armitage School makes me elated and proud for having been part of the school. On graduation day the school shows its full colours and pride in its pupils. Invitations went to parents, divisional commissioners and chiefs of nearby districts. Guest seated, graduates and faculty enter the hall in the most touching and solemn procession. They file into their seats to hear fatherly advice and congratulations from the invocation speaker, normally delivered by the Education Officer for the protectorates followed by the commissioner resident at the island and lastly the principal.

M.D. Sallah was very theatrical and always gave long speeches as last desperate act to stamp his authority on the graduates. With the ceremony over friends and well-wishers attend a reception party given by the School Council and teachers as farewell to the graduates.

I got through then government entrance exam and joined the civil service as trainee Dresser Dispenser, male nurse in 1962 at the Royal Victoria Hospital in Bathurst, now Banjul, Gambia, West Africa.

Chapter 3
NURSING DAYS AT THE ROYAL VICTORIA HOSPITAL, BANJUL

In all former British West African colonies the Gambia was the least developed and worst the least endowed with natural resources. At the time I left Armitage, there was only one 34-bed hospital at Bansang village manned by a single doctor assisted by dispensers and nurses some 180 miles into the interior and the Royal Victoria Hospital (RVH), 150-bed hospital in Bathurst, now Banjul, Gambia's dilapidated capital.

We were the first class of a temporal Gambia Nursing School pioneered by the WHO. My first day at the Nursing School was difficult if not strange for now am to compete girls which was not the case at Armtage's all male boarding school.

At first the girls branded me as male chauvinist because of my not paying attention to them or telling unfounded stories. Nonetheless I was thrown into leadership by the class and I met the challenge with gusto.

Miss Mary Mossop, the UN- WHO coordinator of the school and I got on very well. Sisters Rachael Palmer, Carol, Lady Jawara, along with guest doctors from the Medical Research Council at Fajita taught us medicine, surgery, public health and nursing.

The sisters and doctor jointly taught us along with three UN tutors from England and Canada. Miss Mary Mossop was the longest serving tutor amongst the lot before the school was left to the Gambia cadre of sisters and doctors.

Among the doctors, a very able and congenial Gambian surgeon Dr. E. M. Samba became our mentor in surgery while Dr. Frederic R. Payne and Sam Palmer taught us medicine and obstetrics and gynecology relative to nursing.

Sister Gray handed over the reigns of matronship to Sister William to complete Gambian takeover of the hospital in 1965. Our class started with only nine students but later swelled to twenty-six students when a new set of trainees was enrolled.

The competition grew stiff and here Armitage showed its value. I did so well that at the end the class selected me as its spokes person and coordinator. We had our work cut out but did enjoy our nursing student days.

We competed fierily but remained good friends up to today. Most of my classmates have retired long time ago. I was awarded the best nurse of the class at the end of third year, as we became state registered nurses ready to serve the Gambia.

All male nurses were given another addition year's training in tropical medicine and dispensing to ready them to man the dispensaries in the provinces. Here is where the local villager had misnomer by referring to dispensers as doctors.

True we did most of the minor suturing and dressing wounds along with prescribing initial treatment before referring patients to the RVH or Basang hospital depend which hospital was nearer to the referee. Some mockingly called us glorified village foot doctors. At the RVH, I worked with Drs. Samba, Mackay, Payne, Palmer and Dentist Blain.

While so engaged I managed to do private external courses in Organic Chemistry, Physics and logic from then Rapid Result College Overseas branch in Glasgow, Scotland. My plan was to do a B. Sc degree in chemistry at then Skerise College before proceeding to read for a medical degree.

My training finished at the end of three years earning me a State Registered Nursing Certificate. I was also awarded prize for being the best nurse of the class for that selection.

I still proudly display both in my room anywhere I leaved. Coming from a farming community made me know the hopelessness of healthcare delivery at the region and shortage of doctors in the health service.

Along with the many helpless sick villagers or walking dead I came across trying to get to a far away dispensary seeking medical aid made me commit the rest of my life to becoming a doctor providing quality medicine to the rural sector of the Gambia.

I strongly believe that change and improvement in Gambia's healthcare delivery would only come to our people if indigenous citizens participate positively in seeking solutions to our urgent health problems.

This was the only way I could humbly ease the pain and suffering I saw in those years and up to now. Nursing galvanized my interest in pursuing a medical degree and made me certain medicine help ameliorate the health need of the farmers. At that time only four Gambian doctor and eight British colonial doctors carried out the entire healthcare delivery of the Gambia.

The bulk of the care delivery was left to thirty-five or so health centers located at villages with trading centers. This state of neglect catapulted villagers to and left them at the mercy of voodoo or Witchcrafts. This chronic shortage of doctor would even make the heartless want to do something for the miserably failed villager by both colonial and politicians. Up to today dispensers and nurses who deputized for the equally overworked physician remain asset to the country.

In hindsight, diseases wiped out Africans because colonial administrators simply cared less about the prevalence in the region of malaria, measles, diarrheas, Pneumonia and much more. Sadly enough their inheritors turned worst as they too are only interested in amassing wealth from the people and catering to welfare of those that placed them into power as representatives.

The longer I served at the RVH the more I felt compelled to do something for the rural sector of the Gambia. I had nightmares that would not let me rest from the quest of alleviating suffering I saw daily at the various outpatient clinics, in villages and hospital wards.

These were trying times and I commend African doctors who sacrificed all personal comfort and opportunities developed countries offers and returned to render service to their deprived people. This is much more laudable and noble than gun-totting maniacs now wantonly destroying our continent. I worked for a couple more years before tendering my resignation from the RVH and headed for the Alpena Community College, Alpena, Michigan, United States of America in 1967.

Chapter 4
PREPARING TO SET FOOT IN AMERICA

Cold frigid Michigan would be the last place a true warm-blooded Africa would yearn to go. Providence has it I will have to start my quest for the MD degree at Alpena Community College, Alpena, Michigan in September 1967.

The preparation started after I sent an application for admission to the college's premed courses. I never gave it serious thought or hopeful chance but after five weeks a letter came from the admission's office requesting that I send all my transcripts, two passport photos along with a mare twenty five dollars application processing fees to the office of Foreign Students Advisors at the Alpena Community College as soon as it can feasibly be done.

By the time I reached the last line of that memorable letter my heart rate surged to 300 beats per second, no not beats/minute but seconds for I was taken by a delightful surprise of the year. Yes, I was a bundle of joy filled with great expectations. I ran to the post office to check on how much was left in my saving account.

Luckily I had a mare fifty dollars worth left. I immediately requested a twenty-five dollars money order in the name of Alpena Community College. With this money order at hand I drafted an urgent letter to all my schools and the Nursing School sharing the good news and asking them send my transcripts at the earliest possible time.

All of these were sent at the end of five working days after receiving my request. I took photocopies of all transaction pertaining to transcripts along with passport photos and sent them special delivery to the office of the foreign student advisor at Alpena Community collage in Michigan.

It would be another two months before I would hear from the college. The historical letter simply stated that I have been accepted to start my premed course on the Semester stating the 19th of September 1967.

I was expected to be in Alpena not later than the 29th of August 1967. The letter was a prayer answered for many criticized my forcing my way into school to gain right to Western Education. Loyal friends chastised my father. Some of who never spoke to him after my entering Kinte Kunda Primary School until their death.

During my preparation to start the Simbad the sailor's adventure for a medical education, Drs. Samba and Palmer shined beyond expectation. Dr. Samba provided the bulk of my air ticket to Michigan while Dr. Sam Palmer helped complete the rest of money I needed for books passport and sundry.

With the package completed I tendered my resignation from my nursing job at the Royal Victoria Hospital fearless of possible negative outcome of risk am taking knowing fully well that my parent would not be able pay for my tuition nor would the Gambia government raise a finger if it all goes wrong for me.

I plunged headlong causing Matron Gray to have a serious talk with me to persuade away from going so far away without government participation. I thanked her and assured her only death will prevent me following my dream of becoming doctor practicing in the Gambia.

I assured her that neither arm-twisting nor promises of early promotion in the job would make me renounced my determination to seek the medical Golden Flees for the rural sector of the Gambia. She expressed admiration for my fortitude, bravery and determination to contribute toward health delivery service in the Gambia.

She wished me best of luck. We parted as friends and she gave me her home address in the UK in case I needed help or chose to come to England to pursue my medical education quest.

The Director, Dr. S.H. O. Jones was not happy about my leaving and gave stern warning that let me not expect any help from his office as I fully well know neither my parents nor government would provide support to my ambitious intent.

I in the following week advised my parents and relevant family members of my dream and objective along with moves taken to start the long journey to medical school. Most in the know thought me to be either a compound fool or one out of his faculties for leaving a promising government post in pursuit of an improbable dream.

For once, my parents were very understanding in concert with my desires and goal for the Gambia. I immediate sought Hon. Amang Kanyi's help in securing a Gambian passport. He did by providing with a complete and signed affidavit forms and passport application forms for me to fill and submit to the Immigration. All went without a hitch and I attached all relevant documents and passport as requested by the visa counselor who had been contacted earlier by Hon. Amang Kanyi in my behalf. Ba Taraweleh, a journalist friend gave me Mr. Isidor Gold's name that had promised to assist me whenever I arrive in New York.

Mr. Isidor' reply to my letter made my trip certain. His last telegram to me reads; "Isidor Gold and company would do all we can to assist Alhasan S. Ceesay start his schooling at Alpena Community College when he comes to America."

Destiny had it that I would indeed travel to America sooner than later as the above letter provided documentation of support for my studies. A student visa F1-20 was issued without delay after verifying it with Alpena Community College.

The skeptics wondered how I accomplished all of this by myself. I made it be known that kind Gambians made it all come true for me. With ticket in hand I waited for take off time at 5.25 pm Friday 11th August by Nigeria Airways to Yuff International Airport, Dakar Senegal from Yundum International Airport, Gambia.

I was then to board Pan Arm flight 153 for JFK International airport in New York. On Friday the 11th August 1967 the start of my adventure to the unknown, family and friends came to see off at Yundum International Airport.

Nigeria Airways taxied for take off exactly at 5.25 pm and we landed at Yuff International Airport in Dakar, Senegal in less than an hour's flight time.

I was met by Cousin Isatou Jallow and husband Yoro Bah who were extremely delighted in welcoming as well as hosting me until the next leg of my flight to the big apple, New York. I spent most of Saturday and part of Sunday with aunt Meta Ndow and other relatives in Dakar, Senegal, West Africa.

I said farewell to relatives and Africa when my luggage was checked and loaded into the huge metal bird soon to fly me to the United States of America. We were permitted to board the plane at 3.05 Am. Pan Arm flight 153 taxied for take off from Dakar 3.15 Am Sunday, August 13th, 1967 and while taxing I watched the beautiful Air hostess demonstrating safety precautions and showing us escape routes and location of escape windows in the plane.

The engines roared louder and louder in the dead of night and then we were suddenly air born head for the USA after short taxing on the runway. After a joyful eight and half hour cruising at speeds near four hundred miles per hour at an altitude of greater than 15,000 to 55,000 feet above sea level the captain let the "put on seat belt" sign come on. Very soon we heard his voice reporting that we should be landing at JFK International Airport in less than an hour and that the weather was good. He thanked us for choosing to fly with Pan Am.

The seat belt sign remained on until we landed smoothly on ground. I was eager to see the America I heard about so many times and even dreamt about such magical land of plenty.

It was then I reminded myself of having vowed to always help the needy and sick, if ever I can or get rich to redistribute my riches to family, friends, country and students willing to serve the Gambia pursue their aspirations.

A Piece of paper was handed to me, which became my F1-94 the Immigration and Naturalization (INS) would want from me any time they come across me during my student days. Finally our plane stopped moving and the big engines ceased for the first time since Dakar, Senegal.

The doors were opened for us to leave. One of the dazzling air hoses stood by the door and with a broad smile welcome us to the United States of America.

BR: Dr. Ceesay, Famatanding Trawale and Babucar Dibba, FR@ Fatou Dibba, Baby Penda Dibba and Isatou Dibba, Banjul 1962

Chapter 5
WELCOME TO YANKEE LAND

I had no illusions or expecting to land in the Garden of Eden. I definitely expected enchantment tempered with human imperfections. I read a lot and asked quite a few questions about the USA before heading for the big apple and further into mainland America.

What everyone failed to convey was how cold snow can be and how it mercilessly freezes African bones to the core to say the least of its many treacheries. The massive tall buildings of steel, concrete and glass had already become part of my vision of American cities.

Yet, when I set foot in New York, I marveled more and was overwhelmed by what I saw, at the time, an achievement of infinite capacity of the human brain when put to good and worthy use.

I landed with curiosity and amazement at what stood before me. The architecture and buildings were spellbinding to behold. Hence, my first steps were akin to those of astronaut Neil Armstrong's landing on the moon.

It was a historical giant step for an ambitious village boy and indeed a giant leap for rural health delivery in the Gambia. I joined the arrival line for none nationals to be processed and given permit to proceed to my destination and college.

The hall was massive with endless lines comprising of almost every human being on earth. More and more new arrivals kept pouring in ceaseless from all doors to join the queues.

Being among the few Africans in tradition dress, called attention that I never bargained. I was not scared but eager to get into New York and meet Mr. Isidor Gold. An hour and forty-five minutes of a seemingly creeping queue later it was my turn to present my passport and supporting documents for immigration notation.

I was extremely relieved when I heard the officer say, "Welcome to America." And I wished me success at my studies. Since then "welcome to America" denotes acceptance. The inspection at Customs and luggage retrieval for whatever declaration one wants to make was brief.

A conveyor belt kept going round and round while it brought luggage from our plane. Alas I spotted my suitcase after ten minutes waiting. There was a large crows gathered equally waiting for their belongings. I had only one piece and the Custom officer went through it quickly and again said, "Welcome to America" and bit me a happy stay in the USA.

Being formerly allowed to proceed into greater America I located Mr. Tijan Sallah at the taxi stands, my Gambian contact and temporal host for the few days I will be in New York to allow me link with Mr. Isidor Gold, my would be New York Good Samaritan.

We drove straight to his flat where I met other Gambians among them Ousman Sallah all of who were very kind and did all they could to make my stay enjoyable. The next day we all made it business to locate Mr. Isidor Gold. To my chagrin they were not able to get hold of him through all telephones listed in the reply letter he sent me while I was in the

Gambia. Panic and anxiety started setting in with some of my helpers. They were worried that he might have changed his intent and so was not answering calls. Hence, we decided to drive to the address in the letter.

After almost an hour navigating through heavy New York traffic we arrived at the place. Sure enough there was a businessman going by the name Isidor Gold but he had relocated business in Israel last month. I decided that no matter what happen I would continue to the college and present my findings about Mr. Isidor Gold.

I was left penniless and the boys feared my deportation if the college could not find financial support for me. I was not too perturbed for Americans are revered for their kindness and understanding of worthy ventures like one I embarked upon.

On my way to Alpena, Michigan, on August 18th, 1967, I stopped in Washington D. C. to join a Gambian friend Cheyasin Secka before proceeding to Alpena Community College, Alpena, Michigan. Being in the capital of the most developed and most powerful country in the world I expected to find it much grandiose than it presented me.

It lacked the endless skyscrapers but turned out to be an average beautiful city with very few skyscrapers. On arrival Mr. Secka was there to take me to 3416 Garfield Street, NW, also home of Rev. Bayard Clark where Mr. Cheyasin Secka leaved.

I stayed with him for two days before heading to Alpena, Michigan. I did not tell my family back in Gambia about the loss of my sponsor for fear that it might disturb my frail father.

It was the beginning of a dream coming true, the partial fulfilled effort and even more exhilarating was the fact that I was heading to start Premed course at an American College. Cheyasin and I bit farewell at the Greyhound terminal while I was boarding for Alpena, Michigan. We shed a little tear before the bus sped heading for Detroit Michigan. We promised to keep in touch.

Chapter 6
ALPENA COMMUNITY COLLEGE
(ACC) 1967

At last came August 13th 1967 I was able to board Pan AM flight 153 from Dakar, Senegal at 1.15 am heading for New York, the great Apple city in the USA. It was my first flight and I loved the experience.

There was a young beautiful lady heading to Michigan and she broke the ice letting me know most of what I would encounter or expect upon landing in America and especially Detroit, motor capital of the USA, Michigan.

Having good idea of what things are and how to ask for help I pinched myself out of disbelieve that it was all happening for me despite resistance that shrouded my effort from the days at Kinte Kunda to my tendering my resignation from the Royal Victoria Hospital to head for America.

Now I am leaving Washington D. C. heading for Detroit Michigan and later my final destination Alpena Michigan. We reached Alpena, Michigan at 1.Am after almost twenty-four hours ride on the big Greyhound Bus.

The counselor for foreign students at the Alpena Community College was waiting for me at the terminal. He drove me to 251 Washington Avenue, home of Mr.and Mrs. Howard Riggs.

It had already been arranged that I stay with this family until the opening of the new student resident hall the Russell Wilson dormitory. The Riggs, believe it or not, late as it was for the bus to get to Alpena, were up waiting for me excitedly in their decorated sitting room. Again, I walked into hugs and chants of "Welcome to America." Everyone I met was delighted to see me, even though I was not the first African they had welcomed in 251 Washington Avenue.

I was offered meal fit for a prince. Milk to drink was luxury an African village boy never dreamt could come his way. The house was big but well cared for as it was neat inside and had beautiful green lawn bounded by lovely red roses.

The Riggs were very proud of their home Mr. Howard Riggs owned Ice cream pallor and a restaurant down town Alpena. Mrs. Rita Riggs introduced the family to me the next day at breakfast.

Mr. and Mrs. Riggs from that day on became mum and dad for me. They were very kind and generous to me throughout my American sojourn. They were the ideal Americans to me. They were an average working family who readily shared the little bit they God gave them with others less fortunate.

I remained forever grateful to these kind-hearted American friends. Curiosity made walk to Alpena Community College (ACC) to familiarize myself of the offices and classrooms even though the college would not in cession for week's time.

From here I went down town visiting shopping centers and interesting and where to find the post office. Alpena is a small city and like Njawara village, the business center of most of the surrounding hamlets of farmers and diary production.

I met Mr. Henry Valli and the Director of Foreign Student at the college, Mr. Thomas Ritter two days later to discuss my precarious financial state having lost Isidor Gold my sponsor. Thomas Ritter was afraid that being allowed to continue at the college with a financial uncertainty might in due course cause make the college loose its privilege of enrolling foreign students.

Mr. Valli and Mrs. Viola S. Glennie, wife of Judge Philip Glennie, head of the 26th Circuit Court of Michigan, joined ranks with Henry Valli and asked Mr. Thomas to contain his fears and allow them get in touch with most of who is who in Alpena city to rally behind my quest of a medical education. My plight soon became a household word and it became known to a lot of people dedicated to contributing whatever help they could to others.

Mr. Valli, the Riggs and Glennies speared headed the drive to keep me at the Alpena Community College. Within twenty-four hours after Ritter's ultimatum, Rev. Fr. John Miller of the St. Bernard Rectory came forward as one of those willing to lend me $250 us dollars towards my fee for that semester at the college.

A halo soon followed by numerous donations and loans from people wishing to be anonymous citizens in Alpena. In the end $1200 us dollars were collect enough to pay for my tuition and dormitory fees. I registered for 12 credit hours and started classes as I dreamt of. In another vein the college gave me four hours part time job at the Library.

I had a B average at the end of the semester and everyone was happy even though my financial woes lingered on in the second semester. An appeal to the Immigration for permit to work under section D of the F1-20 gave only four hours a day and need to maintain a 12 credit hours load of one's enrolled course in other to retain the privilege.

My nursing experience back in the Gambia gave chance to work as an assistant nurse at the Alpena General Hospital from 11 pm to 7 Am three days only. This was made possible through kindness of Matron Miss Zona Lee Wilson.

Working at Alpena General gave me chance to observe and learn how U.S. hospitals perform in the delivery of medical service to patients and the communities they serve. I made many more friends at the hospital amongst them was Dr. Charles T. Egli, a surgeon at the both the Art Clinic down Town and the hospital.

   He and others were instrumental in having the Medical Association of Alpena rally to my cause in the second semester. They donated $400 us dollars towards my fees for that period. By this miracle plus other monies I was able to for my second semester fees. In hindsight, I wished I had started at the Alpena High School for one year before embarking into college.

That would have removed the INS pressures, help orient me to the American education system and allow me time to get proper work permit that would let me earn enough to pay school as well as send some to my beleaguered family back in the Gambia. All my current earning went to the school. I had a good advisor and teachers at the time.

My advisor Dr. Elbridge Dunnkel allayed my fears. I became homesick but never let it affect my goal and schooling. Letters hardly come from for me from the Gambia and those that made it came from friends eager to follow my footsteps to America. It got so bad that I thought my parents might have disowned me.

I wrote lengthy letters to my family explaining what transpired and why I was not able to send them money. I had two good and reliable student friends at the Russell Wilson dormitory where I stayed. Charles Traflet and Nelson Herron became good people towards me.

They help me adjust to America, campus life and at the same time maintained a level head with regards to my objectives. There were many distractions in college campuses, e.g. endless weekend parties, and girls and booze, just to name a few of those inimical to scholarly life.

Nelson and Traflet invite me to their home not far from the college and to basketball games. Autumn in Michigan is a spectacle to see. Most of the tree leafs turn golden with some variation of orange tint. It is spellbinding scenery only seeing it conveys the depth of beauty in it.

On the contrary, winter and its snowy days, ice-cold bone chilling winds are not what foreigners look forward to in their lives. The two did lots of pranks on me hoping that I would be entertained by it. The worst was when they stuffed my bed sheets with soft snow and ice and watch me land on it unrepentantly after a long day at school.

This childish prank got me lot of student friends as it removed fears or perceptions they might have about me. Traflet and Nelson made certain I was never left lonely at the dorm during semester breaks. We became inseparable brothers, with me being the gentleman of the lot.

The two left at the end of the year for other universities. Nelson later received national awards and completed a Ph.D. in Chemistry and physics and worked in the computers industry for a while. We prematurely lost Charles Traflet during the Vietnam conflict three years after graduating from Alpena Community College. Nelson and remain in touch today.

Despite turbulent beginnings I too survived Alpena Community College and receive Associates of Art degree in Biology before pro ceding to Olivet College in 1969. Bill and Margate Cruise were the other Alpena family I leaved with for two semesters. The Riggs had moved to some other far away city. Bill Cruise was an engineer at the Jesse Besse Foundation while Margate taught at one of the Alpena schools.

Additionally she was an active civic member of Alpena. She spent most her days helping others get on with life. I later understood that Bill Cruise was instrumental in Besse Foundation awarding me grant to attend Olivet College in Olivet, Michigan. The next Good Samaritan I met in Alpena were Mr. and Mrs. Cloyd Ramsay.

I met Mr. Ramsay while seeking a summer job at the Alpena Arts Clinic where he served as manager. Upon hearing my plight and need of a summer job he told me there was no vacancy at the time but he promised to see what he could do to help out. I left him impressed and very moved by what I told him. He since that day became an integral part of my efforts until my leaving America.

Ramsay contributed and remained lifeline my education by taking several loans on my behalf to enable me complete my Masters degree from Michigan Technological University in Houghton, Michigan in 1973.

However, let us retract and follow the saga of my educational drive from Alpena. A Psychology teach Professor Richard Smith, I met at the end of term suggested that I apply to Olivet College to finish up my B. A. degree in biological sciences. I followed up and was admitted as long as the Jesse Besse Foundation would continue sponsoring me for the two years I need to obtain the B. A. degree.

At Olivet the Jesse Besse Foundation of Alpena offered me full tuition fellowship, which left me to fend money for dormitory fees with measles included.

Olivet city was even smaller than Alpena and it too was mostly a farming community. The campus held no more than a thousand students at the time and I was among a handful of foreigners, a majority of who were Japanese and Chinese, in attendance. I was elected president/chairman of the foreign students club on my first semester.

With help of Professor Cooper Milner, the club gave this little hamlet a taste of foreign culture in the form of films and cookouts activities. Olivet was forty-five minutes drive to Marshall the nearest commercial center of the region.

I spend most of my weekend at Marshall or Lansing doing any available odd jobs or pumping gas for motorists to raise an income for my dorm and food bills at Olivet College. The next summer I secured a full time nursing assistant job at St. Joseph hospital in Flint Michigan.
While at this job I met Mrs. Homer Shepard, a nurse at the hospital. She and her husband offered to lodge for the summer to help defray rent bills.
This enabled me to pay my dorm and food bills when college resumed.
Mean while life on campus aside classes was livened only by activities of fraternities, football or basket ball planed gamed games for week ends. There was always some activity to go to or one offer run into fledgling campus comedian to make one laugh.
Hot off campus debates was the Vietnam War and American global politics or arm-twisting tactics over developing countries. There was fear that Nkrumah and Lumumba might nudge Africa into Communism if given free hand. Even though we had our Vietnam debates our campus was not disruptive.
We worked very hard at our courses despite the relative feelings pervading the air about American involvement in Vietnam. I graduated from Olivet College with a B. A. in Biological Sciences in 1971.
I applied to a dozen or more medical school to start my medical training.
Wayne State University, Loma Linda and Syracuse University School of medicine, replied indicating interest and sent me forms for the second stage processing for my possible admission at these medical schools.

I dispatched completed forms along with requested fees to the three universities. Shortly there after Wayne State University replied and asked that I come for an interview. I met the dean and the interview went well but when we reach at thorny point of who would foot my bills at the university and would I be able to pay the first semester fees affront in a week's time.

My throat dried out and my feet went limb under me. I had no concrete answers for the questions nor did I have anything to show proof of financial sources. I naively told the dean all about my struggles to get money and how my own country neglected my efforts to the present.

I even showed them letters from the government indicate inability to pay for medical aspirants. Wayne State School of medicine dean wrote to the Gambia and the reply was deliberately sent to Alpena Community College even though I had left that college several years ago.

The reply from the Gambia simply stated that, "Because of the number of students on the waiting list there would be no help for Alhasan Ceesay from the Gambia government.

Everyone concern with me was shocked and sadden by the reply. I took the letter to Wayne State and pleaded for reconsideration of my case in the light of my own government refusal to help me out.

I showed letter attesting to the fact friends in Alpena already raised half the amount need for the first semester but the committee felt that I may block someone and not be able to pay or they will end up footing the bill for me.

Loosing Wayne State was a painful blow to my goal, which led to long delays in my becoming a doctor. I had serious depression afterward when college of medicine after college would request that I show proof of residency or being able to pay for my education at their instituted if I were accepted.

By now I lost most friends who were willing to help defray the cost of my medical education at a university should I be admitted to read for Medical degree. I bounced back and took suggestion of a friend and embarked on a graduate degree in biology.

With this cyclical state of affairs along with the shocking reply of denial of assistance from own people sympathizer advised that I do a graduate studies program at one of the universities. Hence I applied to do the M. Sc degree in biology at Michigan Technological University (MTU) at Houghton Michigan.

I was accepted when Mr. Cloyd Ramsay took a loan in my behalf at the Alpena Bank to support my studies at MTU. MTU is one of the most Northerly located university in Michigan.

It is a very conservative school, which started as a college of engineering and mining in the upper Peninsular of Michigan. By this time I have accepted snow and 70 degrees centigrade below freezing point of bone chilling winters.

I failed to ask about winters in the North until when I found myself buried in five to six feet high snow banks during winter. Olivet with its wet cold that penetrate one's bones was not half as severe or had nothing compared to what I ran into in artic Houghton.

Mr. Cloyd Ramsay and Dr. Charles T. Egli became my sole support and sponsors at MTU. I am forever grateful to them and will share their kindness with the needy and the sick of Africa. Autumn follows winter and soon one sees nothing but snow upon snow right through the horizon.

Luckily the region has tool to man the roads and house were well winterized. We had tones and tones of the white cold stuff just a month into frigid winter. The snow banks towered six feet and more to allow an annual snow carving festival and competition at the university.

A whopping three hundred plus inches of snow would have fallen by the end of winter in artic Houghton. I was not a place for hot-blooded Africans especial one from the smiling cost of Africa.

At MTU, I spent the first year at the dormitory but ran out of money on my last year at the university. Dr. Eunice Khan, Drs. Betzi and Alison, professors at the university, came to my rescue.

The Alison's offered to let me stay at their home for the rest of my studies at MTU. This was gracious and equally generous of them as it provided great relief to me. I found them warm, polite, very helpful and sharing the little they have with many more in the area.

This couple like the Ramsays, Riggs and Eglis became my America. I certainly look forward to the day I can welcome then into my home in the Gambia. I worked continuously on my research for nearly nine months before completing the thesis on drug resistance and resistance transfer in Escherichia Coli.

With the thesis finished and accepted by the committee, my candidacy for the Master of Science degree in biological sciences was recommended to the appropriate authorities by the dean of graduate studies and approved by the university.

The devotion paid off and graduation ceremonies were scheduled for December 16th, 1972 just in time for me to leave snowy Houghton before the first avalanche of snowstorms hits. Like the other times, I again applied to several medical schools believing that my current added accolade would help me an edge over many applicants.

Low and behold, the question of finance and residency question would viciously rear its ugly head again and be a painful thorn in my heart, if not a stumbling roadblock for me. Came graduation day, the Alisons and my academic advisor, Dr. Eunice Carlson-Khan, sounded and acted as proud parents of mine.

Mr. Ramsay could not attend of emergency he was to attend. I felt his absence for none deserve to share the joy of the day than him. Ramsay made it possible for to attend MTU and loan he took in my behalf brought this light at the end of the tunnel for my villagers.

I was happy to receive care shown by my professors and Drs Bezabi and John Alison. It was very kind of them for filling the void in lue of Mr. Ramsay and my parents.

They bought all sorts of gifts and took photos of the event and the historic day fared well for all concerned. Lastly they threw a big farewell bash for me after the graduation ceremony. We toasted to each other throughout the occasion.

I left Houghton for Washington, D. C. on December 20th, 1972. Part of me was left behind with those good friends in Houghton, Michigan. I boarded the greyhound bus and headed for the home of Rev. Bayard Clark in Washington, D. C. They Okayed my stay until when I can get an apartment.

Settling was not easy in that city, for the exorbitant rent fees were unbearable and I wondered how one could handle both schooling and work long enough to pay rent and food being only allowed 12 hours a week work permit.

In addition, I worried about where to get little more money to send to my parents now that the Shellie is affecting the farms. The master's degree did not open medical school door for me instead the old conundrum of residency and finance came to hunt me over and over in all my attempts to gain entry into mainland American medical schools.

Opportunity knocks at the door but once and that knock for me was the one missed at Wayne State University School of Medicine. The frustration and disbelieve continued for a while but my determination to become a doctor overcame whatever was the cause of the unforeseen delay toward my being a physician.

Again, it was suggested I enroll in postgraduate program towards a PhD degree. I still have not learnt what the roadblock was all about. Like me, the heart wrenching setbacks did not stop me and I was not about to give up my goal for any obstacle that lay on my way or path.

Chapter 7
RESIDENT STUDENT OF WASHINGTON D.C
DECEMBER 1973 TO JANUARY 1979

On the way to Washington, I reflected on my life and kindness shown by Americans. I prayed for God to let me succeed in getting into a medical school by September 1973. After a lengthy twenty-hour ride I disembarked at the Washington Greyhound bus terminal.

The Rev. Bayard Clark was there to receive me and take me home. Again, there were hugs and congratulations from his family. Though thankful that I had degrees but these were accidental earnings and not the main reason of my leaving Africa for America.

For me only the medical degree would be a job well done that would allow me to take my place as a physician in the Gambian villages. I asked the gathering to pray for my admission to medical.

Washington, D. C. is very fascinating city being the seat of American government.

As in the arrival lines at JFK in New York, there were all shade of the world in this enclave carved from Maryland and Virginia. Most interestingly and to my delight the city was almost like Africa in its social fabric.

Large numbers of Africans from different parts of the continent reside either as students, diplomats or businessmen and women. Unlike Michigan one almost always runs into one's comrade from the same country and at times from Banjul itself. My good friend Cheyasin Secka had then gone to England to read for a law degree.

However, I met Lamin J. Sise, another Gambian brother and alumni of Armitage in my later days at the school who attends John Hopkins University located in Maryland. It was a surprise meeting for both of as years passed since the last time we saw or heard from each other.

Our meeting in Washington was a welcomed relief for as well delightful moment for Land Lamin and I.We went to his flat at 16th Street, NW and reminisced about good old days at Armitage and about the Gambia in general.

Lamin started his university education in Spain and ended up completing his PhD degree at John Hopkins University. Naturally he urged me to move into his flat until a vacancy existed at the building where was living.

He even spoke to the manger and staff of the building to keep me in mind should a vacancy arise. I accepted his offer few days later after discussing it with the Clarks at3416Garfield Street, NW, who were relieved because their elder son was due sooner than expected and I was lodged in his room. I moved to 2440, 16th Street, N. W. to be with Lamin J. Sise three weeks after meeting him.

He was a sociable fellow but tampered all his activities with reasonable discipline and kept a cool head over his shoulders.

Both of us neither smoke nor drink alcoholic beverages, hates gossip and do not get involve in the company of idle students. There were those who were contended working as dishwashers or porters and partied nearly every three nights instead of attending classes.

Because such misdirected goals some so-called students by then had spent six years in the USA without completing junior college. Lamin J. Sise and I are villagers and we thank God for love and discipline instilled in us by our parents and the rugged days at Armitage Secondary School of the 1950s.

I made a deposit towards room 510 as soon as Lamin heard from the management. Getting a job was not difficult if one was not too choosy or lazy. There were lots of restaurants needing waiters, dishwashers, telephone receptionists and desk clerks.

If the worst comes to the worst one could always pump gas for motorists, mow lawns, or clean backyards. I did any job my strength could endure as it was as good as gold and was necessary for my survival.

Lamin Sise and I remained blood brothers. He proceeded to England to do a law degree after completion of his doctorate degree at John Hopkins University. He now works at the United Nations in New York after being refused job in the Gambia. Knowing that a man cannot change what faces him but only, his plans for meeting it.

I continued contacting medical schools admissions offices and meeting organizations seeking financial assistance for my medical mission. I made friends in the city amongst who were Dr. and Mrs. James Adrian Robinson a professor at Howard University Dental School.

The gateway to medical school remained analogous to Dr. Jerkily and Dr. Hyde. The same request of financial proof should I be given place blocked my forward momentum to medical school. I did not want to be a us citizen because of believe that it was time for Africans to be committed to developing Africa and stop the constant nonsensical finger pointing at colonialism or communism.

It was time for Africanism to ring in our African ears and fabric. It is selfish, as long as one is free and safe to go home, to stay because of the greener pasture or easy and comfortable life America and the developed world offers.

I take it sacrilegious to deliberately take up residency in America and let our people die in ignorance, disease and poverty. It is cheap, cheating and dishonouring American kindness that deprived themselves to help us become educated and return to help our people.

This would not be my sin in life nor would it be my cup of tea no matter what personal rewards it might offer. Our presence in Africa despite all her misgivings would foster more appreciation of America, provide hope and jobs for many more than staying in the United States of America would do.

Our skills would bring relief to plenty in Africa who would otherwise never get such privileges or rewards. I choused not to residency or citizenship in the U.S. unlike those who have done great disservice to Africa by pursuing hedonistic lifestyles and personal selfish ends instead of returning home to assist the peasantry.

Worst of all, it is an unforgivable cardinal sin, indeed bestial to marry an innocent American woman or any other, just for the shake of getting residency papers.

Some men throw away their worth and dignity for such unwise ends. None of these would be my sin in this life. I went to Howard University down Town and met with the Associate dean of the Department of Biology, Dr. Clarence Lee and discuss my interest in studying medicine at

Dr. Alhasan Kunsa Ceesay: Badibou Folklore Howard. He recommended that I apply for the university's PhD program in Parasitology as soon as possible. Dr. Lee was an influential member of Howard School of Medicine' Admission Committee. I had believed working under him might just be what would unblock or was needed to boost my chances of getting into Howard University Medical School.

Again like a drowning victim who grabs at the first visible straw in an effort to save his life, I took the chance and accepted the straw thrown at me without a second thought of how long PhD program can be and what happens in the event my age throws a wedge by the time I am able to apply for a place at medical school.

Medicine was my primary reason for coming to America and any other degree no matter how grandiose. I took the Bull by the horn and renewed my commitments to return home whenever I become a doctor.

Friends were skeptical about my joining the Dr. Clarence Lee at the department of biology knowing the opposite of my expectation would do me an irreparable damage. I took up the postgraduate course in zoology with hope that Dr. Clarence lee would use his influence at the medical school to help gain admission.

Two weeks later the admission committee sent me the following acceptance admission effective that very term starting September 1975. The letter read thus:

Howard University
Office of Admissions
Division of student Affairs
Washington, D. C.

Date: October 14, 1975
Date due: November 14, 1975
Semester: Spring 1976

Mr. Alhasan S. Ceesay
2440 16th Street, NW
Washington, D. C.

Dear Mr. Ceesay

Please be advised that you are, by action of the Admission Committee, qualified for admission to the Graduate School, Howard University, an enrolment Fee of $60 (sixty dollars) is required. Your deposit must be made by the date listed above. The enrolment fee is required of all new entrants to the university and is not refundable under any circumstances.
All certified checks and money orders should be made payable to the Treasurer, Howard University and forwarded directly to the Treasurer's office. The university reserves the right to close admission when the maximum number of students has been

accepted. You should therefore send in your enrolment fee as soon as possible so that you may be assured a place in the class. It is your responsibility to see to it that transcripts of all courses completed from this date are sent to the Office of Admissions directly from your college. A provisional permit to register must be cleared not later than one week prior to the date of registration. We look forward to welcoming you to the University.
Sincerely
Mr. A. W. McMurdock
Director of Admissions

Gambian students at Howard were happy to see me but deep down I was not pleased about my decision to take this route. The letter failed to mention the PhD/MD program told to me by Dr. Lee, which was cardinal reason of my risking joining Howard University.

Despite these clouds I gave it a shot and did my best for two years while at the University. Dr. Lee taught me a lot about research but our conversations always comes to an abrupt end as soon as I injected any idea of meeting with the Medical school Dean. This finding depressed me and matters got worst for the more I spoke to former PhD degree holders from the university aspiring to read for a medical degree the gloomier the picture turns out.

It was there and then it became clear to me that my getting a postgraduate degree would place another obstacle. It almost became the last straw that broke the Camel's back for me, as it would be two years since my leaving Michigan and heading no nearer to my goal of becoming a doctor. Stories coming from the Gambia seem to highlight that only thieves grew fat and that things were being turned upside down for ordinary people. In brief, plunder came to gamesters while dissent dissidents were equated to rebels and sank with dishonour.

Washington offered the chance to meet and talk with visiting Gambians and diplomats. I had believe that talking frankly to these folks out side of the pomp and trappings of their offices would bring some change for the better for our country.

I even naively brought to attention about claimed rampant corruption in the country at the time. I pleaded for transparency in the conduct of the affairs of our beloved country.

I was immediately perceived a rebellious student against the Jawara regime and worst of all a political agitator. (See Dr. Sulayman Nyang's affidavit, 1985 and 1986) At the time I really believed that we were having a Gambian –to- Gambian friendly but honest chat about our dear country.

Funnily enough other Banjul students who were present while we were having such debates were never duped political agitators or accused of tribalism. Information about my being a dissident continued reaching the Gambia, unknown to me. It was not until when Dr. Sulayman S. Nyang joined the Gambit Mission in Saudi Arabia as Deputy and assigned the task of sending back reports summaries on Gambians students in North America that I came to know that critics like me were a constant concern of officials back home.

Dr. Sulayman S. Nyang confirmed this later during an Immigration (INS) hearing in my case at Atlanta Georgia, before judge Auslander, while testifying in my behalf. My prayers were finally partially answered on December 28th, 1978 when I received a registered letter from the University Of Liberia School Of Medicine in Monrovia.

I nervously opened it and could not believe my eyes for what I saw and read rapidly if not in half trance. The letter came from Dr. Festus M. Haley, Dean of the Medical School and it simply read:

M. Diglottic College of Medicine
University of Liberia
Monrovia, Liberia, West Africa
Office of the Dean

Dear Mr. Ceesay,

I am pleased to inform you that the Admissions Committee of the Medical School has selected you to be a member of the freshman class for the academic year 1979. Kindly indicate your acceptance of this offer on or before January 15rh, 1979. Otherwise your place will be offered to the next qualified candidate. Congratulations on your achievements so far, and best wishes for a successful completion of Medical College.
Sincerely
Festus M. Haley, MD
Dean, Medical College

I read he letter again and again, perhaps twenty or more times before I came to my senses. The long awaited moment finally arrived.

It was just long overdue. I prayed and thanked God so loudly that I almost scared those nearby. I saw this as the end of my troubles and beginning of fulfillment of my dream for the Gambia and an. I grabbed it with both hands like a drowning man would hold onto a straw or log passing by. Hence, I rushed to my apartment and had the following telegram sent to the Dean, College of Medicine in Monrovia. "Offer accepted with gratitude. I Will be on campus soon.
Will telegram travel plans. Thanks, Alhasan S. Ceesay, 2440 16th Street, N. W. Washington, D. C. "
I acted immediately and so hurriedly that I forgot to check on the political conditions of Liberia.

All I knew at the time was that the Italians started the medical college and that students go either to Italy or Spain to complete their training. Besides, I was in no mood or privilege to throw away a chance I struggled for so long nor would I miss the opportunity of being a stone throw away from the smiling coast of the Gambia.
It would certainly give me chance to be seeing my family after such a lengthy time in the United States of America. The acceptance to a medical school was mercy or unexpected gift rained from the heavens. Detractors reminded me of how in other countries the government shuts down schools just because students demonstrated against certain policies unacceptable to the citizens.
They warned that our new governments were very intolerant of criticism, but Liberia in my mind, was Africa's granddad having gained independence since 1847. I later found how wrong I was in very hard way.

My trusting the Liberia experience since 1847 was a great mistake and I will expand on this in coming chapters. I wrote to my parents informing them of the good news. In the interim I went to the British embassy in Washington and met the Education Attaché.

We had a lengthy chat over a cup of hot tea. He promised to contact the European Economic commission (EEC) for me to find out if that body would be willing to finance my medical education in Liberia.

As back, I contacted Kekoto Manneh, and Kebba Sanneh, friends in the Gambia to personally approach the E.E.C. representative in the Gambia in my behalf. Owning to the short notice of my departure for Africa, I rushed all my moves and travel plans.

Again, the Ramsays, Glennies, and others who wished to remain anonymous, pitched in and helped me purchase my air ticket to Liberia with brief stop in the Gambia. I sold all my furniture and sundries at a giveaway price to enable start medical school in Liberia in the event the E.E. C. failed to materialize or was too late or slow in acting due to Africa's bureaucratic complexities.

The later was the case as it took almost a year before the European Economic Commission acted on my request of a fellowship to Liberia. Terminating the postgraduate program at Howard University angered some who genuinely warned me about the quality of medical education Liberia might offer.

The stigma about Africa in the 1960s was anything concerning the continent, no matter how modern and good it may be was deliberately given thumbs down attitude. Hence to me, the school being recognized by the World Health Organization (WHO) was quality and qualified enough. It has, like most African medical schools, produced highly qualified and well-trained doctors in various disciplines of medicine.

All advice against my going to Liberia fell on deaf ears and I brushed all skeptics aside and went ahead with my departure plans. Coincidentally my return flight to Africa, via Gambia, fell on January 11th 1979. Recall that I left the Gambia on August 11th 1967, twelve years to the day.

I hate to sound superstitious but lost of dramatic events in my life tend to occur on the 11th of the month for some unknown reason or consistent reasons. "Ceesay, be aware of the 11th of the month" a soothsayer would caution.

I kept the trip to myself and only few loyal friends. I dislike being publicized. Those who knew came to see me of at the Washington International Airport by the Potomac River Despite last minutes object of the trip I boarded Boeing 737 from Washington to J. F. Kennedy to connect with Pan Am Boeing 747 bound for Liberia via Dakar Senegal. I was a happy lad that left the USA after twelve years of ceaseless hard work intermingled with studies.

Pan Am 747 flight for West Africa taxied for take off around 6.45 pm, which was aborted because of breakdown in its radio communication system. Later, one of the African Cleaners joked God was trying to tell me to cancel the trip to Liberia.

I laughed and told him he must have had an unusual telephone call from God or he must have been hallucinating at the time.

Shortly after our brief conversation we were asked to board another Pan Am plane for Africa. We finally flew from New York around 8.45 pm.

On take off, I looked through my window for a last glimpse of America, the world's most developed and powerful nation on earth.

Few sentimentally rained in but I thanked God for having decided my life the way it went and the kindness Americans gave me since August 14th 1967. As soon as the plane leveled and the seatbelt signs were off, I went to sleep.

It was the most comfortable and soothing sleep I had for a long, long time since leaving Africa in 1967. I slept like a baby or log because relief I had. We were in contact with Yuff International Airport in Dakar, Senegal, after eight and half hours flight. There of fog at the airport but luckily it did not affect our landing.

Dakar, a city I fell in love with long before traveling to the USA had not changed nor did it have the magnetic effect it had on me twenty seven or so years ago when I first visited the city. I guess after New York, any skyscraper city or developing capital would seem an imitation if not a miniature of the real thing.

My cousin, Isatou Jallow, met me briefly at Yuff International before my flight to the Gambia by Nigeria Airways. We were scheduled to depart at 10.25 am but we instead left after 11.15 am Sunday January $12^{th,}$ 1979 for Liberia. I had a brief reunion with family before heading for Liberia. Thank God for it.

Chapter 8
A.M. DOGLIOTI SCHOOL OF MEDICINE, 1979

My sister Binta Ceesay and friends saw me off at Yundum international airport, a far cry from what current Banjul International airport is, on Sunday January 1979. Te first leg of the flight to Liberia took us to Sierra Leon's Lungi International Airport. Sierra Leon was the sister colony that had once managed the affairs of the Gambia in 1821.
Despite all the diamonds, sierra Leon was not that much better in most of its regions than the Gambia. After forty minutes stop and refueling our plane proceeded to Liberia, the lone star mini America of West Africa.
It was 5 pm when Nigeria Airways taxied to Robert Kennedy International Airport of Liberia. It was lot busier, bigger and better than those of Lungi and Yundum Airports. However, new comers do not easily notice the American presence to Monrovia, Liberia. Nonetheless I was impressed by the look and infrastructure.
Unlike America, there were lines to queue at the arrivals and departure terminals the day we landed in Monrovia, Liberia. Both the immigration and custom formalities took no time before I was on my own heading to Monrovia, capital of Liberia, to start my medical education at the A. M. Dogliotti School of medicine, university of Liberia.
No one from the school came to pick me despite having telegrammed about my travel plans from Banjul, the Gambia. That cable reached the dean's desk a week after my arrival.

It was lying in some drawer at the receiving point in town expecting one of the school staff to collect it up whenever they chanced to pass by. Time is definitely not an asset in leisurely Africa. I hired a taxi for the 35 miles distance to Monrovia for $50 us dollars for the trip.

I later learnt that the actual fare was only a mare 35 Liberian dollars which amounted to s$7 us dollars the most. Any way the taxi driver hastily dropped me at the main campus near the president's resident leaving me to take another taxi to detour for three miles as we passed the college unbeknown to me.

At the College campus I was introduced to Emerson Bull, the student affairs coordinator, who had not been informed of the time of my arrival, even though they were expecting me on campus. I gave him my admission document and Gambian passport to verify.

He apologized and led me to the only dormitory on campus. I was assigned to share room with Akim amao, a Nigerian student and also new at A. M. Dogliotti School of Medicine. The next day I reported to the Dean's office at 11 am. I found Dr. Festus Haley a very warm human being. I liked him on sight for our conversation was more that between long standing friends.

It looked like we had known each other for years before that historic day for me in Monrovia. I guess he was no monster and had much more amiable attitude compared to some in high places. He told me what to do and explained all I needed for registration. I registered at the main campus and felt happy that things seem to be pointing the right directions after so many years of academic preparation to get into medical school. There were many stumbling blocks or treacherous roadblocks that could have stopped my ascent. Being registered at a medical school is still a feeling of elation I could hardly put into adequate language or context. It felt good exhilarating.

I thanked God and prayed for his holly hand of guidance and for health throughout my stay in Liberia, West Africa. Liberia gained independence since 1847 and had been Africa's first and oldest republic.

William Tolbert was serving president at the time of my arrival in Liberia. The True Whig party was in full command and control of political power and the governing of the country. Monrovia, the capital, like Banjul, cannot be compared with cities like Dakar, Senegal or Abidjan of the Ivory Coast.

Despite Liberia's riches in high-grade iron ore deposits and at the time the world's largest rubber plantation, stands amongst the least developed nations in Africa. She lacked the trappings of a modern metropolis and there are very few high ways worthy of comment.

A few shops and below four stars Ducal Hotel were the city's pride. The only paved rood at the time that which ran from the airport to Tubman bluovard, parliament and Side Street leading to the president's residential Palace.

Railways served the mines. Like most African countries Lebanese and Syrians owned most of the shops and businesses in Monrovia. Most of the city was no better than a dilapidated ghetto and the indigenous in the interior were over sensitized to those they consider foreigners.

Dr. Alhasan Kunsa Ceesay: Badibou Folklore
I still cannot imagine calling a fellow African a foreigner while chanting daily for African unity every time our politicians gather. New comers to Liberia were treated with disdain and suspect by the Congo who was then ruling the country. They never consider themselves as culpable part of the inequalities then existing in Liberia.

School went on quietly from January 19th to April 15th 1979 and then hell broke loose with the internal affairs of Liberia. Every thing took a downward spiraling when the True Whig party started to flex its muscles to meet daily resistance presented to it by the demonstrations against the increasing of the price of rice.

Like most African countries rice remains their staple diet for most. Very few Liberians cultivate rice even though it has perfect climate for rice growing. Members of the Movement for Justice in Africa (MOJA), headquartered in Liberia challenged the powers of President William Tolbert, for increasing of the price of rice, which was already unaffordable to the ordinary or average Liberian family.

Monrovia, capital of Liberia, rang with charges counter charges between the government and the governed. On April 15th, 1979, president Tolbert went on national Radio Television and announced the suspension of all university activities until further notice.

This act infuriated the students and made matters worse, for it gave MOJA another tool with which to bring the government to its knees. The university remained closed until November 1979.

It not only set our curriculum back but it created havoc and more turmoil for the country. The students were the only lifeline of democracy in Africa and as such can frustrate a government that wants to stop them or stifle their freedom of expression.

A host of unverifiable newspapers sprung up all over Monrovia Making president Tolbert angry and more determined to curb MOJA. I had no doubts that despite the arrests that followed the students enjoyed every moment of the fiasco or controversy and turmoil Liberia was undergoing at the time. Students and police cashed several times, as each believed it was fighting for democracy.

The whole affair ended in a sad and unnecessary blood bath for democracy in Liberia. Liberia never had general election since it became a republic in 1847 except within the True Whig Party. The farmers were to obey laws enacted by fellows they never chased as leaders.

This gave impetus leading to the type of callus and drastic removal the Tolbert government suffered from the hands of the seven non-commission Liberian Army officers. I had deposited all my money with the university and no provision or transactions were allowed as the solders would not allow any school official or student on campus or near the university.

The university was for the five months of its suspension remained ghost town and no man's land. This made fears expressed by friends and family in Gambia and America well founded observation and predictive of African governments.

I had no money but decided to bite the bullet and stay in Liberia during the whole of the crisis. I at times went for days without food only feeding on berries, fruits, yam and any edible leaf in Monrovia. I remained a lonely foreigner no one cared for under the circumstances and the state of emergency.

I wrote several letters forgetting that the post office was also affected by the demonstration and civil unrest in the country. I kept my nose clean with low profile during the said period.

The long time awaited E.E. C. Fellowship materialized allowing buy a stand-by air ticket to Gambia just in case life became totally unbearable. Allow me digress and talk a bit about A. M. Dogliotti School of Medicine, Liberia.

History has it that the Italian Catholic Mission operated it for many years before handing to indigenous Liberia to man. The school consisted only of one multipurpose building housing office, lecture rooms and laboratories.

Students, during the Italian days, used to attend the fist two years of a five years course or program at the college and then proceed to complete their medical education or degree at any of the Catholic medical schools in Italy or Spain.

Operation of the school was handed over to Liberia in the early 1960s and it since became part of the University of Liberia offering full seven years medical education program towards the MD degree. To help accomplish its goal the World Health Organization (WHO) and other relevant United Nations affiliate along with interested countries send in professors and visiting lecturers to help the skeletal Liberian staff led by Dr. Festus Haley, a

Liberian American trained surgeon, and current dean of the college. Other members of the staff include professors from Sierra Leon, Romania, Egypt and India. A maximum of 86 students, at different levels, attend the school when in full operation.

Clinical courses were held at the John F. Kennedy Teaching Hospital down town Monrovia. It was well staffed by consultants and specialists in various medical disciplines. The days were long and demanded hard work and persistence. My classes kept me glued to the books and allowed little social life or contact in Monrovia.

Alas! School was allowed to reopen but the political climate escalated more and more causing polarization and arrests to escalate. Mr. Bacus Mathew, a Bassa tribesman and leader of the People's progressive party (PP) of Liberia, was already in jail with most of key members of the Movement for Justice in Africa (MOJA).

The signs of sinister events about to happen were written all over the country and walls of the capital Monrovia. The mood of the people was temperamental and turbulent to say the least. Several underground newspaper opposed president Tolbert' regime and ways it handled the crisis.

Increasing the price of rice along with the arm-twisting tactics that followed agitated the masses. The persistence of the demonstrations caused president Tolbert to make the fatal mistake of seeking assistance from Guinea by inviting the republic of Guinea Security forces to help quell a peaceful demonstration against the intended price hike on rice.

The Guinea forces stayed for a week without any incidence or confrontation with the people, police or the Liberian army. President Tolbert continued flexing his government's muscle instead of cooling of and negotiating for an amicable end to the crisis. Now that he was confident of getting help from Guinea he arrested most of the opposition and many others, especially students.

This seemingly tenuous and uncontrollable march to hell was an unbearable situation added to the fact that president Tolbert had already made cardinal unforgivable political sin of ignoring his own solders and relied on help of the Guinean forces.

It fermented the dislike or disdain of foreigners in Liberia and also bitterly angered the lower rank of the Liberian army who could not swallow the bitter pill of being distrusted by their head of and commander of the Liberian Arm Forces.

The army felt its turf being invaded while not able to do anything about it. With this much hurt, Master Sergeant Samuel K. Doe, Thomas Quiwomkpa and 15 other non-commission officers resorted to surgically remove the Tolbert government in which the president, his cabinet and most of his of his associates were brutally executed in April 1980.

The blood bath was ruthless and one sided. Nearly all of Tolbert's followers were killed and most of the True Wig party who could not escape to America were kept under arrest.

The coup was a sad affair and tragic affair in African politics and stability. It's a chaos that blanket Africa's soul. The farmers celebrated in tens if not hundreds of thousands for the downfall of the True Whig Party era which ruled them single handedly since Liberia gained independence in 1847. The borders and main airport were closed for more than two weeks. A 6 pm to 6 am curfew was imposed while the solders combed the country for fugitives. Master Sergeant K. Doe, now Chairman of the Junta, tried hard to keep his men in line and well disciplined, but a few almost became black sheep of the revolution.

There was the incident of high-ranking officer beat up the doctors at the J. F. Kennedy Hospital because of their failure to attend to his girlfriend, who only had a minor laceration on her hand. Only a few foreigners were lucky enough to be spared by the wrath of anger under display by both soldier and commoner.

This venom emanated from the fact that most Liberian believed the foreigners and the Congo contrived to keep them at the bottom of the rug since independence in 1847. I had my first encounter with these gun-totting and trigger-happy fellows in front of the Waterside Market in Monrovia.

I was on my way back to the medical school when I ran into a barrage of insults and accusations being hauled at me by three young soldiers. One of them stopped me and went into litany of accusations that it was the foreigners who supported William Tolbert and made the indigenous Liberian poor.

I innocently and truthfully retorted by letting him know that I was no foreigner but an African from the Gambia in an African sister country. I made it crystal clear that I had nothing what so ever to do either with him being poor or with politics and economy of Liberia during the Tolbert days.

This angered the men and they started to rough me up. I received a few gun-buts in succession and kicks on the sides before a high-ranking officer saw them and came to my rescue. I in pain calmly identified myself as a medical student from the Gambia and told him my side of the story, which the others refuted.

I told the officer to check with the Immigration less than three blocks away. It was then that the officer believed me, for in Liberia foreigners do not like being taken to the Immigration during the Tolbert days. Interestingly enough the soldiers were warned by Sergeant Doe to collaborate with students to allow the revolution popularity and success.

Yet, some soldiers as had encountered did just the opposite. However, I was in end given a warning and allowed to proceed to the medical college in one piece. School continued and I learnt not only how to avoid the path of soldiers but not to respond to whatever they may say against non-Liberians.

My second encounter came on the eve of July 9th, 1980, on my way back to college. The curfew had then been relaxed to allow people some business hours. The new curfew time was changed to begin from 10 pm to 7 am.

On my way back at around 6 pm broad day light, Iran into soldiers in a military jeep, who must have been drunk by the way they were firing their guns needlessly and fowl language coming out of them. They may also have been extortionists or were not aware that the curfew has been moved to start at 10 pm and not at 6 pm as before.

They being from the interior did not care hearing that information from someone they perceived to be a foreigner on Liberian soil. Nor would they take my word as gospel truth at the time of heightened fervour against the Tolbert regime and foreigners. I was roughly and mercilessly thrown amid kicks into a jeep, which then sped to New Kru Town in Monrovia.

Foreigners duped it the new killing town for here victims are killed without any judicial proceedings. They frisked me and found only 25 Liberian dollars, which got them into argument in their local dialect leaving me more worried for my life.

I prayed hard for I had left my student identification card at the school dormitory. Leaving card at school made matters worse for me because the soldiers would not accept my claim without proof.

The more I tried let them know I was in Liberia for a legitimate purpose, such as getting a medical education, the more they snare at me with mockery and laughter. One retorted saying, "Have we not heard it all?"

They searched me a second time and then angrily threw me into a makeshift shed full of accused curfew violators from sierra Leon, Guinea and Mali. We were all foreigners and those unable to bribe or talk their way out of this hell hold were taken by the back door and freed.

Poor ones like me prayed all night for our lives to be spared. We were lucky to have a kind guard for that night, out of the madness of it all. We later came to know that he had just been recruited from the interior into the Army.

One never knows what follows such arrests because lots of stories of brutal killings existed, since the real authorities may not know about them or if they come to know, it would have been too late for the victims.

Dead men do not talk, according to the laws of nature, which afford protection to perpetuators. Sergeant Samuel K. doe normally did not fool around with officers who broke the law. He orders an immediate court marshal as soon as they were exposed.

This stern act by the master Sergeant saved many innocent foreign lives during the early days of coup d'etat of April 15th, 1980. I certain do not agree with coups as proper means of changing governments and this one stinks for everyone in Liberia. The misery continued for a long, long time before abating for citizen and foreigner in Liberia.

Neither Africa nor the world cared to stop the hooliganism. Meanwhile, we were released the next morning when another high-ranking officer came to check for an escaped fugitive.

He remembered seeing me at the school of medicine and through him I pleaded for the release of the rest of the arrested and detained held with me. He relented after a long pause and took some of us in his jeep to town.

God had answered our prayers for the second time. How often is he going to stand by me before these trigger-happy devils finish me? Upon arrival at the campus I told Sierra Leon professor about my experience and he urged me not to talk about it to any others.

I felt betrayed by the school for it showed no interest in my plight and encounters with the security down town. Dr. Festus Haley was in America at time when the terrible bubble busted in the streets of Monrovia and the rest of Liberia. He left a Bassa man acting in his place as dean of college of medicine.

Coup d'etats has become a wild and sad trend spreading like a wild fire through all African countries. I wish was there was a way to put a stop to it before it devours Africa. I prayed for God to bring to an end to such dark and untold carnage so that our countries could map their futures and etched their contributive fingerprints in the annals of world achievements.

Dr. Ceesay receiving residency permit from Solicitor Dr. Angela J. Stull, Lloyds Lawfirm, Stockport Road Nanchester, UK 2013

Chapter 9

FIRST RETURN TRIP TO THE GAMBIA

The two previous encounters with the trigger-happy Liberian security and the cold reaction to it I had at the campus helped me decide on going to the Gambia on December 22, 1980 in time for Christmas festivities in the Gambia.

I needed a safe place where to release pent up feelings about to explode in my tinny chest. Best of all I had forty-five glorious days to be with family and friends in peaceful easy going Gambia.

Kering Marena and friends met me at the Yundum International Airport to receive me when Nigeria Airways landed. Allow me digress and talk a little about these friends.

Latif Sanyang, Kering Marena, and Elhaji Kebba Sanneh and I met for the first time at Armitage Boarding School in 1957 and they became true friends and fraternal alliance since they we set eyes on each other at school.

These gentlemen men turned out to be unique friends who can walk a mile in one's shoes and never judge or accuse you. Yet, in my silence, they knew there was something to share and to be heard. They are among the few friends to whom I impart my grief, joys, fears, hopes, suspicions, counsels and whatever lies upon the heart to oppress it.

These aside my family are that reliable to me. With these gentlemen I am able to communicate myself to a friend who redoubles my joys and cuts into half my consternations. I hindsight they have gone far into replacing my twin brother in my heart.

To Mandinkas, a man cannot speak to his son but as a father, to his wife but as a husband, to his enemy but upon terms, whereas a friend may speak, as the case requires and not as it soothed with the person. Latif, Kebba Sanneh and Kering are indeed kin to me.

There was room ready for me to stay at their homes no matter how short a notice I gave them about my pending visits. At Latif's place friends and well wishers kept pouring in during most of my stay and Dr. Lamin Kurang, Mr. Kekoto Manneh and many more old buddies of mine, outdid each other in keeping me entertained throughout my stay.

They have answered the question, "What are friends for?" It was a very special reunion for us. I later left to join my family at Njawara village in the North Bank Division. Again, the welcoming scenes were very warm, touching and community like.

I stayed at Njawara for two weeks before deciding to tour several places of interest in the provinces. I made numerous stops speaking to villagers and old friends on the way. I even visit relatives at the Senegalese boarder.

I heard all sorts of complains against the ruler of both countries especially the Gambia. I attempted buffer or boost their spirits by urging them to persevere, persist and work harder for the Gambia. I soon found it hard to use those words for the villagers have been, since independence, been doing just that and nothing better seem to come their way. Life for them has been hardship piled upon more hardship since we gained independence from Britain in 1965.

I cried at heart when some wished the return of colonial rule or masters to dear Gambia. I told these it was better to govern our selves and make mistakes than to be under foreign domination no matter how promising that master may be at the time.

There were stories of rampant corruption in high-level offices, which was supported by the type of owned by supposedly very poor fellows who had nothing to substantiate growth of their wealth. Governments of most African nations have the carrot and stick approach in the way they govern. Farmers pointed out that in Gambia things are much more subtle than normally done in other countries.

The curiosity of it was that bank accounts, homes, taxies and businesses were in anonymous names living elsewhere. This allows no direct link or tracing in the event of a public outcry for investigation into an individual's assets.

Yet, it is known fact that there were no way such individuals twelve years salary would be able to by the latest Mercedes Benz model or mansions being built daily at Serekunda and other very lucrative sites in the kombos.

It was open stealing with the pursued thief yelling loud, "Thief, thief!" There was no doubts in my mind that the effect of drought could have been curbed had some of the monies stashed in Swiss banks or wasted on trivial dresses and presents for girlfriends and lucky wives been applied to the much talk about hydro-dam for irrigation and electrification of the Gambia.

There would have been power to encourage industrial growth and water for the crops to enable

us to be self-subtenant of food and we may by chance even export some to other African countries. It would have made the farmers happy and afford more tax revenue for coffers of government.
It was now fifteen years since independence with same promises being rehashed vomited to the starving farmers who end up relying on so-called supper power handouts couched with ideological nuances.
There is always an on going feasibility study that no one sees it result or an end to it. Up to the time of writing this manuscript, neither the foundation nor the building of the promised dam was at sight but was still on the drawing board waiting for another international donor's money to be squandered to put things mildly.
There is no Gambian or African farmer or otherwise, who wants charity or food from any political hemisphere. We just want to be able to grow and sell our produce at equitable and fair prices to the world.
The farmers do not want handouts smeared with most dehumanizing, ridiculous, untold numbers of ideological strings attached. Neither the farmers nor our ancestors ever depended on anyone but God. Previous political struggles between supper powers misdirected a verse number of African politicians. These blindly held onto the coat tails of the supper powers for charity instead of planning for the sustenance and future growth of our dear continent with rich in minerals and natural resources.
No wonder charity and grain sent to feed the African poor never reach the mouths donors intended them for.

These so-called benevolent charities find their way into the black market and become unaffordable to the poor, who in all fairness were supposed to get the donations free, by the time it passes the international black market in the recipient country. My tour brought home to me that democracy was only given lip service in the continent and there was no redress for farmers or the poor.

The so-called freedom of expression, of choosing one's parliamentary representatives, effective franchise or trial by jury of one's peers in proper law setting to which farmers can turn without having to pay exuberantly for use of lawyers, were not for them.

Traditional chiefs are being replaced at will disregard of long standing traditions that created them to foster stability in the communities. Independence, although preferable to colonial domination, did not lease the new life we Africans had expected from our politicians, as well as the military or junta leaders.

I returned to Serekunda after a month's tour of the Gambia and Senegal For some unknown reasons I bit every relative and friend to understand that it would long time before I could come back to the Gambia.

I was expecting to start my clinical clerkships at the J. F. Kennedy Hospital in Liberia. This turned out to be fulfilled prophases with a twist. Now that I have some time in the Gambia, I will digress and tell a bit about my family and warmth found in it in the next few pages.

Chapter 10
MY FAMILY AND MANDINKA TRADITIONS

I am scion of two African tribes, Mandingka and Fulani. Sano Wayeh Ceesay is my great grand father. He hailed from Mali, in Manding and settled at Njaba Kunda village in the Badibous, the Gambia, up to his death in the later part of the 1892.
My father and some elderly scribes of the region told me most what I am putting to paper for you. Sano, meaning gold in the Mandinka language, and his wife Aminata Kassa, who was commonly known as Musolu Bama, a Mandinka from Saba village, had three sons.
They were dembo Bajoja Ceesay, Kekuta Ceesay and Duwa Bana Ceesay. Let me caution readers that birth dates are hard to establish, since none of these village births were attended by modern day doctors or nurses, other than the local old ladies or recorder as happened in some cases.
Time frame implied in this work goes as far back as the late 1820s from Sano Wayeh ceesay, who according to local scribes lived for 96 years. I therefore arbitrarily chose to start with great grandpa Sano Wayeh Ceesay because a lot of people recalled this unique man and told stories about him. Great grandpa Sano, according to legend, was a gold trader and reason why he was nicknamed Sano. His real name was Wayeh Jato Ceesay.
He was said to have had an active boyhood and came from a powerful and pious marabou father in Mali. Among his son were Dembo Bajoja Ceesay, Kekuta Ceesay and Ansuman Ceesay.

Dembo bajoja Ceesay mairied a Fulani lady Sallah Hanti Sey, from Bundu, a former strong hold region of the Fula tribe of West Africa. Dembo Bajoja Ceesay and Sallah Sey had four children, three boys and a girl. Dembo Bajoja moved from Njaba Kunda in the early 1900s and resettled at Saba village, Lower Badibou, the Gambia.

Later, in his energetic fifties, I am told, he moved into his own village settlement near the banks of the miniminiyang Bolong, which he named Panyeki Bajonkoto. Both the new settlement and Dembo prospered and he became an adept trader and politician that gave the chief of Badibou quite a run for their offices' worth.

He was so popular and forthright that he was appointed head councilor for the chief during his days. Wealth in those days was measured or based on the number of heads of cattle, sheep, goats, and money one was said to have.

Dembo Bajoja Ceesay left his mark in this line of wealth. He had thousand of heads of cattle and goats and he doubled as very successful farmer and shrewd trader of the region.

Like great grandfather Sano, Dembo's three children with Sallah Hanti Sey, were Sisawo Ceesay, my father and the eldr of brood, Ngasu Ceesay, who died at an early age and Abdouli Ceesay, commonly called Baba Sallah Ceesay.

The only daughter demobo Bajoja Ceesay had was my dearest aunt, Fatou Sallah Ceesay. Sisawo Ceesay married a Mandinka lady, Famatanding Tarawaleh, of Njaba Kunda village, whose father was Bakari tarwaleh of Mali living in the same village.

Bakari Tarawaleh lost two sons, Fode and Sambou Tarawaleh in the Saitmati civil wars. Sisawo Ceesay and Famatanding Tarawaleh had three sons and one girl. The boys were Dudou Ceesay, my twin brother and I. Our elder sister; Binta Ceesay was the lone daughter they had in addition to the boys. Grandmother Aminata Kassa had a famous daughter called Kassa Jaiteh who, legend has it that she was the talk of the villagers because of her beauty and fame.

She was nicknamed Kassa Nyingma, meaning Kassa the beautiful or radiant. She passed away at the raw tender age of 20 years and rumour has it that the village Witch and demon envied or grew jealous of Kassa and caste a spell, which killed her prematurely.

Kassa Jaiteh was reported to have mentioned the Witch's name during one of her delirium attacks shortly before her death. The later died mysteriously two weeks after Kassa's internment.

I never saw or knew grand ma Aminta Kassa or grandpa Bakari Ceesay since both passed away shortly before I was born in 1942. Dad and mum were reunited in 1947 after father's return from active duty in the Army in North Africa and Burma. He, like all able-bodied men during his time, was forced into service to fight against the Germans in the North Africa front.

Father told horrible stories of how weak soldiers were either left to die under the mercy of the elements and some were eaten by vultures while still alive but too waek to move a muscle to fend their lives.

In addition, they're numerous mercy killings by some who could not bear to watch their friends and kin being torn apart by wild beasts whlte they were still alive. Father explained that these horrible scenes of war and the fact that they brought frightening nightmares made him stay away for he did not want his loved ones to encounter any of the war withdrawal residues that might follow him. We accepted his explanation or version as tangible reasons for the delay of his return to Njawara. Dad later married a Fukani woman from Jokadou, Isata Ndow and had a boy and a girl child with him. The boy who drowned while visiting his grand parent in Jokadou, was call Buba Ceesay and the girl was named Fatou Isata Ceesay.

Father also adopted two widows, Njunji Kanteh with her four children, Wudeh, Binta, Fatou and Momadou Njunji Kanteh. The other adoptee was Binta Sanneh who never had children. These were wives of trusted friend who became casualties of the world war 11 North Africa theatre.

Father adopted these old ladies to help them and their children cope with life. Our Fula genesis came thus. Grandma Sallah Hantie Sey was the daughter of Abdoulie Sey and Hantie Bah. Grandpa Abdoulie Sey married was the son of Malick Sey, a great marabout in Bundu.

Grandma Sallah hantie Sey married Grandpa Dembo Bajoja Ceesay as indicated earlier on. She was an herbalist by trade and was efficient in whatever it was that she mixed for the patients that came to see her about their illnesses. Villagers travel days to bring sick relatives or child to grandma's surgery and it seemed there was no disease on the face of the earth that she could not treat or have a remedy for or some witch to accuse as being the culprit behind all their troubles. I have never seen any patient of her leave dissatisfied.

She never operated on anyone when I used to assist her but there is no doubt in my mind that, given the circumstances she would attempt to operate on her patient at ease if would result to a cure of their ailments.

Grandma Salla Hantie Sey was good, brave and strong lady who would go to any reasonable length to find a cure for her patients. She was my good friend and best grandma, who did her utmost to interest me in her trade.

But fate took her away by the time I developed real interest and curiosity in what she was involved. Sisawo Ceesay, my father, tried to step into grandpa Dembo Bajoja Ceesay's shoes in running what was left his empire but soon found he was not endowed with the heart of a true blood-sucking businessman like his father.

The cattle and money grandpa Dembo Bajoja Ceesay left behind soon dwindled to nothing as father tried to assist too many poor villagers. Father was too kind to those who he lent money or cows and never recuperated half of what he lent out to villagers. He was a benchmark of kindness towards others.

Things he deemed trivial which on the other hand would send you and I through the roof never upset him. He lacked the needed killer instinct to man the empire or legacy his father built before dying.

Dembo Bajoja Ceesay was one of the greatest farmers, politician and trader Badibou ever had.

Father Sisawo Ceesay was other hand tolerant, considerate, kind and an easy going, generous man who at times missed meals to allow an unannounced or unexpected guest to have some food to eat.
These qualities did not make him a weak person. Instead, most saw him as a gentleman who cared very much about others.
This was gift that, up to today, kept his name on the lips of villagers, united the family and brought in help when needed. He was good patriarch of the family who made decisions and judgments only after discussing or hearing opinions from the rest of the elders in the family.
He almost always went along with the pulses of the majority except when it came to my enrolling at Kinte Kunda School as you found out in earlier chapters. Father was never impulsive but was stern once he reached a decision.
Such was the posture, which saved families from disaster in villages like Njawara for accomplishment depended on good judgment from individuals and community at large. Mother was the supportive type. She was kind and a hard working lady who never complained and was good at charming everyone.
She had a gift of being able to make people feel comfortable and relaxed whenever she was around. People just felt at home and at ease when they came to our compound. Mother participated in all family decisions and yet was never too obvious and was never a female chauvinist.
My uncle Abdoulie Ceesay, alias Baba Sallah Ceesay, was the only surviving brother to father and next in command of the family. His first wife Deko Jallow

came from Welingara in Senegal who had Jainaba, Momadou, Omar, Ismaila and Alpha Ceesay with him. His second wife, Amie Ndongo died at childbirth and was replaced by a sister called Hulayi Ndongo, also a Senegalese, who had Mariam, Ebou, Hawa, and Usman Ceesay for him.

Baba Sallah Ceesay was equally and contributed a lot in the development and growth of Njawara village. Recall he was the forerunner founding father of Njawara Primary School in the early sixties. Both he and dad are resting in peace with their maker.

My elder brother Dudou Ceesay is now the current spokesperson and coordinator of affairs of the family at Njawara village.

Family unity is another strength of African life. Males and females are separated early in life before adolescence. The girls interact more with girls of their age group or a bit older. The boys do likewise by being with comrades and other male adolescence. Grandparents are used extremely at these communities to baby-sit the kids while their parents attend to chores of the farms and others.

Grandmas even nurse babies while their mothers are kept busy at the rice fields. Again, this serves to keep the family together and helps the old to feel wanted and to be contributing to the life and welfare of their families and loved ones.

As children, we heard lots of ballads from our grandparents especially grandmothers who provided us with warmth and love no artificial toy or robot could ever give to any human being. It was always delightful to land or run into a grandparent's loving arms. Grandparents can be handy during crises, which they quell easily.

At times they can prevent dad's use of the stick or provide a good alibi for a frightened scoundrel or rascal. Adolescent females are trained to become good farmers, scholars, weavers, housewives and even hunters.

Their mothers and elder sister teach them with a bit nudging from grandmothers. The girls learn all there is to know about womanhood, housekeeping and farming. The school of family arts and survival skills are further engraved into their heads and minds when they get initiated during the circumcision periods.

Circumcision is now being fazed out of requirement for women, as it has no place or relevance in their life or childbirth days. Its practice in this modern day has become controversial and acrimonious even though it was practiced from time immemorial.

One need to gingerly and courteously educate the people if we are going to gain head way in stopping female circumcision in Africa.

The rude rhetoric about rare complications concerning female circumcisions need to stop forth with. It is rooted in our traditions and all must work hard to eradicate its practice through mutual respect and educating the people. One must feelings of women who have had it done already.

I strongly supports stopping it but not by denigrating the cultures that practice it since their inception. Traditionally, men are strictly forbidden from women circumcision camps.

Violators are likely to loose their lives if caught encroaching into such camps. Men have their own initiation also, but is has more fanfare with it.

Ten or twenty villages may agree to have the ceremony at one place. The preparations may take a year or two, as each parent would like to outdo the other parents to show pride in their children. On the designated day, boys for circumcision are picked up by dawn between drumming and dancing. The boys are stripped of their old shirts, after being circumcised, and given those they would wear through the ninety days of stay in the campus. The circumcision camp is normally located far into the bush under sheds made out of rafters and thatched with grass.

It becomes out of bounds area for parents and women alike. This way men chaperons can imposed strict rules on the newly circumcised or initiated without kids expecting sympathy or parental intervention. There are no anesthetic or aseptic methods applied. Fortunately, the death rates are very low, rare and far apart.

Until recently all medications used during the process were from crushed herbs and barks of roots. Joseph Lister would have suffered an instant heart attack were he to ever witness one of these circumcisions, be it female or male ceremonies. Very sharp homemade knives, and at times locally made blades, are used to do the cutting and no wound is ever stitched.

The wound is simply dressed with herbs and left to heal. Luckily the herbs used are very good vasoconstrictor that prevents any bleeding possibilities while triggering the body's clothing mechanism into action rendering it act fast to stem likely hemorrhage.

The poor kid stoped bleeding as soon as he is plastered with the green paste. On hindsight having undergone the same process, I thank God for not having developed tetanus or very serious allergic reaction to the unknown crude green compound plastered on me at the time.

There was always abundant food, singing and training going on daily up to the wee hours of the night before they went sleep. A very unorthodox prayer is performed and then one is allowed to spread out on the floor in rows under the temporal hut.

Chaperons remain awake all night guarding the kids as well preventing wild animals from making a meal out of one or two unfortunate kids, light a big bonfire in front of the hut for use. These gentlemen became teachers, colleagues and indeed disciplinarians for the rest of the camp life. A camp may hold from 150 to 500 adolescents, depending on the number of villages that got together to have their sons circumcised. The wound dressings were normally changed every two days or as need arise near a running stream.

When a person healed completely, he is then allowed to wade into nearby lake or stream and take a needed refreshing bath. Life at village circumcision camps is harsh and challenging, for one is not supposed to be a coward nor a weakling during these days.

One is up by 5. Am and subject to all sorts of trial tests and lessons regarding manhood and how to cope or function within one's environment along with other people.

The chaperons can deliberately set a mock fire drill using real torches late at night to see what type of reaction an individual would make under stress and how fast that person can make life saving decisions. One's final act must always include everyone's safety. This and many other far-fetched events are what is dished out to the initiated until the end of camp, some 90 days from when it started.

On the last day of camp there is cleaning up and ancestral ceremonies and prayers performed by old men before the hut are set on fire signifying freedom and maturity for the kids that stayed in them for the past ninety days of their lives.

The chaperons bring in, a day before the camp ends, new clothes from proud parents of the children. The boys wear these decorated and embroided dresses and then parade down the villages as initiated, matured men.

In the villages parents prepare to receive their graduated sons as brave men ready to follow into their fathers' tradition and footsteps anytime after that day. The parents sacrifice cattle, sheep or goats for food as well give out money to celebrant dancers in honour of their children during the festivities From henceforth, as tradition dictates, the moment the festivities are over a son is given his own hut and treated as an adult.

The proud son now earns more respect from girls, especially his peer group. The young adult male can choose to marry as early as at the ripe age of 21 or later. In times past and even at some quarters today his bride to be would have already been chosen for him by his parents and their life long friends and would be in-laws.

Roughly 65% of village males have cherished chance of selecting their first wives by themselves. Polygamy is an accepted part of rural life and most men marry two or four wives. Marrying more than one wife is neither power status nor is it an imposition on females by any one.

It is all done through individual choice to paraphrase the tradition of Mandinkas. My elder brother, Dudou Ceesay's first wife was typical example of an arranged marriage.

He and his future bride were actually proposed by our parents and their friends when the poor kids were literally breastfeeding babies. My brother was born first so the would be in-laws approached my parents to have their fledgling boy be the future husband of their firstborn daughter.

This was agreed upon and sure enough, when a baby girl was born to our family friend, she was christened with knowledge that no matter what may transpire or happen to the two families, that particular girl and boy are sanctioned and declared future couple.

Villagers and close friends and distant relatives are notified by scribes about the decision in other to minimize future would be suitors. Arranged marriages start as a friendly chat, extension or as a way of cementing links between the two families. It is done only for very special friends and for good reasons.

Parents of future husbands act as in-laws but no formal dowry is discussed until both kids are initiated into adulthood. Meanwhile, the future couples are allowed to grow as natural kids. They may be living in the same village or different district without having any hint of an arranged marriage plans parent have for their futures. By the way the arrangement is binding disregards to where one of the parents may decide to relocate. The Caucasian would call it marriage sanctioned by handshake and true word of a gentleman.

Should the future couple live in the same village, a gradual release with regards to the arranged marriage between them is made as they head into adolescence. It is considered sacrilegious to wrong the family name and houour.

Hence the kids are usually advised by their parents not to defile themselves for any unsavory behaviour by them would earn them permanent stigma in their villages and among their comrades. Well, well my reader, you talk of stress in the Western culture. Here we are and we cannot as teenager boys hold hands with girls with going against taboos and grains traditional norms.

In a majority of cases the couple lived in different villages and only come to know when a little older, say about fifteens going toward their 17th birthday. Parents in those bygone eras had a final say as to which bachelor or man their children may marry. This helps in directing or preparing the children to who is an eligible bachelor acceptable to them and their parents.

At times the poor kid may have their eyes if not hearts set on different persons, but the adage, "Mum and dad knows best" is strictly adhered to in villages and it over rules the childish infatuations adolescence. It may seem harsh at a glance but upon deep reflection it was a great cure for curbing teenage pregnancies and teenage mothers abandoning innocent babies in street corners because of immaturity, lack of experience and moral responsibility of having brought some life that would need their love and full support until when it too can be a viable individual.

The above standard by villagers does not imply rigidity but simply a continuation of guidance and of a practice that had worked well and has prevented lots of heartaches or women spending a lifetime of remorse and without husbands.

Deep down we all love and want to be loved, and marriage was one successful sanction society we lived in embraced. Liberated or not, be fully aware that there is no Miss perfect or mister right knight or miss perfect with shining armour ready to sweep us off our feet to the bridal world.

Every thing in life conforms to laws or suicidal end results such as drugs, crime, prostitution and high alcohol consumption would follow our intransigent decisions. Our girls do not feel left out in these situation, even where they may not end up being with their initial choice, for they have the full blessings and backing of the social fabric.

Any how either one, at the matured age, can nullify the arranged marriage deal where he or she comes up with very solid genuine reasons to the parents and all those initially concerned or involved with the affair.

There is no simple step to it for the outcome may create great rift, discourse and distrust between either party upon a commitment sealed with honour of both families. Marrying into a family makes one a full member of that family and it extended tentacles.

Barring any reasonable alibis for annulment, the male can ask for the hand of his future wife when he reaches 21 years of age. It then becomes the duty of his father, uncles and close family friends with the family scribe to meet the in-laws and discuss the required payments and dowry for the bride.

As a formality, the father or uncle of the gentleman sends his best friend and scribe with some kola nuts to take to parents of the bride and formally ask for the hand of the daughter in question in marriage to their son.

The matter is again thoroughly debated in the most cordial manner and any decision or agreement reached becomes binding on both sides of the isle. There will be no alteration of agreed dowry after a gentleman's handshake, which literally seals the deal for the couple and family.

It is at this stage that the village town crier, then authorized to announce the good news by going to homes asking the elderly to meet at the mosque on a chosen Friday evening, in the event the couple is Muslim, to consummate the marriage between the intended couples.

Christians have marriages in church tradition. Now both peers of the couple pitch in to help the preparation for the forthcoming wedding ceremony. The preparations may take six months to a tear depending on the dowry requested by the bride's family and how elaborate an affair the families and villagers wished.

When every thing is met all adults in the village then congregate in prayer to consummate the marriage at the mosque. Festivities or festive days for Mandinkas are marriage ceremonies, christenings, return of the initiated, and first harvest week and New Year plus the religious festivities of the year.Upon completion of the mosque rituals the bridegroom is then allowed visitation and his friends usually accompany him.

He takes along kola on the first visit to give to parents of the bride. As stated earlier on, it becomes a family affair, hence the fellow's siblings and peers all pitch in to make it a memorable wedding festivities and night to remember.

This does make one liked and relives us from some of life's burdens. Honeymoon can occur before the actual festivities but not before the consummation proceedings at the village mosque and sanctioning of the marriage by the parents, priest, and all those concerned.

Being a virgin is pride and has self-fulfilling reward to Mandinka girls. None pray to be found otherwise. It is guarantee of trust from the onset of the marriage and an everlasting respect from her husband and the community.

Ladies found non-virgins go through great stress and face being ostracized. They are duped a disgrace to their families and friends. This concept is now fading away as the younger generation becomes schooled and acculturated by contacts with young foreign tourists and ideologies.

These contacts have resulted in adoption of different values of morality, style of dress in comparism with prevailing traditional norms and attitudes. I only wished there was a way of testing the virginity of men.

We would, surprisingly, have to throw away so many seemingly angelic men out through the widow into the deepest and hottest part of hell for loosing their innocence and waiting until their consummation to be husbands. Marriage should be of mutual love, trust and translucence of happiness.

Ladies who threw away their dignities in pursuit of modern cheap life faces shameful treatment and eventually becoming the odd one no one cares to marry. In community dependent society no one wants such ugly fate to befall a loved one. Weeks or a month after the honeymoon, a day for the real marriage ceremony is chosen.

The lady is dressed in her traditional bridal costume and now addressed as "Manyo." There is always drumming, singing and dancing all day until late in the evening before the bride finally enters her husband's house. She is help to cross the threshold by either the husband or his friends.

The two had already met on the honeymoon day and its matter of continuing from where they left off the last time. The nights and years to follow never match the ecstasy of the first encounter. Now they stay permanently together for better or for worse as husband and wife.

The ceremony usually continues to dawn before the younger celebrants rest. The bride keeps her bridal dress on for at least two weeks before shedding them for good. Most women store these special dresses for life, giving them only to their daughters if they cannot get their own.

Arranged marriages, like the one mentioned above, hardly ever end up in divorce. It is like safety valve and has commitment ensuring its continuity.

Mandinka ladies consent to be married but do not go around advertising in papers and the internet or looking for husband or getting involved in uncouth experimenting, social exploits or freaky one-night stands, that end up passing Aids or STDs to its participants, as in other so-called developed societies.

Another way a villager could get married without having his wife or her husband chosen is by being a sojourner. One is allowed to look for a suitable partner and then send word to family and relative about one's intention to marry that person. Parents approve and give blessings to the proposal before the marriage is consummated.

Parental concerns and involvement is absolute since the bride becomes full member of the family she is marrying into. The saying "My wife is mine and I do with her what I want," does not exist in village setting.

Here family and community are the basic fabric of life. Hence, there are a host of irreconcilable differences between traditional Mandinka culture and their Western counterparts. Another aspect of life, which is very Mandinka, is the extended family system.

Recall that I mentioned that father adopted two widows. This was an act of the extended family affair. Those widows and their children were not going to suffer as long as father or any of my uncles were alive.

To us a good friend is family until proved otherwise. Therefore, a friend's family and kin need not suffer if one can be of help. So widows and other family members are adopted if there are no known relatives left to stand in for them. A cousin, an aunt or half-brother no matter how far away they may be are part of you and can suggest to you or your household. A relative can come into one's home at any time of the day and is to be welcomed with open hands and hearts.

There is no need to call or ask for permission to visit. A relative one never met was still to be received as though he or she had never stirred away from home. His kin is your kin and responsibility as long as he needs it or the breadwinner was away or disabled.

This understanding and undertaking will definitely not make sense Western cultures and its loose trappings. For us it guarantees continuity and security that is so badly needed when faced with catastrophes.

No one dares be lonely in a village setting for we are each other's keeper and shall remain that way. Simply put, extended families are distant relatives and friends that deserved all we can do for them. They are village assets hard to come by as they would not mind stepping into our shoes and help us walk the distance.

I have no qualms with such rare gift from God. The arrival of a baby is welcomed news. Christen is done at the end of first seven days of the baby's life. Again, a friend or town crier announces the good news of the arrival of a delightful addition to the family and village.

The father chooses the baby's name whatever the gender of it. The chosen name most of the timereflects either one of the in-laws, someone special to both families, or that of an ancestor.

Life is an endless circle or force and to Mandinkas, dying, although a form of painful temporal parting the living, is a joyous reunion of the individual with God and our ancestors, all of who loved us. God had to want us to create us. And our ancestors are the historical part one always looked forward to meeting some day.

I hope this has given a bird's eye view on Mandinka perceptions and believes. Allow me to now regress back to where I stopped about my family. Abdoulie Ceesay, alias Baba Sallah Ceesay, became my best friend in whom I confided many of thoughts.

He was my father's younger brother and his children were lucky enough to be able to attend Njawara School.

Baba is akin to Grandpa Dembo Bajoja Ceesay and spoke several local languages fluently. Had he not been too young at the time of the death of grandpa Dembo Bajoja Ceesay he would have manned the business much better than father did amid sibling competition. Baba was well liked and had talents for business backed by a good salesman's pitch.

With the changing political wind that blew across the African continent coming to the Gambia, Baba Sallah Ceesay stuck it out with his brother, Sisawo Ceesay. There was no division or divisiveness between them because of political affiliation as occurred in other families.

Baba supported the People's Progressive Party (PPP) while their sister, Fatou Sallah Ceesay, remained staunch supporter of the Gambia United Party (GUP). We labeled her as the stubborn, die heart first lady of GUP. On the other hand, no one was ever able to line their brother, Sisawo Ceeasy, with either party. He kept his support to himself because of disdain he has for politics and Western ideals. He once told me that he voted only to make certain he excised his citizenry rights to ward Gambia.

He would not tell which contending parties was a lesser evil of than the others. He laughed when I asked him whom he voted or deserves my vote. He replied, "A person of your age or anyone for that matter should not be told who to vote for.

Do your own home work about the party's stand or manifestos and see which one merit voting for in the forthcoming general election." He must have been juggling my memory to the fact that I had always made my mind and kept my decision, which can hardly be influenced by anyone else besides God.

So father and his brother never discussed politics nor did we ever find then arguing about triviality of life. They had their minds set on keeping the unity of the family paramount despite the current trends in the Gambia. Baba Sallah Ceesay was a gentleman of admirable qualities and he was among the first proponents of Njawara primary School.

He worked hard to see that dream come true for the residents of Njawara and surrounding hamlets. On the day I was leaving to start my studies Alpena Community College, Alpena, Michigan, Baba Sallah Ceesay took me to a quite and private corner and said, "Son you are lucky one to leave the family and travel as far as your journey is about to take you. No matter where you may be or what happens to me, see to it that the family remains united.

You fellows can stay as a team if you put your minds and efforts to that noble goal of oneness for family shake if nothing else. No two are alike but one must learn to tolerate and be considerate to difference obvious in others.

Keep in touch with your siblings for together you become a stronger force impenetrable by evil minded outsiders." He finished with misty eyes by praying for me, wished me well and said, "Goodbye and God bless all of you."

He shook my hand and held it for a while, as if he knew we would never meet in this world again. He turned and walked away without ever turning to take a last look at me.

That, sadly, was the last time we saw each other for he died of a heart attack in my absence before my December 1979 visit to the Gambia. He was among the best of fathers and uncles and he is missed dearly by every one of us in the family and villages. May his soul and others rest in eternal peace and glory in heaven.

A typical day for the family during the trade season starts, as in the days of yore, with a guest or two unloading their belongings in front of the gate. Some ask for my father and others for uncle, while the elderly ones just walk in unannounced. Mother and the rest of the ladies would spend time cooking for untold numbers that show up from other villages.

African women love cooking and do not see the kitchen as denigrating domain specifically for females. No, to them it is way of contribution towards loved ones and friends. It is pride and joy to be able to provide a warm delicious meal to husbands, family, friends, and to even those unknown to oneself from other villages.

Father and uncle both worked in farms as well as traders or shopkeepers during the trade season. Their day starts a bit earlier than the rest for they would be at the shops by 6 Am to prepare for the business day.

They would restock shelves with goods from all over the world, especially as far as China, Hong Kong, Romania, France, Britain, Japan, India and America. At home my sisters became ushers and baby sit the little ones that some guest would leave behind at the house.

Nightfall was always chaotic and rough for us boys. Our rooms were constantly used as standby for those guests who for some reason or another were unable to return to their villages that day. Some stayed for days on end being squarer guests.

This caused my brothers and I to camp with friends in the village until a vacancy existed in our own home.

We loved it as it exposed us to other good kids as well as rascals in the village. We however knew better than anyone to return home with bad tricks we learnt or might have picked from the boys. Indiscipline and bad manners were not acceptable to our parents. Nonetheless we enjoyed playing tricks on our grannies.

Father never spared his brand of bamboo stick or leather whip at any time he caught up with us. He was not sadist but wanted us grown into respectable, decent human beings. The reward this open house policy brought to the family was shown by villagers from nearly most hamlets would come to help us with our rice and peanut farms during the rainy seasons. This was done whether father asked or not. Jubilant farmers report to the farms and rice fields in tens of dozens early in the morning of the first week of rains. The drumming, singing and planting go hand in hand all day.

Father would kill a bull or two at times and a few more goats to feed these kind people helping with the farms. Our Sere friends, who are by trade the best fishermen of the region, would donate tones and tones of all kinds of fish for the sole use of the visitors and helpers at the farm.

At the end it always takes the form of festival than a working day for everyone tries hard to show his or her gratitude to my father uncle. Everything done at the farms that day was free of charge. This is an untold asset in extending oneself to others.

The day's ended was highlighted by an hour or two of continuous dancing and acrobatic performance at our gate. Those who would not or could not return to their villages for that evening always had the boy's rooms on demand.

This taught us tolerance and ability to share whatever we had with others without putting a price tag to it. Sharing and caring will remain the hallmark of my life no matter how short or long it might turn out for me. There was no better reward on earth equal to it in gratification.

As children we dare not disgrace the family name. We were taught to honour, respect and care for the elderly irrespective of tribe or place of abode.

Hence, we grew up respecting and obeying every adult at Njawara and nearby villages.

We even adopted the motto, "Obey first and complain later to mother." Never make the mistake of reporting things to dad. He would call the person you reported and force you to repeat yourself word for word in the presence of the individual(s) what you complained about them.

Father once told me, "I make you boys repeat yourselves before those who you complain about because what you say then will be the truth and only the truth knowing that the person is going to correct you when you lie during this narration of events. An honest person should never be afraid of telling what he said about someone in his presence." We lived by this simple rule and agreed to tell dad a story the informer better be certain of not only the facts but how and what one says to him.

He was the family's Shylock Holmes and detects a lair's face miles away. The more one is able to repeat the same facts before another person with dad listening quietly to whole story the better or safer one's neck

Dad's piercing eyes fixated at your gaze makes you want to confess the opposite and finish with the torturous encounter that transpires between you and dad's eyes. The experience was worse than the whip. Feast days were another challenge as well as exciting for us kids.

Father would sacrifice three or more humongous rams, we used to believe these to be the biggest of all killed, and use at least three or four bags of rice and coos to feed the well-wishers. Visitors do bring more presents for the family. Toboski, nicknamed ram's day and Ramadan are always busy days for the ladies who spend most of the time preparing different meals of the day. These are days when kids gorge themselves with meat and sheep liver. It is meat in all homes for the next one or two weeks after Toboski day.

The visitors from other villages bring bags of newly harvested rice, peanuts, or very nice locally woven cloths laced with beautiful embroidery for the ladies. Some even bring sheep or goat, sacks of millet to make sure meat would be available.

In addition, mats and wooden stools are normally among the presents from villagers rivaling to bring better gifts than others. This was something like what the American call, "Keeping up with the Joneses" in a village style fashion. In short what goes round comes round. Theafore reciprocation by villagers is an African way of life and we are very communal but not communist.

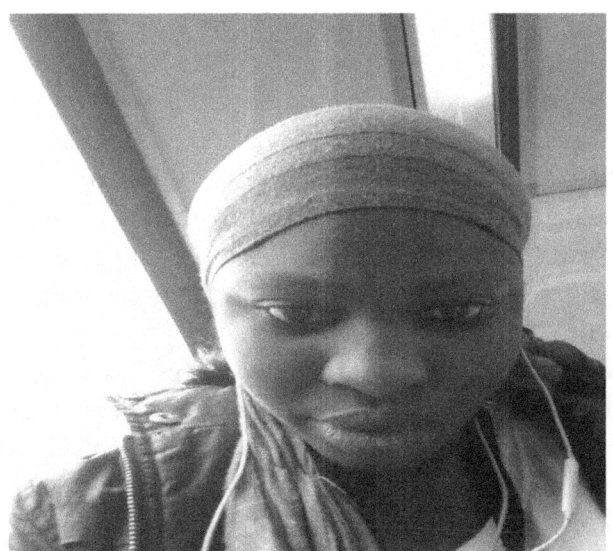

Roheyata Ceesay, Manchester, UK 2016

Chapter 11

THE END OF A VACATION

Let us once more return to our main story. I Flew to Liberia February 16th, 1981 and registered for classes on the following Monday. Meanwhile, the joy of having been with my family and friends buoyed me through most of the school term. I stuck to my books and avoided military men as much as I could at the time.

The situation in the Gambia, my home country, started to show signs of ruptures or political unraveling. The government clamped on the Gambia movement for Justice in Africa (MOJA GAMBIA) branch and as well as the Socialist Revolutionary party.

What made president Dawda Jawara to take this cause was beyond our widest dreams or imaginations. Why is that African governments get so jittery when faced with questions of translucency and good governance? Did not the Jawara regime learn anything from the dissention in Liberia? President Jawara failed to observe the trend that led to the demise of the president Tolbert's' regime in Liberia when he flexed his government's muscles in the extra ordinary name of containing dissident people.

All Jawara achieved by clamping these parties was to give them notoriety they never had or deserved and it made his regime wooing more trouble of higher magnitudes for the Gambia. Moja and the socialist being barred from holding any political or public activities in the Gambia made it easier for these parties to gain more followers if not sympathizers from the silent majority whose voices the Jawara regime ignored. The coup d'etat in Liberia had already sensitized the people in Gambia and made me fearful of what might follow if the Jawara government fails to wake up in time to salvage the country peacefully.

Coups are undemocratic and unnecessary disruptions of life and property in Africa. I hate such means and its willful disregard for human life and rights military governments brings to those they purport to govern.

I despise with passion any so-called supper power guise that encourages or perpetuates dictatorship or dictatorial military rule anywhere on earth. Africa has enough of carnage rained onto innocent people by the military and politicians with help of external alliance in the name of ideology, power, and greed for mineral resources.

On July 30, 1981, while listening to the B. B.C. 6.00 Am world service news, I heard what I feared most for my dear people and home. The broadcast was interrupted with a newsbreak.

It simply said that news has reached London that a coup d'etat was in progress in the Gambia and it was lead by a civilian cum military field force at the barracks in Fajara.

Like majority Gambians I was shocked, dismayed and angered by the possible bloodbath that follows such mindless idiotic acts. It was all madness and a dark day in the history of such peaceful people as we were. The Gambia will never be the same again. Where was Africa heading?

I asked myself in tears. I prayed for Gambia to be shield from the likes of atrocity that followed the coup in Liberia and God to bring international forces as rapidly as possible to quell and minimize the nightmare before it sprouts to an uncontrollable monstrous bloodbath.

An OAU force would have been the choice to step in and stop killers like these but they themselves have military governments and it will be indeed the case of the kettle calling pot black.

Coups ever since their advent swept through our beleaguered Africa bringing nothing but new forms of tyranny because of compulsive, corrupt politicians and inept military men who wallow in destroying institutions and bath the gentle peasantry in pools of blood.

I certainly disliked corruption and government's policies that ignored the plight of the farmers but government must change through the ballot box and not by the cowardly, ruthless way military takeover had done to us.

It was neither the right way to bring change nor was it a civilized means of exercising true democracy were the will and wishes of the majority is supreme. A wrong cannot correct another wrong.

Hence if politicians are behaving wrong the military should not add insult to injury nor demeaning the integrity of the people by adding fuel to fire and thereby hatching more wanton suffering and destruction of property.

I hate coups for they neither cure nor provide innovative answers to Africa's evolutionary and post independence problems and the future of the continent.

Coups and one party government only place further strictures of freedom in the lives of the citizenry. No coup d'etat in Africa ever instituted good and worthy redemption to those they affect.

I became very concerned about fate of my family and friends and Gambians in general. I followed the of events through the B. B. C., world papers and accounts of those returning from the Gambia after the first few days of the blood insurrection in the Gambia.

Gambians in Liberia got more and more worried and frustrated by lack of direct news about one's kin. The coup d'etat attempt continued to hang by slippery slim strings until August 11th, 1981, when Kukoi Samba Sanyang, a Jola tribe's man, and his evil supporters were defeated through the intervention of Senegalese military and Security forces that remained loyal to the Jawara government.

The Senegalese remained in Gambia for three and most of the time acting more like occupying forces instead redeemers of the Gambia we had expected of them.

President Jawara finally told them to leave. Sad stories kept emanating from the Gambia about horrors and charges of untimely deaths of over a thousand people and random arrests of another thousand or more by the occupying Senegalese security forces as an aftermath of the failed coup d'etat led by Kukoi Samba Sanyang and company. Lots of innocent people were caught in these dragnet raids.

The B. B. C. reported 20 people having died while being detained in an inadequate cell. It was also reported that a sort of vendetta and unnecessary purging was being carried out against people who had nothing to do with the coup d'etat in the Gambia.

Subsequent to this I learnt about arrest of a number of friends of mine among who were Alhaji Kebba Sanneh of Japine, my cousin Abdoulie Sarr at the fire service at Yundum Airport, Latif Sanyang at the Cooperatives, just to name a few.

Abduli Sarr was fireman stationed at the Airport who was accused from the blue of participating in the up rise. He was tried immediately and sentenced to death His sentence was later commuted to 15 years hard labour under solitary confinement.

This news lead me to write to president Dawda Kairaba Jawara, the Attorney general, the British and American Emissaries in an effort to protect and secure release of these and all innocent people accidentally napped by the Senegalese forces.

I had no doubts that president Jawara had no hand in what was transpiring because of his human right stance that was claret to all Gambians.

All these arrests may have been likely instigated by people fearful of successful provincials. Below is an insert of a typical letter I sent to the ministry of Justice.

School of Medicine
University of Liberia
Monrovia, Liberia
May 18th, 1981

The Minister of Justice
Justice Department
The Quadrangle
Banjul, The Gambia

Dear Sir,

It will be in the interest of our nation if the Justice department would heed human rights in re-establishing law and order. There was no need or excuse for unleashing the Senegalese troops to arrest Gambians when it was very clear that these soldiers would not be able to tell rebels from the innocent. As a result, indiscriminate arrests have occurred. A good example of which was the arrest and detention of Latif Sanyang of the co-operatives, Abdoulie Sarr of the Fire service and Alhaaji Kebba Sanneh of the Medical and Health along with hundreds of other innocent Gambians lying fallow at the mile two prisons and other unknown holding camps.
Despite appeals from concerned citizens, your department still refuses to free the above along with the innocent. There was no need for the type of purging the government was currently engaged in. In God's name we ask that human rights and justice not suffer in your efforts to regain power in the name of law and order.
Failure to respond will leave me with no choice but to appeal directly to President Dawada Kairaba Jawara and the international world. I look forward to an early reply.
Sincerely
Alhasan S. Ceesay

This and many more went unheeded and arrests continued. As I said before, I never condone coup d'etas but was bitter about the way the civilian rulers were stifling democracy, freedom of movement and expression, which are the very fabric of a functional human society.

By now positive news about my own kin reached from reliable sources that went to my home at Njawara. However they were not able to see my friends who were detained with no visitation rights at any time. My next mail to the Gambia went directly, or so I think, to president Dawada Jawara, the U. S. and British Ambassadors to the Gambia as shown below.

M. Dogliotti College of Medicine
P. O. Box 1018
Monrovia, Liberia
West Africa
September 14th, 1981
Dr. Alhasan Kunsa Ceesay: Badibou Folklore

President Dawada Jawara
State House
Banjul, The Gambia
West Africa

Dear Mr. President:

I commend you for the cool headed approach you gave in bringing solution to the July 29th, 1981 tragic episode for our nation. It was a tragic and dark day in the history of peace loving Gambia.

Serious minded Gambians will forever regret that it took place. Sir, we have seen it occur in most of our African sister countries and I only pray that peace and tranquility returns to my native home.

Such is the wind of change blowing across the continent. Today, I write, with laden heart, to solicit mercy and freedom for Mr. Latif Sanyang, whom I learnt was arrested.

I know Sanyang is totally against violence and that his last name, which he shares with the rebel leader might have landed him in trouble with the Senegalese troopers. It applies to Abdoulie Sarr and Kebba Sanneh among many innocent Gambians.

Mr. President, we admire you for your stand for human rights.

I have no doubts that reason will continue to tamper your judgment as you deliberate over this Gambian nightmare. In Allah's name I beg for the freedom of my friend latif Sanyang along with all innocent persons.

Thank you and greetings. Best whishes for good health and tranquil Gambia. I am anxiously waiting to hear from your office. Wasalam.

Sincerely
Alhasan S. Ceesay
Student.

I sent the following appeal to both the U. S. and British Embassies in the Gambia and Senegal for them to help bring stability in the Gambia and released of the innocent in earliest possible time and way.

M. Dogliotti College of Medicine
P. Box 1018
Monrovia, Liberia
West Africa

The ambassador
U. S. embassy,
Banjul, The Gambia
West Africa
September 6th, 1981

Dear Mr. Ambassador:

Many months have passed since Latif Sanyang introduced me to you. Today, I write to solicit your help to intervene in his behalf. I am saddened by the news of his arrest in connection with the July 29th, 1981 episode.
I wrote several letters to the attorney General's office enquiring as to why Latif and others were held and what they were charged but I have not succeeded in eliciting any response from the Attorney General's office.
Also I wrote to Maimuna Ceesay wife of Latif and an employee of yours. I fear she may be napped for I had no reply from her. I now fear for their lives and I would appreciate any help your office can give to render them their rights and freedom.
Sanyang might have been arrested because of the fact that he has the same sure name with the rebel leader. Latif is totally against violence and it is hard to believe that he had anything to do with the July revolt.

Again, I appeal to you to help these friends and others regain their lost freedoms. A million thanks and I am anxiously waiting to hear from your office. Please extend my greetings to your wife and Mr. Broadway. I am
Sincerely
Alhasan S. Ceesay

This along with many more from Gambians in Liberia and I went unheeded. I suspected mail tampering and decided to write to all Western embassies in Dakar Senegal seeking intervention in be half of the innocent in holding cells. I even quoted the tragic death of twenty persons held in an inadequate cell while waiting action from the department of Justice.
You are now welcomed to my own experience after these letters of relentless contacts in behalf of those I sincerely believed to be innocent in having any hand with the bloody insurrection of July 29th, 1981 call coup d'etat attempt to remove the PPP regime from power in the Gambia.

THE ACCUSATION ENSUING DIFFICULTIES

It was 9 pm; in the evening November 3rd, 1981, when two none uniformed Liberian Security officers approached me and identified themselves by showing what to me were genuine badges and Liberian Security Forces I.D. cards.

My heart rate rocketed and black shades came to my eyes, but I still managed to remain calm. I remembered one being tall and slim and the other looming huge, standing between the only dormitory and I at the college.

I stared stupidly at them as though I just woke up from a nightmare, unbelieving what I had the officers say, until I took it all to be a big mistake. I prayed for God's protection and vindication from the hands of Satan and these menacing unknown elements before me.

I am not a Liberian and had nothing to do with their internal affairs. I started wondering why I was accused rather than all the other politically active Gambian in the Movement for Justice in Africa (MOJA) down town Monrovia.

I was speechless when the big fellow told me of the request from the Gambia concerning sending me back for routine investigation in connection with MOJA Gambia.

The contemptuous news became real to me when the officers asked me to follow them to a quieter or more private place on campus. I cautioned myself to do exactly what they asked, as long as I was not to leave campus grounds.

I always believed a military man with a warrant for arrest was no longer a man, to say the least a human being, but a robot claiming to be the stature of the law. They are usually cold, deaf and mute or impervious to reason.

These fellows proved me wrong, as will be revealed by the following episodes. Hence, I followed the officers, animatedly, to the place of their choice by the Catholic Hospital on Campus grounds.

We sat on one of the free benches under a big almond tree away from would be listeners, but secure enough for me.

Even though they acted as if we were having normal conversations, I was under the watchful eyes of too many people, students included, for the two none-uniformed Officers to brutalize me.

They offered me cigarettes and I told them that I do not smoke and would appreciate it if they would some day stop smoking. They laughed and started their gentle interrogation about my previous political activities in the Gambia and if I had any connection what so ever with the Movement for Justice in Africa (MOJA).

The calm composure they kept throughout the meeting made it easier for me to recall events and answer their questions to best of my knowledge. Still they kept on asking if I have anything to do with Moja in the Gambia or if any of the leaders in the Gambia coup d'etat attempt were familiar to me. Then they revealed to me that the Gambia government wanted me be returned to the Gambia for routine questioning for one of my friends, Latif Sanyang, who had just left Liberia before the episode was arrested.

They emphasized that the request was only for a routine processing and that the Gambia would allow me back to finish my schooling pending the outcome of the inquiry. I naively asked the huge fellow to show me proof that all they had been telling was true and that such heinous request did come from the Gambia.

He laughed immediately at my naivety, further relieving my tension. He then told me to meet them the following morning at the same bench in front of the dormitory.

He warned that I was not to tell anyone about my meeting him or her and that campus undercover Security have been detailed to keep an eye on me and those who I talk to until the next day of our meeting after 10 Am.

They would take from the campus decoy would be taken seriously and will make them not help me out of the country. Whether that was intended to keep me silent I really could not tell so by obeying their command to the letter I might save my life.

Suspicious and interested fellow students told me they have noticed the security officers talk to me. They promised to help if I were in any trouble with the law in Liberia.

To that offer and request I turned and denied being in trouble and told them that the officers were long time friends. I took this stand because I feared that one of those so-called helpers might just be the undercover fellow the officers told me would be keeping his eye and ears open about me.

hould I slip, these officers, who now seem helpful would be left with no other choice or course but to ship me to the Gambia.

Came the next day and at the agreed time and spot these men arrived in a different car. I became worried, but kept my composure and did exactly just what I was told to do. We drove away from campus to the outskirts of Monrovia.

I had left a note stating my current predicament under the pillow at the dormitory just in case these trigger-happy fellows decide to finish me or repatriate me to the Gambia. When a safe place was located, they parked the car in the bush and we walked into a thicker canopy.

I prayed at that juncture for believing they were going to finish me. The slim lad laid out conditions under which they could help me if I wanted to escape to any country of my choice.

Then I was shown a memorandum from the Gambia Justice Depart to the Liberian Government requesting the arrest and return or deportation of some twenty Gambians.

My name was on the list. The only thing that came to mind was that perhaps the Gambian authorities mistook me to be a member of the Movement for Justice (MOJA).

I told the officers that I was no member of Moja-Gambia and that the whole thing was a big mistake and that the government in Gambia was clamping down on all Moja suspects.

I would justice to myself by accepting their offer to help before higher officers know that I am still in Liberia when they were told that I had been sent back two weeks ago in the first raid.

The officer told me that if I wet their hands they would do their best to help me escape to any country of my choosing.

They guaranteed to go the extra mile with me as long as I did what they suggested to me. We then drove to the nearest bank where I Withdrew $400 us dollars and paid each of them $200 leaving my account closed.

This was big money in those dark days, especially when converted to Liberian dollars. However all I cared for was to get out and head back to the United States of America.

All of a sudden fears expressed by my sister while I was in Gambia became obvious to me. She asked, "Are you out of your mind to leave America to study medicine in Africa? Have you not heard about the cat and mouse games between the government and students?"

I now had no doubts about the officers' intention to help me out of the darkness. I had no money left and yet they did all they promised except provide me with a copy of the memoranda from the Gambia.

They insist that giving it to me would not only implicate them but would compromise the work of other colleagues and higher up officials may court marshal them if the document was found with me. It will blow their cover and reveal them giving it to me as there was other way I would be able to lay hands on it.

We compromised to have it sent to me while in Sandusky, Michigan, USA. I never received it nor were the numerous letters I sent a given postbox ever elicit a response from my Liberian Security friends. I called them friends because unlike my previous encounters these turned out to be an exception for they kept their side of the deal we had agreed on and remained trustworthy throughout the time I was under their watchful eyes in Liberia. They then reported to their new superior officer that I had fled the country by the time they got to me at the campus. I moved into the interior and stayed at a farmer friend's secrete house.

The farmer became life between the town, officers and I. This gracious farmer sent word to the officials whenever I needed their assistance in mailing letters or sending telegrams to friends in America.

Thursdays were my meeting days with the officials. In one of these meeting came the most surprising confirmation of the request to be deported to the Gambia.

The acting dean called me into his office and told me of the termination of my studies with the university and that was all he could tell. He then bid me goodbye and asked that I take care of my life and act fast.

This was the last piece of the puzzle left to convince me of the perilous state I might be facing. I took a few shirts with me and left the campus immediately to join the friends helping me make a get away to freedom before it is too late to do so.

We drove past the airport and rubber plantation before detouring into one of the obscure huts in that area. This location "X" was my designated hiding place until all transactions for my flight to America were completed.

Their village farmer friend was alerted and told of my arrival. The farmer was told not to talk to any other person or official about my being in the vicinity and that my location and lookout post must be changed whenever things looked suspicious or about to be compromised. The farmer kept his promise and I began the most excruciating experience of my life at the time. From that moment in 1981 on, I never knew a day's or night's peace. Every place, person or time became equally suspect. I feared Liberians, military men and any other farmer who might run into me by accident.

My security friends agreed not to put on uniforms when coming to visit me or bring messages. That was the only way I could or would be seen by anyone other than the farmer friend of mine. It guaranteed avoiding mistakes taking another uniformed man as an emissary for the officers. My farmer friend would move me to a different location or to an abandoned hut quite out of reach of unsuspecting intruders.

I applied my heart to the instructions given and ears to pick up any unusual sound or approaches during the night. This lifestyle continued for the rest of the month of November. Meanwhile, now that I was certain that my life was in jeopardy, I drafted a telegram to friends in America asking for their help. Numerous letters I sent after the telegram reinforced my request. My security friends moved me secretly into Monrovia the day I needed to make visa application to the United States.

Mr. Cloyd Ramsey, Michigan friend of mine, had already sent a round trip air ticket as requested for the B2 visa to Detroit, Michigan. I almost declared my request for asylum at the U.S Embassy in Monrovia, but remembered what happened at the French Embassy with regards to Tolbert junior.

I decided to accept the B2 visa under the circumstances.

The visa officer had no inclination or hint as to why I was nervous. She calmed down by letting me know that she will issue a visa to me. And this was done promptly. Back in the Gambia, arrests continued of persons opposed to the government or identified with elements supporting the coup d'etat attempt and prosecuted under emergency powers and special tribunals of judiciary proceedings.

By December 17th, 1981, all my flight arrangements had been completed and carefully reviewed and alternative escape routes put into place. I telegrammed Cloyd Ramsey of my pending arrival time in New York and Detroit on the 20th, of December 1981.

The flight was scheduled to leave at 11 pm on December 19th, 1981. We followed our plan to the letter and I was met at the airport by one of the clerks working at the departures terminals.

She saw to it that my luggage was among those checked in at the counter and loaded aboard the Pan Am flight to New York.

I passed through immigration and costumes without a hitch and les delay than most would normally be encountered in an African departure lounge. My Security friends in Monrovia did every thing I needed for the flight back to America.

No one worried about me or asked questions. Instead those who spoke to me only wished me a pleasant flight to America. Up to now flying from Africa to America connotes going from extreme poverty stricken to endless riches.

The American goldmine was all there to grapple with as some imagined America. Having been there, I know better that the riches of America came part

from hard work, investments and respect of law and order that allowed fruition of industrial ideas.
Nothing goes forward in a place where banditry and gun buts are the art investments and rule of the day.
I made certain to be among the first to board the huge metal bird about to set me once more to freedom and reality.
Meanwhile my security friends were on standby incase they had to resort to our second alternative escape route in the event of an over-booking of the flight or some unforeseen developments.
None the less everything went as planned and I felt lighter when I stepped into the giant Boeing 747, very soon to be air born to America. It was difficult moment for me as I was heading for exile in the United States in contravention to all what I believed in or expected in my life.
The airhostess did not notice fear and uneasiness in me of being discovered until after take off. I prayed for God to bring peace to Africa and give a rewarding end to all my nightmares.
I was numb inside and I cried like a baby for I was leaving my parents, family, friends and above all land I loved dearly behind until God would have me return safely to be with family while serving the Gambia.
I loved the Gambia and had hoped that I would be able to contribute to her growth and reward my aging parents. I did not sleep throughout the flight to America. I just kept ruminating about my future that of Africa and what would happen to my family when my escape to America comes to light.

It could land those security men who helped escape in trouble if discovered. Do I deserve their blood on my innocent hands? I had asked the officers to send someone overland via Sierra Leone to inform my parents of my escape to America, the champion of freedom, at Njawara village at the North Bank in the Gambia.

I also begged them send me photocopy of the request from the Gambia Justice Department for my extradition from Liberia to face routine investigations regarding my possible involvement with Moja-Gambia.

It was supposed to be sent to me at Sandusky within ten days of my arrival the United States. Were they going to do it or would forget? My B2 visa was only good for sixty days, after which I had to make the most painful decision of my life.

I must request asylum from the government of the United States of America or return directly to the Gambia. Another civic lesson was about to unfold in my life even more challenging than previous encounters.

Late Auntie Meta Ndow with Alasan Mballow Jr.

WELCOME TO AMERICA

It was 1.15 pm, December 20th, 1981 when our plane started to descend. My vision of the future turned blurred if not bleak and uncertain. I kept praying for solutions and also repeated several quotations from Samuel Sharp but the most frequent was, "Even so the Lord doth pour upon them His blessings manifold."
I took a last look over my window and there it was, New York and her abundant skyscrapers beckoning me with the outstretched hands of the lady of freedom, Stature of Liberty, ready to welcome me once more to America, the pillar of freedom and human rights.
The landing was smooth and we taxied to the arrival terminal in fifteen minutes after touchdown. I pinched myself to make certain that I lived to see this day come true and had flash back of my last hours at the village in the Liberian jungle.
There were no doubts in my mind that I was back in the United States of America beset with serious problems that cried out loud for solutions. I have no reason why the Lord kept me sane through my ordeals in Liberia amid swam of mosquitoes and crawling insets not to mention various poisonous snakes that passed my way.
At the same time I was very grateful and thankful to God, my Liberian friends and Mr. Cloyd Ramsey for having helped me escape to America despite ignominy of being on exile The immigration and costumes check points did not take too long nor was I asked any out of the way probing questions.

I caught my next flight to Detroit, Michigan from LaGuardia airport around 3,15 pm the same day. The Ramseys were at the Detroit Metro-International arrival terminal waiting for me. They must have noted the strain and fatigue in my face, if not the sorrow of leaving my beloved Gambia and people behind for an indefinite time.
They welcomed me graciously and at baggage retrieval I took what I thought was my luggage to the car. It was not until we made it Sandusky that we realized the re had been a mismatched in the boxes. I had mistakenly taken some else blue Samsonite suitcase identical to mine instead.
I was so embarrassed by it but Mr. Ramsey phoned the airport and informed them of the mix up or as he put it, "The accidental exchange of luggage." The official he spoke to agreed for the suitcase to be returned to Metro Airport the next day.
Sandusky, Michigan is a very small rural town located in the Southeastern region of Michigan, where most people are farmers. The Ramseys had moved from Alpena to Sandusky by my second trip to the United States.
I became part of the Ramsey family since my early days at Alpena Community College in Alpena, Michigan in 1967. Life has it that when some of us were created the mould broke. Most give time and energy to their own families or to work that brings them some happiness and some money.
Clyod and Noreta Ramsey are among a few who give themselves wholly and unselfishly to others. I can be able to tell you enough how devoted this family is in sharing their lives with the needy unless you meet them.

In brief, the Ramseys fed me, sheltered when I needed it until I got my feet back on the ground. They are salvation voice in the wilderness of life's rugged road. I stay at the guest room while in Sandusky. I slept soundly on the first day more than I ever did for months.

The family and I went over the horrors of my African encounter several times. I wrote to my parents, the Gambia government and friends hoping that someone trustworthy would reply to let me know that the whole fiasco was a mistake.

I guess a drowning man hangs onto any straw that passed his way in his effort to save his precious life. This never happened; instead, we later found out that the letters were never delivered.

I kept hoping that my case was a mistaken instructions or identity that a reply would soon lay to rest or affirm my hunch. Days passed into weeks and soon into months and February 1, 1982 were the deadline for my filing an application for asylum or leave the United States of America forthwith. My arrival in Sandusky became public when the Sandusky tribune published an article about the Christian gesture of the Ramseys at the end of my first week in the town.

The Tribune had or pictures and dwelt on the political instability, the corruption and emigrational difficulties ahead me. Life's enemy time kept ticking away towards expiration date of my B2 visa. There was no other situation less tense and so empty of hope than this in my entire life. Life became an abyss of despair which only God and good friends like the Ramseys, Dr. Egli and Viola Glennie pulled me of from underneath.

Below is one of several letters I wrote to the Gambia just in case someone made a mistake in Liberia. Most of my letters were addressed to then Establishment Secretary of the Gambia Government.

Sandusky
Michigan
U. S. A.

Establishment secretary
The quadrangle
Banjul, The Gambia

Dear Secretary,

I am still shocked and perplexed by the Gambia's termination of my studies in Liberia because of letters I wrote in behalf of detainees. I have since my return to the United States, written several times jut to find out if it were one of those cases of mistaken instructions.

I hope this note, unlike several before it, will elicit a response from the Gambia government. Like most serious minded Gambians I am willing to serve our people as a physician despite all the difficulties I encountered in Liberia.

I have been readmitted to a medical school in America but could not start because of visa problems that are blocking my enrolment. I have sought temporal protection until things are clarified from the Gambia.

Again, if there be any chance that the whole affair was a mistake please kindly have the government reinstate me at any medical school it wishes to have me complete my training.
No matter what the Gambia decided my dedication and determination to contribute modern medical aid to our people, especially the farming community, shall be cornerstone in my life.
 Sincerely
Alhasan S. Ceesay

This too fell on deaf ears. The fact that all attempts to get direct verification from the Gambian officials failed sent me into the most severe depression of my life. I was so devastated that I broke into uncontrollable tears on New Year's Day when Ramsey and all their friends and nearby relatives came to dinner.
I was not able to handle the constant reminders and questions regarding Gambia's inhumane treat and the horrible experience I had while in Monrovia, Liberia, West Africa. It was difficult to take difficult take in and likewise equally difficult for me to believe the trend my life followed.
I still remained embarrassed for having ruined that New Year's evening for the Ramseys and the guests. Cloyd and Noreta were so understanding and forgiving that I got over it and was able to overcome numerous more surprises life had awaiting me at Sandusky.
From that moment on I gained strength to survive and plan for my freedom and eventual return to medical school either in Africa or America. On January 15th, 1982, I was prompted to make a last

minute ditch effort to elicit some form of response from the Gambia by sending via the Director of Medical Service the following telegram, "Ran into serious problems in Monrovia, Liberia. Please try and have me transferred to Nigeria or any other medical school.

My Fellowship from the E. E. C. is transferable to any medical school in Africa. Reply waited." Again, Gambia did not care to reply. I lamented that virtue cannot live me out of the teeth of emulation. William Shakespeare stated my condition well when he wrote:

"Between the acting of a dreadful thing and the first motion, all the interim is like a phantasm, or a hideous dream. The genius and the mortal instruments like to a little kingdom, suffers then the nature of an insurrection." Indeed an insurrection had been going on in my head since the day of my first encounter with trigger-happy Liberian uniformed men during those horrible days of the coup d'etat of April 15th 1980 which got worse when I was in hiding in Liberia.

I became fully aware of the need for courage, persistence and strength with endurance to prepare my mind of the coming exile days and the form it may turn out to be for me. Meanwhile Mr. Ramsey telephoned both ministries of External Affairs and of Health Services in the Gambia as an attempt to verify and correct any possible misunderstanding that may have occurred.

This too having failed, Ramsey called several friends and representatives seeking advice on how to request asylum should I decide to file for political asylum in the United States of America.

On January 6th 1982 we received a package from senator Carl Levin's Washington, D. C. office containing three copies of Form 1-589 for my use in seeking asylum in the USA. I filled them immediately with as much detail and documentation as possible.

The only crucial missing document being photocopy of the request from the Gambia to Liberian authority asking for my repatriation to face routine questioning about my being involved with Moja-Gambia.

The mere fact that I filled the forms without the help of a solicitor was a mistake that came to roost home at later date in our processing the asylum request. Mr. Ramsey and I kept receiving sad news from the Gambia from television reports.

No one from the Gambia government cared or dare reply to our enquiries. Friends and relatives who dare write made it clear that I would be arrested and incarcerated just as happened to my friends, when and if I ventured to return to the Gambia at that time. Further more students in America corroborated eminent danger should I be forced to return to the Gambia at the instant. However, when my lawyer Francis Conti, asked them to appear before the immigration officer in Detroit in my behalf or sign affidavits in support of my effort these students backed away for fear of what may ensue or be done to their relatives in the Gambia. With everything neatly typed Mr. Ramsey and I agreed to take the bull by the horns and go to the Immigration and Naturalization Service in Detroit, Michigan, USA within a week's time. On the night of February 21, 1982, I asked myself, "What is the essence of existence if one cannot bring peace and happiness to family, friend even mankind? I surmised that the agonies of history could find their justification only in the realized freedom and happiness that is ultimately made for humanity. I then renewed my covenant with God and Africa. I assured my maker that I would return to serve my people no matter how long this ordeal may take to resolve.

I prayed for peace and tranquility to my beloved Gambia, Africa and the world at large. It was well after 2 Am and so the Ramsey on hearing loud voice ran from their room to find out what was happening.

I apologized and told them that I was thinking loud and not aware of the disturbance. I decided, after praying all night, to file a request for political asylum in the United States of America before my B2 visa expires on February 23rd 1982.

A true insurrection went in my brain. On February 22nd 1982, I made my decision to seek asylum, come what may, known to Mr. Ramsey. Right after it I seemed to have an untapped well of power and control I never dreamt of possessing.

I kept singing to myself that freedom; democracy and human rights are worthwhile sacrifices for my strength. To make African governments respect instruments of peace, service and of progress one must stand for human dignity.

Mr. Ramsey and I headed for the Immigration and Naturalization Service (INS) at Mount Elliot Street, Detroit, Michigan the same day. We submitted the asylum form 1-589, on February 22nd 1982, to the receptionist and kept photocopies of all accepted documents and her name just in case I am asked whom did I submit my claim to and where among many INS branches. I moved to East Lansing few weeks after submitting my asylum claim or petition and attended Michigan State University as guest student.

Here I met my old friend Nelson Herron, my former Alpena Community College colleague and friend I mentioned in earlier sections of this work. I stayed with Nelson who was instrumental in getting some help for me.

Both he and Mike Bennett of Alpena Community College, made life in East Lansing tolerable during those dark times of my life. I remained eternally grateful to them for their kindness and generosity. Also easing my life was Dr. Norman Robinson, and Dr. Charles Coy both of the Veterinary Laboratory at Michigan State University.

Four months after submitting my request for asylum I received a letter May 20, 1982, from the Acting District Director of immigration and Naturalization Service, Mr. Ronald A. Brooks. It specifically stated that my examination day was set for July 8th 1982 and that I should see a K. Dawson, Immigration Examiner and that I should take with me my passport, Form 1-94 and any and al evidence to support my request.

In small print it said, "Failure to appear as scheduled may rest in denial of your request for lack pf persecution per 0.1.103 2(o)" Ramsey and I reported at the INS Detroit Office at 7 Am on July 8th 1982 as scheduled by the appointment sent us. It became one of the longest vigils of my life. I was nervous but very confident of my facts and above all else my perception of the United States' Justice system buoyed me. Finally Mr. Kenneth A. Shillair, the designated Immigration officer on the case, called me and showed us his office. He eased my fears when he smilingly asked Mr. Ramsey to take a seat by his table.

He began the examination by asking me extensively all that transpired and why I fear persecution if asked to return to the Gambia at that particular time. I told him everything I knew, giving an account of my experience with the Gambia and while in Liberia.

He was vividly and equally disturbed by the way I had to be kept in hiding in Liberia and the fact that the Gambia continued to ignore our inquiries or to deny the allegations. He after grilling me for an hour and half turned to Mr. Ramsey and questioned him about what he knew and how and when did Mr. Ramsey meet me.

Ramsey gave an honest understanding of my plight and the help that he and other Americans citizens contributed to my education. We left letters, newspapers and all pertinent evidence concerning my case with Mr. Kenneth A. Shillair at the end of the interview.

He looked at his watch and asked if I had anything more to add to what had been said and deposited at that time. I told him that was all I had at the time and would certainly send more as I receive information from either the Gambian or the Gambia government in due course.

He saw to the door and promised Mr. Ramsey that he would certainly do the best the law permits him to do with my request. The warm and friendly

handshake left hope trickling down my throat. I could taste freedom by his promise to do as much as can be for my case. Good people are not difficult to tell and this was one good Immigration Officer. Mr. Kenneth A. Shillair and Mrs. K. Dawson reported their findings to the District Director, Mr. James H. Montgomery, who then sent the following letter to the Bureau of Human affairs with a, "A brilliant Grant recommendation" for my asylum application.
United States Department of Justice
Immigration and Naturalization Service
Detroit, Michigan 48207
October 8th 1982

Bureau of Rights and Humanitarian Affairs
Department of State, Room // 7802
Washington, D. C. 20520

Dear Sir,

Reference is made to the request for Asylum in the United States, Form 1-589, submitted by Alhasan S. Ceesay, a native and/or citizen of the Gambia. In accordance with Title 8, Code of Federal regulations, part 208.7 your opinion is requested regarding the validity of applicant's request. Copies of the request, addendum, all supporting documentation, and the interviewing officer's memorandum of the interview, with recommendation are forwarded herewith. Based on my review of the officer's report of the interview and documentation in support of the request for asylum. It is my opinion that the case is meritorious.

Therefore, the service intends to approve the request. Please advise if, in your opinion, the application has or has not established a claim to asylum. Your continued co-operation in this matter is greatly appreciated.
Sincerely
James H. Montgomery
District Director
I remain eternally grateful to Mr. Kenneth A. Shillair, Mrs. K. Dawson and Mr. James H. Montgomery of the Detroit INS branch 1982 for solidifying my faith in the American system of Justice.
However, fighting injustice nowadays is like wrestling a sea of putrefying sea of mud while in it to up to one's armpits if not the neck. Political cronyism normally masks and stifles justified decisions.
It took seven months, April 8, 1982 to be exact, before I received a reply from the Detroit INS office. It did recommend me for grant of asylum in the USA as above but president Jawara's shameless, boot-liking tentacles at the Gambia Embassy went to work on making sure that such opinion did not surface by painting unfounded stories about me and heaping high praises of Jawara being democratic and strong supporter of human rights.
The Banjul Charter was a joke fumigated by the tsars of the city with Jawara penning it. On Saturday, February 23 1982, a blast, which was later found to originate from the nearby Mooney Oil Cooperation service station next door to my apartment on Clement Street, Lansing, blew up shattering my bedroom window and those of fourteen other

buildings. I at first thought that someone was sent to finish me before I could embarrass the Gambian government. It was later proven that a tanker truck was delivering gasoline into underground storage tanks when a stray spark set the explosion and demolished my building.

The blast left me shaken for days. I moved to another apartment on 127 Shepard Street, where Nelson Herron and other friends stayed, I remained at Shepard Street until May 1983 before returning to Sandusky, Michigan. District Direct, Mr. James H. Montgomery, had just sent a second letter from the INS. It read:

Date: April 7th 1983

Dear Mr. Ceesay,

Reference is made to your request for asylum in the United States filed on February22, 1982, enclosed is a copy of a letter dated February 8, 1983 from the State Department wherein it is stated that you have failed to establish a well founded fear of persecution within the meaning of the United Nations Convention and protocol relating to the status of refugee should you return to the Gambia. You are hereby advised, pursuant to title 8, Code of Federal regulations 103.2(b), that this service intends to deny your request based upon the opinion of the State Department.

The evidence and other articles are insufficient to establish a claim to asylum unless they relate directly to you and provide insight into reasons for seeking asylum.

In the absence of a response from you during this period the service will proceed with the evidence on record.
Sincerely
James H. Montgomery
District Director

I naturally rushed to see what the attached pages from the State Department purported. I was eager to know what reasons it gave in rejecting my asylum petition. USA was a place I acquired most of my ideals. Here is that conundrum from the Department of State.

United States Department of State
Washington, D. C. 20520

RE: Alhasan Siswao Ceesay

Dear Sir,

This is in reply to the request for an advisory opinion concerning the asylum request of the above named individual. According to information contained in the application, the applicant, who entered the U. S. most recently in December, 1981, alleges that because he wrote letters to the government of the Gambia protesting the detention of some of his friends following the July, 1981 attempted coup in the Gambia, he would be persecuted upon returning home.
The applicant was in Monrovia as a student at the time of the coup attempt in his homeland. While the coup attempt in the Gambia resulted in the arrest of

about 1000 people, approximately 800 were quickly released without trial. The government of the Gambia published list of detainees, released detainees, and those cases where disposed off administratively.

The remainder is receiving due process of law. Of those tried some have been convicted and others acquitted. Trials are stilt continuing in a reasonably open and correct manner and as of October only 97 persons remained in detention.

The applicant claimed that his open support for Latif Sanyang and others would endanger him. According to our information, Latif Sanyang has a brother with the same name as the alleged leader of the coup.

The brother, who was in the United States at the time of the coup, was mistakenly assumed to have been cause of Latif Sanyang's arrest on suspicion. He will return shortly to his government job.

Since the applicant was not in the Gambia at the time of coup attempt, and as his post coup involvement was on behalf of a person who has been cleared and released, we are of the opinion that the applicant does not have a well-founded fear of persecution in the Gambia within the meaning of the United Nations convention and protocol relating to the status of refugee.

Sincerely

Lawrence Arthur

These two letters were like double-edged daggers trusted simultaneously into my heart. It was akin to surprise stab inflicting a mortal gash by a brother. It was the unkindest cut of all and last straw that could break the donkey's back or vanquished me.

They spelled and herald doom for me and magnified my fears. It showed that I just an insignificant minor if not an ordinary who does not deserve U.S. because he does not belong to bigger boys or Banjul power. It almost said justice was relevant to which quarter one belongs.

It clearly showed that governments cared only about opinions of counter part governments, no matter how ill-treated their subjects, and it does not matter whether one stands for the common weal or justice. I still had no doubts that had I been affiliated with the Banjul tsars, married to or with those in high office in the Gambia the outcome of my petition would have been totally different.

Wondering in thought, I asked silently, was life, which has thrown so many foul balls at me, in another process of delivering one more nightmare to me. The advisory opinion did not consider the fact the Gambia had been discussing me and had already recognized me, from dubious sources, as one of the political agitators in North America. According to testimony of its former diplomat in Saudi Arabia, Dr, Sulayman S. Nyang, the Gambia had already labeled me as tribalist and political agitator well into my undergraduate years.

He testified that the government was finding ways to contain me at all length during my undergraduate years. Dr. Nyang not only wrote an affidavit to the fact that the Gambia been nervous about me but also testified before an INS judge hon.

Charles Auslander to that effect in my behalf. Dr. Nyang's testimony and affidavit states thus: During the period I was Deputy head of the Gambia Mission in Saudi Arabia, I was present during discussions by Gambian government officials about political agitators and dissidents, On a number of occasions, Alhasan Ceesay was identified during such discussions as a political agitator and one of the members of the Mandinka tribe who repeatedly expressed dissatisfaction with the Jawara government's policies.

I am confident that Alhasan still has a reputation among Jawara government officials for being a political agitator and a tribalist. At the time of the coup, Alhasan and a number of other students from the Gambia who were identified with a radical political party, the Movement for Justice in Africa (MOJA).

After their return to the Gambia, a number of Alhasan's friends were placed under arrest." Dr. Sulayman S. Nyang summed up his affidavit saying, "I am aware that this affidavit will be used in support of Alhasan Ceesay's application for political asylum in the United States and believe that Alhasan Ceesay's fear of being persecuted, if forced to return to the Gambia, is reasonable.

I am certain he would be placed under arrest anyway. At least, he would be ostracized or blacklisted by the Jawara government and his activities would be monitored. In addition he will not be permitted to continue medical school." The state department disregarded this crucial affidavit from the very horses' mouth, forgetting that Dr. Sulayman S. Nyang used to oversee such meetings and knows more about the mentality of most of the officials he was testifying against.

They were his colleagues and he knew all about the government's covert behaviours. The Bureau of Humanitarian Affairs had ears only for the cronies of the Jawara government in Washington, D. C. They were freeing their relatives and leaving provincials like Kebba Sanneh and other lounging in open air holding camps.

President Jawara, through the Banjul tsars created an illusion of practicing democracy and respect for human rights while his opportunist tentacles did otherwise. It took quite a while before the real Medusa government surfaced.

Nonetheless let me state categorically that it did not warrant a coup d'etat and carnage that followed in those dark days in the Gambian history. The State Department insistence that my life was not in jeopardy from the hands of a bunch eager and ingenious to do anything to keep them in power as long as it continues to net money raised by poor American, British, French or German tax payers to spend lavishly.

Aid sent by supper powers to most developing sountries end up being stashed in some internal banks like the Swiss banks; while leaving citizen it was intended for go hungry or eats crumbs.

Another fact not addressed by the state department advisory opinion was that those accidental detainees given administrative reprieve belong to families in high office or came from relatives married to these who exercised their privilege as those above the laws of the Gambia.

It continued to gall me and any other just person when it stated, "Trials are continuing in a reasonable open and correct manner." How could they make such blanket statement without being there to witness draconian kangaroo court in process. Was the state department aware of the fact that the Gambia hired foreign judges and attorneys to mockery of our judiciary? Why where judges not offered chairs in such important affair for the citizens?

These foreign judges and attorneys, in my humble opinion, were nothing but hired guns that would carry out the government's dictate. Perhaps most of them were unemployed in their homelands and like hungry hyenas seized opportunities to their share of the carcass left behind by a heinous attempted coup d'etat of July 1981.

Why were these so called arms of judiciary recruited under elaborate arrangements at considerable cost to hungry Gambia? It would have been proper and cheaper if Gambian Lawyers and judges were allowed to oversee and decide the guilt or innocent of the accused in accordance to our Gambian laws than using foreign buccaneers.

It was not because the government or city click wanted to see justice meted out impartially but because those at the throttle wanted to purge innocent people they believe or suspect to dissidents to the Jawara regime. They were scared of their dirty laundries being exposed to public view.

This disguised use of the Gambian judiciary was a farce lower than the lowest. The whole fiasco was not to assure fair trials because none Gambian hired by the regime, would most likely, be more interested in earning a living than caring whether legal reviews of the cases or the events filled with endless corruption that lead to the unholy uprising of July,

1981, were meticulously reviewed. The policies of government and over high handedness might have lead to the cause of the undignified and unholy attempt to remove the regime from power. Coup d'etats are a disgrace, disdains and demeaning debacle to human beings.

The perpetrators most have to be less than the lowest animal on earth to cause such carnage and suffering to people it claim fellow human beings and citizens.

It would have suited the purpose had these hired hands or government's life guns but neutral volunteers offering legal help expertise to their Gambian counterparts trying the accused.

Tell me where in Africa a hired foreign judge is not an instrument of the president of that country? Hence government became indirectly jury and judge over lives of innocent people it was already concerned or angry at in the first place.

Instead of a free judiciary as opinioned by the stat department that purchased justice was, "Open and correct law," for Gambians to be tried by such gimmickry.

Will the Americans ever allow Gambian judges, bought or hired by the U. S. government during an uprising, to try citizens of the United States? I hope not.

The Gambia government distrusted its own British trained judges and lawyers and the legal system by which its subjects are being sent to jail. Was it giving open and correct law or justice that will not stand against whims and wishes of tsars in power? Can hired judges or personnel go against their employer or are they likely to do as told by their employer.

In my humble opinion the state department's opinion was bias and hastily or deuced from cover up information supplied to it by the then Gambia Embassy officials.

Did they tell the state department that Dr. Sulayman S. Nyang was assigned to covertly report on students in America or the fact that I was considered a political agitator and tribalist? The state department opinion makes me want to puke or ponder when it said that the Gambia thought it was Latif Sanyang's brother, Samba Sanyang, who led the attempted coup d'etat of July 1981.

How can the Gambia of think such rubbish when Samba Sanyang was in class in America at the time of the July coup attempt? Samba is a peaceful person who would never be involved in such atrocity like an overthrow of the Gambia government.

Did the government look at their student list or was the inclusion of Samba Sanyang a deliberate ignorance of the facts that cause the uprising which gave the city tsars an opportunity to nap those they fear will out root from their post for being honest and better qualified persons?

The only list they had was that kept on those they deem political dissident, as they kept persistent none blinking hawk-eye and record on me while I was in United states of America.

Does it in the name of justice and fairness, have to take eleven months to establish contact with the U. S. Schools, U. S. in the Gambia or the state department to find out whether poor Samba Sanyang, who was by the way busy with his studies in America, had time for such drastic and inhuman plans for his fellow citizens? It was flimsy gimmick from or by certain quarters to keep level headed provincials out of circulation to create posts for their own. Can the advisory opinion explain why Latif Sanyang and others were kept for eleven months under detention while the government pretends to correct what was later admitted to be case of mistaken identity?

Finally, was the state department aware of the fact that Latif and all I wrote in protest for were never allowed to return to posts in the civil service? Does this equal punitive damage for my friends who lost their jobs for no fault of theirs?

The state depart should have never allowed itself accept that arrest and detention of Latif and others was an error that was corrected shortly there after as the opinion implied in the letter to INS District Director at Detroit, Mr. James H. Montgomery. I will now let you read Latif Sanyangs letter to the Rt. Rev. Coleman McGehee, Bishop of Diocese of Michigan in Detroit, for you to find out if the Gambia was telling the state department truth and nothing but the truth surrounding the arrests of these and numerous other innocent victims of the purge so help it God.

Below is Latif's letter to Bishop McGehee.

P. O. Box 2469
Serekunda
The Gambia
West Africa
August 29th 1983

Dear Sir,

I am writing to thank you very much for the invaluable service you have been rendering to Alhasan Ceesay since his return/arrival in the U. S. A.

Your kindness towards Alhasan Ceesay has been made known to all his relatives and friends throughout the Gambia. It is in this regard that I am writing this short letter to express our appreciation of your genuine love and concern for Alhasan's welfare.

Alhasan and I have been very close friends for over twenty years. We are all children of poor rural farmers. We were in the same class at high school. I am positively and confidently speaking of him as a harmless person with a pleasant and charming personality.

He loves people and is extremely sociable. If there is any odd against him, it is because he is too much full of ambition to achieve his desired goals. He really is harmless. Like most African countries, the Gambia also received its share of instability on the 30th of July 1981, when some Gambians attempted to overthrow the government of the country.

Through the intervention of the Republic of Senegal, the rebellion was crushed. The aftermath of the attempted coup was the arrest and detention of over one thousand innocent persons as suspects and measure to enable the government to locate the culprits.

In this mad state of confusion, I was personally arrested and detained for almost a year. I did not know why I was arrested, detained and up till now nobody has told me the reason for the move. During my period of internment, distance was no handicap to Alhasan Ceesay in fighting incessantly for my release. He communicated with our head of state and with other persons of authority or influence.

This endangers his position on returning to the Gambia. Although I committed no crime at all, yet my arbitrary arrest and detention cost me losing my job. I had my appointment terminated.

The state of emergency is still in force and gives government a lot of sweeping powers for arrest and detentions. I have got my experience and would not want to see Alhasan Ceesay passing through the same trauma.

His poor old father and mother are so worried about Alhasan's safety in the event of any premature return to the Gambia. Please kindly prevail on him not to return now until the situation turns normal. Please give my love and warmest regards to your family.

Sincerely

Latif T. Sanyang

If this leaves any doubts about my safety being in danger should I be forced to return prematurely to the Gambia, then I do not know what the opinion of the state department was based upon.

It has also made it clear that Latif's arrest and eventual detention was no case of a mistaken identity as claimed by the Gambia to the state department.

Why was his job terminated if the government exonerated him and others? Was the list of released persons or detainees a bamboozlement of the international community into making it believe that there was attempt on the part of the government to correct the crisis without over-reacting? How come it took a year before the Gambia can establish the where about of Latif's brother, Samba Sanyang? Would placing a call to the U. S. Embassy in Gambia to find out if Samba Sanyang was in school or traveled to the Gambia at the time of insurrection take 12 months to verify?

Many questions in the state department's opinion begged to be questioned and investigate to not only to allow the truth come out for justice to prevail in my case and innocent Gambians caught in this dark dragnet.

My dear reader, this must have been the longest international telephone call ever made between two governments. I believe it deserves nomination to the Guinness Book of world Records.

Does not this tell that the advisory opinion was clearly based upon what the Gambia Ambassador told his diplomatic colleagues at the state department who swallowed it wholeheartedly and regurgitated it in the fashioned letter with regards to my asylum request sent to Mr. James H. Montgomery, District Director of the INS branch in Detroit Michigan?

Friendly nations are only friends if they practice moral democratic principles of justness in their dealings and must refrain from supporting tyrannical rulers and laws.

Was the state department aware that writing to the president Jawara's men or cronies enquiring or requesting releases of detainees was considered a serious threat and confrontational challenge to authority of tsars of the government having strong foot hold on the Gambia? I sincerely urge Lawrence Arthur and all those who gave the aforesaid above state department opinion to District Director James H. Montgomery, to polish their freshman courses on Africa and attitude of African leaders when in power.

Their policy follows a modus operandi of one man, one voice, one dictator for life and no rights or place in affairs of state for opponents and dissidents alike even if they were telling the truth about the national state at the time.

Hence my innocuous letters were perceived as second voices the tsars would not accept no matter how reasonable the intent. My writing was certainly perceived as a challenge worthy of being detained if the tsars were able to lay hands on me.

I have been disfavored for a long time and according to Dr. Sulayman Nyang this would have been most opportune moment for the Gambia to settle scores with me.

They would utilize the emergency powers against me to their extreme limits. Was the state department aware that Latif Sanyang was re-arrested shortly after his initial release? If the Government acknowledged the first arrest as that of due to a case of mistaken identity what was the reason for the second short-lived arrest of Latif?

With the advisory opinion issued me, I found I only fell on Scylla while trying to avoid Cherubic. It made my heart as cold and numb as snowball for the dept of the North Pole. It is numerous numbing experiences like I went through that lead to the believe that a serious double standards exist in interpretation and application of laws to protect human rights and democracy by the developed world. These powers do not use stringent applications of democracy or human rights when it comes to the developing world or so-called third world countries.

Shortly there after received the following letter from my parents in May 1983 which said:

Njwara Village
Lower Badibou District
The Gambia
West Africa
May 2nd 1983

Dear Son,

We have heard about the difficulties you are encountering and we are very concerned for your safety. Please persuade your American friends to protect you for a while. From the surface life seems to be normal but where is smoke there is fire underneath.

We cannot say much but do send you prayers and love from all of us. Members of the family are very worried for your safety upon a premature return to the Gambia.

Greetings and please write when you can.
Your father
Sisawo Ceesay

Another letter came from a long time Liberian friend states thus:

Monrovia
Liberia
West Africa
April 17th 1983

Dear Alhasan,

I am sorry for the break in communication between us. The reason was that as soon as I received your last letter I decided to go to the Gambia and inform your father about your situation and what may be your fate if things go wrong.
Your parents strongly advised that you not come to the Gambia at the present moment. Your father said he was questioned about you but he told that he never heard from you since you left Liberia.
He is certain that you will be tried if you show up in the Gambia because friends you wrote about are suspects and that could incriminate you. Some of these are still under detention.
Letters you sent during the disturbance of July 1981 angered very powerful elements in the Gambia government and its tsars. Two of your friends, Latif Sanyang and Kebba Sanneh, who were recently released and promised a return to their jobs, have never had their job, the were instead served with letter terminating their appointments.
This was effective February 15, 1983, and is regrettable indeed. Friends have that they keep a low profile and not discuss politics with anyone, friend or foe. Alhasan, we are all concerned about your safety. We hope that you United States friends will be persuaded to protect you for a while.

We send you our prayers and greetings. I have to run to class but my girl friend will mail this letter to you today. Good luck. The family is really worried about you. Write soon.
Your Friend
Samuel Siafa

All of the above supportive documents reached me at a very confusing moment in time. Recall that the INS District Director at the Detroit branch had by then given me fifteen days in which to come up with additional evidence or be deported back to the Gambia.

My anxiety heightened and I wrote to nearly all American friends asking for advice and help about nightmare and plight about to engulf me. It was at this time that I wrote to one of my very good friends, Dr. Harvey I. Sloane, Mayor of Louisville, Kentucky, asking for his help.

Meanwhile my location at Sandusky made transactions I needed done very difficult and at time replies reach me too late. The distance between Sandusky and Detroit became an impediment for communication and too far from any government agency or would be helpful organization.

On April 11th 1983, I told Mr. Cloyd Ramsey that it would be best if I move to Detroit to fight my case. On the morning of April 15, 1983, Mr. Clyod Ramsey and I drove to Detroit to search for a sanctuary or help. I wrote the following farewell letter to the Ramseys on paper blotted with my tears. It read:

Sandusky, Michigan
April 15th 1983

Dear friends,

Each of us has a path to follow. I am, today, set on one that will be trying but I will do all I can to make the rest of my life useful and functional for the Gambia and man.
I am forever indebted to you and again I express profound gratitude in behalf of my village, and my family. Thank you. I will succeed in life. God bless you. God is my guide.
Sincerely
Alhasan S. Ceesay
Mr. Ramsey and I drove to Detroit in an unusual or what I called a rare emotional silence. The Ramseys are more than friends to me. They are cherished family among the cardinal part of my American experience.
It was 1.30 pm when we stopped at the Greyhound bus terminal where I checked one of the phone books and picked at random on the Episcopalian Diocese of Michigan on Woodward Avenue thinking it one of the catholic missions in Detroit. When we stopped at the given address it showed St. Paul's Cathedral of the Diocese.
I told Mr. Ramsey to drive to the back entrance for me to check whether that was the Diocese. Lo and behold it was the Diocese of Michigan. Still believing it to be a Catholic mission, I went in and asked the guard for directions to an office to help me. Mr. Ramsey helped unload my things and then took off immediately because he had a long day before him.

He was going to drive to California the next day. My reasons for coming to Detroit were very clear. These were days of doubt about my future and those of innocent Africans. It was a sorrowful time when African politicians and military had hay day in wrecking innocent lives thoughtlessly.

Hence, American sense of justice was the only humane salvation, if not the only avenue of hope and protection left to me.

Over a grim blackness of an impending denial of my request for political asylum, I walked into the hallowed halls of St. Paul's Cathedral, Episcopal Diocese of Michigan on April 15th 1983, I found Hugh Davis, the security guard at the entrance.

He helped me put my luggage at safe place and then directed me to a Mrs. Patricia Kobylski, commonly called Pat, Refugee coordinator for the Diocese. After a few hurried flights I was on the second floor where I met Muncel Kyle, who showed me Mrs. Kobylski's office. As soon as I reached the office, Patricia stopped her typing and asked what help she could give me.

I narrated my mission in a nervous way and showed her all the papers along with notice of a pending denial by the District Director at the INS in Detroit. She read everything or every piece of article I gave her and then telephoned Rev. Virgil Jones at Wayne State University and followed with another to Rev. Hugh C. White, assistant to the Bishop, who came to her office right away.

Pat, Hugh and I went over all aspects of my plight and the eminent danger if forced to return to the Gambia prematurely. At times, I broke down into subs and tears but later picked up my sanity and continued telling my sad experience and lost I encountered since 1981. The very day Rev. White and Pat were able to contact Mr. John Cannon, the Chancellor of the Diocese about my case.

Mr. Cannon in turn contacted his colleague Robert Duty at the Dykema, Gossett, Spencer, Goodnow and Trig law firm at the Renaissance Centre in Detroit. Meanwhile, Pat and Rev. White continued to contact friends at the refugee legal aids department in New York.

The Cots on Trumbull Street, Detroit agreed to lodge me for that night. Rev. Virgil Jones returned the telephone call that was placed earlier on by Pat Kobyiski.

He was already contacting an attorney who once helped him assist a Ugandan in a similar need. Rev. Hugh C. White and John Cannon having made arrangements for me to see Mr. Robert Duty at the Renaissance Centre down town Detroit on Monday 8 am followed this.

We ended the day with Mrs. Pat Kobylski, Theresa and Sharon Forster giving me a ride to the Cots on Trumbull Street. I was ushered into the cots after ten minutes drive through Detroit, motor city of America. I found it jammed with people, all of who are indigent and looked like a collection of lost souls, men and women, old and young.

Some were talking to themselves while others stared at the ceiling if part of another world. Most residents looked like zombies from ghost lands. The sight was unbelievably sad one. The air in the hall was filled with cigarette and tobacco smoke from cheap cigars and all kinds of nicotine products in the market.

I was interviewed by the manager and told to go to the food line. The meal consisted of fish, mashed potatoes, stew and a cup of tea or coffee. I was totally at lost being in such an ungodly place. People stared at me and asked each other what I was doing in a place like the cots.

One had the nerve to ask if I were a junkie or some African drunk. I tried hard to eat the food but was unable because of the stress I was under. Tears welled and ran down my cheeks uncontrollably. It was a depressing experience.

I grew lonely amidst plenty of people who looked more like figurines. I prayed hard for God to help me survive the night at this hell hold of the cots on Trumbull Street, Detroit, Michigan. The experience was hard to bear but it further made me value life more and savoured everything I can.

It made me determined to be of help to my fellow beings. By ten in the evening I was led upstairs to the men's section and shown a bunked near a very seriously ill man with exfoliating dermatitis, as a place for me to spend the rest of the night.

I felt sorry for the poor fellow whose skin seemed in the process of peeling from his body and he smelled like a hospital than anything else. I was later told that it some unknown chemical he took that caused the skin reaction he now manifests.

It was sad case and hopeless case as he could not sleep free of pain. At 11 pm the fellow on the top bunk came in. He was a husky tall fellow who seemed to delight in talking ceaselessly and not care if anyone was listening to him. Worse of all he snored loudly whenever he chances to fall asleep.

This man had been at the coy for just two weeks and everyone in the room was fed up with him. Luckily he was not violent and does not talk to any except himself. I did sleep a wink the whole night because my state of mind would not permit it and the environment was not conducive for me.

I could not tell you how relieved I was when the manager told me that my friends at the Diocese were on the way to pick me up. I thanked God for letting me bunk in the cots for an unusual and unforgettable first night in Detroit, Michigan.

L-R: Tigida Nta Kady Fatoumata 2017

THE EPISCOPALIAN DIOCES OF MICHIGAN

The Diocese, as I came to know, is the administrative headquarters of the Episcopalians of Michigan and is led by a presiding Bishop. The Editor of the Record, Mrs. Lois R. Leonard, in the March 1985, issue of the Record described the Diocese as follows: "The Diocesan office in sense is a bunch of secretaries, bookkeepers, church administrators and other paper work types, not social workers, political experts or lawyers."
Let not this simple reinvasion of the Diocesan fools you. They are to be precise, a gift of devoted warm hearts ready to share their lives and stand by justice whenever called to do so.
They are my America I would like to share in these pages with you. It was here and from these unique people, that I learned that there is a special strength that can sustain us through almost anything. It come from God and from kind hearts as occupies the Diocese of Michigan in Detroit.
The strength come from partly within but even more, it comes from the faith and love of those close to us. I am here in Detroit today partly because I would not give up. But more than that, I am here in America because a lot of kind people would not let me give up even if I had wanted to. A few persons gave themselves wholly and as unselfishly to other in need of the Episcopal Diocese of Michigan.
They devoted their time and dropped self-interests aside to help me fight my case while I was up to my neck in legal and political mud. With their help I completed petition to God and family for giving me

blissful moments when confronted by trivial and vicious sides of life. The Episcopalians fed and sheltered me while I continued fighting my case at the immigration courts. The Diocesans were open minded enough to debate contradictions regarding justice, moral and religious believes which guide and shape world order.

We agreed that slavery as well as injustice is immoral and so was the case when governments ignore justice for ideological or earthly power postures, which in most cases destroys innocent lives, and property for self-aggrandizement.

One should be numbed by killings, horrors and heartaches ordinary people have been enduring from so-called cavaliered governments The supper powers in their East-West tug of wars encouraged dictators, tyrants and inept military men to rule Africa and elsewhere.

These tentacles of evil debauched and deceived us in the name of ideology, while human dignity continues to be denigrated at will. Heads of governments in most of our countries and inept military men who forcefully lead coup d'etat in their lands, are praised and considered heroes instead of puppets.

Should such lowly bestial elements of society be considered heroes of our time? Real democratic and civilized people should not ever recognize tyrants or ruthlessly imposed governments no matter how seemingly friendly they might turn out to be.

It is wrong to force governments on helpless people and wrong should mean the same for all people anywhere on earth. Our people do not deserve these self-style military regimes.

These military governments survive only because the world supper powers give them credence and recognition, despite knowing that their hands are drenched with blood of the innocent that makes feel powerful demons over the people.

One should never forget that one only have a short time to leave on earth and that we need to leave admirable footprints on the sand of time so that another new earthling like us would take heart and continue the good work from where we left.

Allow me return to the Diocesans of Michigan in Detroit. It is said that whosoever is delighted in solitude is either a God or beast.

My friends at the Diocese not only helped me make the past year bearable but they made me certain I am invited to most if not all social functions and movies to avert my becoming lonely. Special thanks go to Rev. Hugh White and family for relentless efforts to keep me sane and mingling with Americans.

In a village no one goes lonely but in big cities like Detroit, the Latin adage "Magna civitas, magna solitudo" applies. Simply stated, the larger the city the greater the solitude. Rev. Hugh C. White championed social aspects for me throughout my stay in Detroit.

The world would have turned into wilderness of solitude without true friends like Hugh White and his family. Meanwhile Mrs. Patricia koblyski, Rt. Rev. Bishop McGehee, Rev. Hugh White, Rev. Virgil Jones, Rev. David Brower, Rev. Bill Wood, Rev. Walter White, Mrs. Ann Kenzie, Mrs., Lois R. Leonard, John Cannon, Mary Hattle, Betty Howitson, Mrs. Shella Garner, Theresa VanGorder,

Alexandra Manshour, W. Y. Gard, professor Francis Conti, Robert Duty, Beth Sax, and Bishop Mason and a host of Episcopalians translated their deep faith, concerns and love of humanity and continued to be my Good Samaritans and a bridge over troubled waters.

These warm hearts were led by the Rt. Rev. H. Coleman McGehee, jr., who was true believer in God, the sanctity of life, and power of knowledge and justice over ignorance, He, like me, defies authority that supplies swords to defend and strengthen ignorance and oppression.

Today, when some one kills he must die but he who kills the spirit goes scotch free. Should friendly oppressive governments continue to be left to cover crime with crime and more crime and not be answerable for their ugly deeds?

Is this international law and justice for the beleaguered? Bishop McGehhe's weekly radio commentaries are a clear picture of the spiritual force leading the Episcopal Diocese of Michigan in Detroit.

I only wish that I lived long enough to take him and his people to be serenade in the Gambia. This bird's eye view of the Diocese suffices at the moment. On April 16th 1983, Patricia Koblyski came to pick me up from the cots at Trumbull Street.

I was relieved to see her. We drove to the Diocese and continued searching for solutions to my problem. She took me to the Renaissance Centre Monday where I met attorney Robert Duty.

Mr. Duty turned to be very friendly and also eager to help me tackle my asylum problem. Again, as before, I narrated every aspect of my plight to him.

He listened very attentively and would at time only interrupt by asking questions to clarify the picture as presented to him. At the end he sent me back to the Diocese to write out all about my political activities from my undergraduate days to the very minute I came to see him.

I went to work on the request the moment I reached the Diocese. Being a novice at typing I spent the better part of the day on the trying to type it until when Sue Coburn came to my rescue. She did a good job for which I am eternally grateful.

However before the Diocese closed for the day Mrs. Patricia Koblyski had set up an ad hoc committee consisting of herself, Bishop McGehee, Bishop Mason, Rev. High C. White, Rev. Virgil Jones, Rev. William Wood, Rev. David Brower and Mrs. Lois R. Leonard, Editor of the Diocesan newspaper, The Record to help me in my fight against deportation to the Gambia.

These ladies and gentlemen became the brains the brains behind my fight with the immigration courts. While gathering more evidence for the INS I took sanctuary at the Mariner's Inn on Ledyard Street. It was time to close and I was taken to the Mariner's Inn on Ledyard Street in Detroit.

THE MARINER'S INN LEDYARD DETROIT MICHIGAN

This is an alcoholic and drug rehabilitation center of the Episcopalian Diocese of Michigan and is administered by a board, an executive director, and an assistant to the director with a bunch of dedicated staff, whose only goal is to help another person.

The Inn offers food, shelter and moral support service to all who needed it. It deals with "common every day problems that beset mankind", according to the current Director Miss Mary Ellen Robertson. She describes the Inn best when she said, "Among our residents are skid-row winos and corporate executives whose alcoholism achieved the upper hand, the former heroin addict now clean and seeking both employment and his lost sense of self respect, the parolee bewildered by the outside world, the physically and mentally infirm, who are so often and so easily rejected from that which they need most, a home."

She continued her statement as thus, "Mariner's Inn is neither their home, it is shelter, refuge and sometimes sanctuary." Yes, indeed, it was my sanctuary for almost three and half years. I walked under its protective umbrella on April 16th 1985 seeking, in effect sanctuary until my case was cleared or ruled upon by the immigration.

Rev. Walter White and Mary Ellen Robertson were director and assistant director respectively of the Mariner's Inn. They and the staff became a gift of God to me. I never had better friends.

Of all those helping me, the staff at the Mariner's Inn among my Good Samaritans and true friends, were left to endure the painful depressions and panoplies of life I would encounter while at the Inn. Mary Ellen Robertson became Director of the Inn when Rev. Walter White fell sick and Miss Sharon Forster took over as program director.

Mr. John Carey was another of those rare friends I had at the Mariner's Inn. He is in his unique ways, had done a lot for me and he shared my pains privately.

How can the amiable, laughing and singing but compassionate Mr. David Crain? Rev. Walter White was equally magnanimous. He and John Carey gave their ears and hearts to me. They used to listen to me narrate my story for endless hours without showing any boredom.

I met Sharon Forster the first day I came to Diocese and she has been warm and friendly person ever since. Among the auxiliary staff was Mrs. Dorothy Robertson, Mary Ellen Robertson's mother from whose genes came the kindness of Mary Ellen Robertson. The nurse, Miss Audrey Chute, also showed love and concern for my plight. She had been friendly and persistently looked for ways of getting me out of my nightmare. Audrey epitomized compassion and was indeed an indispensable hand that rendered voluntary service to the Inn.

Mary and Walter allowed me to help at the desk in the office, once on a while. They were right in letting me help as it made me feel useful and one of them even though I was not paid for it.

I was happy to give back some service to the Mariner's Inn. Rev. Walter White's departure come new faces, Gonzolo Rodriguez, Mrs. Lateena Pryor and Chuck Gibson as counselors. The resident and I attest to the dedication and hard work these people have from the bottom of our hearts.

It is rare to find people so willing to share their lives with others. Hazlit wrote, "One cannot expect people be other than they are." However, with a bit compassion and sincerity the Cass Corridor Street dreary ranks can be helped if not nudged back to a worthy life.

A coy panhandler, in my early days at the Cass Corridor near Ledyard, once stopped me and pleadingly said, "Brother-man, would kindly read the note?"

I stooped and he handed the note of carefully written which stated that he had not eaten for two days, that his children were sick and worst their mother had deserted him and the small ones. It went about rent difficulties and water being turned off because he could not pay the bills.

The final line said, "If you believe in God and that He created me and those little mouths I want to feed, will you donate whatever you can? Thank you." I had only five-dollar bills and so I gladly put one of them into the cup he had wisely labeled, "Help the little ones eat."

He smiled and we each went our separate ways. I never considered the Cass Corridor Scene as that of vagrants and addicts but only people needing some form of help. On the same day just by Chris and Carl's Restaurant on Cass Corridor, I met another young looking man who was very seedy.

He too stopped me and in almost a whisper said, "Can you let me have a quarter to buy a cup of coffee?" I told him, you do not need coffee but do need to head to the hospital and seek treatment. You are definitely very sick and weak. He admitted being sick but needs coffee very badly.

The day being hot and humid made me suspect that he was craving for a cold beer than a hot cup of coffee. I gave him a dollar and saw to it that he took the bus to the hospital.

If he needed the dollar for bus fare then chance has delivered it to him but I still suspect him stopping at the next stop and get his beer from the nearest liquor store on the way. To this very day my coffee craver hugs me any time we meet.

He has become a friend even though he never went to the hospital as promised. When one becomes acquainted with the Cass Corridor folks, a revelation of dignity shines through the rags of most of the so-called bums and winos of skid-row valley.

Having lived and known these folks, I developed care and feeling for them and their sufferings. I kept clear distance from the muck and drug pushers so prevalent by the corner near where Mariner's Inn was.

I found most of these drug peddlers wanting to stop dealing but one has to be careful whom one deals with in such areas. Guns and knives are their pens and working tools. Shootings and stabbings are every day's scene on Cass Corridor.

Life on this corridor, nicknamed death valley 2, at certain times of the day was like walking on a sharp edge of a steel sword as one lied through the rows of violent addicts meandering about.

Similar one was liable to be mocked, mugged and or hurt anytime during those wee hours despite police patrols. I was accosted a number of times coming from evening classes by addicts who would not hesitate to leave one with an everlasting scar on the face just to get one's money.

I thank God that I survived Cass Corridor's Death Valley. At one death meant nothing to be afraid of because one saw bodies daily. The murders were never known and are hardly caught as it takes years for the police to find the culprits involved in such heinous deeds.

As bleak as life was on this side of Detroit I was never too frightened or afraid of death, I had made up my mind that death will come when it will. However, I was very careful and circumspect whom I dealt with and length of time I allowed them to be with me.

I would deliberately change topics or have an excuse to leave immediately as soon as I sensed disagreement or danger. One does not argue these senseless minds or brutes.

Those who wanted to change their lives to a dignified one would ask, "Brother, how can I get out of Cass Corridor?" Some of these are very intelligent former executive hooked on drugs and hence to these I quote Albert Schweizer as a response.

Schweizer exhorted us to "Try to moderate your habit and learn new skills, engage in new jobs and new environment and devote yourself to a good cause for your fellow men." I suggested that they change for the positive and stop being negative about themselves.

The need to pull the guilt cloak out and burn it for good. I made it clear that vacillation in life was their greatest enemy. I made it very obvious that human growth means ability of encountering of many difficulties on the way before one great door can be opened.

This I called the door of maturity and success. Sometimes I would paraphrase the sayings of Marcus Aurelius thus, "God Lord of the universe heap worthy gifts to the feet of foolish men, Give me gift of untroubled mind," Albert Schweitzer said of life best when he said, "From a feeling of embarrassment, we hesitate to approach a stranger. The fear of being repulsed is the cause of a great deal of coldness in the world, when we seem indifferent we are often merely timid.

The adventurous should and most break the barrier, resolving not to mind a rebuff. If we dare with wisdom, always maintaining a certain reserve in our approach, we find that when we open ourselves we open doors in others."

I would like both my Cass Corridor friends and those who look down upon the skid-row family to be grateful for life and to render in return some sacrifice of their own life for others. At the Mariner's Inn, poverty and solitude, and doubt about outcome of my appeals oppressed me on every side.

It was lurking in the walls of my cubicle where at times Nymphs dance the Spanish Sara for me making feel like I tool was becoming victim of Cass Corridor as these illusions bothered me. Josh Liebman wrote, "If we acquire the art of proper self-love, if aided by religion, we free ourselves from shadows of fear, and learn honestly to face grief and to transcend it, if we flee from immaturity and boldly shoulder adult responsibility, if we appreciate and accept ourselves as we really are, how then can we fail to create a good life for ourselves? For the inward peace will be ours."

In short, I was sustained at the Mariner's Inn by believe in God, love of human rights, freedom and by the endless encouragements and generosity of the Episcopalians of Michigan. In general, despite the disparity of reasons for being at the Mariner's Inn, the residents had been kind to me.

I only wished that I were able to be more help to them. I lived at the Inn, except for brief six months when I went to Louisville, Kentucky, since 1983 to December 1986 before heading for the American university of the Caribbean in Montserrat. First let us check Robert Duty and colleagues at he Renaissance Centre in Detroit, Michigan.

Alasan Mballow Jr. and Rohreyata Ceesay 2015

DYKEMA, GOSSETT, SPENCER, GOODNOW
AND TRIGGS

By this time the Renaissance Centre became a common place I go to every other day or week to meet with my attorneys, Robert Duty and Beth Sax. These two agreed to stand in for my legal struggles with the Immigration and Naturalization Service (INS).
Beth Sax submitted the following letter to the District Director, Mr. James H. Montgomery in response to their April 7th 1983 notice of pending denial in my request for asylum in the United States of America The letter states:

April 13th 1983

Dear Mr. Montgomery'

On April 13, 1983, Mr. Alhasan Ceesay, a native of the Gambia, asked us to represent him in his effort to obtain political asylum in the United States.
In a letter dated April 7th 1983 your office indicated that it intends to deny Mr. Ceesay's request for asylum, but granting him fifteen days within which to provide additional supporting evidence.
In view of our recent involvement with this matter we ask that the service extend the fifteen-day period by allowing us an additional thirty days to submit evidence.
The extension will enable us to review the record and familiarize ourselves with the case. It will also enable us sufficient time to obtain pertinent records and documentation.

An immediate response to our request will be greatly appreciated, Thank you for your corporation in this matter.
Very truly yours
Robert L. Duty

This letter gave my lawyers and I breathing time to regroup and plan a defense approach strategy. Attorneys Robert duty and Beth Sax worked hard on the case. We were able to obtain an affidavit from a former Gambian Deputy Head of Mission of the Gambia Mission to Saudi Arabia, Dr. Sulayman S. Nyang.
On March 28th 1983, Robert Duty submitted his rebuttal for my case. It was an in-dept review of the record of the facts to James Montgomery, District Director, INS, Detroit, Michigan.
The review pointed out that the state department based its conclusions upon incomplete information, lawyers ways saying it lied, as it failed to recognize that I was involved in political activities before the coup attempt on July 30, 1981.
He made it clear that I was already subjected to persecution and to support this position he submitted an affidavit from Dr. Sulayman S. Nyang and me. These two affidavits outlined in great details a well-founded fear of persecution I had about the Gambia. Mr. Robert Duty made it very clear that the deputy head o Gambia's Mission in Saudi Arabia had stated that I will be arrested upon my return to the Gambia and that even if I were eventually released, I will be ostracized, blacklisted and monitored.

Also, it stated that I would never be permitted to continue my medical education or practice medicine in the Gambia. Dr. Sulayman S. Nyang's affidavit concluded that I had a well-founded fear of persecution at the hands of the then Gambia government.

After a lengthy point counter point rebuttal and discussion of the advisory opinion, Mr. Robert Duty concluded by stating that, "Based upon the information provided, we submit that Mr. Alhasan Ceesay has established a well-founded fear of persecution should he be returned to the Gambia at this point in time.

We would direct your attention to the recent case of Reyes vs Immigration and Naturalization Service 603 F2d (A6, 1982) wherein the sixth Circuit court outlines the appropriate burden of proof in situations like the one addressed herein. Based upon the standards set forth in Reyes, and the additional documentation submitted, we are confident that Mr. Ceesay.s request will be granted."

In addition to the above documents and letters in my behalf Mr. Cloyd Ramsey, my friend at Sandusky, Michigan, provided the following in support of my effort to gain political asylum in the United States of America,

Sandusky
Michigan

RE: To whom it may concern

This letter is to acknowledge my association with Mr. Alhasan Ceesay over a period of fifteen years.

During that time I found him to be a young man of very high ideals. His only interest in life has been to obtained an education and return to his home country to help his people.

I have personally invested thousands of dollars in Alhasan because it seemed to me to be a very efficient way to help the impoverish people from his country that have had a great deal less opportunity than I have.

If anyone were to follow the course of his life, he would see that his motives most certainly were not to simply escape the futility of his country and live that, "good life" here. There is no doubt in my mind that the dangers that he described do exist for him. Even if there were less than perfect proof, would you like to take the chance of being wrong and find out later that he had been imprisoned or worse for no reason at all?

Please save this man. If you cannot do it for his shake, then consider the investment made by concerned individuals, other organizations and myself. Thank you for your serious considerations of this matter.

Signed: Cloyd Ramsey, Sandusky, Michigan

Throughout this saga or nightmare the Ad Hoc became the Ceesay Committee and my Pegasus wings at the Episcopal Diocese.

We held regular brain storming meetings every three weeks and all efforts were made to help me collect additional needed evidence for my case as requested by the district director, Mr. James H. Montgomery of the INS at Detroit office, Michigan.

The Committee became God's eyes and hands for me as would be revealed in these pages. We developed a unique bond based on respect, friendship, strong commitment to God and human rights. People like these bring out light in our souls. They understood that the cause I stood for was the cause of all mankind for where complaining becomes a crime hope turns to despair.

They knew me as a dissenter though not the rock throwing kind but a responsible opponent of injustice. Mrs. Patricia Koblyski, and at times rev. Hugh C. White, normally chairs the meeting, which took place in an atmosphere of cordiality underlined with great concern for my life and my derailed goal of becoming a physician.

It would be almost ten days before I met Rev. Virgil Jones and Rev. Bill Wood at the Wayne State University Student Centre in Detroit, Michigan. I made it very clear on the first day the Ad Hoc, also duped the Ceesay Committee met, that I was ready to use the anvil to forge history for my people and that I would rather die for the cause but there was no cause I am ready or prepared to kill a human being for.

I reiterated my total abhorrence of the wave of coup d'etats sweeping across Africa. This declaration was intended to clear any doubts as to my being a murder seeking their help. Patricia Koblyski, Rev. Hugh White, Rev. Bill Wood, Rev. Virgil Jones, Rev. David Brower, and Lois, R. Leonard were regular members, with Bishop Mason popping in at times, and attended every session and above all proved that love is the glue holding the world together.

Like any normal human gatherings we had different ideas to how to approach the problem but all our meetings steered toward or sought better ways to meet the challenges and the enigma about to end what I stood for and worked hard for in life. The meetings start at 1.30 pm on Wednesdays and are over by 4.30 pm.

The brain storming sessions were very lively, pragmatic and were over all well-intentioned discussions. One of these exploratory approach or searches for a solution even led us to Mayor Harvey I. Sloan of Louisville, Kentucky.

I met Mayor Sloan in 1976 when I was trying to get into the University of Louisville medical school in Kentucky. Also we used to write a lot to each other when I was at the A. M. Dogliotti School of Medicine in Monrovia, Liberia, West Africa. I venture to Mayor Sloan's office early February 1983, and was given opportunity to talk with key aids at city Hall while the Mayor attended other state affairs.

His executive assistant, Sharon Wilbert and Mrs. Blanche received and reviewed my case along with the information already in a file that was opened in y name. They concluded that I did deserve help and I was asked to speak to Mrs. Joyce J. Rayzer, Director, Health Affairs, for the Mayor. She took the challenge immediately

and called the medical school Dean and gave him a thorough and in-dept briefing of my background and the situation I was faced with. The Dean asked to be given a few days to talk to admissions office and those who have to be a part of the decision-making concerning my admission to the University of Louisville Medical School. She then promised to do her utmost for me and indeed two weeks later on February 28th 1983; I received the following letter from Mrs. Joyce J. Rayzer in behalf of Mayor Harvey I. Sloan.

Office of the Director of Safety
City Hall
Louisville, Kentucky 40202
February 28, 1983

Dear Mr. Ceesay,

It appears, as the old saying goes, I have good news and bad news. I have been in contact with the University of Louisville School of Medicine with regards to your admission at the fall term.
I have spoken to Dean Donald Kemetz, Dean of the Medical School, and Mr. Harold Adams, special assistance to the president of the University of Louisville.
Both of these administrators, upon receiving the information you sent me, feel that you are a very good candidate for the minority admission program. There is however, one issue, which must be resolved favorably before your admission to medical school at the University of Louisville, or the financial aid packaging necessary to begin this endeavor can be given serious consideration.
The issue, which must be resolved, is the financial determination of whether you will be granted asylum in this country. Without political asylum the University's admissions or financial aid cannot be considered because your legal status in this country

is too tenuous for them to invest hard cash in your future medical development whey your entire future in this country is nebulous. I cannot reiterate enough the importance of your getting an affirmative statement from the Immigration Office regarding your asylum.

It is the triggering mechanism to begin the process of matriculation at the University of Louisville School of Medicine. Another bit of news, which I am certain you could go without hearing, is that it appears you must begin Medical School anew. The two years of study, which you successfully completed at Liberia, cannot be accepted for transfer to the University without documentation it even appears that with adequate documentation there is still some questions with compatibility between those courses you completed in Liberia and those at the University of Louisville School of Medicine.

The final result is that it is almost certain that you must start medical school as a freshman in the fall. Again, try to get the final determination as to the granting of your asylum. I have been assured that everything that can be done for you will be done immediately upon a favorable notice of your asylum. Everybody in the mayor's office says hello and we are all sending you our prayers.

Sincerely

Joyce J. Rayzer

Director, Health Affairs

Mrs. Joyce J. Rayzer turned out to be a very kind and unique sister to me. With this encouraging news from Louisville, my attorney, Robert L. Duty, submitted additional evidence in support of my claim for asylum in the United States.

These favorable grounds lead me to move on June 6, 1983 to Louisville, Kentucky to make need more obvious to officials at the University. Mrs. Joyce Rayzer lodged me in exchange for my baby-sitting her five-year-old son.

I did just that until October 26th 1983 when circumstances required that I leave and wait out my asylum ruling in Michigan. Meanwhile, Bishop McGehee continued the fight for me and wrote the following letter to Mr. Edwin Chauvin, then District Director at the Immigration and Naturalization Service in Louisville, Kentucky.

Office of the Bishop
4800 Woodward Avenue
Detroit, Michigan
October 24, 1983

Dear Mr. Chauvin,

As Bishop for the Episcopal Diocese of Michigan, located in Detroit Michigan, I write you this letter on behalf of Alhasan S. Ceesay, a petitioner for political asylum in the United States.

As you may note from the file Mr. Ceesay seeks political asylum base on his fear of political persecution and danger to his physical safety and well being by the government, were he returned by the INS to his country the Gambia.

As Mr. Ceesay's life will disclose to you, he was active opponent of the political regime in the Gambia.

After protesting incarceration of his friends, Mr. Ceesay was placed on a list of individuals who were allegedly involved in criminal activities and who were involved with Movement for Justice in Africa (MOJA) and were sought for interrogation by the Gambia government.

The Gambia government has singled out Mr. Ceesay because political opposition and has prevented him from continuing his medical education in Liberia by cutting off his financial assistance from the E. E. C. and by asking the Liberian government to return Mr. Ceesay to the Gambia.

I am personally acquainted with Mr. Ceesay, and believe him to be an individual who is worthy of support of the Episcopal Diocese of Michigan. I feel that it took great courage for Mr. Ceesay to stand up for human rights and to publicly oppose the political regime in the Gambia.

I am convinced that Mr. Ceesay is an altruistic individual who deserves to pursue his medical training to benefit both the United States and perhaps the Gambia or elsewhere, those individuals who might be helped, in due course, by his medical ability.

Mr. Ceesay has already demonstrated or established his medical science aptitude in his studies at the A. m. Dogliotti School of Medicine in Liberia. He has applied to and been accepted by the school of medicine at the University of Louisville, Kentucky, with tuition to be paid by that institution upon his authorization to remain in the United States Mr. Ceesay has also authorization to engage in employment pending the outcome of his asylum request, he proposes to assist in medical research at

the university should his employment authorization be granted by your office. Therefore, on behalf of Mr. Ceesay as well as the members of my Diocese, I would urge you to give very favourable considerations to Mr. Ceesat's request and expedite his request for political asylum petition and employment in every possible way so that his efforts you enter the University of Louisville School of Medicine may not be delayed any longer than may be necessary by legal and administrative procedures which your office follows.
Please feel free to contact me if I can be of any assistance in helping you reach your determination on this urgent may matter. I fervently believed that, upon your investigation of Mr. Ceesay's case, you would reach the conclusion that he would be an asset to the United States, and that his fears as to his personal safety should he return to the Gambia, have a firm foundation in fact.
Very truly yours
(The Rt. Rev.) H. Coleman McGehee, Jr.
Bishop of Michigan

While at Louisville, Bishop McGehee, Rev. Hugh C. White, Rev. Virgil Jones, Rev. Bill Woods and Mrs. Lois R. Leonard kept an open line between us. They continued to contribute as well as advice about unfolding developments in the Gambia and of the emergency state in that country.
My INS file was finally transferred to Kentucky because I was hopping to continue my medical schooling at the university of Louisville, Kentucky. It was later brought to my attention by mid 1984 that Detroit INS was much more willing to stand its

recommendation for asylum but was relieved of taking further action by my transfer of my file to Louisville, Kentucky. The law is at times of slow process and the wheel of justice turns even slower. At some time and point in life everyone faces a decision, which will determine out fate.

I knew I would not escape the Judge's hash ruling minutes after my encounter with a coldhearted INS officer at Louisville, Kentucky. He told me forthwith, "Sorry boy.

We cannot help in your case." And he like a bulldog sneeringly added, "Perhaps our INS judge would do something about aliens like you wanting to stay in the United States." He was unlike the kindhearted INS officer I met at Detroit, not professional, courteous or civil in the way he treated me.

His unkindly statement went through my heart as if a dagger was trusted in it. It left me bewildered and standing on the cross road to hell or freedom. The constant delays and disappointments now started to wreck my nerves.

Up to then my strong believe in America and her stand for the underdog never wavered. Now my mind wonders and I started contemplating suicide as the only way out. I prayed and fervently begged God to help me bring an end to this misery and confusion I had been shrouded with.

Interestingly enough I fell asleep right after that prayer and woke up fresh and more determined to fight as well wait for whatever the judge's ruling turns out to be. Such euphoria and relief that followed made me forget about carrying my suicidal plans to this day.

I now feel ashamed that my faith and will could be that shaken but it reinforces the fact that I was no angel and that having gone through the length of time of mind bungling experiences as much as I did one was bound to breakdown at some point in time. I hope God will forgive me for being a simple human being trying to overcome trying earthly events.

For months, telephone calls frightened me for they were each a matter of utmost importance to me. With simple ringing of the telephone I might be getting results of ruling on my political asylum petition.

Denial would result to my being deported to the Gambia to regime I was running from. I world not am until the passing of 16 months before I received the dreadful to my life and goal on November 2, 1983.

I thought, after reading the order denying me asylum in the United States, everything would now be catastrophic if not cataclysmic of some torture month after month until my life wanes in a little dark and amp cell in the Gambia. The dreadful letter from Jsmes H. Montgomery, district Director at Detroit INS office read thus,

November 2, 1983

Dear Mr. Ceesay,

Attached is the order denying the request for asylum in the United States filed by Alhasan S. Ceesay. You may depart the country on or before November 14, 1983.

Sincerely
James H. Montgomery
District Director.

Uncontrollable tears of pain and disappointment ran down my cheeks as I read the following attached material and denial by the above official due to pressure from the state department, which believed the Gambia government side of the story. Bear with me and read the following letter from the INS.

IN RE: ALHASAN S. CEESAY APPLICANT: REQUEST FOR ASYLUM IN THE UNITED STATES.

DISCUSSION: The applicant is a single 37 year-old native and citizen of the Gambia who last entered the United States as a non-immigrant visitor for pleasure, class B2, on December 20, 1981. On February 22, 1982, the applicant filed the instant request for asylum in the United States based upon alleged fear of persecution should he return or be forced to return to the Gambia because of his political opinion, and membership within a particular social group.

Request for asylum in the United States are filed pursuant to section 208 of the Immigration act, as amended, and may be granted if the alien established that he is a refugee within the meaning of section 101 (a) (42) (A) of the Act. Section 101 (a) (42) states: The term refugee means (A) any person who is outside any country of such person's nationality or, in the case of a person having no nationality, is outside any country in which such person last habitually resided, and who is unable or unwilling to return to, and is unable or unwilling to avail himself or herself of the protection of that country because of persecution or a well-founded fear of persecution on account of race, religion, Nationality, membership in a particular social group, or political opinion Title 8, code of federal regulation 208.5 provides that the burden of proof is on the applicant in asylum proceedings. On July 8, 1982, a service examiner interviewed the applicant in order to allow him an opportunity to present his claim.

He stated in July 1981, there was an attempted coup in the Gambia, which was successfully put done by the government. In the aftermath of the coup, some of the applicant's friends were arrested and jailed. In an attempt to obtain his friends release the applicant wrote letters to the government in their behalf. He now believes these letters will result in his persecution should he return home because he is viewed as a sympathizer of the Movement for Justice in Africa (MOJA-Gambia), an organization his friends belong to and which supported the coup d'etat.

The applicant was closely questioned regarding his assertions and stated that unnamed friends had told him he would be killed or jailed if he returned home. In support of his claim he submitted copies of letters he had sent to the Gambia government along with letters from friends warning him pf reprisal should he return home.

At the conclusion of the interview, and after careful review and consideration, the service forwarded the request to the Department of state, bureau of Human and Humanitarian Affairs, with a recommendation of approval.

In a letter dated February 8, 1983 the State department advised that it disagree with the service recommendation because the applicant was not in the Gambia at the time of the coup and his letters of support were in behalf of persons who were exonerated by the Gambia government and released. Therefore the applicant does not have a well-founded fear of persecution as required by the United Nations Convention and protocol relating to the status of Refugees.

The service thoroughly reviewed the state department's opinion and concurs with its rationale. In a letter dated April 13, 1983, the applicant was furnished a copy of the opinion and told that the service intended to deny the request based upon the information therein.

In a letter dated May 26, 1983, the applicant's counsel submitted additional evidence for consideration. This information was forwarded to the state department for review on July 20, 1983. The state department pointed out that the applicant's political activities did not bring him into disfavour with the Gambia government because he was awarded a five-year scholarship by the Gambia office of education.

Further more, supporters of the Movement for Justice for Africa (MOJA/Gambia) have been appointed to high-level positions with the Gambia government.Finally, the judiciary system in the Gambia is considered to be open and reasonably correct with legal proceedings observed.

While the applicant might be questioned upon returning home, the observance of due process by the Gambia government greatly diminishes the chance of persecution and harassment. To establish a well-founded fear of persecution, the applicant must present substantial evidence, which shows a likelihood of persecution directed at him individually.

See matter of Eilus Dec. 2914 (A) 1982). The applicant must either demonstrate that he actually has been a victim of persecution or that his fear is more than a matter of conjecture.

The evidence submitted by the applicant and counsel is insufficient in the light of the state department's opinion dated February 8 and August 29, 1983. The instant request for asylum has been carefully reviewed and considered.

The assertion made by the counsel and applicant as well as the supporting evidence is insufficient to establish a credible claim to asylum by the preponderance of evidence test outlined in matter of William, and matter of Chumpitaze, supra. Therefore, it can only be concluded that the applicant has failed to meet the burden of proof and does not come within the meaning of section 101 (A) (42) (A) of the Immigration Act supra. Accordingly, the following orders will be entered, ORDER: It is ordered that the request for asylum in the United States be denied. It is further ordered that any permission to be employed either granted or implied be rescinded effective 15 days from the date of this order unless written evidence is received showing that the applicant qualifies for employment under other part title 6 CFR 109(b).

Dated 02 November 1983
James H. Montgomery
District Director

PREPARATION FOR IMMIGRATION COURT HEARING

The above statement from the District Director of INS and opinion of the state department were not only playing lip service American Justice but were bias and involved with East-West political as well as ideological interpretations of the United Nations Convention and Protocol relating to the status of refugees.
Let me point out here and now, that as far as Gambia government was concerned, the perpetrators of the July 1981 attempted coup d'etat in Gambia were highly suspected of being communist and as such anyone caught in the dragnet of the recuperating Gambian government or Banjul government was, whether one like it or not, automatically considered a communist sympathizer and the tentacles the Gambia government did not mince their words in nudging the West, especially America, to swallow that notion wholeheartedly. This stance by the state department would have to be the cardinal reason for the persistent refusal to grant my request for asylum in the United States in 1982.
As far as they were concerned their golden boy was in power and they do not give a hoot if the polices left the villagers wretched and at times starving because of escalating corruption in that era. Let us sail through the opinion of state and see if they were not wrong in the evidence or decision made on my request for protection from persecution by the Gambia.

America is one place whose ideas and principles I cherished dearly and people who, despite the current cruel dagger trusted at my back, I still believed to be champion of the underdog and of freedom and human rights in comparison to other nations.

Hence, both the state opinion and that of the INS totally disregard the affidavit from the horse's own mouth, submitted by the very Gambian Official at the Saudi Arabia Gambia Mission, Dr. Sulayman S. Nyang, who was assigned to monitor students like me in North America was wrong and deliberate refusal that I would be persecuted had I return to the Gambia at the time.

It showed blatant refusal to recognize my experience and plight at the medical school in Liberia and how I eventually landed in America. Does the INS and state department believe that I would throw away my medical training for an uncertain state of life like that of a refugee?

I negotiated the European Economic Commission Fellowship while in Washington before leaving Washington, D. C. for Liberia in 1979 and not as stated by the opinion letter. The letter wrongly stated or implied my friends being supporters of the July 1981.

This cabbage feed to them by the Gambia High Commission in Washington D. C. May I categorically state that neither I nor any of the people I wrote about were ever members of the Movement for Justice in Africa (MOJA-Gambia) or supporters of any coup d'etat attempt in the Gambia. MOJA was banned by the Gambia government but if the state department opinion had looked carefully it would have found that being member in MOJa, which it believed me to be, entitles me for grant of asylum. Boys who were in Liberia upon returning to Gambia were arrested and interrogated at the prisons for spurious connection with Moja. So to say that I was not going to be persecuted when I return to the Gambia was fallacious if not malicious murderous of an innocent like me.

Refusal only meant that it deliberately ignored the point of the Un Convention as applied to refugees regarding the term refugee and its reference to membership in a particular social group, in my case Moja, or political opinion for which the Gambia gave me the most coveted title of a tribalist and political agitator as per Dr. Sulayman S. Nyang's affidavit.

If the state department believed me to be a member of an organization banned in my country and I am seeking the application of the UN Convention Protocol as stipulated in the letter, what were the reasons of the opinion based upon? Certainly the opinion was not that of the UN Convention for refugee status.

It should have just said that the state department likes golden boy Jawara's government and hence it does not care if people were hurt or jailed as that government tries to consolidate its lost power back. Believe me up to the time of writing this chapter Latif Sanyang and other friends never got their jobs back.

One can see clearly that this intransigent position taken by the state department was based on lies and trumpeted or false information furnished by the Gambia embassy in Washington D. C. The embassy viciously if not maliciously wrote letters to U. S. officials in an effort to destroy my character and the principles I stand for. Secondly, I was not told that I would be killed by any unnamed friends instead it was the Liberian Security men that told me and showed me a copy of a memorandum from the Gambia requesting my being returned to the Gambia to be questioned.

This was followed by the acting Dean of the college of Medicine informing me of the Gambia's termination of my schooling at the University of Liberia. The friends I wrote about were in detention at the time the state department' opinion was hatched. Some were in jail while the state department belatedly told us these were released or pardoned.

In fact one can confidently argue that had it not been my writing and exposing the government's dirty laundry to the international areana/woarld, Latif Sanyang and others would not have been released for quite a while as wide range of emergency powers were enacted for us by the agent of the tsars and security forces.

Fear of loosing its lucrative aid from America and the West, upon continued incarceration of those I wrote about made the Gambia government to let go of these innocent people. My cousin, Abdulie Sarr, was accused of shooting a Mauritanian dead while on duty as a fireman at the Airport on the day of coup attempt.

He denied having shoot at anyone but was none the less found guilty by foreign mariners calling themselves judges and give a first class kangaroo trial and sentenced to death which was later commuted to 15 years hard labour in solitary confinement. Why was he not released? Finally, the opinion said that, "While the applicant might be questioned upon returning home, the observance of due process by the Gambia government greatly diminishes the chances of persecution and harassment."

Does the state department imply or mean safety for someone whom the government had already labeled "Political agitator" well before the attempted coup d'etat? Does the state department the adage that prevention is better than cure or does it even cares about my life? Has it declared my life expendable in favour of friendship it had the Jawara regime?

As far as the state department was concerned I should have returned to the Gambia directly from Liberia and wait for a Kangaroo court to place the noose around my neck at an unknown place in the bush, before I can cry for help from a people or America whose system and ideals I believed in. Yes, despite my encounter in 1983 with the ruling of the INS and state department slanted opinion against my plea to be protected from impending doom, I continued to, in my humble opinion believe that America stands out as the champion of freedom and for the underdog. The support I got from ordinary American citizens reinforced this believe in my mind. Hence, let the record read that I bear no malice or hatred for any human being. Thank you America!. Thanks a million to all those who genuinely believed in human rights and the sanctity of life. Please stop the human carnage going on in our world of the innocent.

With the state department's in hand I telephoned the bad news to all my foot solders to ready them for a bigger skirmish with the INS and state department in my fight against deportation at the Immigration and Naturalization Service course. Mayor Harvey I. Sloan and Mrs. Joyce J. Rayzer wrote strong supporting letters in my behalf to the district director at the INS Louisville branch in Kentucky.

None of the INS officials were willing, even though they have authority not to accept the state department's opinion, to reverse their colleague's or the opinion of the state department. The opinion was nothing more than a wreath based upon the protocol relationship between the Gambia and America instead of standing by democracy, good governance and accountability to electorates, human rights and use of egalitarian laws for the people. Should the United States sacrifice its principles of freedom and justice for all in other to remain loyal to sham governments that not only steal from the poor but also thrived on the blood of the people that brought them to power?

Any how by now, because of delay after delays compounded by unexpected rulings, I had lost my chance to start medical school at the University of Louisville in Kentucky. I plummeted into a gigantic major depression, which lasted three months. Hence, I had to return to Michigan and fight my case in the INS courts. Bellow is Mayor Sloan's letter in my behalf. I remain profoundly grateful to him and his warm and wonderful staff at City Hall, Louisville, Kentucky.

Office of the Mayor
City Hall
Louisville, Kentucky 40202
November 7th 1983

District Director
INS, Louisville
Kentucky 40202

RE: In support of Alhasan Ceesay's asylum request

Mr. Alhasan S. Ceesay of the Gambia has contacted this office in an effort to gain political asylum in other to complete his medical education at the University of Louisville. I know that he is dedicated individual and is more desirous of providing need medical aid to his fellow man.
Mr. Ceesay petitioned for political asylum in February 22, 1982 due to a purge, which followed a failed coup in the Gambia. The Medical School at the university of Louisville is currently processing his application for the 1984/85 academic years. It would be most helpful if you could assist him in expediting his papers.
He will not be admitted unless a written statement confirming his residency status in available. Since he has already lost two years awaiting residency confirmation, it would be deeply appreciated if you could assist this young man in any way possible. If my staff or I can be of any further assistance in the matter, please do not hesitate to contact this office.
Sincerely
Harvey I. Sloan

Mayor Louisville

This and numerous other letters not only fell on deaf ears but made maters hairier. City Hall never received any of the promised calls despite several follow-ups of the above letters from Mayor Sloan. Life grew so unbearable. Disappointed I returned to Detroit Michigan, on November 11, 1983 and went back to the Mariner's Inn at Ledyard on Cass Corridor in Detroit.

The Ceesay Ad Hoc Committee, and the Diocesans felt equally bitterly disappointed and sorry for me. The Committee convened at the earliest possible time the following week to discuss the withdrawal of attorneys Robert Duty and Beth Sax from being my legal representative in my quest for asylum in the United States.

They had to withdraw because the firm they work for demanded a large sum of money that the Diocese was unable to cough up to meet the latest payment deadline given by that law firm. It was during that session that Mrs. Lois R. Leonard, Editor of the Diocese newspaper, The Record, suggested that we contact a Canadian Movement she knew that was helpful to people in my situation. She suggested out contacting Professor Francis Conti, an attorney, at the Detroit College of law, who was a member of that movement or volunteer group. The committee concord and Lois got in touch with Prof. Conti.

He returned the call indicating desire to help in whatever capacity and legal advises he could give at the time. I met him the following day 9 am at the Detroit College of Law.

This gentle and caring person listened to my story, at times interjecting here and there to have a clear picture of my contentions and then he went to work on the case. First, I was to document a complete history of my political activities, provide names and political organizations I was ever affiliated with and what positions I held in said organizations.

I went back to the diocese and typed out a ten-page history of my student days in America and made it very clear that I had no party affiliation because I was busy trying to become a doctor and then return to help the Gambia reduce some of her existing health problems.

I made it clear that I wanted to contribute in a positive way by helping provide modern medical aid to the villagers. This compilation was submitted on our second round of meeting two days later.

Professor. Francis Conti came to our regular brainstorming meeting held the next week and everyone embraced him and felt very confident and comfortable about outline he made in fighting the case at the INS courts.

That meeting was also one of the liveliest and educative eye openers to Immigration nuances. He made it clear it will be a long, and hard up-hill battle with the INS courts because the blockage was coming from higher ups in the state department. This was why INS officials were taking careful approaches to the matter regarding my request for political asylum in the United States of America. I said silently to myself, "Professor go get them and teach them American stance for justice."

Professor Conti wrote to let the INS at Louisville know that he was taking over legal defense of my case and he should be contacted should they need any further information regarding my request for asylum in the United States.

In that letter he suggested many possible ways in which the case could be untangled without further a due. He said in part, "We believe that there are compelling reasons for the district director to so act under CFR 242(a) (2) vii.

If either of these forms of relief, or asylum or other approach relief could be granted, the service would be able to relieve his fears, satisfy the personal altruistic needs of a talented young man, and provide the people of Kentucky with very valuable public health service, without any encroachment on the basic policies underlying our Immigration laws. Mr. Ceesay is sincere and worthy young man.

We hope you are fit to reconsider his claim for asylum or to provide him with an alternative form of relief. I look forward to meeting with you on December 22, 1983, at 9.oo am. Thank you for your consideration." With this letter having been sent earlier to the Louisville Immigration and Naturalization Service Office (INS), we drove to our scheduled meeting with Mr. Schrimp in response to an earlier demand that I appear before the Louisville INS for processing. Upon arrival on December 18, 1983, in Louisville, Professor Conti spent half of the night preparing me for whatever may evolve out of the meeting.

He reassured me but avoided giving me any guarantees or unrealistic or false hopes. He promised to fight this case to the best of his ability.

On the morning of December 22, 1983, at the INS office of the enforcer, I broke down because of the cold attitude of the enforcer, whose professionalism, courtesy or civility was not endearing, and humiliation of being treated like a criminal. Americans in general are among the warmest, mos open and friendly in the world but this one reminded me of Hitler. He treated like a bucket of anthrax or shit from the pit latrine.

I was finger printed and photographed and told that I will give thirty days voluntary departure notice unless other legal maneuvers indicate otherwise. I will never forget the face of that junior Immigration officer who was finger printing me.

He was very cold and showed no interest in whatever I was saying to him nor did he care about my worries or what throwing me out to the invisible, as far as the INS and state department were concerned every aspect of Gambia government was immaculate, wolves would mean for me and many other concerned people.

This potbellied figure just said, "Boy, let us get on with it. The INS judge would be pleased to get aliens like you out of the United States." This statement left me mute and bewildered and I just said to myself he was just doing what higher ups told him and so I was able to, there and then, forgive him for the mannerism he exhibited.

I followed this chain of thought with a silent prayer for something worthy to come out of my struggle for the Gambia, human rights and man. There were no answers to all the questions and suggestions raised by Professor Francis Conti in his letter to Mr. Schrimp.

The fellow we met gave deaf ears to all the suggestions and the good service I could render not only to Kentucky but also to mankind in due course. He was not interested in anything said nor did he worry if am forced to return at that particular time or day.

I am certain that had Professor Conti not been present my fate would have been decided in the Gambia the following day. I asked myself if I did not fall into wrong hands. My nerves were no longer able to stand the negatives and impermeable responses coming from that officer.

He treated me like a rock the whole time I spent with him at his office. It was painful experience that, along with numerous others, will go to the grave with me. I saw myself being treated less than a cow for asking that we stand together by the principles of democracy and human rights.

All I ever did, which now seem to be a crime, was to call my country's attention and requested that it respect human rights in its effort to restore law and order in the aftermath of the abhorring event of July 30, 1981, coup attempt.

This was my crime to the Gambia and reason why I am still begging to be left to pursue my goal of becoming a useful person not only to the Gambia but also to all who can benefit from my medical skills. I am not suicidal but rest assured that despite this, whatever the end, dreadful experience, I vow to continue to stand for my principles and for the right of all of us anywhere on earth.

With the record entered Professor Francis Conti told the Louisville INS officer that we were going to file another request for a hearing before an INS judge and at the time we would renew our plea for asylum to be granted to me in the United States. In the following days and months, Professor Conti became an integral and indispensable part of the Ad Hoc committee in Detroit, Michigan.

This new addition not only continued to impress every-one of us but also had represented me in the most exemplary manner since his taking over the case. He and I became friends and worked together on the case ceaselessly.

I found to be easy going and an impeccable character. He is very sincere and an ardent supporter of law and justice for all people. On our return to Detroit, Michigan, a week after, on December 30, 1983 we received an order to show cause and notice of hearing from New Orleans LA INS office.

This was the divisional headquarters for all cases coming from the Louisville region of the Immigration and Naturalization Service. This meant going through my nightmare all over again before a body that might still chose to tow the state department's line and incarcerate me rather than caring about the service I can render mankind.

That information read: "You entered the United States on December 20, 1981 in New York. At that you were admitted to the United States as non-immigrant visitor for pleasure and authorized to remain in the United States until February 23, 1982, with the authority of the INS.

And on the bases of the following allegation, it is charged that you are subject to deportation proceedings pursuant to the following provisions of law. Section 241 (a) (2) of the Immigration and Naturalization Act in that after admission as a non-immigrant under section 101 (a) (15) of the said Act you have remained in the United States longer than permitted. Wherefore, you are ordered to appear for hearing before Immigration judge of the INS and the United States department of Justice at the date and time to be determined and to show cause why you should not be deported from the United States on the charges set forth above. Stated December 28, 1983.

Signed: Eugene M. Ditus
Assistant District Director
For Immigration
New Orleans, LA.

The order failed to realize that I was not illegal in the country but was up to my neck in a plethora of asylum requests and denials. Mr. Eugene Ditus failed to realize that the law allowed my stay in the United States until my INS court proceedings were over.
Hence to charge me as above was clear indication of how little the INS could or was willing to do to release the handcuffs the state opinion put around me. In a nutshell, there was no officer who dares or willing to be seen to take the risk and call attention worse and low people are less harassment than I currently deserve.
They do not care whom I would be much help to nor were they ready to let me stay until the current political dust settles down in Gambia.

MY FRIENDS AT FORKS OF THE TROUBLESOME CREEK

One of the many ways or approaches and avenues to finding a solution to my plight and roadblocks was exploring the possibility of using the third-preference category from the INS Ina frantic effort to get me started at the medical school at the University of Louisville, Kentucky, by September 1984, we contacted a Rev. R. Baldwin Lyod of Blacksburg, Virginia as indicated by the following letter from Rev. Hugh C. White, assistant to the Bishop at the

Diocese Of Michigan.
4800 Woodward Avenue
Detroit, Michigan 48202
January 24, 1984

Dear Rev. Baldwin

Greetings! Looking forward to having time with you in the near future. You will be interested to know that Mike Mullin of Hyndman Settlement, Kentucky is now in communication with Alhasan Ceesay here in Detroit waiting final disposition of his case with the Immigration Department.
I believed it would be best if Ceesay made a trip to wherever Mike Mullin suggested working out the details of whatever job they might be able to offer in Kentucky.
It is important to both parties, Ceesay's and the Immigration that hires him, to know what will be entailed. His story is best understood face-to-face

for there are several complications that are understandable yet easily confused on the telephone or in letters. The sooner arrangements can be made for his work the better for the reasons that time is running by and he will likely be obliged to go before an Immigration judge in early March, 1984.

I hope you have the opportunity to meet Ceesay for we are confidant and persuaded that his case is worthy of whatever we can do. We will likely be talking on the phone sometime next week in regards the Louisville conference and what can be done for Mr. Ceesay.

Devotedly
Hugh C. White

Mike Mullin and I had several more conversations over the telephone and the outcome was an invitation for me to come to his settlement area and talk to a few hopeful and prospective helpers interested in doing something to lighten my burden. Sure enough, like rabbit shown carrots, we took the implied aid and I left with the first available Greyhound bus to Hindman Settlement in Kentucky to meet it Director, Mr. Mike Mullin. Hindman, according to an article by Mercy Coogan, residents of the settlement at the time is located in Knott County, Kentucky.

It is small and is settled by people who, "Embodied the social notion and consciousness that the imbalance between the nation's rich and poor citizens could no longer be tolerated." They believed in the proposition that the haves processed a moral obligation to give of their time, energy and resources toward improving the lot of the have-nots.

The founder of the settlement of Hindman, Solomon Everidge in 1899, invited Mary Stone and Katherine Pettit it to join him. He said, "Women, my name is Solomon Eve ridge. Some folks call me the granddaddy of Troublesome. Since I was little shirttail boy hoeing corn on the hillsides, I have looked for somebody to come in and learn us something.

My childhood passed, and my manhood, and now my head is blooming, h'aint to come. I gowned up ignorant and mean, my offspring was wuss, and my grands wusser, their maneuvers, God knows. Come over to Troublesome, women, and do for us what you are doing here."

Old Solomon learned to improve his settlement and people of Troublesome Creek and the present generation lived up to his call or credence. For in 1902 the settlement founded a school to, "provide an education opportunity for the youth of the mountains and keep them mindful of their heritage."

Who would not be impressed by old man Solomon's efforts? This what each and everyone should aim at not marauding, mayhem and leaving footprints on the sand of time for a new generation to pick up courage and continue doing well to themselves and others of their time.

Here at Hindman Settlement was where I met Mr. Mike Mullin, Director, utilizing all his knowledge or know-how and energy for his people. He and the settlement were more than happy to see me and to give all the help they can to get me a job in their region in order for me to put a stop to my misery and plight shrouding me.

Mike Mullin got on the phone and spoke to a host of others and the hospital administrator at Our Lady of the Way, in Martin, about the plight that beset my life and need to help me put an end to the agony. I spent the night at the guesthouse and the next day morning Mike and I drove to Martin to seek help from Sister James Edward roach, the administrator. This hospital by the way, subscribes to the policies and philosophy of the Sisters of Charity of Cincinnati.

The sister and her assistant got to business the moment Mike Mullin and I arrived and after almost an hour reviewing my case and capability along with need to help me break out of the circle and clutches of despair, Sister promised to study their findings and get back to me as soon as possible.

I have no doubts that it would have been a rewarding exchange and a learning experience for both of us had it not run into union difficulties and resistance to foreigner in my situation being employed at the hospital. Back at the settlement, I was treated like I had been with them for a longer period.

Everyone wanted to say hello, shake hands or reassure me of their desire to help me and that I was more than welcomed among them. It was wonderful to know that people needed my help at the Appalachian instead of wasting me in some darkened cell in the Gambia. Indeed, Sister and her staff wanted me onboard but the nurses union, as I am told, would create problems and the request for asylum made it impossible for the hospital to work out arrangements that met criterion for the Immigration aspect of the deal.

Here with out further a due, is Sister James Edward roach's letter in regards to the above decision.

Martin
Kentucky 41649-0910
March 13, 1984

Dear Mr. Ceesay,

Thank you for your letter of March 4 1984. I am very sorry we were unable to work out an arrangement that met all criteria for the Immigration. Our prayers, thoughts and best wishes go with you through out these trying times. Please keep me posted, as I am very concerned for you.
Sincerely in Him
Sister James Edward Roach
Administrator.
Despite this bleak setback, Mike Mullin continued to search for another opening for me. Finally, he sent the following letter in June 1984.

Hindman settlement school
Appalachia,
Kentucky 41649
June 24 1984

Dear Mr. Ceesay,

Thank you for your letter. I have thought about your situation a great deal. We were depressed over the fact that we could not work anything out. What little we did for you was more than welcome.

I hope the Immigration bill passes so that the question of your residency in this country will be assured. It seems that it is in for rough sledding but I do feel that it will pass.

I am glad that the judge you met was sympathetic. It would be very depressing to have had a negative hearing. If we can be of any assistance please let me know. We pray that every thing works out well for you.

Sincerely
Mike Mullin

I remain in touch with Mike Mull for many years until my return to the Gambia in 1992. He was a good friend who was concerned about my well being.

I later numerous series of interviews but was never lucky to land a job specific enough to be applicable for me to use in a petition for a third-preference category consideration by the Immigration. Employer turned my request because of the same fears by would be employer about my future in the United States.

This being the sticky point in the case the committee and I braced up fight my cause at the judiciary level of higher courts. Professor Francis Conti and I collected many newspaper articles about the July 30, 1981 attempted coup d'etat in the Gambia and its ramifications to people like me. Professor Conti spoke to several Gambian students who at one time promised to testify in my behalf but had to later on, back out of that idea for fear that official records of their testimonies against the Gambia government were certain to jeopardize themselves and their families in the Gambia.

Prof. Conti, my attorney, put it this was, "Several Gambians whom I have approached have, when appraised of my client, either wholly refused to talk with me or have expressed an unwillingness to talk about the Gambia's political situation, based upon fear of personal and economic reprisal by the Gambia government officials upon themselves and their families."

I sent someone to meet the students in my behalf and this was what response he reported back, "When some fellows were told that my attorney wanted to talk to them about the Gambia and my case it was reported that the fellow was visibly trembling and obviously frightened for his and his family's well-being should the Gambia government discover that he talked with me."

This sort of reaction placed serious blow, if not a setback to our efforts to gather as many Gambians to testify in my behalf before an INS judge hearing asylum request case.

In paraphrasing our experience with the Gambian students, I would say that many of these wanted to come forward and present more startling and mind bewildering activities and behavior of the Gambia but since there was the risk that governments listens to governments, as was apparent in my case, they stayed clear of the idea or suggestions of testifying in my behalf.

Out of the many Gambian officials who labeled me apolitical agitator and tribalist, only Dr. Sulayman S. Nyang, in general honesty thought of the common good I stood for the Gambia. By the way, at that time in Gambia, when one tells the bitter truth or "plain-spoken truth or disagrees with the rampant corruption, which was an art of the day, one was branded a political agitator and tribalist. On the other hand if one come from the so-called elite or tsars of the big city and agrees with the dirty plundering, epitomized by the wolf crying out loud or saying, "Where they tie the sheep is where it feeds."

One was considered a loyal fellow. These are thieves deserving nowhere less than the penitentiary. Dr. Sulayman S. Nyang was not happy with the assignment of reporting student activities to the Gambia government.

Writing about or keeping dossiers of student in North America was not a dignified or contemporary admirable diplomatic post for such intelligent and descent fellow like Dr. Sulayman S. Nyang to cope with.

I knew him as an honest and forthright person who would not want to be used in any seemingly spy-like capacity. There are very few Gambian officials who would dare the tsars as Dr. Sulayman S. Nyang did in exposing the truth about the power-wielding fake Gods of the Gambia government in those days. Along with other explorations, Professor Conti wrote, through advice of Rev. Virgil Jones, to Congressman George W. Crocket, appealing for his assistance.

Upon receipt of the letter the representative's office decided to send all the documents and letters to none other than the Gambia Ambassador in Washington D. C. asking for the Ambassador's opinion on the matter. Even a political novice will not be caught doing such a mistake of asking opinion of an Ambassador who could be removed

from his post the moment he was found to have said anything against his country's regime. Up to the present day, we at the Diocese did not know what was the Congressman's objective in such an exercise. It only pointed out his naivety or gullibility for the Ambassador would not be willing to risk his career or his head under the guillotine to tell any that things were as stated in my affidavit.
Hence, the Gambia Ambassador took the opportunity to malign me and wrote very damaging letters to all parties at the state department, the Immigration District Directors in Detroit and Louisville INS offices, and finally he sent of president Dawda Kairaba Jawara in the Gambia. This was to show his boy in Washington is pulling all strings in his government's favour and not for the ordinary folks who elected them into office.
My parents were summoned to the state house in the Gambia, questioned and asked to give me very stern warning. My father was lucky to receive a small tap on the hand because the government fear of loosing the lucrative financial aid it craved from America.
And any hash treatment of my parents would have boosted my defense before the INS judge hearing my case. Father never said a word about my case to anyone again until his death in 1991. He was afraid of wrong information filtering back to the official in Banjul.
Father told me to tell the officials that they are forgiven for they know not what awaits them in the next world. To add fuel to fire and to everyone's dismay, shock and regrets we on April 30, 1984

received the following reply from representative George W. Crocket.

Congress of the United States
House of Representatives
Washington, D. C.
April 30, 1984

Dear Professor Conti,

In response to my request for information regarding the status of Mr. Alhasan S. Ceesay, a resident of the Gambia who is seeking political asylum in the United States, the ambassador of the Gambia to the United States sent me the enclosed letter.
Given the response that Mr. Ceesay is in no danger should he return to the Gambia, I am not disposed to pursue my involvement in the matter.
Of course, should events or information come to light, which would have a relevant bearing on the case, please let me know. I look forward to working with you on other mutual concerns.
Sincerely
George W. Crocket
Member of congress
Congressman George W. Crocket was certain held hostage to the whims and caprices of the Gambian Ambassador in Washington, D. C. The Ambassador surreptitiously gave unfounded lies about me in defense of the regime he represented.
He was hardly ever ready to divulge the truth that I had already been dupe, "political agitator and tribalism" by government he swore allegiance to uphold its protocol. George W. Crocket at the time

took the views of the Ambassador as sacrosanct and inviolable when it comes to unknowns like me. Again the Gambia has silently dealt another blow while pretending to be innocent of being the culprit causing my plight.

All other attempts to have a tête-à-tête with the Congressman failed. No one acquainted with my case expected that such an outstanding legal and political mind, as George W. Crocket was, would be so easily bamboozled by the very devil ruining lives of our people.

These were the new tsars and cronies reaping by both left, right and center the benefits of the Jawara regime or what could be simply labeled the city boys government. Was Crocket aware power-wield by these tsars? For sure the Ambassador will not spill the beans of wrongdoing he might be privileged to know, as did Dr. Nyang in an affidavit in my defense.

I was discouraged and fearful of this new development especially of the letter furnished to president Jawara. I knew it would not help my family breath the air of freedom in under the regime.

I was certain of it being used as exhibit XXX by the Gambia prosecutor against me in a kangaroo trial for the benefit of the International and local press whenever I return to the Gambia. Not giving up we decided to try our luck and asked for help from none other than America's second most powerful man with highest political cloud or office in the land.

Friends had repeatedly told the members of the Ceesay-Committee and I that then Vice president George Bush, Sr., was a very kind and sympathetic man who upon knowing my plight would certainly help me continue my medical education or schooling so that some day I can return to my people as a useful medical officer.

I still remained convinced of his humanitarian ness and that had I been privileged to personally meet him things would have turned differently. Instead underlings handled the matter in behalf of the Vice president Bush in an effort to boost their ambassador friend from the Gambia.

History has it that I became doctor in 1992 and served at Royal Victoria Hospital at the time the very Ambassador Njie's admission at the private block at the Royal Victoria Hospital.

I had at one time intended to bring his letter to his face to let him know what God ordains mortals cannot stop. I stop short of doing it because he was a patient and secondly I had forgiven all involved in making my life painful during those dark days in America and Africa.

Not one member of his family knew I was the Ceesay he had written so nastily in an effort to offset chances of my asylum request being granted. I have forgiven him.

With gut feelings I begged the Rt. Rev, H. Coleman McGehee, Jr, Bishop of the Diocese of Michigan to write to the vice president of United States of America, champion for the underdog, freedom and human rights, on my behalf, This was the Bishop's appeal in my behalf to vice president Bush.

Office of the Bishop
4800 Woodward Avenue
Detroit, Michigan 48202

Dear Vice President,

I write in a final to present the life of Alhasan S. Ceesay, who I am convinced from careful investigation, would likely be imprisoned indefinitely or suffer execution for treason if he is forced to return to the Gambia at this time. All things considered, detailed in the, which followed, and by the attached documents, Mr. Ceesay deserves political asylum.
This past, December, 1983, I was asked to assist Alhasan S. Ceesay, a citizen of the Gambia, in his efforts to remain in this country, due to real fear of returning to the Gambia, and, in part, to enable him to attend medical school at the University of Louisville, Kentucky while here.
At the time, as a result of advisory opinion from the state department the Detroit Immigration and Naturalization Service Office had denied him his request for political asylum.
A brief recent background of Mr. Ceesay is in order. He had received his B. A. and M, Sc degrees in Biology at Olivet College and Michigan Technological University, between 1967 and 1973, and completed some course work for a PhD in parasitology at Howard University in Washington, D. C. by 1978.
At that time however his ambition to become a doctor lead him to return to Africa and seek scholarship from the European Economic

Commission (EEC) and entered the University of Liberia Medical School in Monrovia, where for approximately two years he was a student in good standing. In July/August 1981, there was a coup d'etat attempt in the Gambia, which was initially met with considerable support, and then was put down when President Dawda Jawara invited the Senegalese Military and security forces to intercede. Approximately 1000 people were killed in the coup efforts and its aftermath and over 1000 arrested. In its aftermath, Senegalese forces remained in the Gambia, the coup virtually led to the confederation of the two states and the continued support of the Gambia government by Senegalese forces.

In any case, among those arrested were friends of Mr. Ceesay. Believing them wholly innocent he wrote numerous letters in their behalf to high government officials pleading for mercy and justice. Among those pleaded for were Latif Toure Sanyang, who spent over a year in detention without reason given, Kebba Sanneh and Abdoulie Sarr, a first cousin who was a fireman at the airport, who has been sentenced to death by a special tribunal employed in the coup's aftermath.

Shortly after this, Liberian Security personnel who questioned him about his political activities and informed him that he was on a memorandum list of twenty Gambians in Liberia whom the Gambia government wanted returned quietly to the Gambia Justice Department approached Mr. Ceesay.

At about the same time, the acting Dean of the medical school informed him that the Gambia government had terminated his scholarship and indeed, he was no longer considered a student at the medical school. He was given no explanation. However, he was advised to take care for his life. He went briefly into hiding until he was able to secure a tourist visa from the United States embassy in Liberia and airfare from an American friend, Mr. Clyod Ramsey, from Michigan.

He came to the United States fearing for his if he were to return to the Gambia. Although reasons for the government's action are of course not documented, there is a strong likelihood that Mr. Ceesay, who was viewed as a political agitator prior to the coup in the Gambia, and was probably, also identified with the Movement for Justice in Africa (MOJA) although he is not a member, was perceived as, "dangerous" to the Government. These perceptions, together with his correspondence to officials probably lead the overly sensitive government and security forces to unjustified conclusions. Mr. Ceesay applied for political asylum just before his tourist visa expired. Although the Immigration officer who originally examined and considered his case recommended that asylum be granted, after an advisory letter from the state department was obtained, the district director denied his asylum request.

In addition to the above, Mr. Ceesay has been virtually assured acceptance to medical school at the University of Louisville in Kentucky, however in order to obtain the necessary financial assistance he would need to commit himself to serve in physician shortage areas in Kentucky for several years subsequent to graduation.

Although he would like eventually to return to the Gambia to serve his people, and I do not at all question his sincerity in this regard, continuing conditions there do not make that now advisable. Mr. Ceesay needs to obtain some form of legal residency status whether through the granting of asylum, a private bill, or third preference status. Ideally, Mr. Ceesay would like to obtain some assurance of legal residence status very soon so he might be admitted to medical school for the September class.

Mr. Ceesay is sincere, altruistic fellow entangled in a web of unfortunate circumstances and laws. We hope that you can see fit to help him obtain an appropriate residency status. If you have any questions, please feel free to continue to contact me at your convenience.

Sincerely

(The Rt. Rev.) H. Coleman McGehee, Jr.

Bishop of Michigan

Hope surged into my entire system for we thought at last someone with a voice has an opportunity to review my case. My dear reader, brace up for here is the saddest and most unexpected political lesson and surprise of all my life and disappointments. Like Mark Anthony said of Brutus's dagger in Julius Caesar's body, "It was unkindest cut of all."

It was not until April 25, 1984, that we received the following communication supposed to be from the office of the Vice president of the great United States of America. The first country to challenge Britain's right to colonize or dominate another country.

I like to raise glass to the clans of the Boston tea Party of yesteryears. Could this be the America I want to take to my people to relish as their friend, champion of the underdog and bastion of hope and freedom? Let me not take any more of your time for the letter simply read:

The Vice President
Washington, D. C.
April 25, 1984

Dear Rev. McGehee:

Thank you for your recent letter concerning Alhasan S. Ceesay. It was thoughtful of you to write and I appreciate your having taken the time bring Mr. Ceesay's case to my attention I have asked the state department to review all asylum cases and human rights violations, which are brought to my attention. I have, therefore shared your letter and the enclosures with officials at the department of state and asked that they review Mr. Ceesay's request and write to you directly. I have also asked that a copy of their response be forwarded to my office. With best wishes.
Sincerely
George Bush
Well America, there you have it. It was the most diplomatic answer to a Bishop who could rock the electoral boat at his port. We had indeed enclosed the letter from the state department with letter that was sent to the Vice president. Hence, the opinion of the state department was clearly know to him and one asks what was the reason for redirecting our

request for his assistance to the very body that already rejected the case in the firs place? The state department, at the time, had ears only for the cronies of the Gambia Embassy were not interested in the pursuant of justice or democracy in a Banana or Peanut Republic like the Gambia.

Minors like me are expendable in preserving corruption of comforts of the tsars in the Gambia. This the way little clean guys are treated by superpowers and their cronies.

It would have much different had I arrived in the use with hands reeked with blood of the innocent multitudes deliberately sent to their graves as one seek to forcefully dethrone a democratically elected government.

Oh yes, there would be the faithful red-carpet spread end to end for me to shamelessly walk and have my warm hand shake from a start department representative. These hands would later be washed with gilders of state as grant for being a perfect blucher cum terrorist.

In simple current political lingo a "strong man needed to carry out dirty games for so-called friendly supper power(s). This was not what humble American citizens want to see nor believe that such butchers, who wallow in carnage, deserve American recognition.

Simple villagers like me only want to learn from America and return to help their people's development like the rest of the world. We never heard from the vice president or the state department despite several reminders from that April 25, 1984 bombshell to this very day.

We are still patiently waiting from a response from the state department. Perhaps one will drop from Mars in due course over my old tired fighting bones or grave. The long delay in reply to the vice president's ported request for review of my case was unprecedented.

Americans, unlike other places, do reply in reasonable time, especially when it is a matter of life and death. I had no doubts that had Bishop McGehhe reached the vice president directly the outcome would have been Different and a much favourable one that would allow me complete my schooling and is the good contributing human being I aspired for the Gambia.

Friends still attest to the fact that vice president George Bush, Sr. to be a good man who cares about human rights in the developing world. Personally, I have not had the chance to meet him but do look forward to having the opportunity to do so some day if we live long enough.

I am almost certain he was party to the letter released in his behalf and to Bishop McGehee in Detroit, Michigan. However, it was under such bleak circumstance that the Ceesay Committee and I continued our preparation and collection of data to use for additional evidence in support of my claim for asylum in the United States, Two months later we received the following notice of hearing in deportation proceedings.

Francis Conti
RE: Alhasan S. Ceesay

Please take notice that the above caption case will be heard by an Immigration judge on June 199, 1984 at the office of Immigration Judge, Richard Russell Federal Building, 75 Spring Street, SW, Room 1354, Atlanta, Georgia.

Failure to appear at your hearing may result in any or all of the following actions: Forfeiture of your bond, your deportation hearing being held in your absence under section 242 (B) of the Immigration and Naturalization Act, an order of deportation being entered against you or an issuance of a warrant for your arrest and deportation.

Office of the Immigration Judge
June 1, 1984.

With the hearing date set we redoubled our efforts to rally witnesses and collect money for the trip to Atlanta, Georgia. Bishop McGehee donated a thousand dollars and Bishop Irving Mason gave one hundred and fifty dollars toward our cause. Bishop Irving Mason is another gentleman to whom I owe a lot and I am grateful having met him in my life as experienced at the Diocese.

Even though he could be at our regular meetings he had been with us spiritually and has kept himself abreast of developments in the case I made it duty to solicit help by telephoning friends and would be sympathizers for more donations to help cover the fare for those of us to be flown to Atlanta, Georgia. It was during one of these phone calls I spoke to Doris Masko who kindly donated another two hundred and fifty dollars towards the trip for transportation of my witnesses.

God bless her heart. The Ceesay Committee and I agreed that Dr. Sulayman S. Nyang, Professor Francis Conti, Rev. Hugh C. White, Mr. Cloyd Ramsey and I be at the hearing if not one else can go with us to Atlanta, Georgia. Dr. Nyang was to leave from Washington, D. C. He was also our key witness since the other Gambians from Banjul had backed out from testifying before an Immigration judge in my behalf.

Mr. Cloyd Ramsey and others were back-up character witnesses and people who dealt with me on the case for a reasonable length of time. The strategy was to show the judge contribution that most of these people of statue made towards my mission then, as an undergraduate and graduate student during my student days in the United States. Mr. Cloyd Ramsey is a longstanding friend who supported me extensively throughout my college years.

He was a clinic manager turned into building houses and motel business. Rev. Hugh C. White served as consultant to the Bishop of Michigan. He is someone with whom I shared a great deal of ideas about life. He is a kind and religious and sociable man.

Hugh White, as he normally wants me to call him, chairs our meetings when Mrs. Patricia Koblyski is away or unable to attend. Allow me as a sidetrack; let me point out that Mrs. Patricia Koblyski is one of the few kindhearted and mindful of the need of others and someone you would like to have on your side.

No wonder she was designated Refugee-coordinator for the Diocese of Michigan at Detroit. Unfortunately neither she nor Bishop McGehee was unable to the hearing at Atlanta with us. While talking about the Ceesay Committee members, let me acquaint you with a few more of the wonderful people of Michigan.

Rev. Virgil Jones reminds me that both science and religion teaches us, at least in part, that obstacles to serenity are not that external. They are within us. Rev. Jones was an engineer turned priest and studied at the Oxford University Seminary for his priesthood.

He has a sharp mind and is well versed in scripture. These qualities beguile the man. He is a gift I never came across and found him not serving others, be they American or foreigner. More often than not these are the bewildered street people needing direction in their lives and to get some relief.

No matter how tired Rev. Virgil was he showed up for most of the Ceesay Committee meetings we had in the last three years of this asylum request petitioned by me. Rev. Bill Wood was another outstanding figure in the committee, who was very active behind the scene.

He normally goes the extra mile with me when I feel very in spirit. I tease him as, "Bill Africa" because he stayed or served for many years in Liberia ministering to members of his Parish in Monrovia, Liberia.

Hence, it did not take convincing to bring him aboard the venerable group working to help solve my political nightmare. Rev. Bill Wood is a gentleman at heart that is equally concerned about human rights and social Justice. He had come to my aid when I showed up at his office. We have constantly debated and sought help with regards to my asylum request in the United States. More of the Ceesay Committee members like the Rev. David Brower and others will be touched upon in subsequent chapters.

Dr. Sulayman S. Nyang is a Gambian and professor of political science at Howard University, Washington, D. C. He is an exceptionally unique and good friend who served as deputy head of the Gambia Mission at Saudi Arabia where he and others, designated to monitor activities of Gambian students in North America.

They met frequently and is was in such forum and capacity, on more than three occasions, when Gambian officials discussed and labeled me as a "political agitator and tribalism" With professor Conti, Rev. Hugh C. White, Mr. Cloyd Ramsey, Dr. Sulayman S. Nyang and I booked to fly to by Republic Airline to Atlanta, the battle lines were drawn.

Mr. Cloyd Ramsey from Sandusky was to join Rev. Hugh White and I at Metro Airport in Detroit, Michigan. Mr. Ramsey was nowhere to be seen when Hugh and I got to the Airport. It was tense moment for us but I knew Mr. Ramsey would show up. His love and concern for my safety is immeasurable.

Time ticked and we had to leave his ticket at the reception desk for him to pick another Republic flight slated for Atlanta. What we did not know was that Mr. Ramsey had instead gone to Mississippi and flew from there to Atlanta ahead of us earlier in the day. We were confused and grew very worried and concerned for there we are in Atlanta with two key witness members of our plans to fight for freedom and eventual chance of my getting into medical school.

Where these events a bad omen or just jitters due to the tense atmosphere cum our determination to get it over with to allow me move to better things in life? My nerves and those of Professor Conti were unsettled.

He was tense for he had not faced a judge for many years as a law professor, now he is faced in defending life and death as my case presents him.

Dr. Joyce Inyang RIP, a true friend 2016

Chapter 20
INS HEARING IN DEPORTATION
PROCEEDINGS: ATLANTA, GEORGIA,

Our host for the evening, Fr. Vincent P. Harris of the Episcopal ministry to the Atlanta University Community Centre, met us at the Airport. The Republic flight from Washington, D. C. was delayed se we waited until 8.30 pm at the terminal for Dr. Sulyaman S. Nyang's arrival.
The plane came without Dr. Nyang. We paged him several times but no one replied. Finally, almost discouraged, we decided to proceed to our hotel in down town Atlanta. We left a message for Dr. Nyang to call us at the Paschal Motor hotel upon arrival in case he had to take a delayed flight from Washington, D. C. that evening.
Fr. Vincent drove us to the Paschal Motor hotel on 830 Martin Luther King, jr. Drive, NW, Atlanta, Georgia. At the hotel we found that the promised reservations or down payments were not made. Thank God Rev. Hugh C. White had brought three hundred dollars with him and with that we were able to book for one night occupation for five people at the hotel.
It was well after 9.00 pm when I received a call from Dr. Nyang. Evidently he too had arrived at 3.00 pm from Mississippi and proceeded twenty miles north to a friend's place. You can imagine the sigh of relief my attorney and I gave when Dr. Nyang phoned to say he was in town and would join us shortly at the Paschal Motor hotel.

He arrived at the hotel very late that night and shared room with me. Fr. Vincent left us at the hotel the moment our rooming arrangements were taken care of. Being the only Gambian willing to help we spent most of the night talking about my case and the political state of our beloved country the Gambia.

I had a lot to share and discuss with Dr. Nyang. Our topics ranged from our families, politics and student friends in Washington, D. C. His presence lightened my day enabling to relax and ponder more on my future including the likelihood a noose placed around my neck at the gallows. It was scary but I sailed through it all.

The phone rang at about 11,30 pm. It was Mr. Cloyd Ramsey calling from the Airport. I was not surprised for I had expected him early in the morning before we were to go to the hearing. I just knew that my Mr. Ramsey would do all he could to be at the hearing in Atlanta, Georgia. We gave him directions on how to get to the Paschal Motor Hotel from his vantage point.

Ramsey joined us half an hour later adding more calming effect on all of us for it now completes the team for our defense plans. Professor Conti began his preparation sequence as soon as everyone was present. He rehashed probable questioning line the government attorney might take and admonished us not to fall into traps he might lay while cross examining us during the hearing.

He reassured us that there would be no jury and it would only the INS' Hon. Judge Charles Aulander, the attorney for the government and ourselves. Professor Conti went all over the details with me and later with Mr. Ramsey, after which we went to bed around 1 am. Dr. Nyang and talked until he fell asleep. I was so relieved seeing Mr. Ramsey knowing that he was not involved in the accident that slowed the traffic in Michigan. I tried to sleep but it would not come to me that night.

My mind was wandering for a while then I prayed for help and protection from God. It was hard to believe I was dressed and ready for the hearing by 5.00am that morning The hearing was schedule to start at 1.30 pm, June 19th 1984. I woke everyone before 7.00 am and we went to the Cafeteria for breakfast.

Hugh did his best to lighten my spirit but the more he made his one-line jokes or slipped into general conversation the more I grew frightened. It was my life and future that were at stake and about to be tried, reviewed and weighed, so to speak, by a complete stranger who might not want rattle the state department.

How could this judge, this person, weigh the burden, heartaches and need within for justice me? No man will ever know the amount of pain I felt having lost my freedom or my grasp on a medical education in the United States. Dr. Nyang joined us at Cafeteria breakfast table later.

I had nothing more than respect and admiration for Dr. Nyang because very few Gambians officials would help anyone, worse still to stand in a court of law and give evidence or testimony against the unholy behaviours of the Gambia government.

Dr Sulayman S. Nyang knew that my criticism of the Jawara government were based on constructive democratic grounds and done in the interest of the common man or the general good and not of malice against anyone in particular. Again, after breakfast, Nervous professor Francis Conti re-examined Dr. Nyang's testimony and former position in the Gambia Mission at our Saudi Arabia Embassy. All things reviewed and considered and set, we left the Paschal hotel for the United States Immigration Court on 75 Spring Street, Atlanta, Georgia at 12.30 pm.

We left early to give allowance to possible traffic congestion problems or in the event we got lost on our way since we were all strangers to Atlanta. Luckily we made our way through traffic without any problems and reached the Richard A. Russell Federal Building, and took the lift to room 1354 by 1.05 pm.

We sat in the lobby and kept company with one of the lady lawyers for some time. My heart rate increased several fold due to fear and uncertainty of what influence the state department might have on the decision I might walk out with from this building.

We later, just before the start of my hearing, learnt that this lady lawyer had just defended another Mr. Ceesay from the Gambia and that the fellow was ordered deported by the same judge I was to present my case. This bit of unexpected or unpleasant news caused my heart rate to surge and my pulse almost fluttering rate.

I wondered how I survived that news without collapsing or going in syncope for good. This bad news became very bad omen for me I now fear I may likely be perceived in the same light as the other unfortunate fellow deported by judge Charles

Auslander. Hearing this sad new for my fellow country man made me offer another silent prayer while the lady conversed with the rest of the team. I still wondered whether the judge would have given the type of decision you are about to be familiarized with had he taken my case before the other Ceesay's hearing.

We continued to nervously wait at the lobby until the U. S. government attorney called us into room 1354 at 1:45 pm, a day I will never be able to erase from memory. The room was simple and had all the decorum of a mini-courtroom. There was a judge's section decked with microphones and other gadgets for recording of the proceedings.

In front of the judge were five rows of chairs for witnesses to use and right at the front row were located areas for the defense and his client, and a similar setting away from the defense was the territory of the government lawyer or what one calls the prosecutor who speaks and defenses the government's position in a case such as mine before Judge Auslander.

There were no stenographers for everything said in the courtroom was taped-recorded and transcribed later.

Chapter 21
THE HEARING, JUDGE AUSLANDER PRESIDING

Honourable Judge Charles J. Auslander, a youngish looking gentleman, walked into the room at 1.55 pm. We all stood until he took his place above us before we were seated. He advised both attorneys that every aspect of the hearing would be tape-recorded and that he would be glad to receive and all evidences presented to his court.

The proceedings began after he tested the mikes or shall I say the entire electrical recording system, as if to place emphasis on the weight of the case before him, in the courtroom. He then recorded the following statement, "United States Immigration in the matter of Alhasan Sisawo Ceesay respondent in deportation proceedings, presided over by Judge Charles Auslander, Jr. at Atlanta, Georgia, June 19th 1984."

I was then called to take the stand or my place near the judge and facing the two lawyers. He swore me in that I will tell the truth and nothing but the truth, so help me God. I repeated this half-dazed, with my left hand raised at first. The judge corrected me and asked that I raise my right hand in taking the oath, which I did.

He began by asking me state my name, country of citizenship and date of birth. My attorney then asked me to tell my story as I lived it. I narrated my experience at length and reasons why I feared persecution if forced to return to the Gambia at that time. Professor Francis Conti noticed that I was getting nervous and afraid and he tried his best to establish my background, the hard work put into the years to get medical school, the investments American friends had in me and the fact that despite my constructive criticisms of the Gambia government polices in agriculture and other matters I was deliberately labeled a political agitator and of tribalism by a regime now wanting to contain me. I dwelled on the pain and difficulties I encountered after the termination of my medical education by the Gambia government.

Judge Charles J. Auslander would now and then as a question or two either to clarify a point I made or to ask that I elaborate on an aspect of my testimony. I became so nervous and tense that when my attorney asked me to tell the court the anguish I went through in my efforts to flee to safety, I broke down and cried for at least five minutes.

Every horrible thing that happened to me in Liberia came before me and pierced my heart and the emotions that I could not contain welled out. The room became dark and all I could think was why was I going through all these types of punishments? Will Judge Charles J. Auslander ever care that I wanted to be with my people and not as a client in his court?

Shame and embarrassment made it even worse for me to look at myself. I love my people and do know that my pains were only due to few who believed in power than serving the people who elected them as their representatives.

Judge Charles J. Auslander made me feel even worse when he followed my recovery with such questions asking if I believe that the Gambia would, for the sake of letters I wrote to its authorities, persecute me if I were asked to return to the Gambia. I answered affirmatively but wondered he too did not care about the background, which lead to my being labeled and then quietly removed from medical college. Cannot he realize that the letters tie the action taken clandestinely against me by the Gambia government?

The officials were confident no one would see that they were behind the scene of this drill. The other such questioning brought to my mind was whether anyone believed such a nitwit or crazy fellow to throw away thirteen years of hard work plus two and half years of medical school just to point an unnecessary finger at the Gambia government. Why would I choose to be a refugee instead of the doctor I have since been struggling to be all those years?

The line of questioning made me feel that the judge had already made up his mind about my case from the dreadful advisory opinion of the state department. He in fact on two occasions asked for us to get a recent opinion from the state department.

This and many others off the wall questions were the straw that broke my back. I grew more and more scared, not of the judge, but about the future about to unfold before my very eyes. I was helpless and from the look of things, the Gambian regime seemed to be getting its wishes.

My attorney, Professor Francis Conti, continued his presentation of the case and the arguments in support of my contentions and plea for political asylum in the United States.

After forty-five minutes or so of presentation by my attorney he rested his defense and gave the court additional letters to be considered along with what was said in court. Judge Auslander went into the motion of accepting everything we gave him despite a pretended objection from the government attorney with regards to one of the letters written from the Gambia.

The Judge told him that he would accept unless the government was willing to bring the writer from the Gambia to disclaim the authenticity of the letters. The objection was overruled and all my added evidences were entered as accepted by the court for use in future consideration of the case.

This act by the judge made me feel that he might be sympathetic after all but my suspicions of the weight of the state department opinion never left me. Honourable Judge Charles J. Auslander took over the cross examination as soon Professor Conti was through presenting his side of the case and the evidence supporting it.

Judge Auslander asked about my political activities and affiliations, if any, while I was in the Gambia and the United States. He let me elaborate upon the nature of my sudden departure from Liberia. How I obtained a B2 visa from the U. S. embassy and other matters relevant to the court were dealt with to the best of my ability and emotion at the time.

Quite a bit of time was spent on my family and if my state had repercussion on any of my family members in the Gambia. I told him to best of my knowledge I had no idea as what was or became of them and that I was not getting any more letters from them after the ones that were presented him that day. I made it clear that the Gambia will wait until he, Judge Auslander, had decided about the matter before him before my actions would be taken against them in a similar clandestine fashion.

I reiterated that even if they were suffering from the hands of the tsars of Gambia government it would not be revealed to me for their own sake for wanting to protect me from further possible harassment.

I was asked to define tribalism and also state if I was tribalist. My gut response was that tribalism is similar to nepotism in that the group only cares about or favours its own but pays lip service to the other Gambian tribes.

In Gambia it is a smear tactic in which the perpetrators are accused of being devious and deceptive while the accuser is equally swinging with the same fiddle. It was a cloak used to smear the innocent people while the accuser engages in similar dirty nepotism activities.

It was, for heaven's sake, the case of the pot calling the kettle black for as soon as the accuser steps into power or government they do worse than those they were pointing fingers at.

Simply put, the very people busy labeling others guilty of tribalism are themselves in the mud up to their necks. It is a social cancer inherited from the days when everything revolved around the tribe. This why up to today most African politicians offer a majority of government posts to their clan's men than the others even though they would not be ashamed to canvas for the votes of other tribes.

So tribalism is unacceptable and as far as I am concerned it's a great hindrance to progress. I reiterated my strong commitment and believe in equality and that Gambian officials were sticking an unfair label on my back. The judge the asked a few more questions and then asked the government attorney to take over the interrogation.

My protagonist, the attorney representing the U. S. government's side looked like he was not prepared for the case. Perhaps he was certain that the court was just going through the motions having allowed me present my case but there was no reversing of the state department opinion.

He nonchalantly asked if I belong to any political party in the Gambia, and if so to state its name before the court. I replied that I had no affiliation with any political groups in the Gambia and that medicine and my eventual return to provide much needed medical aid to the people were the only things that interested me.

To my utmost surprise he still wanted me to clarify the meaning of tribalism to the court. This really turned me off for I was not there on a socio-anthropology 101 teaching course. His line of questioning did not address any salient point in my presentation nor did he care that my life and future were on trial. Atlanta, Georgia, U.S.A. was my Nuremberg.

After several requests that I elaborate on this already stale tribal topic, I reminded him that it was the Gambian officials, as per testimony and affidavit of Dr. Sulayman S. Nyang, that coined the term or phrase.

Why did he not ask the Gambian Ambassador to define a term his government officials coined to Labelle students and the innocent it disagrees with? I told him it was my life, my career, and all that I ever stood for that was on trial.

I had to remind him that I was an asylum claimant seeking decision from Americans via this forum, as privileged by section 208 and 241 (b) of the Immigration and Nationality Act. I also pointed out being surprised that he was not dwelling on my experience but he was trying to attach me to a group or idea I have nothing to neither do with nor have I the foggiest idea what he was looking for in the word tribalism.

He laughed at me and continued to ask more irritating questions. There was no direction in the questioning he embarked. The line of questioning neither established nor disproves my experience and need to be granted asylum until things get safe to return to serve my people and better in the Gambia. He cared little about my seeking political asylum.

In a nutshell, I lost my cool and told him that I sought asylum from America because it was here that I learned some of the democratic ideals I wanted practiced in my country, the Gambia.

I pointed out to him that under colonial life we in Africa lived within the rules of an external master who introduced nothing in its right form to us, or does so in such a haphazard manner that it becomes worthless to emulate.

He glossed over that and continued to ask more and more trivial questions, which were very frustrating to me under the circumstances. It was then that I realized that no matter what his time consuming questions were, he was not going to deviate from the state department's stance and he was just carrying out instructions given him by his bosses at the round table.

After a few more exchanges between him and I he abruptly terminated this exercise of futility or cross-examination of my case. He simply said in an abrupt manner, "Your honour, the government stands by its previous position in this matter."

We all simultaneously let a sigh of relief from his lack of feeling for the gravity of the case. Hon. Judge Charles J. Auslander stepped in and asked a few more questions and then he asked me to step down, unless I had something else to add to what had already been heard in court.

My senses and nerves were so numb at the time that I felt relieved to be asked to step down. Our chief and key witness, Dr. Sulayman S. Nyang, Professor of African studies at Howard University in Washington, D. C., was then called and sworn to tell the court the truth and nothing but the truth about my case and all that he knew concerning me that would be of interest to the court.

Dr. Nyang took the witness chair and narrated or told most of what he knew about the Gambia government's activities towards me while he was deputy head of our mission to Saudi Arabia. At this juncture Prof. Francis Conti presented Dr. Sulayman S. Nyang's credentials and asked him to tell the court what he heard the Gambian officials discuss about me during his tenure or term as deputy head of the Gambia mission in Saudi Arabia. Dr. Sulayman S. Nyang stock to his affidavit and in addition gave an apologetic definition of what tribalism meant. It sounded as if the answer was coming from one of those who coined it.

The judge stressfully asked if Dr. Nyang really believed that the Gambia government would persecute me because of those innocent letters and is so does he still stand by the fact that I do have a well-founded fear of persecution and in being afraid for my life?

Dr. Nyang answered in the affirmative and tried to qualify the answer at one point. Fear that Gambian hearing about him testifying struck for a short time but I noticed, he picked up his courage and composure and continued his lecture-like testimony. He talked at length about tribes, especially the Mandinka tribe, which I thought, like the government attorney's tactic, a waste of the court's time and unnecessary for what we were concerned with all the time. Nonetheless Judge Auslander and the Americans may have been interested in hearing about tribes in the Gambia.

I, on the other hand, hoped the court would continue to address and stay on course with the matter before it instead of taking an anthropological swing about Gambian tribes. Suspect the judge was getting bored at this juncture about tribalism and after a few more questions he handed the cross examination of Dr. Sulayman S. Nyang the U. S. government attorney.

The attorney again picked up on the line of tribes and tribalism in the Gambia. The conversation between him and Dr. Nyang continued. It never turned to my case. At one point I thought my attorney would raise strong objection to overly beaten, irrelevant aspect of my hearing.

I believe we were not there because tribalism but because the Gambia government had persecuted me to the point that I had to flee for safety and seek asylum in the United States. The government attorney casually asked a few more boring and irrelevant questions that were already dealt with. He even at one point wanted to have the hearing adjourned till the next day but the judge ruled out the motion and insisted we complete it since only two more witnesses were left to testify.

The attorney ended his questioning and thanked Dr. Nyang, who impressed him. Judge Auslander again asked Dr. Sulayman S. Nyang if he still was convinced that I was in trouble should I be forced to return to the Gambia.

The response was affirmative as given before but only this time said with more confidence. "Yes, he will be persecuted if he forced to return at this moment." Dr. Nyang was then told to step down unless the government attorney had a question to ask him. It was now well after 3.00 pm. Mr. Cloyd Ramsey followed and was sworn in to tell nothing but the truth about our association and his knowledge of the case.

Like all of us he took the oath and told the court how we knew each other as early as 1967 when he was a manager at the Medical Art Clinic in Alpena, Michigan. He testified to my honesty, hard work and the single most desire in my heart, i.e. to return to serve my people as a physician.

Judge Auslander asked if Mr. Ramsey believed my contention against the Gambia. To which point Ramsey replied he would bet his life on it because he had known me for more than fifteen years and throughout those years I never told him falsehoods. He assured the judge that even he and I were not fishing or drinking buddies, we have become great friends and he and others invested in my education as a means of helping the impoverish farmers of the developing countries."

Mr. Ramsey gave a glowing picture of me from 1967 to the present day at the court hearing. I was moved and bashful at the same time, hearing him pour out concern and love for me from his heart made me relieved.

I said to myself, here is an honest man the judge should pay attention and believe that my future was seriously at stake that warranted help and his kind consideration for reprieve. Mr. Cloyd Ramsey stepped down after another ten minutes of friendly exchanges and presentation of when and what he knew about me.

The U.S. government attorney did not care to ask Mr. Ramsey any thing, which made me very worried and scared as well fearful of the outcome of this hearing. To me it seemed as if the court was just going through the motions of a having heard my side or some thing on record but decision about my fate had been taken at the state department.

And it would need true believers in democracy and human rights to over turn ruling made by that bias opinion wasting my life and court's time for nothing.

I knew Mr. Ramsey would have put the government attorney in his rightful place had he been asked questions by the attorney. He would have pointed out the fact that both the attorney and the state department were ignoring the history of harassment and labeling I experienced at the hands of the Gambia Government. The U.S. government attorney's stonewalling in court was based upon probably instruction to turn down my request for asylum in the United States.

On Mr. Ramsey's way to his seat our eyes met and his seemed to say to me, "Ceesay, I tried my best but I do not know what the system will decide. God help you my friend." I wholeheartedly thanked him in silence and watch Rev. Hugh C. White the stand in my behalf.

It was by now well after 3.45 pm when the judge called our last witness, Rev. Hugh C. White, to present his version to the best of his knowledge of the case.

My attorney, Professor Francis Conti, presented Rev. White as a representative of the Diocese Michigan's interest in my case and as a respected consultant to the Bishop of Michigan.

He assured the court that Rev. Hugh White had been up on the case since it came to their attention and he was qualified to attest to my character and integrity. Rev. Hugh C. White was sworn in testify on my behalf. Rev. White testified that he and others at the Diocese had looked into my case very carefully and are convinced that my fears are legitimate and that I do deserve asylum in the United States.

It was now getting well beyond 4 pm and again to everyone's surprise the government attorney raised a motion suggesting adjournment until the next day. Judge Auslander ignored the request and asked Rev. Hugh White to continue delivering his statement or testimony. Rev. Hugh C. White stressed that the

Dioceses had no doubts about the seriousness of what has been revealed to the Immigration court. The judge then asked a few more questions regarding the letters I wrote to the Gambian officials.

Judge Auslander asked if Rev. White thought that these letters had any significant bearing to warrant the action the Gambia took against me or to disrupt an effort such as I have put into my life?

Rev. White told the judge that he had no doubts to what I had already experienced from the hands of the Gambia and that consideration of favourable type would be worthy response to the unjust treatment I encountered or endured from trying to be a useful person to the Gambia and mankind.

Judge Auslander stopped questioning and the government attorney, in a haphazardly manner, was fretting and cared very little as to what was being said about me.

Judge Auslander then asked the U.S. government's attorney to give its summary argument. The attorney summed up by stating that the United States government saw no relation with the letters and my claim of fear of persecution and that it will stand by the state department's advisory opinion issued me in February and April, 1983, that in view of those arguments I should be deported forthwith.

He then rested his case for the government. His last words were, "Your honour we contend that this has not met the required evidentiary proof and presentation for asylum under section 208 and or withholding of deportation under section 243 (h) of the Immigration and Nationality Act.

They did not establish a well-founded fear of persecution in the Gambia." These lines still echo into my ears for they and only they pointed out why the attorney lacked interest in the proceedings and also these lines multiplied my fears, regrets and remorse beyond description.

America is my bastion of freedom and has now turned its back against me, an admirer and has just reaffirm its preparedness or determination to hand me over to the hounds and enemies of democracy in Africa to be torn alive with their razor sharp dirty claws.

I, at the time, wanted to remind the court that I was not the only one on trial but also the practice of democracy in Africa which was about to be dealt a severe blow more devastating than slavery. I wanted to make it clear that if the court's ruling is unfavorable to the practice of democratic ideals and allows stifling voices of justice then independence for the developing world had no meaning then and for eons to come.

I wanted it known that I was not asking to be given United States citizenship but requesting a temporal protection from the political quagmire that was about to kill my spirit, if not my soul. I thought I had made it very clear that I would return to my people as soon as the climate was safe for me to live in the Gambia.

That, to me, was the only way I can share the kindness and education provided me by the Americans. My attorney noticed some uneasiness on my part and he got up before I did and stated his own summary. Prof. Francis Conti reminded the court that the Gambia had already singled me out and persecuted me by terminating my medical studies in Liberia, that the deputy head of mission of the Gambia in Saudi Arabia, Dr. Sulayman S. Nyang's presence and testimony in support of my fears cannot and should not be ignored by the court, and that letters received from family and other friends in the Gambia and Liberia do show that I had a well-founded fear of persecution if I were to be forced to return to the Gambia prematurely. Francis Conti stressed that all the correspondence presented to the court supported the case and strongly advised that I not return to the Gambia at present.

He further pointed out the fact that the INS initially recommended granting asylum and Americans have invested in me and have vested interest in what happens to me and that it was good and descent citizens who came to testify in my behalf.

These and a hope for democracy in the developing world or countries would be served if a positive ruling were given to my request for political asylum in the United States.

Professor Francis Conti concluded by saying, "Your honour, based upon the information provided and my personal encounter of the Gambian students' fear of reprisal should they just been known to have talked to me, counsel for Mr. Ceesay, submit that Mr. Ceesay has established a well-founded fear of persecution directed at him should he return to the Gambia at this time.

For all or any of the above reasons, the applicant respectfully asserts that he qualifies for a grant of political asylum in the United States and request that he be provided with political asylum under section

208 and 243 (h) of the Immigration and Nationality Act." Professor Conti then handed the judge the following letters from respectable Americans concerned about my saga with the INS since February 1982.

Diocese of Michigan
4800 Woodward Avenue
Detroit, Michigan 48202
June 7, 1984

Dear Judge Auslander,

I write on behalf of Mr. Alhasan S. Ceesay who is requesting asylum in the United States because it would be dangerous for him to return to his country of origin, the Gambia.
I have known this young man for somewhat longer than one year during which time a number of us in the Episcopal Diocese of Michigan nave been concerned about his case. He is a rare young person, unusual in his steadiness of character, his truthfulness, and his high ethical standards.
There is a stereotype of the third world student who seeks residency in the United States in order to enjoy our standards of living and to avoid working under difficult conditions in his country; we have all met such people.
Alhasan Ceesay is the diametrical opposites of this stereotype. He would be happiest if he could use his considerable education and training for the benefits in his people and country. Some day, if there is a change in the political configuration in his country, he will work for its growth and development.

However, if he is forced to return now, to face political charges for guilt by association and probable incarceration, the potential contributions of this truly unusual young person will be sacrificed for no reason or purpose.
It is my believe that granting asylum to Alhasan Ceesay is, in effect, an investment in the coming generation. Neither the Gambia nor any other nation produces any surplus of young men of his caliber.

Faithfully Yours
Lois R. Leonard
Editor, The Record

United Ministries
Wayne State University
Detroit, Michigan 48201
June 11, 1984

Dear Judge Auslander,

As Episcopal chaplain to Wayne State University, I have known Mr. Alhasan Ceesay for approximately one year. He was referred to my office because of my familiarity with West Africa and West African students, and because I have lived in the region and continues to work with Africans.
During the time that I have known Mr. Ceesay, and in my many contacts with him, I have become impressed by his intelligence, honesty and sincerity. I find no sense of hustle or guile in Mr. Ceesay.

His care and concern for his people, his family and all those who are without power seems to be a main theme in his life. We have talked on a number of occasions about his sense of justice foe the poor, and I have suggested as the devil's advocate, that he should accommodate himself to the prevailing system of power in his country, which appear typical of the entire region.

Almost to the point of naivety, Mr. Ceesay continues to put the interest of the poor above his own self-interests. Indeed it is this concern, which lies at the heart of Mr. Ceesay's difficulties.

By expressing his hope to the president of the Gambia that due process of law would be followed for those arrested following the coup attempt of the Gambia, he, in African cultural context, questioned the leader.

I Africa, one does not directly confront the leader, but rather accommodate oneself to those more powerful and claims rule over the less powerful. What may seem a mild and trivial or worthless at within the American legal and political context is perceived as a treasonable act in Africa.

I sincerely believe, based upon my experience in West Africa, that Mr. Alhasan Ceesay will be imprisoned or suffer a worse fate, if he is deported to the Gambia.

One element of our national experience has been to provide a place of refuge for those who would be charged with treason in their own country for wishing to have a system of equal protection under the law.I am proud of this tradition.

I pray that this tradition will remain alive in the case of Alhasan Ceesay. Thank you for your consideration in this matter.
Sincerely
William Fames Wood
Episcopal Chaplain

United Ministries
Wayne State University
Detroit, Michigan 48201
June 11, 1984

Dear Judge Auslander,

I have been the University Minister of the United Christian Ministries at Wayne State University for the past twenty years. I first met Alhasan S. Ceesay April 1982, after the U. S. Immigration and Notarization Service had rejected his plea for political asylum.
Even though I am a Presbyterian minister, some Episcopal Church officials suggested that he should contact me. From then until now I have been ministering to his needs. Alhasan Ceesay is one of the finest persons that I have ever met at home or abroad.
His lively intelligence, his gentle and humane spirit and his sense of humor endear him to all who have the privilege of meeting him. He is a dedicated and God fearing man. Even though he is a Muslim and I a Christian, our friendship is based on our respective commitment to God. His religious faith has enabled him to endure the many hardships, which he has undergone these past three years.

He has deep passion for freedom and justice, which come from his belief in God and from his exposure to our democratic policy during his student days in our country. Coming from a farming family, Alhasan has been always concerned about the well being of the farmers in his native land.

On a number of occasions, he protested to the officials of the Gambia government about the injustice the farmers in his country were suffering. Professor Sulayman S. Nyang of Howard University, a former Gambia government official at the Saudi Arabia Mission, and still a Gambian citizen, informed me in a long telephone call that the Gambia government has some time looked upon Alhasan Ceesay as a "tribalism and political agitator," because of his championing of the farmer's cause.

Ceesay's troubles mounted when he wrote letters to his government protesting the illegal arrest and detention of innocent people shortly after the attempted coup d'etat of July 30, 1981. Two factors, however, have caused Alhasan Ceesay to believe that his government feels that he really had something to do with the Movement for Justice in Africa (MOJA) and the attempted trouble in Gambia, that his own government requesting the medical school; he was attending in Liberia to drop him from its enrolment and request the Liberian government to secretly send him back to the Gambia to face charges of crimes committed against the state. He, thus, fears for his life if he should have to return to the Gambia at this time.

Mr. latif T. sanyang, for instance was with Alhasan Ceesay in Liberia a week prior to the coup. Yet he was arrested and detained for eighteen months. Alhasan felt that he had to speak up for those whom he knew were non-violent persons who had nothing to do with the political troubles in the Gambia. Alhasan Ceesay loves his country dearly and has sought for years to prepare himself to serve his people' medical needs.

He has assured me that he had nothing to do with the attempted coup, which occurred in the Gambia while he was in Liberia in July 1981. It has been his dedication to truth, and justice that has placed him in the predicament in which he now finds himself. Given his circumstances, I highly recommend that our government should grant him political asylum. With his dedication to democratic values of freedom and justice and with his learning and professional training, he would be a valuable contribution to American life and Africa.

Sincerely
Virgil L. Jones
University Minister

The Mariner's Inn
Ledyard Street
Detroit, Michigan 48201
June 18, 1984

Dear Judge Auslander,

I am writing to commend Mr. Alhasan Ceesay for your favourable decision regarding permission for him to remain in this country, if not under any circumstances, at least until he has completed his medical schooling. Mr. Ceesay has been living in this residential facility for the past fourteen months. My familiarity with him from day-today contacts and conversations, lead me to affirm that man, a very discerning gentleman, is caught up in circumstances which will lead to life and, hope not, or death and destruction.

A valuable medical school has offered him the opportunity of a four-year scholarship in medical sciences. Such is an affirmation of his obvious intelligentsia capacities. I would hope the United States of America could see fit to grant Mr. Ceesay the opportunity of preparing himself to become a positive factor in the health needs of his generation. Of course I am a neophyte in Immigration policies and politics; however, if it fails me to see.

In the realm of human rights and the need of mankind in the world today would there be any constructive use of this life by refusing him a positive opportunity?

My constant contacts with Mr. Ceesay bring me to affirm to you his integrity, his honesty, and his unswerving commitment of himself to leading a life, which contributes to the common good of mankind. I do not find a political radical in him.

I rather confirm him to be kind of moral thoughtful person in addition his presence has brought and served as source of encouragement to this agency and men in it.

Mr. Alhasan Ceesay clearly opened up the minds and hearts of the residents to appreciate the tremendous values of life and opportunities, which lie waiting, and around them in this nation.
Again, it would seem to me, that offering a quality person the opportunity of preparing himself for a particularly needed service to mankind is a formidable position for us to take as we seek for a peaceful, healthy co-existence in this world.
With respect and Sincerity
Walter W. White
Executive Director.
With these and more letters in hand Judge Charles J. Auslander asked if there were anything further. With no one answering he said, "This court is declared adjourned." He remained at his desk for while talking to the government attorney.
When he left for his chambers the government attorney came to us and spoke with my attorney and had the nerves to shake my hands and said, "I had to do my instructed duty."
I could not at the time understand what prompted him to dos or say what he told me openly before all my defense team. Was it guilt by association with the state department?
Did he realize that justice and human rights were not going to take precedence in this case? Whatever it was, I still remember shaking the hands of my foe for the respect of decency. On hindsight, I have never before been involved in court proceedings but on that day I observed United States judiciary in action.

The judge left us with the impression that he knew what I stood for and was in sympathy with us and even told us that he would hand a ruling on the matter in four weeks from June 19, 1984. Some of us left the Immigration Court with feeling that judge Auslander, was considerate, but deep down in me I was very suspicious.

Why was the judge talking to the government lawyer after the hearing and not include my attorney in that discussion? And the broad smile from the government lawyer after wards made feel oh heck the Gambia embassy and their cronies at state department are at work again.

All these and the attitude of the government lawyer left me skeptical of the outcome of the hearing four weeks from then. It was a pure mockery of the U. S, judicial system. Why were we not what the ruling would be at the end of the hearing? All I needed from and was a simple line that says it was okay for me to start medical school in America.

This was what the University of Louisville in Kentucky was asking for but I was unable to get any form of statement from the judge. Most likely he too had to send everything to the state department. I just felt that the Judiciary was a free arm of the people of a country.

My lawyer never tried to pursue that aspect and so my chance of admission to medical school in America went down the drain by the end of that hearing in Atlanta, Georgia. A day I duped, "Alhasan Ceeasy's Nuremberg. With the hearing over, we headed for the airport immediately. My friends, who did not see the writing on the wall, were in a celebratory mood when we reached the airport in Atlanta. I was, on the other hand, in a state of shock, for my future remained quite uncertain if the Judge Charles J. Auslander or the government ruled against my request for asylum. Given the news about the other Mr. Ceesay whose case was heard earlier in the day and his eventual deportation order issued by the same judge Auslander did not go well with me.

I felt nauseated and completely confused why such darkness shrouds me of all people. Could judge Auslander rebuff the state depart as he is empowered by the Immigration Act or would he rather safe his own skin and tenure and acquiesce to the whims and caprices of the almighty state department?

Will he side step the political powers above him and give me protection I sought from the United States? Today, in my mind, the United States seem to stand on the flimsy pedestal that the judiciary in the Gambia was correct and open even if it was used as a tool for the president' men and government officials in their attempt to regain power in the Gambia.

Again, where complaining becomes a crime or a treasonable offence, then hope becomes despair. All it pointed out was that it was all right for friendly nations to act hypocritical about democracy and human rights as long as it or they remain under the big ideological umbrella.

It was okay for the Gambia to pretend to be practicing democracy while at the same time engaged in flagrant violation of human rights amid rampant corruptions.

Why the detention of mostly innocent provincial people for more than fourteen months and refusal of these people from being reinstated to their former posts after the insurrection? Why the sweeping emergency powers?

We cannot have a two-tier society in the Gambia nor would we accept the colonial yardstick of divide and rule mentality. The Gambia government must only respect the rights of the governed but must serve them with accountability and transparency in all government transactions. Governments belong to the people and not clicks or tribes.

Nor does it belong to an individual a tribe or party and it must serve the common objective, rich or poor, of a nation.

The people must be allowed to exercise the high ideals and principles embodied in democracy and that such basic human rights as freedom of speech, freedom from arbitrary arrest or harm, have a choice in who governs them, freedom of movement and right to good health service, right to earn a living and an education must be fundamental right of all citizens of the Gambia.

For me a president is subject and servant of the people he heads and must be accountable to the people. Most Gambians were aware of the lip service given to farmers while plundering of the nation's meager till went unchecked.

Be reminded that all that glitters is not gold and the Gambia's spin-doctoring propaganda led the world into believing that the government was by the people and for the people. At the time of July 30, 981 insurrection the new tsars have succeeded in reducing president Jawara into a nominal figurehead not aware of the affairs of state. Dr. Sulayman S. Nyang was among few Gambians officials willing to break ranks from the political clan to put a stop to some of the covert activities of our fledgling government.

Hence, at the airport in Atlanta, we lamented about dear Gambia for half an hour before boarding our flight back to Detroit, Michigan via Washington, D. C. Dr. Nyang was so concerned that the last thing he said to me at the departure terminal was, "Please take it easy with yourself. These dark days will come to pass. "I was thankful he came but at the same time sorry to see him leave.

He was the only one who dare come forward and join me in telling America the truth about the state of affairs in the Gambia. We still wondered why my plight kept falling on deaf ears. The rest of waited for another hour before we left Atlanta for Detroit, Michigan.

We finally landed at Metro Airport at 11.35 pm. Mr. Cloyd Ramsey bid us farewell and drove back t Sandusky, Michigan the same evening, while Rev. Hugh White, Prof. Francis Conti and I drove heading down town Detroit.

Mr. Ramsey went with my heart to Sandusky and I almost asked him to let me stay with him at Sandusky while I wait for the judge's decision due in four weeks. Life at skid row by then had made me feel terrible and such encampment did not help my nerves.

I remained in serious anxiety the whole night upon returning to the Mariner's Inn. I jus could not stop worrying about my family back in the Gambia and the way my medical school prospect were being derailed by the limbo created as I waited Judge Charles Auslander's ruling on my request for asylum in the United States. Also most of my supporters were getting discouraged and loosing interest because it has already taken two years plus and we were still at the first phase of the struggle to disentangle me.

There was no sign of a resolution of the case as the judge's silence only left us afraid of getting bad news from that end. I thank God but then went into severe depression and remained so for a whole week despite the interventions of Mary Ellen Robertson and the Mariner's Inn staff that made life a bit tolerable.

The next day at the Diocese despite the uncertainty, most of my friends thought that it was the end of the nightmare chapter of my life or asylum request. How wrong they were. It was a forgone conclusion in many minds.

Not so in mine. I kept asking would Judge Charles Auslander be human enough to grant me asylum in the United States? Would people stop seeing this world in the perceived and deal with the realities in the developing world? Most of our leaders, like their stooges and bullies, do not believe in democracy or human rights.

Chapter 22

THE SLUGGISH WHEELS OF JUSTICE

The wheels of justice turns very slowly in matters like this petition for asylum in the United States. I called for meeting of the Ad Hoc Ceesay Committee the same week after our return from the INS hearing in Atlanta, Georgia.
Everyone attending gave an upbeat and hopeful report from Judge Charles J. Auslander based on the fact that he did take into record all the evidence and letters we took to the court. From that time on our meetings became fewer and months apart.
We tried meeting once every three months and it was during one of those meetings of trying to attempt to refresh my mind at school was raised. I accepted and followed it up by meeting the Dean of Admissions at Wayne State University Medical School about such a possibility.
It was by now three years since I last attended classes, Hence, the dean suggested that I do a post bachelor's guest student program in sciences until the outcome of the INS ruling or at least for two semesters while the medical school tries to find out how it can best accommodate my case.
Despite my heavy heart and confused state with depression, I started classes as recommended in spring of 1985. It was a step in the right direction but impact of the series of delays and serious disappointing had started leaving their scars on my brain.

I will tie this aspect of my experience with a sequel when I graduate from Medical School. With Wayne State University accepting as a guest student in sciences everyone in the Ceesay Committee relaxed except Mrs. Patricia Koblyski. She right away wrote the following letter to Rev. William Wood soliciting financial assistance to help me pay for my preparatory course at Wayne State University, Detroit, Michigan. It read:

Diocese of Michigan
4800 Woodward Avenue
Detroit, Michigan 48202
March 4, 1985

Dear Rev. Wood

I am writing you, as refugee coordinator of the Diocese of Michigan, in efforts to preserve the life of one Alhasan S. Ceesay, who we are convinced from careful investigation, will likely be imprisoned indefinitely or suffer execution for treason if he is forced to return to the Gambia at this time.
All things considered, detailed in the letter, which follows, Mr. Ceesay deserves asylum and our support.
Within the past month Mr. Ceesay has been admitted as guest student to a post of bachelors program in sciences at Wayne State University, which would assure him entrance into medical school when his appeal for asylum has been granted. As strange as it may appear, with the long delay by the Immigration, we are hopeful that asylum will be granted to Mr. Ceesay.

The minimum cost for his studies at Wayne State University for one year will be $1000 per semester9Spring/Summer, Fall/winter) totaling to $3000. This is the bare minimum. We really need $4000. The Bishop's fund at this time is practically depleted, so obtaining financial support for Alhasan Ceesay is needed.

A brief recent background of Mr. Ceesay is in order. In December, 1982, Bishop McGehee was asked to assist Alhasan Ceesay in his efforts to remain this country, due to real fears of persecution on returning to the Gambia, in part to enable him attend medical school at the University of Louisville in Kentucky or Wayne State in Michigan.

At the time as a result of an advisory opinion from the state department, the Detroit Immigration and Naturalization Service had denied him his request for political asylum.

He received his B.A. and M.S. degrees in biology at Olivet College and Michigan Technological University respectively, between 1967 and 1973, and completed some course work for a PhD in Parasitology at Howard University by 1979.

At that time, however, his ambition to become a medical doctor lead him to return to Africa to seek scholarship from the European Economic Community (E.E.C.) for him to attend medical school in Africa.

At the beginning of 1979 he entered the University of Liberia A. M. Dogliotti College of Medicine in Monrovia, where for two years he was a student in good standing. In July 1981, there was an attempted coup d'etat in the Gambia.

Among those arrested in the aftermath were friends and relatives of Mr. Ceesay. Believing them wholly innocent he wrote numerous letters on their behalf to high government officials pleading for mercy and justice. Among those pleaded for were Latif Sanyang, who spent almost a year in detention without reason given, Abdoulie Sarr, a first cousin, who was a fireman at the airport, and Kebba Sanneh, a health superintendent, Department of Health.

Abdoulie Sarr had been tried and sentenced to death by a special tribunal employed in the coup's aftermath. Shortly after this, Mr. Ceesay was approached by Liberian security personnel who questioned him about his political activities and informed him that he was on a memorandum list of twenty Gambians in Liberia whom the Gambia government wanted returned quietly to the Gambia. These security personnel actually showed him the memorandum from the Gambia government. About this time, the acting Dean of the medical school informed him that the Gambia government had terminated his scholarship, and indeed, he was no longer considered a student at the medical school.

He was given no explanation; however he was advised to take care of his life. He went briefly into hiding until he was able to secure a tourist visa from the U. S. Embassy in Liberia and airfare from an American friend from Michigan.

He came to the U. S. fearing for his life if he were to return to the Gambia. Although reasons for the government's action are, of course, not documented, there is a strong likelihood that Mr.

Ceesay, who was viewed as apolitical agitator prior to the coup attempt and was probably also identified with Movement for Justice in Africa (MOJA), although he was not a member, was perceived as dangerous to the government.

These persecutions together with his correspondence to officials probably lead the overly sensitive government and security forces to unjustified conclusions.

Mr. Ceesay applied for political asylum just before his tourist visa expired. Although the Immigration officer who originally considered his case recommended that asylum be granted afterward an advisory opinion letter from the state department was obtained. The district Director denied his request for asylum.

In addition to the above, Mr. Ceesay has been virtually accepted to medical school at the University of Louisville, Kentucky. However, in order to obtain the necessary financial assistance he would need to commit himself to serve in physician shortage areas in Kentucky, or Michigan for several years subsequent to graduation.

Although he would like to return to the Gambia to serve his people, and we do not at all question sincerity in this regard, continuing conditions there do not make that now advisable. Mr. Ceesay still fears for his life and safety if he were to return. We are convinced that he is right.

Mr. Ceesay is a sincere, altruistic fellow entangled in a web of unfortunate circumstances and laws. We hope that you see fit to help him. If you have any questions, please feel free to contact me.

Thank you in advance for your willingness to take this on. Peace.
Pat Koblyski
Refugee Coordinator.
The response to this forthright letter was a generous grant of $500 from Rev. William Wood. Pat Koblyski in addition, also contacted the Diocese's New York office or branch, which responded as follows:

The Episcopal Church Center
New York, NY 10017
May 16, 1985

Dear Mr. Ceesay,

Recently, the scholarship committee of the Presiding Bishop's Fund for the World Relief met to review scholarship application for the academic year 1985/86. As previously arranged, your 1984/85 applications were held for reconsideration at this time.
I am pleased to advise you that the Presiding Bishop's Fund for Refugees and Displaced persons scholarship program has warded you a $3000 scholarship for your studies next year.
This is onetime award and has been granted in support of your preparation for medical school at Wayne State University during the academic year 1985/86.
Unless we hear from you otherwise, checks for $1000 will be disbursed twice a year in July 1985 and January 1986. Checks cannot be disbursed in fewer than two payments. If you would let us know to

whom the checks should be drawn, we will forward the first check in July 1985. All best wishes to you as you continue your education.

Faithfully yours

Ian T. Douglas

Associate For Overseas

Leadership development

I was overwhelmed by this kindness and constant generosity. It made it possible for me to participate in the program at Wayne State University. Another effort to raise money was done in the form of a moving article by Mrs. Lois R. Leonard, Editor of the Diocesan newspaper, The Record.

It dwelled on my dilemma and the need to join hands and help me fund my schooling. Allow me a moment to tell a bit about Lois R. Leonard. She is a human rights advocate and a dedicated journalist to the struggles of the underdeveloped or shall I say the underprivileged.

She is the type that would stand between a giant and a midget to protect the later weakling. She does not hesitate to call to attention to the miss use of authority or responsibility wherever it occurs. Yet, despite this fierce believe in justice, she is a kind-hearted person and more than willing to share with others the little she had.

She champions freedom of expression and of human rights. She came on board the Ad Hoc Ceesay Committee as soon as she was told about me and never missed a meeting until my departure from the U. S. in 1987.

Rest assured that she was an asset to have on my side. Believe me, she kept our Ad Hoc meetings lively and well balanced. She never hesitated to say how she felt about an approach we were contemplating during discussions or suggesting some sort of contact to propel our objective forward.

Lois was amongst our think tanks during those brainstorming meetings at the Diocese of Michigan in Detroit. It was she who led us to professor Francis Conti who became my subsequent defender at the U. S. Immigration court. Here is, without further ado, the moving appeal article Mrs. Lois R. Leonard wrote on my behalf.

Professor Sulayman S. Nyang, Washington D. C

Chapter 23

HOW YOU GET INVOLVED SOMETIMES WITHOUT INTENDING TO

Two year ago most of us never heard of a country called the Gambia. Some of us still aren't sure where it is in Africa, somewhere. We did not expect to know anyone from there, and we surely didn't care about the Gambian political situation. That was before Alhasan Ceesay.

Two years ago he walked in off Warren Avenue because he thought this was the Catholic church/mission. He came seeking, in a sense, sanctuary. The Diocese' office isn't set for that sort of thing. We are a bunch of secretaries, bookkeepers, church administrators and other paper types, not social workers, politicians or political experts or lawyers.

But here was Ceesay, small, wiry, dark-skinned, fluent in English with a little accent that you can't quite place. Ceesay with eyes that can look sorrowful, a dazzling smile, a person of intelligence, humor an invincible determination.

Alhasan Ceesay wants to practice medicine in his country, the Gambia, where Western trained doctors are scares. He is the only member of his immediate family who has had schooling.

He has studied in this country, graduating from Alpena Community College and Olivet College, then earning a Master's in biology from Michigan Technological University and doing graduate work in Parasitology at the Howard University.

With that good start towards his goal, what on earth went wrong? Why was Ceesay walking the streets of Detroit without a dollar in his pocket and no place to stay? After his successful experience as a foreign student in the U. S. Ceesay had returned to Africa and got himself a scholarship to go to medical school in Liberia.

The Gambia had no medical school of its own. During his second year of medical school there was trouble in the Gambia. The president of the country invited military and security forces from Senegal, his neighbour on the other side, to put down the July 1981, uprising.

About 1000 people were killed in the attempted coup d'etat and another 1000 were arrested, some sentenced to death for treason. Ceesay was not even there when it happened, but imbued western ideas about justice, fair trials, and democratic principles, he wrote letters in defense of some of those arrested.

He got himself on a black list of Gambians whom the still edgy governments wanted for suspected subversion. The Liberian Medical School acting Dean told Ceesay that his scholarship. Financed by the European Economic Community (E. E. C.) for Gambia, had been cancelled. He warned him, unofficially, that his life was in danger.

Ceesay managed to get a tourist visa and some money from an American friend and escaped back to the United States of America. The tourist visa had long expired, and Ceesay's application for political asylum has bounced from one jurisdiction to another.

The first Immigration officer to who examined his case recommended asylum but a higher up at the state department turned him down. His case is now pending before a federal Judge, who heard the case on the evidence nearly a year ago but who has not yet handed down an opinion or ruling in the case. Under the law, Ceesay cannot hold a job while his Immigration status is unsettled.

Because of this delay, he has been obliged to forfeit a full scholarship to the University of Louisville Medical School, which had been awarded on condition that he promised to practice medicine for six years among the poor in Appalachia, which he could not do without residency status.

Time is passing, Alhasan Ceesay a roof and food at the Mariner's Inn where the aged men and recovering drug addicts and alcoholics have found him to be warm, helpful friend. He comes around to see us all at the Diocese office every week.

Some times he brings letters from the Gambia, from relatives who warn him desperately and urgently not to come home.

We all ask anxiously, "Any word from the judge/" if the judge rules against him, deportation is the next step. A Detroit law school professor, Francis Conti, who has been acting as Ceesay's legal counsel without compensation, promises there can be a delay by appealing for to higher court if he ruling is negative.

But time is fleeting and lesser person than Ceesay would have given up. Sometimes he is depressed, but more often he cheers us, reminding us that it is all in God's hands. A way has opened up that would give some of us a chance to serve God's hands.

Wayne State has agreed to admit Ceesay to take some necessary refresher courses in biological sciences. We have no doubts of his abilities. He has a mind like a like a steel trap and a dogged determination of an Olympic Marathon runner. But Wayne State is not offering him scholarship, at least not yet.

So we are going to try to make up our scholarship for Ceesay. We have no resources for raising money, and we are pretty sure that foundations would not be interested. We could get Ceesay into medical school and some judge still sends him back to the Gambian prison or firing squad. But if you know Ceesay, you have to gamble on him.

He is too intelligent, too determined, and too courageous to be abandoned. Somewhere down the line after a different government comes into power. We can see him setting up clinics in the Gambian villages.

It is this picture we cannot get out of our minds. The other picture, the one that frightens us, is armed gauds picking up Alhasan Ceesay at the Airport in the Gambia if he were deported.

There are a lot of black Africans who need the help of people of good will, millions of them. We are digging in our heels on this one. Simply because we know him and he has become, "Our Ceesay."

Signed: Lois R. Leonard

Editor, The Record

This article generated a tremendous response to our appeal besides being signed by more than half the staff of the Diocese of Michigan. In response to it, I sent the following letter to the Editor of the Record

Ledyard Street
Detroit, Michigan 48201
March 26, 1985

Dear Editor,

Kindly allow me space in the next issue of the Record to thank all of the signatures of the moving article about my dilemma published in your March 1985 issue.
Special thanks are also due to the editor and efforts members of the Ad Hoc Committee that has been working with my case so assiduously and steadfastly since I stepped foot at the Diocese in April 1982. Many thanks go to Mary Ellen Robertson and her staff at the Mariner's Inn.
It is an unprecedented case in which my counsel professor Francis Conti of the Detroit College of law has represented me in the most exemplary possible manner. God bless you professor Conti. Simply put, God has indeed come to my aid through all of you.
I am most grateful to the Episcopalians of the Diocese of Michigan and their parishes for standing by my case. As an African, I am very concerned about the future of my continent and man. While the world advances in rocket leaps and bounces, my people are still miserable, oppressed, hungry and unable to enjoy the simple fundamental rights like freedom of choice to a government and who rules them.
The new tyranny in independent Africa is sheer compulsion of corrupt politicians and inept military men who wallows in destroying the institutions and

the gentle peasantry. Coup d'etats are neither the cure nor the answer to the evolutionary problems facing Africa. Coups and one party states, be they overtly or covertly instituted, communism, as been the case in most our countries, including the Gambia's sham multi-party, all the other current Gambian parties are from the ruling PPP, only places restriction of freedom in the lives of the citizenry.

So far no coup has ever instilled better and worthier redemption to those they affected. Hence, dear friends, take advice from a sincere African. All that Africa needs from you are teachers, agriculturalist, engineers, businessmen, and technicians to help her uplift the masses.

I have prayed daily for God to stop the West and East from preserving few rich tsars and coup leaders in the midst of the starving multitudes of Africa. Stop propping the devil that pokes the peace progress and tranquility out of Africa.

Yes, we the peasants are grateful for what little that has trickled down to us by accident, but more would have been touched if the tsars of Africa were forbidden from ever coming near or touching the "loot" sent by foreign government grants in aid and other banking gimmickries. Friends, I am very happy with what you did for me.

I have a covenant with Africa and I will return to help when the time comes. For me, freedom means simply to belong to earth and feel at home in a democratic framework. I certainly agree with Benjamin when he said, "In free governments the rulers are the servants and the people their superiors and sovereigns."

In current Africa the reverse is the case. Your stand has been a reward to freedom and human rights. I thank you for uplifting my heart and spirit, for the encouragement and sacrifice with which you met the unusual nature of my case.

Your act goes to uphold that the human heart is born good, sensitive and feeling and above all we are all eager to be approved and to approve. In life, we are hungry for simple happiness and a chance to live.

We neither wish to kill or to be killed, as in my case. I reiterate my commitment to return to Africa and do declare, before all, that my whole life, whether it be a short one or long, shall be devoted to the needy especially the sick. I shall share your kindness with Africa.

Again, I am most grateful to all of you and so are the Gambian villagers. Thank you. I am touched and humbled by your generosity and its uniqueness. God bless you.

Sincerely Your Friend

Alhasan S. Ceesay

I, literally, under duress, continued schooling at Wayne State University and at the same time searching for ways to disentangle myself from the grips of the INS. The 1983 letter of the United Bishops illustrated the spider's web on which my very life and future hung.

The United Bishops defines hope as, "The capacity to live with danger without being overwhelmed by it, hope is the will to struggle against obstacles even when they appear insuperable." Danger awaits me if the Federal Judge rules against me.

God and hope were my only self-consolatory avenues. At the same time I could not remove the premonition or feeling that the Judge would not be able to over rule the state department's advisory opinion based upon protocol interest than human rights and law.

It was the advisory opinion versus the need of an ordinary and an unknown fellow like me. I was just too certain that the judge would not risk his job, even if it were going to land him the noble laureate in law, for the exercise of justice and upholding of human rights in my precarious case.

Sure enough, after 16 months waiting and when I lost all grants and interests of the schools willing to give me a second chance to complete my medical education, we received the following heart wrenching, bombshell decision from Judge J. Auslander concerning my request for political asylum in the United States of America.

When it rains it pours and I am now drowning in deep sea of despair and further disappointments. The ruling left me with the daunting task of surviving a stigma placed upon me by the denial. From now on most American satellites or allies will consider me an undesirable fellow and God knows what falsehoods the Gambia had in the state department files about me.

The decision came at a very hard time for my family and I. It was another humiliating snag on my way to the M.D degree and it placed my life at the whims and capiases of the Gambian tsars to who I will never bow. Here is a summary of the six-page decision.

IN THE MATTER OF
Alhasan S. Ceesay In deportation proceedings
Respondent

The respondent is a male native and citizen of the Gambia who last entered the United States at New York on December 20, 1981, as a visitor with authorization to remain until February 22, 1982. He remained beyond that date without authorization of the Service and is deportable pursuant to section 241 (a) (2) of the Act.
The respondent's persecution claim is lacking in detail and coherence that it simply does not demonstrate sufficient and satisfactory reliability. The claim constitutes nothing more than mere speculation and conjecture, and does not raise to the required level of concrete, believable evidence having some objective corroboration, Rejair v INS 691 F 2d 139 (3d cir. 1982).
Therefore the, I must conclude that the respondent has not met the statutory standard of eligibility for asylum whenever the claim is assed in terms of demonstrating a clear probability, realistic likelihood, a reasonable possibility or good or valid reasons to fear persecution.
Further, I conclude that he has failed to demonstrate eligibility for withholding of deportation. It does appear that the respondent is eligible for voluntary departure and merits a favorable exercise of discretion for that relief.
ORDERED: It is hereby ordered that the application for asylum and withholding of deportation be and is here denied. It is further ordered that the respondent be allowed to depart

the United States voluntarily on or before January 1, 1986. It is further ordered that if the respondent does not depart when and as required, that he shall be deported to the Gambia.
Charles J. Auslander, Jr
Immigration Judge
Dated: December 18, 1985

Alhasan Ceesay and Bishop McGehee at the Diocesan Center. photo credit: Lois Leor

Chapter 24

AN APPEAL TO U.S. SENATORS AND INS BOARD

The doors of justice seemed slammed shut at my face when I read INS Judge Charles J. Auslander's decision with regard to my request for political asylum in the United States. It left me feeling that life is worthier with descent treatment and personal exploitation designs of others.

The Gambia government seemed to be getting their wishes every step or time hope tend or attempts to surface on my way. The Ad Hoc Ceesay Committee convened horridly and we rolled our sleeves and went to work on for possible appeal of the decision rendered by Judge Auslander.

My attorney Professor Francis Conti responded to the ruling with an appeal petition to the INS Board of appeals. Naturally, my friends got more worried and concerned for my life.

Everyone was taken by surprise with the rendered negative ruling. Most wondered whether this great nation has not compromised its usual stand, ideals so to speak, against tyranny, oppression and oppressors.

People started to ask or felt that there seemed to be a broader issue, which underlines my asylum request denial. They frequently ask, "Will the United States government reaffirm its tradition of granting political asylum to refugees who seek protection from their governments and who flee from the oppressions of the non-communist governments?"

Others categorically stated that the present policy was one of granting political asylum to those fleeing communist regimes, but denying the same asylum to others. Worrying like a rocking chair does not carry us any further than where we are seated.

So we called a hurried general meeting where after a great deal of brainstorming, it was unanimously agreed at that meeting that we decide on another approach to unravel my puzzle.

During that emergency deliberation we concurred with appealing the case to the Immigration and Naturalization Service Board of Appeals.

This was done on December 13, 1985. Because time, the thief of life, flees, I in desperate need of help wrote to some of my most admired U. S, Senators Carl Levin, Donald Reigel and Edward Kennedy of Massachusetts.

I had high regards for these senators and was literally that if my case had been brought immediately to their attention the story would have had a different ending or turn for the better. The last, Senator Edward Kennedy, has been a member of the clan that further ignited my interest in democracy and respect for America.

I was in America during the days of "Camelot" And it was the elder brother, late president John F. Kennedy, who said, "Ask not what your country can do for you, but what you can do for your country." Putting it mildly, I am an admirer of the Kennedy clan for the stand they took in support of the little guy or people as well as the power wielders.

Who other than Robert Kennedy would speak on the topic; "What if God were black?" to then South African parliament entrenched in apartheid.

Like any who care and love descent people, I suffered the bullets that ran through Rev. Martin Luther King, Jr, president John F. Kennedy and lately my great senator from New York, the late Robert Kennedy. These were stalwarts of America during their days. The following appeal was sent to senators mentioned above.

Diocese of Michigan
4800 Woodward Avenue
Detroit, Michigan 48202
November 14, 1985

Dear Senator,

I am Alhasan S. Ceesay, a Gambian citizen, who for the past four years has been fighting for his life. The enclosed documented facts will show that I did nothing other than asking my government to heed human rights and dispense justice equally and fairly. This angered some powerful authorities for, today and since 1981, I stand homeless and unable to complete the medical training I started in Liberia. I was removed from medical school because of the enclosed articles I wrote seeking justice and freedom for the innocent who were wrongly arrested in the aftermath of the July attempted overthrow of the Gambia government.
As you will notice I have been offered scholarship in the U.S. by University of Louisville School of Medicine and as well as Wayne State University in Detroit, Michigan. The scholarship and my eventual admission to medical school can't be finalized until

reasonable resolution of my asylum request in the United States. If judge Auslander's November 18th, 1985 ruling stands it would render a final nail to my coffin and a terrible blow to all that I stood for and democratic ideals I learnt from America. It is in this vein that I write to solicit your help.

I only want America to be a protector until when the political climate in the Gambia is safe for my return. Despite this setback to me, I am fully determined and committed to returning to serve my people as a physician when my life would no longer be in jeopardy.

My continent is going through an evolutionary period and I will not renege on my obligation to contribute to her development and growth. Senator, I assure you of my determination to succeed and eventually to serve the Gambia. This is an unbreakable covenant I have for my people and between God and I.

Returning to serve the people, at a later and safe day, would be the only way I can share your kindness and skills America taught me. However, should I be forced to return at this time, all my goal and life will go unrealized, for the current government is like a wounded Leopard and will not hesitate to purge or silence those whom it considers, "political agitators", or worse enemies of the State. I am no enemy to my people and have never been involved in any criminal act, implied or otherwise. I have no party affiliation nor did I ever have knowledge of or participatory association in any attempt to overthrow the Gambia government. All I have catered for is to be able to contribute positively towards the health service delivery to the most deprived region of the Gambia. Hence, I beg to be protected from wanton destruction, as I witnessed in Liberia during her uprising in president William Tolbert's overthrow, and be allowed to stay in America and finish my medical education so that some day I can be of use to Africa, America and mankind.

I certainly plan to return to my motherland as a productive human being and not as a jailbird. Kindly review the enclosed and give a helping hand to my cause. Finally, American medical schools are willing to allow me start all over if allowed to stay in the United States in the United Sates.

Your, assisting me in this case, because of being a believer in the American system of justice, a respected representative of the people will go a long ways into calming the rough seas for me. I reiterate my total commitment to overcoming this roadblock and with yours and God's and good friends I came across in this land, nothing is unconquerable.

Thanks a million for whatever consideration and help you can give to my plight.

Best wishes for good health and extend my greetings to your family and friends. I am anxiously waiting to hear from you at your convenience about what can be done for me.

Sincerely
Alhasan S. Ceesay
Gambian student and asylum Seeker

A covering letter was also sent to each of the above senators by (the RT. Rev.) H Coleman McGehee, Bishop of the Diocese of Michigan to reinforcing the gravity and need to help bring resolution to my asylum request at the INS.

Again high hopes were raised, only to be dashed by the long trail of silence that followed these appeals to U. S. Senators. Only Senator Carl Levin replied and asked his Detroit office to look into the matter and report back its findings and any suggestions that would bring relief to me. Here is the Bishop's letter to the Senators.

Office of the Bishop
4800 Woodward Avenue
Detroit, Michigan 48202
November 18, 1985

Dear Senator,

I am writing on behalf of Alhasan Ceesay, a Gambian national who is seeking political asylum, whom I have personally known and helped for over two years. I have enclosed copies of material describing his situation and Judge Auslander's decision.
In seeking all possible means of protecting Mr. Ceesay, my Diocese and I would appreciate your looking into the possibility of sponsoring a member's private bill on consideration for third preference status on behalf of this dedicated human being.
Mr. Ceesay deserves the attention and humanitarian consideration, which your office might give. He is a sincere person entangled in a web of unfortunate circumstances and laws. Mr. Ceesay needs to obtain some form of legal residency status not only to protect him from being wasted but also to allow him to complete medical training, which will be useful to

his country in due course. I hope that you will see it fit to help Mr. Ceesay obtain an appropriate residency status. I very much appreciate your concern and effort in this matter, and look forward to hearing from you. If you have any questions, please feel free to contact me at your convenience.
Peace
(The Rt. Rev.) H. Coleman McGehee, Jr.
Bishop of Michigan

Senator Carl Levin, fortunately, personally received his copy of the above letters and package I sent to his Washington office. We never heard from the rest of the key senators we contacted.

I sent reminders, which went unanswered. I then suggested my making a personal appearance to the various senators' offices in Washington in an effort to bring them aboard this case.

It never happened because we literally ran out of funds and most people have started getting bore by intransigence of the Immigration Service and its handling of my request for political asylum in the United States.

Interest in the case just waned tremendously after Judge Auslander's ruling on the case. Again, most felt that only the state department can resolve the matter and it will in no way turn around and say the hastily made advisory opinion was based on information given to it by the tentacles of the Gambia government in Washington.

At Detroit, senator Carl Levin's office reacted immediately and asked that my attorney, Professor Francis Conti and I meet with Miss Jane Jeffery, chief liaison for the senator at the Detroit, Michigan office the following Monday.

This was done and we met Miss Jane Jeffery and Mary green very eager to meet with us, explore possibilities of a third preference category and perhaps for me to meet the Senator when he comes to Detroit the following week.

The two liaisons diligently officers took note of all information concerning my situation and suggested or confirmed that the third preference window would be the best approach since the INS could drag the case on infinitely.

We left senator Carl Levin's Detroit office very hopeful that something would turn up from that angle. Again hope faded as time passed by without much being achieved. By now I had almost became immune to disappointments.

I ended up telling my friends to wait and see what emanates from promises to help made by various offices and officials. I was a poor village boy who believed in the American system but do the American politics allow its proper judicious exercise for a foreigner fight for human rights of his people abroad.

The pendulum continued to swing begging for a fast resolution of my misery. In one of the meetings it was suggested that I write to Chief Justice of Michigan, the honourable G. Mennen Williams because he not only served in Africa but, as legal scholar and a respected citizen he might be able to get someone to look into the case for the shake of my life and the future I sought for my people.

I left no stones untouched or uncovered and followed any lead we were told if there grew more skepticism about the outcome of that pursuit. Here in a nutshell is my letter to Chief Justice G. Mennen

Williams. You know, on hindsight, I wished we had written to the governor of Michigan. It was just when I made up my mind to leave the United States that someone called attention to the fact that I should have written to the governor of Michigan. Some suggested writing to the nearest whip that none of us at the time dreamt of doing.

We were just inundated by series of time consuming disappoint which ended up numbing our judgments and even strategies. However some in the know told me the governor would not risk or be able to persuade influential INS and political figures to take a second look on my behalf to bring a speedy resolution of my asylum request in the USA.

Diocese of Michigan
4800 Woodward Avenue
Detroit, 48202

November 14, 1985

Dear Chief Justice Williams,

I am Alhasan Ceesay, a Gambian citizen, soliciting your help in a life and death situation. I have asked the very Rev. Bertram Herlong, dean of the Cathedral, Church of St. Paul to talk to you. I also submit the enclosed documentation to provide detail background about me and pending case with the INS.

I would be most grateful if your honour would grant me an audience upon reading this material and at your convenience. The enclosed letter from INS judge Charles J. Auslander shows I do need any help

one can give to me to remain free so as to complete my medical training. Thank you for taking your valuable time to look into my case. God bless
Sincerely
Alhasan S. Ceesay
Few weeks latter I was given chance to tell my story to Chris Church on Military Road, Dearborn, Michigan. Mrs. Edwina Clay of Dearborn spearheaded it. She and her Parish wrote supportive petitions for me to their representatives and Senator Carl Levin. It feel good to know that there were people willing to stand by justice and human rights for all the people on earth.
By this time the Chief Justice's office had called me several time to reassure me that, even though he was powerless in handling the case, since it was a different jurisdiction of the Justice Department, he would write to let responsible persons look into my case. This he did in the following letter to senator Carl Levin.

Chief Justice of the Supreme Court
Detroit, Michigan 48201
January 10, 1986

Dear Carl,

This letter brings to your attention the disturbing circumstances surrounding the refusal by the Immigration and Naturalization service to grant asylum to a Gambian citizen, Alhasan Ceesay, who is presently resident in Detroit.
A brief summary of Mr. Ceesay's history, as I know it, follows. Gambia is small West African Country.

Mr. Ceesay's long-term goal is to practice modern medicine in his homeland. Between 1967 and 1978 studied biology at the undergraduate and graduate levels in the United States.

During this time, he frequently criticized the Gambia governments' agricultural policies and official corruption. He was labeled a political agitator in government circles. In 1979, Mr. Ceesay enrolled in the medical school at the University of Liberia after receiving a scholarship through the European Economic Community.

The following year an attempted coup d'etat in the Gambia was defeated through the intervention or intercession of the Senegalese military forces and security, which remained in the Gambia today. Mr. Ceesay wrote letters to government officials in the Gambia protesting arrests and injustice associated with them.

In November 1981, Liberian security official questioned Mr. Ceesay about his political activities and told him that the Gambia government wanted him returned. His name appeared on a list of students belonging to the movement for justice in Africa (MOJA), a radical political group, although he was not a member.

A number of these students and suspects were arrested upon their return to the Gambia. The acting Dean of the medical school informed Mr. Ceesay that his scholarship had been discontinued and that he should take care for his life. Ceesay secured a visa and airfare to the United States.

He has learnt through correspondence with friends and close relatives that he will be incarcerated if he returns to the Gambia. It is alleged that something in the nature of witch hunt for critics of the Gambian and Senegalese government officials continue in the Gambia. At the expiration of his visa, Mr. Ceesay pursued a request for asylum. Attorney Francis Conti has represented him in this endeavor most recently.

The Detroit office of INS originally concluded that Mr. Ceesay was entitled to asylum. However, that decision was reversed after the Gambia Ambassador wrote to the state department, and after the state department sent a report to the INS indicating that since Mr. Ceesay was not present in the Gambia at the time of the attempted coup, since some of the people on whose behalf Mr. Ceesay had written letters has been cleared by the government, Mr. Ceesay does not have a "well founded fear of persecution" upon his return to the Gambia. Mr. Ceesay has appealed this decision in Federal court and is presently awaiting the court's decision. He will be deported back to the Gambia if his appeal fails. The uncertainty of Mr. Ceesay's status in this country has resulted in his loss of educational grants and employment opportunities here. While I am not personally acquainted with him, those whose opinion I trust informed me that he is a person of great intelligence, courage and integrity.

You may wish to investigate Mr. Ceesay's case further. He can be contacted through the very Reverend Bertan Nelson Herlong at the Cathedral on 4800 Woodward Avenue. Thank you for taking the time to learn about his case.

Sincerely
G. Mennen Williams
H. Chief Justice

At the time in my wishful thinking, I wished that I could use the stair of heaven as short cut to the chemist's shop. The only thing that had happened for me so far is that the INS' ultimatum date of January1, 1986, as the set forceful deportation to the Gambia had gone uneventful and I am now in touch with even higher authorities of the United States. However, with continued support from friends, the ad Hoc Ceesay-committee, my patients and ability for endurance, I am able to float above these tempestuous waves about to swallow me. Frustrations heightened but I had to continue to struggle or work hard, with the committee as guide, for the golden days of opportunity to help the needy and the sick in the Gambia.

At time I had to swallow my pride and endure privation with gusto because it would be worth it if my people and I reap rewarding benefits out of these sad, ignominious dark days of my life. Hence, in response to Chief Justice G. Mennen Williams' kindness and to show my deep appreciation of his taking time to write in my behalf, I sent him the follow short note.

Diocese of Michigan
4800 Woodward Avenue
Detroit, Michigan 48202

Dear chief Justice Williams

This is to thank you for the humanitarian assistance given to bring relief to my dilemma. It has been a painful four years but with efforts like yours a ray of hope penetrates my heart and life.

Despite the odds I am committed to working hard to someday return as a physician to the Gambia and Africa. Your honour, I never perceived independence for Africa to be of milk and honey, likewise I never dreamt of the current lingering effect of coup conflicts and corruption by power-intoxicated individuals and politicians.

The Africa I wish to see exist is that governed by the rule of law, free speech, accountability and transparency in all government transactions, be it in trade or civil service activities.

Africa must thrive on democratically selected governments that would heed the principle of human rights, civil and the political rights of all the tribes in our nation states. Today's Africa pays only lip service to democracy.

No true opposition or public dissent exists that is not met with brutal and even fatal consequences to the participants. What was my sin? The mere questioning and criticism of the Gambia's agricultural policies, of rampant corruption and embezzlement of public funds by senior officials and politicians led to these painful days of my life. I love my people and will eventually return to them when it becomes safe for my life.

In short, I have asked of America the privilege that any and every oppressed person would do. I beg to be protected from wanton destruction. I will do all I can to complete my medical training and return to share with or serve the needy and sick.

Please help me make this current liability into an- assert for my people and mankind. I have already been persecuted, even though I did not commit any crime what so ever against the Gambia.

And if returned home at present worse awaits my arrival. The political asylum has requested has now sharpened the talons of Gambian official and their determination to contain me. Thank you for reading this and I appreciate all the help you gave. God bless you.
Sincerely
Alhasan S. Ceesay
Be it whatever the policy the current U. S. administration, I am convinced that the Gambia government has whitewashed the state department into believing Gambia to be a democratic nation. Here is a bird's eye view of the current inner gimmickry of lip service paid to democracy in the Gambia.
In effect, elections are forth coming in the Gambia early 1987, the ruling PPP now allows former Vice president and others to form an additional new party, the Gambia National Congress party.
This in addition to the few splinter parties in existence, on paper and to Westerners, constitutes multiple parties but in essence it was the PPP fooling the West and at the same time guaranteeing return of the president and tsars to power.
We in the Gambia do not want lifetime presidents who perpetuate their tenures under guises of a seemingly democratic balloting.
The truth is there was only one party in the Gambia and it was the ruling PPP. The NCP and the rest were all birds of the same feathers compromising for the PPP to, in effect, remain in power as long as they can get their share of the coffers. No matter what name one chooses this can only be called a one party state and so was the Gambia.

One has to belong to the PPP or get nothing. This one party state in disguise has been the state of affairs, the judge and jury over the lives of Gambians farmers for the past thirty odd years. The former vice president, Hassan Musa Camara, in one of his reasons for leaving the PPP said, "I did not leave the PPP because I did not like it.
I left because the PPP is no longer what it used to be." This simply implies that the PPP has been seriously compromised by cross over tsars who care very little about the farming community of the Gambia.
As indicated previously by the time the soul of the PPP had been over run by the cross elements from the other big city parties that had no iota interest in the farmers. In reference to misuse or mismanagement of the economy, former vice president Hassan Musa Camara stated, "The aid was consequently mismanaged in my opinion. And that resulted in the situation which we are now in." This sounded like the pot calling the kettle black. All these so-called leaders were mute for dozens of years while the farmers endure their errors.
The power struggle within the party and new city tsars lead to bitter rivalry between former vice president Saikou Sabally and Bakar Darboe creating a big crater in the PPP. Where was the vice president all the years prior to the heinous July insurgence?
Why were they not talking or standing by the farmers when they were holding high lucrative cabinet posts? These elements, now said to have formed new parties, are nothing other than shadows of the PPP and they were doing it only to split the

vote between NCP and PPP. They were no better than the PPP, their benefactor for more than twenty years for some, nor were they more innovated now than before. These were only helping, by so acting, to perpetuate the ruling party of the day and to seek favour from president Jawara latter after gleefully returning him to power.

The West and the super powers should refuse to recognize life long presidents and military juntas for these have become forestallers of democracy and progress in Africa.

Meanwhile, when the sad news of the denial of my political asylum request in the United States reached the Gambia, some loyal friends wrote letters to senators in my behalf urging them to preserve my life. One of such persons was Latif toure Sanyang who sent this letter.

P. O. Box 2469
Serekunda
The Gambia
January 6, 1986

Dear Senator,

Please allow me permission to write you this letter to seek your indulgence in regards to the impending case of my dear friend, one Mr. Alhasan Ceesay from the Gambia.

Alhasan went to the U.S. several years ago in search of higher education. No doubts he has achieved something during his stay in the U.S. Alhasan and I were together in the same class during our high school days.

I have a profound knowledge of him. He is an ambitious person and always aiming for higher things. During our high school days and also during our stay together whilst he was working in our main city hospital, Alhasan had all the time been very ambitious to become a medical doctor.

It was with this aim in mine that he left the Gambia for U. S. I personally left for England to study business. Alhasan in his pursuit of medical education was rather unfortunate to have to go to Liberia.

Perhaps it is too superfluous to say anything about the instability and unrest in Africa. Only few countries can claim to have any semblance of peace. The frequent uprisings and sudden changes of governments also have their corresponding effects on learning institutions.

More often than not such institutions become victims of unforeseen circumstances. Such was the case in 1981 when our own country received its share of instability. There was an attempt to over throw the government by unconventional means. The attempted overthrow was foiled through the intervention of the Republic of Senegal whose interest was also at stake.

The aftermath of the events saw the mass arrest and detentions of so many innocent persons. I was also a victim of such arbitrary and unlawful arrests. In this letter I do not wish to bore you with full details of the indignities and dehumanization processes we underwent during our detention.

As an American of such international reputation, you are no doubts aware of the excesses of African governments, especially during so-called emergency periods. Our country is no exemption to these phenomena. Among the people who raised their voices to condemn this violation of human rights was Alhasan Ceesay. He wrote to our president personally and all those Gambian authorities who were in a position to wield opinion in this country. He fought relentlessly to establish my innocence and to facilitate my release.

I am in possession of all copies of these letters and can send them to you if the need arises. This humanitarian gesture by Alhasan was not well received by the Gambian authorities. Some unknown persons gave the government the impression that these were external forces of the attempted coup.

Some countries including Liberia arrested such suspects and deported them to the Gambia. Under such an atmosphere of the fear and suspicion and Alhasan felt unsafe and therefore made his exit to the U. S. his medical studies were interrupted and he also forfeited the scholarship awarded to him by the European Economic Community (E.E.C.)

His return to the U. s. has brought more trouble to Alhasan Ceesay than he must have anticipated. In fact since 1983 or thereabouts Alhasan had been having problem with the U. S. Immigration.

Since he put me in the picture, I wrote to some people in the U. S. to assist him out of his dilemma but without any success.

Recently he sent me a cable informing me that he lost his case. What a pity! It is in this respect that I am writing this letter to seek for your personal intervention to redeem Alhasan from his present plight. Since the start of this episode, Alhasan's

friends and relatives have had sleepless nights. Alhasan's case is having a lot of psychological affects in the family and I can vouch that he would return to the Gambia as soon as he finishes his studies and it being safe for him in the Gambia. There is no opportunity whatsoever for him to do medical studies here.
The chances of getting a scholarship to study abroad are almost nil. Alhasan's premature return to the Gambia will be quite disastrous, I look forward to your kind assistance to save this fellow. Thank you very much and I wish you the best of luck and happiness in 1986. Goodbye
Yours faithfully
Latif T. Sanyang
Latif Sanyang, Kebba Sanneh and those whom I wrote about remained sincere friends. I shall always be indebted to them. Latif Sanyang and I have always been outspoken for the farmers of the Gambia.
Recall that the state department's advisory opinion letter to the INS district director said that Latif Sanyang would be reinstated to his post in the Gambia. Well, this letter and numerous others attested to the fact that was not the case and that all detainees who had no clique, tsars, or higher up affiliations lost their jobs for having committed no crime against the Gambia.
In the U.S. friends as far located as Alpena, Michigan and Riverdale, Georgia, wrote to their representatives seeking for a reputable voice that will stop the pains I have been enduring since my requesting political asylum in the U. S. in 1982.

All of them spoke of the impending danger in my premature return to the Gambia. So far the INS still stuck to the advisory opinion of the state department regarding my case, which in its own admission said, "He (meaning me) will be questioned upon return to the Gambia but we foresee no harassment or persecution of him."
Will the state department be there when I am taken, overnight, to Senegal and dealt with to confess to unfounded accusation and crimes I never committed?
This might be the type of questioning or sequence the state department does not know could take place easily in the even of my premature return to the Gambia. Many ill begotten things do happen in these so-called democratic countries of Africa, which if brought to the notice of the world will appall the American people, including the state department, which is currently raising the Gambian flag in darkness instead of that of the ideal of the USA I hope someday or when daylight come the state department will not be embarrassed by the shameful deeds of a rotten egg it is holding on high pedestals of good governance.
I love my people and will never run away from them, nor throw away my medical schooling in Liberia for the life of a refugee in the U. S. if my life was not in danger. Let tell readers that I would have taken the green card after ten years in America if I were interested in the pursuit of the greener pastures and personal comfort. Left alone, I will return to the Gambia but it is not politically safe for the moment. However among those who added their support were Dr. Charles T. Egli, Judge Philip and Mrs.

Viola S. Glennie, and a long time friend, Mr. John Dale. I met the Glennies while attending Alpena Community College in Michigan and they had since been an integral part of my American experience and life. They treated me in many generous and Christian ways.
They were an admirable couple that simply believed in justice for all people. Dr. Charles T. Egli also met at the Alpena Medical Arts Clinic while I was searching for a summer job in 1978' A unique chemistry of friendship developed between us since that day to today.
Dr. Charles T. Egli spearheaded a lot of admirable assistance and approached a lot others to seek help in an effort to try and get me out of plight. Here are some letters from friends in support of me.

Medical Arts Clinic
Alpena, Michigan 49707
November 14, 1986

RE: Deportation Notice on Alhasan Ceesay

Dear Senator Levin,

Alhasan Ceesay was a college student at Alpena many years ago when I first met him and was very impressed by his sincerity and enthusiasm. He went on to graduate school at Michigan Technological University I Houghton, in hopes of getting into medical school.
He tried very hard to get into medical school in this country. He was receiving no support from his own country because it considered him a political agitator

and tribalism. Alhasan Ceesay, on his own initiative was able to get into medical school in Monrovia, Liberia and succeeded in taking two years medical education before he fled for safety to the U.S. He later sought political asylum in the U. S. for fear of persecution due to the aftermath of an attempted coup in July 1981.

It has always been his dream and desire to complete his medical training and return to the Gambia when the climate warrants. For almost five years now, Alhasan has been trying to receive asylum, during which time his chances at medical school are affected.

Most recently, he received a letter from the INS judge ordering his deportation. The deportation of Alhasan back to the Gambia would result in his certain death or imprisonment and would constitute another sorry tragedy in the way our government handles people like Alhasan S. Ceesay.

In a country where there are so many illegal aliens it seems that there must be some place for one more refugee. I beg you to personally consider Alhasan's case.

Sincerely
Dr. Charles T. Egli, M.D.

I have had moments of despair, however I remained optimistic. Americans are part of a pyramid of people whose approach to self-rule is just and admirable. John G. Dale from Riverdale, Georgia wrote representative Net Gingrich to also add his weight and seek relief for me.

Riverdale, Georgia
February 21, 1986

Dear Representative Newt,

I am a Georgia Tech. Graduate of 1972. With a little humour in mind, despite this obvious handicap with any political training, I have decided to be a more active citizen.
I request your indulgence for you to kindly contact the INS in behalf of Alhasan Ceesay for them to allow him stay in this country until things calm down in his native country.
The enclosed collaborates his current dilemma which I seek your help. I knew Alhasan while we were at Alpena Community College. I have never known a finer individual of impeccable character in all respects.
It is my opinion that if he is not granted political asylum and is deported to the Gambia he would be grave danger. Thank you kindly for your consideration in his behalf. I am,
Yours truly
John G. Dale
True friends like John Dale are rare gifts from God. I followed this kind note with the letter below to representative Newt Gingrich of Georgia, on May 4, 1986. I had gone to Alpena and seek legal advice from Judge Philip Gleenie and there I renewed my acquaintances and had a lot of people to write to the INS and their representatives in both the Congress and the U. S. senate.
Professors I met at the College in 1967 had left at the time of my visit. Only class records and albums remain in storage.

Diocese of Michigan
4800 Woodward Avenue
Detroit, Michigan 48202
May 4, 1986

Dear Representative Newt,

My former Alpena Community College colleague and good friend John G. Dale of Riverdale, Georgia just informed me of having brought to your attention the enigma marring my life. It has been four painful years and total waste for the Gambia and man.

Medical schools are willing to let me start all over again if my status can be determined. All I ever begged for from America is to be granted a temporal political asylum until it is safe for my life in the Gambia.

The Gambia is good at paying lip service as well as cosmetic democracy to guarantee their getting grant in aid from the West. Already lots of splinter parties are formed ahead of the forthcoming elections of 1987.

By so doing it will virtually guarantee the return of the ruling party as none of the other parties would be able to garner enough votes or even agree to canvas under one umbrella. This on paper and to the perception of the West constitutes multiple parties.

But in essence it is the ruling party bamboozling the West to believe that political plurality or democracy exists in the Gambia. All the parties allowed standing, whose leaders it can easily embarrass, were part and parcel of the PPP government.

We do not need life long presidents or military dictators ruling in Africa. They and their cronies personalize or usurp the authority vested in them by the people if allowed life tenures. This in reality is one party state where the leaders eventually consider themselves no less than God.

These fronts were mare tentacles of the ruling PPP. In Africa every vice president wants to become the next president and every president lingers on for life. This personalization of the post leads to compromises of human rights, justice, and freedom of choice in who governs us, the little people.

The world should never recognize or assist such sham governments nor life long presidents for they are a disservice to Africa, just as military juntas or governments of AK47, anywhere, are an insult to human integrity and civilization.

Our farmers are proud and hard working people who rather contribute than receive dole from the world. However, corruption at high levels of our governments and civil service now deprive these farmers of the simple life that was theirs since the genesis of life in Africa. My case has been appealed to the INS board of Appeal since October 1985. Meanwhile, I have lost all grants to medical school due to negative rulings by the INS.

This note is not only to thank you but to reaffirm the need of a voice(s) that would stand for the American tradition of protecting oppressed ordinary people like me, even if they are from so-called friendly governments to America. Friendly governments should be so designated only if they respect human rights and democracy under rule of egalitarian laws for all citizens.

Finally, I am appealing to you to help me in my quest to become a physician serving the Gambia. I assure you of my determination to return to provide medical aid to my people. However, I need to be freed of the INS' entanglement to accomplish such a mission. Time is ticking away for all of us.

My service would be lot better for the government than my rotting in jail or being shot to death by a group that wants to rule indefinitely.

Again, I believe in government by choice, a million thanks and I look forward to receiving your kind support in my efforts to gain temporal political asylum in the United States until it becomes safe for my return to the Gambia. God bless you and yours. Please reply at your convenience.

Sincerely
Alhasan S. Ceesay

Chapter 25
THE FIZZLED CANADIAN TRAIL

In Detroit, the Ad Hoc Ceesay support committee continued to look for alternative solutions to my intransigent plight. Here was an attempt to have Rev. John Rye of the Anglican Church of Canada help us bring an end to this enigma. Rev. William Woods wrote this letter in that direction and objective.

United Ministries
Wayne State University
Detroit, Michigan 48201
November 28th, 1986

Dear Cannon Rye,

It was a pleasure to have met you during the consultation of American Diocese with African partnership in Washington, D. C. earlier this month. I very much appreciated your thought and comments on the workshop I conducted on Ministry with African students.
During the conference there were items, which we informally discussed, that I would like to pursue with you further and seek your assistance. It concerns Alhasan Ceesay, a Gambian, who has applied for political asylum.
I have enclosed a copy of a letter from the Detroit Diocese of Michigan, giving some of the background of Mr. Ceesay's case. Since the time that this letter was written, Mr. Ceesay's appeal to be granted political asylum has been denied.

His lawyer has filed another appeal to the INS board of Appeal, however, we are told that the appeal process may take another two years before it is heard, and that the likelihood of receiving a reversal of the lower court opinion is nil.

At present, we are in a holding situation while Mr. Ceesay, his lawyer, and those of us in the Diocese of Michigan including Bishop H. Coleman McGehee, explore alternatives.

Meanwhile Mr. Ceesay has been supported by donations, while he lives in an "ecclesiastical flophouse" run by the Diocese and takes some courses at Wayne State University.

So that eventually he can resume his medical education. One of the alternatives that we want to explore is the possibility of Mr. Ceesay going to Canada.

It is our impression that the Canadian government's policy towards those seeking political asylum is more open and humane than that of our present U. S. administration.

Before Mr. Ceesay makes such a move it will have to be examined, contacts made and reasonable assurance made for Mr. Ceesay's safety. I will be happy to provide further information, or have Mr. Ceesay's lawyer contact you, if you are willing to assist us in this case. All of us, who know him and are concerned about Mr. Ceesay, have found him to be a man of integrity, warmth and talent, who seeks, primarily, to contribute to the betterment of his people.

He has admirable witnessed to the African characteristic of patience, endurance, and hope. Yet as he turns forty years old, and is away from his

family and country, we realize that the legal limbo placed upon him by the INS and government, can break anyone's spirit. We need help. If you consider that a meeting between us to discuss both of these matters would prove useful.
I will be very happy to come to Toronto at a date and time convenient to you. Again, it was a pleasure to meet with you. The presence of members of the Canadian Church at the consultation added much to the event. I look forward to hearing from you.
Yours in Christ
William James Wood
Episcopal Chaplain
This letter evoked a not too surprising response from the Anglican Church of Canada. As I tried to allude earlier on, once the United States rejects an asylum application it seem to pick up a mushrooming cascading negative reaction from other Western allies.
The U. S, fails to realize this pivotal position it's ruling has upon those it denies help. So we received the letter below from Kathleen Ptoleny, development and Refugee Consultant at Rev. Rye's Office, the Anglican Church of Canada.

The Anglican Church
Toronto, Ontario,
Canada

Dear Rev. Wood,

John Rye has asked me respond to your recent enquiry regarding the possible immigration to Canada of Alhasan Ceesay. I would suggest that as a preliminary step to exploring Canadian possibilities that Mr. Ceesay, along with someone from your office, request a meeting with a Canadian visa officer at the Canadian Consulate in Detroit.

As a result of that interview you will be able to determine the government's position on Mr. Ceesay's ability to meet Canadian criteria and to determine whether or not the offer of Canadian Church support, either informal or through a private sponsorship, would be contributing factor in Mr. Ceeasy's selection.

I must caution you that people with medical background and career experience often poses particular problem and the path leading to recognition of medical qualifications and right to practice in Canada can be slow and painful.

His need for protection in Canada should be the most prominent aspect of his request for resettlement in Canada. Subject to a favourable indication from Canadian visa officer, we will certainly attempt to find a parish willing to assist with Mr. Ceesay's resettlement.

Yours Sincerely

Kathleen Ptolem

Dev. & Refugee Consultant

For someone in my state needing immediate solution to a long dragging problem, this sort of winding letter was no help. Simply, it was a very long way of saying they were not willing to consider my case unless the Canadian government gives the green light.

It that was made available it would not be necessary crediting anyone other than the Diocese of Michigan. The Canadian Anglican Church wanted us to do all the dirty or hard work before I can receive their coveted help.

It is obvious that finding people ready to assist in the resettlement of a refugee after gaining Canadian government's approval was no problem We were seeking immediate relief from my nightmare not starting the ball rolling all over again at the Canadian Consulate in Detroit.

It was repeating of immigration laws rather than addressing our request as stipulated in Rev. William Wood's letter to Cannon Rye. We were aware of people being helped without the route Kathleen suggested.

It was utterly incomprehensible to the farmers back home that even were we are taught in the U.S., it still prefer to back the type of regimes as in the Gambia and the continent, against people trying to practice its own teachings and doctrine.

I imbued every aspect of American ideals and am now rejected by proponents of those ideas. The farmers wonder what surety the Gambia had been to America.

My deportation back to the Gambia will only ring in a somber day for the farmers who banked on America standing by my cause and quest. Some times we wonder why super powers lend support to those who sponge out the last drop of blood of their citizen who stand for democratic ideals like me. Did the state department care to visit the Gambia and sample the feeling of the farmers and to find out if the Gambian Ambassador was telling the truth about release detainees, Like Latif Sanyang and Kebba Sanneh, and job reinstatements? One would be surprised at their findings had they venture to put the Gambia to acid test. Majority of villagers were sick and tired of the rampant corruption and deprivations levied upon them by high officials with president Jawara unable to stop the constant pilferage.

Has the Gambia government any program to bring economic relief to farmers? I see no reason why the Gambia was not producing rice or any other cash crop to the level of self-sustenance had it just used a quarter of the millions of dollars donated or lent to prop up agriculture and the irrigation of arable farmland for cultivation.

Instead farmers were told lots of political hogwash programs that raised the hopes of farmers but not line up their pockets with money or provide good crops to them.

Do not enterprising farmers deserve better opportunities for themselves, the country and a future for the new generation of Gambians? My agitations and concern for improving the condition of the Gambian farmer has been construed by certain elements as tribalism.

May I remind the reader that PPP was the party of the rural people that, unlike its counterpart urbanite parties, embraced all Gambians, but it has sadly since 1968, drifted too far towards the urbanites and now fails to deliver its promises to the founding farmers.

All the farmers ever asked for was to be given equal shares of the county's endowments and the way the pendulum of corruption was swinging.

The Gambia should have never been surreptitiously divided into the districts of the urbanites and rural. We are all Gambians deserving equal treatment from our government. Today the farmers, especially those from the Badibous, dissenters of the party are dubbed tribalism by roaches of the defunct parties. Those who portray the Badibous, as Trojan Horses must read their histories again.

What was to be gained by spying on students and labeling the one the tsars of Gambia fear or do not like, as political agitators or tribalism? I believe it takes a thief to notice as well catch a thief. They were just pots calling the kettle black for one tribal clique (yours) was to horde government post for their tribe than distribute it fairly to qualified persons.

Thanks for using Jawara infavour of your clan. Farmers will not accept a mediocre citizenship. These were undemocratic acts and I have no doubts that the cronies and opportunists of the government will sharpen their fangs and claws to tear my innocent flesh for having exposed the inequalities and disrespect for human rights with random illegal arrests testified.

You will be wise to clean up your laundry before you force the hand of the majority of Gambian farmers. The Gambian farmer is kind, law abiding, and peaceful but far from being passive to slavery. A united Gambian front will be more beneficial than the current hypocritical posturing.

We most be governed by the choice of the majority and not by a clique or a tribe. The developed world advanced only because people shared knowledge and skills.

Division or divisiveness like seen in the continent only keeps Africa in the dark if not into the first century instead of the twenty first century marching along with the rest of the world. My dream for Africa is a simple one.

I would like to see us govern by rule of law and not by cliques or individualization of any post or by tribe, nor by the whims and caprices of life long presidents, military juntas, of power, corrupt and conflict mongering, or marauding tribes.

Our people deserve governments based on the principles of human and political rights of all the tribes. These should be able to have free press, trade, and rights to collective government systems. The constant jailing of or holding of people incommunicado just because of their standing for the truth and the believe in proper democratic approaches is political sacrilege.

The world, especially the super powers, would help if it stops recognizing undemocratic African governments or regimes, be they politician or military juntas, before the catastrophe reaches unmanageable proportions.

I am writing today because believe in your fairness, American foresight and readiness to stand by and for justice. I have heard your representatives in the days of Camelot propound just principle and ideals of democracy that made America tick and admired. Please allow us the same rights and let me reiterate that I choose to seek temporal political asylum in the United States only because of my believe in democracy and human rights and will return to serve my people when it become safe for me in the not far future.

Today, I walk the streets the most-free nation on earth, with fear of arrest in my heart. This note below from my attorney Francis Conti is the only element that prevents my experiencing unnecessary arrest by INS enforcing officials while criminals are free to do what pleases them in the United States. This thus reminds me of "Pass" in South Africa during heydays of apartheid.

TO WHOM IT MAY CONCERN

I represent Alhasan Ceesay in his efforts to obtain political asylum in the United States. His case is presently on appeal before the Board of Immigration Appeals.
He is no legal jeopardy at the present time. If you have any further questions please contact me at your convenience.
Sincerely
Francis J. Conti
Professor of Law

Back on the Canadian trail, I still continued to look for reasonable and positive way to bring solution to my INS plight. Sometimes the sight of the above note makes me feel low and want to beg to free of the need for such a pass in my life.
As I look back on my American experience during my student days, I am moved by the kindness, understanding and encouragement and wisdom I gained as well as came across. Americans not only stood up against injustice but also did their utmost in trying to make it possible for me to continue to rely on democracy.

Support like this made it possible for me to continue the struggle for my goal of providing modern medical aid to the villager whenever the current dark clouds or situation is disentangled. In short, my American experience was rich in love, educative and overwhelmingly generous.

Today my life has been garnished with challenging lessons from the panoply life throws at us. As it stands today, mine had been harried enough and believe it or not neither success nor failure has been its attributes.

These are trying times for my soul, which has been tested for more years than I care to remember. My life has been torn apart by politics and twisted circumstances caused by the strictures of the political world.

I am desperate and fearful but despite it, I am going to return to the Gambia as a physician and will continue to dedicate my entire life to the easing of the health plight of the farmers and common people.

America's support by dogging their heel on my side is deeply appreciated and welcomed relief. The challenge is not insurmountable. It just seems insuperable but with a little hard work it is conquerable and an end that could be met. With your help I might not need to use the stairs to heaven as a short cut to the Chemist shop.

Chapter 26

IN COMMENDATION OF PROFESSOR
FRANCIS J. CONTI

In one of the meetings of the Ad Hoc Ceesay Committee, we decided that it was time to pay attention to the outstanding work my attorney, Professor Francis J. Conti had done up to then despite the Canadian rebuff.
It was unanimously agreed that we write a note of thanks to him, which was to be published by the Detroit Free Press and the Diocesan Newspaper, The Record. The Record and also other newspapers in Detroit published the following article.
All of us who have struggled with the case of Alhasan Ceesay, a Gambian refugee, realize that he was legacy for us from Thomas Jefferson. Alhasan came to us to call us back to the principles of justice and equality, which our government honours in the breach.
The experience with Alhasan provided us with opportunity to see a distinguished and prudent law school professor demonstrate, in a modest and determine way, the kind of faithfulness to principles for which we honour the men who wrote the Declaration of Independence and the constitution. Alhasan's Detroit years after the Immigration and Naturalization Service had denied Ceesay's first petition for asylum.
Conti responded to a phone call from out of the blue. I called him because his name had been mentioned at a meeting of Detroit/Windsor Refugee Coalition, a group engaged in helping

Central American Refugees. It was early November 1983, and Alhasan was scheduled for deportation in a few days, Francis Conti agreed to see him the next morning. Alhasan described that visit as one where he felt "rejuvenated."

Francis listened closely and carefully. "He was rare, impeccable, and thorough: Alhasan said. He gave Alhasan the names of two other practicing attorneys in Immigration Law, but Alhasan was too smart to go shopping. Having undertaken the case, Francis Conti never turned back.

First, he went to Louisville, Kentucky, with Alhasan in December of 1983 for an appearance before the INS official who processed deportations for the region. Conti filed a request for an appeal before the INS judge and thus delayed the deportation.

Then he took up the strategy of appeal to Congressmen, which unfortunately, were unsuccessful because the legislation refer such matters to the state department and the state department rarely has an encouraging word for anyone except refugees from Communist countries. The hearing before the INS judge was scheduled in Atlanta, Georgia, the regional pattern for these adjudications must have been devised by the airlines, In June of 1984, Alhasan, Francis Conti and Hugh White gathered in a motel on the outskirts of Atlanta.

Two key witnesses were missing. At midnight one turned up and Francis Conti worked on outlining the strategy for the next day. Alhasan who did not sleep at all, got others up at 7.00 Am for a hearing that would start at 1.39 pm.

The other missing witness, Dr. Sulayman S. Nyang, a Gambian professor at Howard University, showed up late at night and joined them at breakfast.

When all the testimony was complete, Francis asked the court's permission to enter his own testimony. The judge looked startled and advised against this unusual procedure. But Francis said he wanted to do it anyway, and he made a moving appeal.

That was June 1984. It was sixteen long months before the judge's ruling came down. During that time, Francis Conti patiently counseled, patience. He gave Alhasan a "To Whom it may concern" letter to carry in case anyone tried to apprehend him.

The rest us might have done something ill-considerate or rash during those sixteen months if it had been Francis' counseling of patience. When the answer finally arrived, it was negative asylum had been denied. Francis immediately filed an appeal to prevent Ceesay's immediate deportation.

Ceesay felt too old to postpone his training any longer. It was decided to pursue a different strategy, to continue his education at a medical school in the Caribbean. Francis helped us investigate this possibility. The project became one of fund raising rather than seeking political asylum in the United States.

Alhasan is now a student at the American University of the Caribbean, in the West Indies. Working on the case of Alhasan Ceesay has provided all of us with joys and frustrations, and with opportunities to learn more about others and about ourselves. Not the least of the benefits for us has been working under guidance of a thoughtful, considerate, conscientious and principled legal advisor.

We have all learnt from Francis Conti, and to be unflinching in dedication to the spirit of the law.
By: Mrs. Lois R. Leonard
Editor, The Record
For Alhasan S. Ceesay Support Committee
Bishop H. Coleman McGehee, Jr. Ex Officer
Bishop Mason Mrs. Patricia Koblyski, Rev. Hugh C. White, Rev. Ward Clabuesch, Rev. William Woods, Rev. Virgil Jones, Rev. David Brower, Rev. Richard Smith, Mrs. Evelyn Bayer, Mrs. Lois R. Leonard, Mrs. Ann Kinze, Mary Ellen Robertson, and Professor Francis J. Conti.

Chapter 27

AN APPEAL TO AMERICAN LAWMAKERS

I am neither a politician nor an expert on international law. However, I would like to direct these few lines to the honourable ladies and gentlemen of the bastion and mainstay of the lofty ideals and principles inscribed in the Declaration of Independence and the American Constitution.
Most of Africans educated in America do so at great personal cost and sacrifice by our poor peasant parents who risked allowing us explore as well as learn your system.
We are obliged to return to serve our people back in Africa and are committed in returning to share education and skills learnt from you. At times, because of sad and unfortunate or unforeseen events, it becomes necessary for us to ask for temporal protection to stay longer needed due to coups and political evolution a particular country might be experiencing.
These sad events are most of the time off shoots of East-West ideological tug of wars, greed that disregards human values, e.g. minerals versus natives, and from blatant disregard of human rights and rule of equally applied laws.
Conflicts reign in any society where two-tier systems of law exist. The mutant politicians that took over from the colonial masters turned out equally heartless, if not more brutal, to the people who entrusted power to them.

It is with agony, great concern and hope that I seek you help, consideration and contribution to justice not only in my case but also for all oppressed people of the fledgling dictatorial governments of Africa. As people we share bond in life and God.

My cardinal sin was the directing of the attention of my government towards human rights and exercise of equal justice for all Gambians under the law of the nation.

Because of this simple act, I today know what it means to live in frustration, imposed limbo, in constant agony and the humiliating but humbling life of a refugee. I braved the unknown since 1967 in quest of modern medical skills to serve my villagers in Gambia.

The record will show that I made a progressive move and in-roads towards that objective but the last four years have been a tragic waste for the Gambia and I.

All other doors for the realization of my goal were open but the main gate remained closed for reasons based upon the desire of a few tsars in the Gambia willing to use any guile to remain in power for life. The sufferings of many a peasant in the developing world, especially Africa, would be reduced if only the super powers and legislators like you would refuse to recognize or contribute to any military or civilian president maneuvering for a life long reign over his citizens.

Africans will be most grateful if America and her compatriots would bell the cat and proudly declare such a posture with regards to the third world people. We are sick and tired of the carnage and destruction of property brought onto the people by politicians and inept military as well as so call rebel groups. These thrive because of being certain that no other force, like yours, was going to blow them off the surface of the earth to wilderness they rightfully belonged.

These are not part of the civilized humane world but modern sophisticated vicious vampires. Today, coups jump back and forth over the blood of innocent victims and we see super power ambassadors rushing to shake the reeking and bloody hands of murderers and ardent foes of democracy while they present so-called credentials of diplomacy.

Do not give your hard earned taxpayers money to inept military men as long as they came to the presidency using force and removal of properly elected civilian governments unconstitutionally. No God or religion condones what is transpiring in Africa.

Hence, stop recognizing these political novices, rouges, and opportunists from ruining Africa. This humanitarian act by you will dampen or kill the impetus that causes half-baked non-commission recruit or officers to overthrow governments and then with dark ignorance turn into tyrants that sink the countries into despair and hopelessness.

My friends, I do not mean to bore you by repeating that we are sick and tired of the bloodshed and carnage in the third world. Coup d'etats and life long presidents as rein Africa serve no good to the populace they rule.

Let me assure you of our being communal in nature but will never be communist in thought or deed. No communist regime thrives in Africa, as people will always revolt against it. Please interact with true Africa to note believe and admiration farmers have for American principles of democracy and egalitarian justice for citizens.

Let your envoys go to villages and have tête-à-tête with the villager and above all let these emissaries supervise disbursement of money you send to these countries. It is your taxpayer's money and hence you have all right to know how the last cent has been used.

Was it used for the purpose donors intended? Rather than the usual relatives, friends of politicians and businessmen who wallow in cheating the farming communities of the third world, have the villager do the distribution under watchful eyes of your representatives in that region.

This will minimize or even stop the governments and their cronies from interfering with the donations thereby letting the intended group benefit from your good will gesture.

Most of the high government officials have enough money to send their children to be educated in Europe and America while farmers can hardly afford to feed their families moreover to meet the cost of educating a child abroad.

The make do with mediocre school systems brought into force since independence for political exigencies than academic excellence. This unfairly keeps farmers' children at the bottom of the ladder of progress and worst of the continent's advancement.

We the sons and daughters of the farmers are made to attend mediocre experimental primary schools while the others go abroad for their education and return to be hired as heads of departments in the various ministries.

How can a nation develop if the majority is surreptitiously deprived of contributing in its life and growth? The governments you are familiar represent a very small fraction of real Africa.

Most officials enrich themselves before being forced out of power leaving the poor farmers poorer than a church mouse.

The officials are the ones who always want everything and at times cause the most trouble by mismanaging of the economies of their respective countries. I wonder why America and Europe sits watching Africa being destabilized.

Please take more indigent indigenous children of the farming communities as a marshal education plan for Africa, from the third world to study in America and Europe at reduced school fees and maintenances.

Divert your grant in aids and loans into this approach and you will in less than ten years provide for advancement of the continent far more than all the millenniums of regular unfulfilled flowery promises made about educating the African child spewed out by canvassing politicians and governments. Help us create stability in Africa and we will do the rest without the prevalent carnage and bloodshed.

But we need a crop of dedicated honest Africans to spearhead and pioneer the way forward for the next generation. We need inspiring footprints as foot solders of Africa development. The Africa military's rampant destruction of institutions now results in our having fewer worthy universities able to accommodate influx of student and maintenance of classes.

Helping educate the developing world will also reduce disadvantages endured by children from poor farming communities and will put your taxpayer's dollars into better use rather than being stashed in some equally corrupt and mindless international bank while the people are left to suffer from starvation and illiteracy.

The youth you would educate are the backbone of Africa and developing them will move the continent' advancement faster into the twenty first century. It will certainly reduce the illiteracy as well as provide the continent with needed skills and technology for advancement.

A friend, whilst we were discussing the super power involvement in the East-West tug of wars and effect these had in Africa said, "Ceesay, we do send peace -corps to your jungles to enlighten the natives." In deed you do and we are very grateful. But these too thinly spread and usually overwhelmed by bureaucratic juggling by our governments and yours respectively.

It would be much more productive if money spent to run such ivory tower programs was used to build schools and skill training center so that many more villagers would benefit. This sort of input will be rewarding to both Americans and Africans, as it will enable the hinterland child to be guaranteed some for of standard education be it formal or skill oriented.

We, the farmers, want democracy and human rights to have a foothold in the continent. But your marauding pilfers would not allow such left alone. Without democracy there will neither be rule of law or stability and progress in Africa for a foreseeable time.

We are satisfied and very proud and thankful for the African God created us from the beginning of genesis. Let the world accept one-man one vote to be equally applied in Africa as it meant in London, Paris, and Washington, D.C.

We wonder why the world, being fully aware that a regime in Africa is in total flagrant of the rule of good governance, looks the other way and to add insult to injury give aids and support to such inept and despicable entities as if saying, "Carry on novice.

We are behind you as long as we can destroy your forests, exhume your minerals, and have our puppets destroy the rest that we could not." It is a pity that such double standards exist in this day and age of human civilization.

We in Africa yearn for real patriotic leaders and not puppets voting against the will of the people at the United Nations sessions because of nudging of aid from super powers. We want leaders who can stand by the truth even if it would make them feel lonely in a full house.

The truth is only thing that last in life and comes to hunt us if not said. Educating us will help form some form of a unified political development based on agreement, as in the olden days of the gentleman's handshake deals, on democratic fundamentals.

We will not be polarized flag wavers for any super power but will live in peace with all humans. Please invest in the farming communities to help them improve their lot. The application of a common prudence and wisdom will help the world grasp the forces of change that overpowered colonial continuity in Africa.

It would be wise to accept that Africans can achieve organizational, educational as well as professional pinnacles previously unimaginable. We are an integral part of the world. Educate the children and there will be longer be sham-governments.

The children of the commoner are bound to take their rightful places in Africa, as they constitute the silent majority.

Hence, no matter how poor, if a student shows some intelligence and desire to learn, West and, especially America should be willing to invite these to your colleges and universities. Do you know a poor farmer's child, no matter how brilliant, finds it hard to secure a visa from your embassies of lack of substantiating financial sources or sponsorship, requirements nor easily available to these aspirants? Democracy in my view is rule by the majority while respecting the rights of the minority.

Would not your grants in aids be better utilised by directing such resources in a Marshal Education plan for Africa instead of relying on politically manipulated scholarship committees not interested in the education of farmer's children?

I strongly believe and do urge you to note that we are your investment in the future of democracy and stable world living in peace.

If I had waited for Gambia's scholarship committee to select me, having come from a village, or had I allowed the notion that poverty prevents one from doing worthwhile things foe one-self and country, then I would never have been to school nor been able to write in your language as you experience and see before you.

All I am trying to say or convey to honourable lawmakers of America is that there are more brilliant and more determined youths than I in the farmlands of Africa who with little help from you could one day become renowned and rewarding scientists, educators, agriculturalists, doctors, and even missionaries that would contribute positively to Africa and the world.

The disease of the child from wealthy African families has been that of complacency because the comforts of life are almost always guaranteed to them by virtue of their parents' position in government or business. Aside from the above fruits of thought I now want to call your attention to the case before you.

I came to America in 1967 as a self sponsored student with sole purpose of becoming a medical doctor and returning to provide much needed medical aid to the Gambia. A few innocent protest notes or letters I sent to Gambian officials have now become a nightmare for my family and me for the past four years.

If the trend of negative rulings from the INS with regards my request for political asylum in the United States, continues then all years of hard work I put into schools shall be in vain just because a few tsars want to remain in power and continue to shamelessly lavish themselves hard earned taxpayers money you dole to them as grants. No head of state anywhere should run for more than three terms. Doing so makes them personalize reins of government as theirs blindly.

Now that my case has reached such critical levels, the Gambia and all involved in the derailment of my education, will do all they can to connive to keep themselves in your favour. Why would the Gambia Ambassador go to such extreme pain, on March 29, 1984, to write against me to the district director Detroit INS office, to Kenneth Scott of the state department and to president Jawara?

This resulted in my father being summoned to the state house in Gambia, questioned and threatened by officials representing the government. God knows what threats were made but one thing was certain father never felt safe or free until his death in 1991.

My father was spared jail only because doing so would have unveil their dirty laundries more than already know by my exposing this case to the international arena. Why all that panic, if not paranoid, trouble if they were not hot after my heels to contain me?

My friend, the communist scare tactics has become an unfailing tool, weapon or technique of these hopeless undemocratic governments used in gaining power and remaining there for life despite the contrary wish of the people they forcefully governed. When will America and the West be awake to this unfair use of your citizen's money?

Life presidents never improve the lives of the lives of people they pretend to be having their confidence and support. We would appreciate your helping us institute democracy in our communal communities but please do not ever support self-aggrandizing elements. You can make the perplexities of democracy simple by preventing despots and tyrants that unconstitutionally come to power in Africa and the third world.

The gross misuse of authority, wealth, social injustice and repressive polices that follow coups are intolerable, evil and undemocratic. Is it progress or egalitarian to have less than 0.2% running the affairs of the Gambia?

Are the talents and resources of the country being developed and utilized? Does the world believe such mall, selfish, self-styled, self-centered quasi-aristocracy will last in Africa? The vestiges of colonial democracy must go to oblivion with the colonials.

The skeptics of democracy in Africa point out the passengers of a ship would perish if they insist that problems of navigation be solved by majority vote. This is the illogical excuse normally given for allowing unholy murderous governments in Africa. It is beyond witticism if I say that the "African ship" would sail to safe harbour if the majority of the people were allowed to participate fully in its affairs. Democracy in its correct form should not be excluded from Africa due to false complexities of instituting it in the continent.

Many a time we hear others accuse or blame our setbacks on the vestiges of tribalism. Nonetheless, persons making such remarks proudly assert claims of being English, French, and American or any other Caucasian group or tribe.

If tribal differences of these countries or groups did not prevent them from advancing under democratic governments why should there be tribe as an issue when it comes to Africa or be so falsely used as excuse or veil for refusing to accept and stand for democracy in the continent?

The tribes in Africa behave exactly like other tribes of the world. It is insulting to perceive us as a people whose organizational achievements or abilities rest upon tribalism and slavery. Why not accept the fact that colonial destruction of all our institutions and replacing them with haphazard systems that supported the principle of conquer, divide, and rule empires.

The blame for Africa's political instability and backwardness lies squarely on these historical interruptions of our lives and culture. We will resist both external and internal totalitarianism at all cost in our quest to maintain democracy in Africa.

Those who think it foolhardy and that one would not succeed to try to introduce traditional forms of Western democracy in Africa should also justify the ease with which colonization got its roots in Africa. Could it be that critics of instituting true democracy in Africa have themselves moved away from those forms of lofty egalitarian democracies or dreams? On the hand are they afraid that when full-scale democracy exist in Africa she might cast a shadow over them, given the great capacity and untapped wealth of the African continent? We are by no means relics of musty myths. You can help democratize Africa by educating the children of the masses and by refusing to shed blood for self-perpetuating regimes.

Do not be implicit supporters of ancient regimes and power-intoxicated people who rule by whims. Please not perceive our nations as in the primordial community-building stage of political systems. Be part of a nurturing of true democracy in the continent.

Refrain from supporting juntas, rebels, and politicians not interested or committed too good-governance and the development of African people. Educating us will create a free and innovative people with good governance under majority rule as a yardstick. He us supplant knowledge in place of ignorance or fear of communism and tribalism as the obvious roadblocks to Africa's progress into modern day advances.

Again, the communist do not deserve the crown of fear, as in the early 1960s, you are giving them or making them wear with regards to Africa. Be happy to note that the few countries that tried their hands at communism in Africa failed miserably and it spiraled to their doom.

Africans are communal but not communist oriented. This is the plea from the heart of Africa. Back in the Gambia, the president will point out that he is fighting corruption and that he has formed an "Evaluation of Assets and Properties Commission" that would look into as well prevent corruption in the Gambia.

This was a cheap exercise in politics for we are yet to see him declare his own assets and properties or agree to answer questions regarding his properties before the Evaluation Commission. In Africa emergency laws and Acts are normally intended to curb the opposition.

Could this Evaluation Act be a disguised extension of the tsars' arms in behalf of the president? According to the Act, the commission can only act when, according to provision C of the Act, "The dealings of any non-public officer or any public body are referred to the president of the Gambia." The Commission is selected from the city cliques or cronies and worse the president oversees their work. In Africa, who dares argue with the president at the round table?

Would you consider the Commission as an open and fair democratic way? In real democracies the judiciary is independent of the legislative and this includes the head of state. This is country to which the state department said it has, "correct and open judiciary."

The Commission, like many of its predecessors, is not allowed to publish any finding, especially if it concerns the president or his cabinet members and all its reports are channeled to the president who decides what is to be published.

I used the case of the Evaluation of Assets and Properties and the prevention of corruption practices Act to demonstrate to you how laws are for the convenience of the head of state in Africa. At times the presidents are the judges, jury and administrators of the law over the lives of Africans. Corruption escalates at higher levels and farmers have to bribe to have civil privileges given them or their children.

The perennial request of these pages is for you to take a moment and look into my case and those of numerous other students like me in Africa.

Students are the pillars of democracy in Africa and despots and military juntas have not spared jailing them in the name and pretext of national security and on half-baked false judiciary grounds.

Is it wise to consistently back dictators and tyrants and at the same time expecting friends among those whose children are subjugated by these bloodthirsty hounds?

Abraham Lincoln once said, "What is morally wrong cannot be politically right." Our African governments should not be allowed to destroy the peasantry and not replace it with worthwhile avenues for the displaced farmer. Again, the enclosed package speaks for itself and outlines my achievements, current experiences and my request for political asylum, and request for your kind intervention in my case.

I reiterate my desire and determination to work hard and to return to the Gambia to practice medicine in the villages. You can help in the fulfillment of this dream by allowing me stay or the granting of political asylum in the United States until it become politically safe in my country. My friends, with all humility and confidence in the American sense of justice, I do submit my case to your judgment, and that righteous judgment shall be based on facts and the granting me temporal asylum to allow me complete my medical education in the United States of face a bleak future if there would be any. With this appeal made I decided that it was time to find an alternative to this foot dragging limbo my life had been since 1982. At one of the ad Hoc Ceesay Committee meetings we decided to try getting into one of the good Caribbean Medical School.

Chapter 28
AMERICAN UNIVERSITY OF THE CARIBBEAN SCHOOL OF MEDICINE

Sir Isaac Newton once said, "If I have seen further, it is by standing on the shoulders of giants." The road to the medical frontier was an unbelievable huddle against numerous unforeseen obstacles. It was a daunting task I was committed to over coming despite the odds against me.

I never flinched nor regretted taking the step I took to become a physician. I admit being totally ignorant of God's design for my life but I shall not cease to believe in them because I cannot fathom them, and I rather mistrust my own capacity than.

His justice. I know of no way to succeed other than my determination to elevate myself by conscious efforts to become a physician serving the rural sector of the Gambia. I had by now lost my case for political asylum in the United States and had opted for a medical school outside of the USA.

Meanwhile, my lawyer and I agreed to appeal the case to the INS Appellate Court. The Ceesay Committee contacted the American University of the Caribbean in Montserrat, West Indies, seeking my being enrolled at the school of medicine at the university.

Some members, amongst them Rev. Richard Smith, fell put down that I decided on this alternate route but they failed to realize that time was ticking away and fast against me and that our appeal with the INS Appellate Court may take from two to three years waiting with no guarantee that it will be in my favour.

Time and my age would not allow me entry to most medical schools because I was well over forty years by then. This called for raising nearly 430,000 required to cover the cost of my studies at the American University of the Caribbean School of Medicine at Montserrat.

This had to done quickly and indeed in a very short time to enable me start school ahead of deportation deadline set for me by the INS. Left at the Bishop McGehee Ceesay account was $750.

First, I submitted the following application letter, reinforcing information that had already been given the school, to the Dean of Admission at the American University in Montserrat, West Indies.

Admissions Committee
American University of the Caribbean
School of Medicine, P.O. Box 400
Plymouth, Montserrat
British West Indies

Dear Admissions Committee,

Until very recently my life was caught between the jaws of unforeseen circumstances and intractable laws. I am more than please to report that the newly passed Immigration bill signed by the president may remove impediments to my case and objectives. Enclosed is verification attesting to the fact that I did register for the MCAT offered during the 1986 sitting but could not do so because of Immigration restrictions and hearings at the same time. It one time got so difficult that I had to take sanctuary at a church until when some temporal relief was obtained for me. I have learnt my lesson and I assure you of my determination to excel and to keep my nose onto my books and schooling, when given chance at your school. This note is personal appeal to all of you to help me help my villagers receive modern medical aid.

I will return to serve the Gambia when I complete my training. In my village, disease and death are more familiar visitors than quality medicine or qualified doctors. While in sanctuary, I read my medical books and wrote an autobiography to be published in 1987.

Portions of the proceeds from the book will be used for establishment of scholarship in medicine and agriculture for candidates from rural communities. Your giving me the chance to be trained at your medical school will enable me serve my people as a physician when I return to the Gambia.

I herein, reiterate my interest in being trained at your medical school and do seek your kind consideration in view of all the unforeseen experiences I have endured during these trying times of my life.

The Diocese of Michigan has already raised $30,000 and other interested party assures us their commitment to helping finance my studies at your school if you would give me the chance to fulfill a dream for my villagers and man.

Thank you for taking time to read this appeal and I look forward to receiving your help and consideration for this unusual case. The Gambia and I will forever be indebted to you for giving us the chance for me to be trained at your school. God bless and best wishes to all of you.

Yours Sincerely
Alhasan S. Ceesay
Meanwhile more pledges were solicited. Mrs.
Patricia Koblynski reported having collected
$15,000 on October 16, 1986 in addition I released
the following appeal thus

82 Finchingfiels Way
Black Heath
Colchester
Essex, CO2 OAU

Dear Sir/ Madam,
RE: Seeking help to build village hospital
I am Dr. Alhasan Ceesay, a Gambian, currently on
study lreave in the UK. I am writing in behalf the
North Bank region villagers and Manding Medical
Centre, village self-help health organisation I started
since 1993 and remained head of the centre.
I set it up because of sheer shortage of medical
services and healthcare delivery in the region
resulting in prepondarace of premature deaths of
children from malaria, diarrhea, worm infestationds
and other childhood diseases.
The organisation is now well over thirty thousand
strong enthusiastic members mostly of farmers,
local villagers, chiefs, and local business persons.
The centre compliments the health services in the
Gambia additional to promoting preventive
medicine.
We are deicated to providing medical aid to villagers
and children. There are no doubts that service
offered by Manding Medical Centre is gradually
denting the infant mortality and morbidity rates in

areas covered by the Centre. We enjoy recognition and support of both the Gambia Government and the local authiry in the region. The Centre has since inception tread 90000 villagers free of charge. Building the children's hospital would go far to providing a permanent service at closer proximity for the villagers who, at present, have to travel long distances to seek medical aid for their children. This adds to loss of life before help arrives, a short coming which has devasitating effect on children who die in their their hundreds because of lack of medical facilities and services.

We need lot of input from interested persons and organisations and financial institutions to help build the Children's Hospital. We would appriate monetary help of any amount and equipments amongst others. £30 will buy ten bags of cement. Building of the entire children's hospital comforming to modern standards will cost £96,000 sterling. Some of which is being currently raised through bimonthly fund raising activities such as raffles, dances, sales and various community donations.

Contributions and participant should through contacting Dr. Alhasan Ceesay via e-mail: alhasanceesay@hotmail.com or call him any time conviniet to you on +447398022675.

Finally, the villagers do need the help and would appreciate any kind gesture that would help them raise their dream of a medical service for them and their children.

Please feel free to contact me at the above addres should you or any one needs further information

about Manding Medical Centre and Friends of Manding, Colchester.
Yours Sincerely
Dr. Alhasan S. Ceesay, MD
Director/Co-ordinator
Manding Medical Centre

Chapter 29

AN APPEAL FOR MEDICAL EDUCATION ASSISTANCE

I am Ahasan Ceesay, a Gambian, whose asylum petition, despite INS initial recommendation for approval, has been turned down twice by the State Department and INS Judge Auslander. An appeal is now before the INS Appellate Court but it may take two and half years before a ruling is handed to me. We believe the United States INS Judge upheld the earlier decision due to protocol or diplomatic relationships the United States may want to maintain with Gambia making justice in this case its casualty. In view of the fact that six years have already been wasted, one must now turn to alternatives that will correct today's errors and make me a useful and productive person to my people and mankind.
I have, with God's and friends as guide, decided to explore the possibility and opportunity of being trained as a physician at the American University of the Caribbean school of Medicine, at Montserrat, West Indies.
All other avenues to make it possible for me to have my training in the United States were made improbable by intractable if not inhuman INS and State Department Roadblocks and residency permit requirements.
At this school, I can ear my medical training in nine and half semesters and do my residency at accredited teaching hospitals in the USA or Europe. The World Health Organization (WHO) along with

other foreign medical schools recognizes the American University of the Caribbean (AUC).
It opened its doors to students in 1978 and now has its graduates as residents doing advance medical specialties at universities like Michigan, Wayne State, Ohio, Missouri, Maryland and the University of Chicago, just to name a few schools that deal with the American university of the Caribbean school of Medicine. The program covers nine and half semesters with the basic medical sciences done on campus and clinics are done at accredited teaching hospitals in England and America.

This note is an appeal to you and al those who can assist me help my people receive fundamental medical aid. By helping you would also become integral in my evolution as a physician dedicated to serving the needy. Enclosed is the semester breakdown of what it will cost to attend the American University of Caribbean School of Medicine. I will be indebted if you can join me in this venture. Rest assured that I will repay all loans accorded me when I complete my training. Classes start in January 1987, and if assisted I should depart for the American University of the Caribbean (AUC) by middle of December 1986. The only thing holding my admission is the financial proof to maintain my studies at AUC. I will enter as regular foreign student. Please feel free to contact me or through Rev. Hugh C. White in case you need any questions answered. I will be most grateful for whatever helps or consideration one might give to this plea for financial assistance. Thank you for sharing a dream with me. God bless.
Signed: Alhasan S. Ceesay/Gambian

As the momentum gathered pace the Ceesay Committee also sent out the following letter to a large number of Parisians and would be possible contributors to my case.

The letter from the committee made it possible for us to pick up an additional $15,000 before our scheduled committee meeting of October 23, 1986. Bishop McGehee wrote to the Dean of the Medical School requesting consideration for my application before the admission committee of AUC. It said:

Eugene A. Arnold, MD
Dean of Medicine
American University of Caribbean
School of Medicine
P. O. Box 400
Plymouth, Montserrat
British West Indies

Dear Arnold,

It is my privilege to commend to you Mr. Alhasan S. Ceesay for admission this coming January 1987, to the American University of the Caribbean School of Medicine. I know Alhasan personally.

He is a person of integrity, intelligence, human sensibility and God knows perseverance against formidable inequalities. We have provided Alhasan Ceesay personal support and financial assistance for his living in the past three years. Alhasan is a person who we are proud to sponsor for admission to your school of medicne.

It is our understanding that the only obstacle delaying your acceptance of him is a financial statement verifying that he will be able to finance his education at the American University of the Caribbean. We presently have $15,000 pledged towards the $30,000 required.

We are making a concerted effort to raise the balance. If the required funds are to be raised within the next ten days, donors need to be certain that Mr. Ceesay will be admitted to medical school this January 1987.

I will phone you personally regarding this inquiry next Tuesday, October 28, 1986, between the hours of 19.00 Am. This is an under taking of an urgent matter for Mr. Ceesay and we do hope that we can give you assurance that the money will be available to Alhasan. Peace.

(The Rt. Rev) H. Coleman McGehee, Jr.
Bishop of Michigan
Detroit, Michigan

In another front, the Bishop's assistance, Rev. Hugh C. White, dispatched the following to various personalities and other professions asking for their help. His message says,

Dr. James Lightbody
12580 Van Street
Grosse Point Woods

Michigan 48236

Dear Jimmy,

I believe you have had the opportunity to meet Alhasan Ceesay, the Gambian who we have provided sanctuary for over three years. You will recall that I contacted you regarding his possible placement for work, but we learnt if was not possible for him to take such a position being on visitor's visa to the USA.

Alhasan is a person that we have come to know well. He deserves whatever help we can give him. Unfortunately, the new Immigration bill did not include his class of alien. This has prompted a small group of us to raise the needed funds for Alhasan to attend the American University of the Caribbean School of Medicine, Plymouth, Montserrat, British West Indies, beginning January 1987.

We would, naturally prefer that he be admitted to a medical school here in the states or Canada but this is not possible. Your being in a position to appreciate both the financial and human cost involved in going through medical school, as well as the importance of supporting black Africans at this juncture in our history.

I invite you to consider participating in the support of Alhasan Ceesay. We are requesting potential sponsors to consider a pledge of $1000 to be paid over next eighteen months, beginning December 15, 1986 and going through to July 15, 1988. This is a substantial request for the reasons that we cannot make a general campaign for this money, the time is too short, and the potential donors too few who would understand.

The medical will not accept him without certification that $30,000 will be available for his support and medical education at the university. Be assured that you can say no to me in regards to this solicitation without in any way my interpreting it as a refection.

I am enclosing a brief narration of Alhasan Ceesay's life and accomplishments and a copy of Bishop McGehee's letter to the Dean of the Medical School. You will likely have questions. I will give you a call regarding this early in the morning coming week. I am writing a similar letter to Laurence.

Sincerely
(The Rev.) Hugh C. White
Consultant to the Bishop of Michigan
For Public Affairs

The narrative ran in part thus, "I am Alhasan S. Ceesay a citizen of the Gambia, West Africa. My parents are peasant farmers and I am the only schooled in the family.

I completed high school at Armitage Secondary in December 1961, in the Gambia before enrolling at the Gambia Nursing January 1962. I received the state registered nursing certificate after three years of training and continued to serve in a nursing capacity at the Royal Victoria Hospital, Bathurst, now Banjul, until my departure for studies abroad in 1967.

I first attended Alpena Community College, Alpena, Michigan (1967) where I matriculated with an Associates of Arts degree in biology (1970) and the proceeded to Olivet College, Olivet, Michigan the same year and again earned a bachelor's of Science degree in 1971.

I later earned a Masters degree in biological sciences in 1973 from the Michigan Technological University at Houghton, Michigan. I spent most of those summers working as nursing assistant at Alpena General hospital and also at St. Joseph Hospital in Flint, Michigan.

I did serve as laboratory assistant at the department of biology during my final year at Michigan Technological University in Houghton. I worked for a year to raise funds for my studies and then in 1975 enrolled at Howard University department of Biology on a PhD program in Zoology.

I pursed this avenue until my eventual enrolment at the A. M. Dogliotti College of Medicine at the University of Liberia in Monrovia.

It was at the end of my second year in medical school (1981) that an unsuccessful attempt to overthrow the Gambia government occurred. In the process, some of my relatives and close friends were arbitrarily arrested and I was accused, out of the blue, of anti government activities for having written letters inquiring the state of those arrested. The Gambian government became irate and suspicious of my activities.

It then withdrew my scholarship, with the assistant dean confirming it to me, forcing my removal from medical school. I went into hiding when it was confirmed that I might be returned to the Gambia and face possible questioning, trial, imprisonment or even death.

Thank God, I am safe in the USA because of the kindness and prompt action of Mr. Cloyd Ramsey, a friend who saved my life from wanton destruction.

When I left the Gambia the infant mortality was very high and life expectancy in the rural area ranged from 43 to 57 years. The health budget was woefully inadequate and it was complicated by lack of qualified physicians and hospitals with which to serve the country.

In the villages disease and death are common visitors and are more frequent than physicians. Mosquitoes and malaria, diarrhea, pneumonias, and tuberculoses were almost accepted neighbours. I committed myself to being part of the solution of the health problems in the Gambia and will do so as long as I live despite the current dark experience I am faced.

I am now seeking to be given a chance to attend medical school at the American University of the Caribbean in Motserrat, West Indies in 1987. Considerations would be given to alternate arrangement one may come up with that would help me complete my medical education but time is ticking against me.

The current twist and dilemma only make me more determined to become a dedicated physician to mankind. My long-term goal is to practice medicine in the Gambia when and if the political condition or atmosphere becomes favourable to my life.

Finally, I appeal to all of you to give me the chance to fulfill my goal and dream of becoming a dedicated physician to my fellow man. I do look forward to being your student at the above university in 1987. Thank you for you kind considerations.

Signed: Alhasan S. Ceesay/Gambian"

Bishop McGehee having concurred with the Ceesay Committee's judgment in sponsor or supporting my studies at the American University of the Caribbean School of medicine (AUC) left us all geared up and made more contacts for financial assistance before our next scheduled meeting of October 23, 1986.
A lengthy discussing pursued identifying what was needed to be accomplished in meeting the university's requirement for my entrance.
Some of my friends never wanted me to go away and hence, it was later agreed that the decision to attend AUC was to be the committee's and mine. It agreed to go along with the Bishop in being my sponsor.
Folks like Rev. Richard Smiths were very angry that I choose to go to the West Indies for medical schooling. We were not certain whether the INS Appellate Court would rule in my favour for grant of political asylum in the United States.
We received several differing opinions as to how the Appellate normally hardly turns INS judges finding or rulings down. Besides it might take another two or three years before the appeal reaches these INS Appellate Board Judges.
Given my age at the time and all of falling into another Immigration judge confrontation should a school in America risk taking me on board its classes before the ruling from the appeal board. Hence, the American university of the Caribbean was the only next logical avenue left for me to hold onto my medical aspiration and complete my training in due course.

This declaration made, we agreed that each person in attendance would contact four or five persons to help raise the $30,000 needed within the next sixty days. On the morning of November 16, 1986 I received the following letter from Patricia Litwin, Liaison Officer for AUC. It read:

Medical Education Office
2801 Ponce de Leon Boulevard, Suit 800
Coral Gables, Florida, 33134-6923 (305-446-0600)
November 11, 1986

Mr. Alhasan S. Ceesay
C/O The Episcopal Diocese of Michigan
4800 Woodward Avenue
Detroit, Michigan 48202

Dear Mr. Ceesay,

The American university of the Caribbean School of Medicine (AUC) in Montserrat, West Indies, is pleased to offer you admission to the first semester of basic medical sciences, which will begin January 7, 1987.
To secure your acceptance to the September 1987 class you will need to send the Medical Education Information office $400 non-refundable inscription fee. Receipt of this fee will be acknowledged provided that you type your name and address on the enclosed postcard and return it with your payment. Please note that if your inscription fee is not receiv
ed in this office by November 25, 1986, your acceptance position will be awarded to another

individual. Registration and general information materials have been enclosed with this letter. Please feel free to contact this office, in the meanwhile, if we can be of any further assistance to you prior to your departure for Montserrat.

Congratulations upon your acceptance and I wish you success with your education endeavours at the American university of the Caribbean School of Medicine and future career in Medicine.

Sincerely
Patricia Litwin
Liaison Officer

Joy and thrill of pleasure ran into my heart as I ran to tell Bishop Mcgehee of the good news. He had already been told by telephone but was waiting to see the letter before letting the cat out of the bag for everyone relief.

The letter brought relief and good tidings into my life and effort that the Ceesay Committed invested for the past four and half years while at their sanctuary in Detroit, Michigan. I completed the formalities requested in the letter and enclosed the inscription fees and sent the package special delivery to AUC in Plymouth, Monterrat, West Indies.

That night I prayed and thanked God for opening the doors of medical school to me. I begged Him to guide more all the way to graduation and help me return to serve or provide modern medical aid to the villager in rural Gambia.

I phoned all my American friends and indefatigable foot solders and told them of the good news and when I should depart the USA. I thank them and each was delighted and relieved about the new dawn my life embarked upon Issuing out of Mariner's Inn into medical school I felt an unimaginable thrill of pleasure and readiness to meet the challenges of medical school for my people. Such please is only experience as when a captive is delivered from his dark dungeon.

The Ceesay Committee hastily arranged for our final meeting to on November 7, 1986. We met with Bishops McGehhe and Mason in attendance We went over the last bit to noted and Mrs. Evelyn Bayer reported on the amount already at hand. It was agreed that the rest of the money be collected in the remaining 18 months while I am at Montserrat. This done we came to final agenda, which was, and address by me.

I began thus, "Ladies and gentlemen, today marks a historic phase in my life. First, let us thank God for this day. There are few things neither riches nor power can buy. Without true friends the world is wilderness.

We all know or have experienced that a crowd is not company, and faces are but gallery of pictures and talk is a tinkling cymbal if these lack love or caring. Today I emerge from darkness of the trouble past into the dawn of a future, which years I hope, shall never be severely over-riding.

I therefore thank you for the ease and discharge of fullness and warmth of your hearts. Your strong believe in human rights and justice for all made today possible.

You and your Diocese not only stood with me throughout this struggle against injustice and its obstacles when it appears insuperable, but provided me with the best you have to help me fight my case. Profound gratitude and appreciation goes to you and the Diocese of Michigan for providing me with shelter, support and for generously overwhelming me with kindness and compassion. Freedom never had better or truer champion and I never had better friends.

Let me reiterate my gratitude to all of you for making the daylight out of darkness and confusion, which blanketed me through these past four and half years at the Mariner's Inn. These are dark and difficult times for Africa.

The Continent is marred by sad events to which the politicians, inept military men and rebels (beasts) wantonly wreck lives and property in enhancing themselves. These devils mellow in destruction of the land and the peasantry.

Coups places fundamentally strictures of freedom in the lives of the people and worst of all it destroys life and property without replacing or instituting better and worthy administrations or to the original state it blasted.

Tears of shame run down my cheeks any news of coup d'etat reaches me. It has no redemption but only causes damnation. I only wished there were a peaceful way of getting reed of these dictators and thieves now ruining the lives of my people.

Freedom is belonging and feeling at home in a democratic framework. Friends, "wars and coups", according Thomas Man, are only, "A cowardly escape from the problems of peace." I believe in peace and human rights and good governance for all of us.

Today belongs to justice and human rights and likewise a reward to freedom. I reiterate that I did no wrong and will never deliberately hurt another human being. I only asked for justice for all Gambians and fair sharing of the resources with the hinterland farmers. Thank you for lifting my heart, for ceaseless encouragement, and sacrifice with which you brought this meeting into being.

Today is a mix bag for me for I cannot be truly happy while my people are miserable, oppressed, sick and hungry, unenlightened, and unable to enjoy freedom and the beauty of the world.

Colonial rule, as uncivilized and barbaric as it was, has come to be preferred than the new tyranny in independent Africa. The new rulers seem to forget God to be above all and that governments are not deities but servants of God and the people.

In my country dissidents farmers are duped as Trojan Horses even when they are telling the truth or asking for what was due them.

I have been asked many times why I wrote in behalf of the detainees in 1981. I did so because I was certain of their innocence and because for me human beings, human rights and justice are more important than power or money and what it can purchase.

I believe in freedom pf the individual and I am convinced that when justice accompanies freedom individuals can then realize their fullest potentials. In essence, we must have the right to worship freely, have companionship, enjoy music, the right to think and reason, to pursue ideas, to seek truth, the right to read and write, protect the weak and helpless, to honour and cherish good.

When we work together with our fellow men to build a better universe, then our status is deserving and worthy of human being.

The human heart is born good, sensitive and feeling, eager to be approved and to approve. The human heart is hungry for simple happiness and chance to live. It neither wishes to kill or be killed.

Tears came my eyes when I behold the statue of Liberty on Liberty Island. I was moved by the inscription which simply said, "Give me your tired, your poor, your humble masses yearning to breath free.

The wretched refuse of your teeming shores. Send these, the homeless, tempest, toast to me. I lift my lamp besides the golden door." Herein America has spoken to me and showed me the worth of spirit and human rights.

Is freedom not the child of truth and confidence? Some say the world is nothing but a place dog eats dog or the big fish feast on the little ones. I do not subscribe to these and I feel obliged to help my neighbour.

True freedom, equality and justice must be cherished and guarded carefully within our souls. Africa will strife to survive these inhuman insults and we will contribute toward world progress and democracy and it's spiritual as well as its principal values.

Edwin Markhan said, "There is a destiny that makes us brothers, none goes his way alone, all that we send into the lives of others comes back into our own." Ladies and gentlemen, friends and fellow warriors, I have a covenant with Africa and I will return as a physician serving the villagers.

Those of us schooled must have moral obligation to, by destiny and choice, help the hinterland Africa out of darkness and ignorance. It is a responsibility we must have courage to face squarely, eyeball to eyeball for the enlightenment of our people. Friends your presence elates me and makes me feel richer. Thank you for contributing and for helping me to withstand the vicissitudes of this insecure and unpredictable era of African dictators.

In my short live I have heard about so many inhumane acts, cheatings, corruption, sordid and out right selfishness but be rest assured that I have not become cynical.

The presence of descent people like you, kind and noble in act, gives me faith in the possibility for a far finer existence than yet known to my people.

Finally, I am most grateful to all of you and so is the Gambian villager.

In short, allow me to reiterate that I will do all I can to share the fruits of your kindness with the sick and needy, especially at the village level in Africa.

Charles Lewis Slattery sums up my feeling when he said in his prayer, "Almighty God, we thank thee for the job of this day, May we find gladness in all its toil and difficulty, in its pleasures and successes and even in its failures and sorrows.

We would look always away from ourselves, and behold the glory and the of the world that we may have the will and strength to bring the gift of gladness to others, that with them we may stand to bear the burden and heat of the day and offer thee the praise of work well done- Amen."

At this stage, we dispersed with everyone hiding their tears for we have become one and have fought vehemently hard for a worthy cause. The years brought closer to each other more than we ever dreamt.

It is true that he who understands you is greater kin to you than your own brother. For even your own kindred may neither understand you nor know your worth. The Diocese of Michigan became part of me as I their fabric for life.

The following editorial about my new direction and life was published both in the Diocesan newspaper, the Record and local newspapers down town Detroit.

My stunning Princesses at Brusubi Gambia 2016

Chapter 30

ALHASAN CEESAY LEAVES OUR SANCTUARY FOR MEDICAL SCHOOL: A WORD FROM BISHOP MASON AND REV. HUGH C. WHITE

You will be delighted to learn that Alhasan S. Ceesay was accepted yesterday (Tuesday, November 11, 1986) into the medical school of the American University of the Caribbean, Plymouth, Montserrat, West Indies.

Alhasan is hoping to commence his studies at the medical school this coming January 7, 1987. You know that Bishop McGehee and the Diocese have given Alhasan sanctuary for more than three years. Mariner's Inn has provided him with housing and sustenance.

Bishop McGehee in his letter to Dean of the Medical School in the West Indies said, "I know Alhasan personally. He is a person of integrity, intelligence, human sensitivity, and God knows, perseverance against formidable inequalities."

For the past several weeks a small group of persons in the Diocese have raised $15,000 towards the $30,000 required for his medical training. You may wish to join in the support of Alhasan. The purpose of this memo is to give you that opportunity.

You do understand that every dollar raised will go directly to his personal support.

You may make a monthly or quarterly pledge to be paid over the next eighteen months, beginning December 15, 1986 and going through to July 15, 1988. All monies received for this purpose are tax deductible.

Evelyn Bayer at the Diocese Centre (4800 Woodward Avenue, Detroit, M! 48201) will take your pledges or your money. We are confident that Alhasan Ceesay will serve all people wherever he is. He is personally committed to returning to the Gambia as a doctor to his people.
Signed: Bishop Mason and The Rev. Hugh C. White
A copy of my letter followed for Editor of the Diocesan newspaper to print in The Record.

Dear Editor,

I will be most delighted if you would kindly publish this note in the next issue of the Record for me to extend deep appreciation and gratitude to the Diocese of Michigan, my support group, Mariner's Inn, and all who steadfastly stood by me to seek resolution of my intractable INS case.
Thank you is awfully inadequate and words cannot aptly convey to you what the help you rendered meant to my villagers and me. I take this opportune moment to express profound gratitude for your generous and the overwhelming support accorded me.
The fruits of your benevolence will be shared with the sick and needy in due course. To those not aware, I am pleased to report my being accepted at the American University School of Medicine in the West Indies effective January 7, 1987.
Most relieving is the fact that I will be able to meet with my family in Guinea Conakry on my way to the school. All of this would have been impossible had it not been for love, encouragement and support you provided me during these difficult times of my

life. Therefore, allow me to convey to you, in advance, sincere appreciation of my family and villagers for the kindness you always touched us with during my exile days or years. We are very grateful and a million thanks to all of you who one way or the other contributed to make this chapter and day possible for my villagers.

Thanks for being true friends of human rights and for being so kind and helpful to my mission and me. I will certainly return to serve the Gambia as soon as that is possible for me.

Thank you! My gratitude to this country (America and Americans) is immeasurable. It is here that life taught me how to forge ahead for my people and for nothing more I am thankful for the love and friendship of the people from whom I learn the true meaning of sacrifice and good will towards others. The French capsule my feeling best in the saying, "Tout est bien, qui fini bien."

All is best that ends well. God bless all of you. "Au revoir mon ami." Goodbye my good friends. I will see you in the Gambia. We certainly look forward to welcoming you in our villages to thank you for your stand in this unusual case.

Sincerely

Alhasan S. Ceesay

With this newfound relief I braced myself for the task that lay ahead. I got my little possessions, I had, all packed, bought my air ticket to Guinea Conakry via Amsterdam and the London and Antigua to Montserrat, West Indies.

I made my last pilgrimage to the Diocese of Michigan early on December 19, 1986, the day of my flight out of America. Everyone seemed to want to hug me and wish me well and a safe journey. They were also relieved that life has now signaled progress for me and that the prospect of meeting with my family was super.

The Bishop broke down, at his office, when I shook his hands for the last time. He and I have grown very close and are now parting for, possibly, for good. I took a last look at him, with tears dripping on my cheeks, and walked out saying thanks, goodbye and God bless you sir.

I heard his footsteps behind me up to the end of the corridor and I disappeared into Rev. High C. White's officer who was then on the telephone making final arrangements for me at Detroit Metro Airport for a 1.00 pm flight from Detroit to Chicago for both of us.

The scenery of well wishers repeated itself at the corridor where I met a throng of people wanting to see me for the last time. I will never forget (The Rt. Rev) H. Coleman Bishop McGehee, Jr, Patricia Koblyski, Hugh White and the Ceesay-Committee, Lois R. Leonard, Evelyn Bayer, Marry Ellen Robertson, and Rev. Walter White, executive director at the Mariner's Inn. Rev, Hugh C. White and I entered the car amidst tears and cheers from those onlookers and good friends of mine. This was the beginning of the closure of my life in exile and the Mariner's Inn saga.

At the Metro airport and after the formalities, Hugh and I bought few soft drinks but none could finish his because of the Erie feeling that we are now about to separate for long, long time to come, or perhaps forever.

We arrived at O'Hare International Airport in Chicago two hours early. This gave us time to browse around and renew our commitment not to loose contact of each other, especially the Bishop and my friends at the Episcopal Diocese of Michigan.

Time flew rapidly and soon we had the PA announcing boarding time for Amsterdam. The Rev. Hugh C. White and I shook hands for the last time at O'Hare International on December 19, 1986 and I broke down for the first time since I left Diocese of Michigan in Detroit.

I have bid farewell to the last of the true friends I had in America. These were friends who uphold the doctrine of human rights and justice for all. We prayed together and I joined the boarding queues. Hugh too had a tear or two escape him.

He stood watching for a while before he disappeared into America and I headed for Africa and the Caribbean. Very soon elation took over my sadness for leaving behind such good friends I made during the saga of my exile years.

The flight was routine and went smoothly. I landed at Amsterdam, Holland, 5.00 am, the next day. I could not believe that this time the sun has risen for me and that I am not in the Mariner's Inn but on my way to motherland Africa.

The thought and feeling of relief I had at that December 20, 1986, can never be repeated. I prayed and thanked God for letting me survive the ordeal and for the kind people He brought into my life during those trying moments. The transit took seven hours instead of the four I was told while booking the ticket for the flight.

At the end of the waiting and having gone through the Airport formalities for Conakry we boarded a KLM flight destined for Guinea Conakry at 1.00pm. I was so eager to leave that beads of sweat ran down my face in wintry Holland.

My adrenaline was surge supper high and all I wanted was to be in Conakry with my family. The iron bird finally started to taxi for take off from Amsterdam for Conakry International 5.00 pm and besides a few air turbulent moments the flight was calm and steady and I did manage to sleep most of the nine hours flight.

KLM taxied at Conakry International 5.oo pm, December 21, 1986, nine hours after my first trans Atlantic flight for five years. The blue skies and warm breeze or climate was a dramatic relieve from the dreary wintry weather I just left behind in frigid Amsterdam, Holland.

Once more life was familiar scenery and the people were cheerful as they welcomed us to Guinea Conakry. I took two or there deep breaths cool evening tropical fresh air and praised God for letting me this far and for freeing me from the torturous trial my life had seen in the past six years since Liberia.

I then went into the arrival formalities almost dazed for my mind could not accept that such fortune could be mine. I picked up my luggage after the arrival rituals or formalities and only to find out that my suitcase was missing.

It had all the presents I brought for my family and fiancée Fatou Koma. Two hours passed before Fatou Koma and her friend came for me. Evidently, she had been at the Airport on arrival of an earlier

KLM flight, which originated from Dakar Senegal. At that time she was told that I was not onboard the one from Dakar but should check back for the KLM flight from Amsterdam. She returned to Conakry hoping that I will call while I was already at the arrivals.

Luckily she return at 7.00 pm and we hugged and kissed several times before anyone of us could utter a word or two in. She was just delighted to see me well and back in Africa. It was a momentous ecstasy and indeed exhilarating for us.

Every second seemed unbelievable. It shows that I was free and at last with the woman I ever loved in my life. It was to us like a dream and we held onto each other not to be separated again for the rest of our lives. It all happened on an African soil. We prayed and thank God for being kind to us and for letting us see each other in good health, even if our spirits were broken by the threats that lingered over me in the past six years.

We took a taxi and headed for Conakry, capital of Guinea, West Africa, through which journey we kissed incessantly right to our destination at the International Hotel at the outskirts of town.

I spent the night at the hotel and told my future wife all that happened to me, and the luggage caper, even though KLM promised to try and locate it. She was just happy and felt lucky and thankful that I was alive and was in Guinea with her.

The next day I moved to Alhaj Saikou Omaruff Nimaga's home down town Conakry. He was my fiancee's uncle and he had insisted I stay there for the rest of my short stay before I head for Montserrat in the West Indies.

The reunion with some of my family members from the Gambia and would be in-laws was an unbelievable dream. My uncle Alhaj Sherif Sey arrived on Wednesday from the Gambia to brief me about the family.

He told me father was too frail and could not come but he was there in spirit with us. The entire family in Gambia was concerned about my state and urged that I keep up the fight to clear my name. They were convinced that God would vindicate me and that I will one day return to serve the Gambia.

Uncle Sey told me that father always prays for my progress and fulfillment of my dreams in life.

I was happy to see him and to know of the state of the family back in the Gambia. I did not sleep that night. I was worried about my poor aged parents and impact my case might have had on them.

It might be the reason why my parents were afraid of meeting me in Guinea.

However, on Thursday evening a delegation of elders was sent to Fatou Koma's parents asking or seeking the hands of their daughter to marry to me. This delegation of twelve, at the behest of my fiancée, Fato Koma, insisted that we be married before my departure for Montserrat in the Caribbean.

She told her parents that she would a sphincter if they deny her the choice of a husband. The parents acquiesced and I paid the dowry and all that was asked or required for the marriage to be blessed and consummated. At first, Fatou's father, Alhaj Ousman Koma was hesitant about my marrying his daughter, in view of the prevailing history, and he pretended to block the proceedings hoping to get higher dowry offer. I assured him of the eternal love I have for his daughter and that I will never let her suffer or ever dreamt of divorcing her. I told him that Fatou Koma is my soul and mine even in death. We will remain one person should he give her hand in marriage to me.

Hence, Alhaj Marruf Nimaga, Mohamed Dansugu and a group of elders, between who was my future father-in-laws' best boyhood friend, all assured Alhaj Ousman Koma that the marriage was going to be sanctioned.

With this pressure on he finally recapitulated and let what God wanted between Fatou Koma and I materialized. Fatou Koma-Ceesay is of the Sarahule tribe and Daughter of Alhaj Ousman Koma and Jalian Ture of Kindia village, Republic of Guinea Conakry.

We met in 1979 while I was a student at the A. M. Dogliotti School of Medicine, University of Liberia in Monrovia, West Africa. It was love at first sight that never faded but grew daily for both of us, up to the present day of our lives.

She is the beauty of the world in my eyes. She is stunningly beautiful, sexy, young, intelligent and all I like or wanted in a woman. The romantic fantasies of life become reconciled with reality when one meets that one individual that stands out in our hearts of hearts and emotions.

It is much more than a feeling, which removes protective barriers one may have erected. Fatou Koma-Ceesay was the unquestionable love for me the moment we laid eyes on each other. I finally realized a soothing or comfort and sharing I hardly experienced with others.

As time grew we developed and matured into being twins that loved, struggled and shared everything in life. One look at her will allow you class her as the queen of the palace of beautiful queens. With her beauty goes an exceptionally well-mannered, sociable and intelligent lady.

Her father, Alhaj Ousman Koma, always teases me by accusing me of having stolen the jewel of his compound, which is an under-statement when one sees or meets my Fatou Koma-Ceesay.

I am yet to hear anyone utter objectionable remarks about my dream girl. Her mother said that I must have had very long arms that reached out from the Gambia to Kindia in Guinea Conakry and snatched their princess's heart.

In short, this lady is my dream wife turn real and I will never allow her escape me. Hence, I wrote the following letter to my parents on 2/21/1980, while in Liberia, informing them about Fato Koma and my intention of marrying her in due course.

A.M. Dogliotti College of Medicine
University of Liberia
Monriovia, Liberia
West Africa
2/22/80

Dear Parents,

I have through my life aimed at bringing joy to your hearts. Unfortunately circumstances seem to impede me. However, I am today pleased to report that, despite my bewilderment, I have met a lady in Kindia, Guinea Conakry whom God made our hearts and spirits as one. She is called Fatou Koma, a Sarahule and Muslim daughter of Alhaj Ousman Koma, the Imam of Kindia.She loves me and has refused to marry anyone since I met her.

In view of the unusual determination and love we have for each other I as you to kindly bless our proposed marriage and for you to send letters of appreciation and concordance etc to her parents, especially Alhaj Ousman Koma and Jalian Ture in Kindia.

Fatou and I met in 1979 and she and her family have since remain kind to me. I fully understand your difficulties but I beg for your approval of my eventual marrying of Fatou Koma as soon as possible.

This is one woman I love more than any that came to my life. I have already written to her father about my intentions. A copy of which (the letter) is being enclosed herein for you perusal. I will upon hearing from you finalize the formalities.

I am asking her hand in marriage not only because we love each other but because she has also been an honest, lovely woman to me and had stood her grounds for me. If everything seemed puzzling and untimely then that is what God has planned for Fatou Koma and I.

I have reached an age where a good lady partner will be normal and advantageous if not realistically traditional. Again, I love Fatou Koma and do know what I am about to get into.We await your unquestionable approval of my marrying Fatou Koma. Bare with me I know what I am doing and if all it all ends you will be happy with my Fatou Koma.

I will return with a good wife on my side and a good skill to serve the Gambia when I finish my studies. Regards, God bless and reply soon.
Your Son
Alhasan S. Ceesay

My parents wasted no time in writing to Alhaj Ousmab Koma and all those concen in the above request. But as fate had it Fatou and I had to seat it out until my return to Guinea in December 1986 before we could finally marry.

I had sent the following letter to my future father in-law, Alhaj Ousman Koma during the same period that I contacted my parents requesting their approval of my wedding Fatou Koma. It read:

College of Medicine
University of Liberia
Monrovia, Liberia
West Africa
2/23/80

Dear Alhaj Ousman Koma,

I am Alhasan S. Ceesay, son of Mr. Sisawo Ceesay and Mrs. Famatanding Tarawaleh of Njawara village, Lower Badibou, District, the Gambia. We are Muslims and of the Mandinka tribe. I am currently studying to become a doctor of Medicine when I complete my training.

I met your daughter, Fatou Koma in Monrovia, Liberia in 1979. God made our hearts one and indeed very close at heart and spirit. It is in this light that I write with deep humility and courtesy to ask you, your wife, Jalian Ture, and all relatives of yours to give me the hand of Fatou Koma in marriage. My father is now 90 years old and cannot travel to Guinea as would be required by tradition, so he would be writing to you shortly.

Upon hearing from you my uncle Alhaj Sherif Sey, will be deligated by the family to travel to your place in Guinea to formalize the consummation. Fatou Koma and I love each other very much and would like your approval of our marriage.

Islam will be the corner stone of my house and all I can assure you is I love your daughter and believe she is good enough to be my wife for life. Let the record show that I commit myself to doing all I can to maintain her well and give her all the love and protection I will give to myself. In Allah's name, Fatou Koma and I, anxiously await your reply and tacit approval.

Your son-in-law

Alhasan S. Ceesay

If I were to come into this world again, I would prefer the convenience of the two that brought me into earth. They were the most befitting parents and the Gambia is my Garden of Eden in which Fatou Koma is the perfect match for me in my heavenly life.

Hence, after almost eight years of waiting Fatou Koma and I got married at a mosque in Conakry on December 23, 1986. My uncle Alhaj Sherif Sey deputized for my parents since they were too old and for fear of alerting authorities as to my where about in Africa, did not come to witness the low key ceremony we had agreed on.

My uncle left for the Gambia the following day, after consummation of the marriage, to report to my family and reassure them of my being well and committed to return to the Gambia when the proper time comes.

Fatou Koma, now Mrs. Ceesay, relaxed in my arms like a tender baby. How sweet it rings in the ear to hear people call her Madam Koma-Ceesay or Mrs. Koma_ceesay.

Our honeymoon was very short for I had to be in Medical School by January 7, 1987 in the West Indies some twelve thousand miles from Conakry. We agreed that she stays in Guinea until my situation improves or when I finish my clinical rotation.

I wrote the following letter to Bishop McGehee and Hugh White while in Guinea informing them of the new change in my life etc.

Kindia
Guinea Conakry
West Africa
24/12/86

Dear Bishop McGehee & Rev. Hugh White

RE: Surprise permanent union

It gives me great pleasure to inform you that my fiancée Fatou Koma and I were married today in view of the circumstance known to all of you and love being the paramount reason behind the enactment.

Her's and my parents insist that time had it for us to marry come what may as both of us are advancing in age. Hence, I would be most grateful if you bring this low-key wedding to attention of the Diocese, the Ceesay Support Committee and Parishes and well wishers in Detroit.
I will be enrooting to the American University in Plymouth, Montserrat, West Indies in two days time. Will write or call while in Plymouth. Again share the joyful news with friends. Regards
Your friend in Christ
Alhasan S. Ceesay
I later in the saddest fashion, through Rev. Richard Smith, found out that either mails never left Conakry because of poor service or were lost while on international transit to USA. Rev. Richard Smith harped on it to destroy my integrity before the Bishop and company.
It worked but let us follows the Richard saga at a later section of the chapter. So I took my return flight to medical school on the 5/1/87 heading via London, Antigua and my final destination Plymouth, Montserrat in the West Indies.
The flight took 14 hours by the time we flew across the Atlantic from Guinea Conakry via Paris, London and then Antigua into Plymouth, Montserrat. Motserrat is a very small volcanic Island of no less than 6000 people in the West Indies.
The Northern sector was occupied white residents while the rest of the island indigenous West Indies. On arrival to Plymouth, using Lait flight, we were given permits and then we took a taxi ride to the ultra-modern campus of the America University of the Caribbean (AUC) after ten minutes ride of

winding and hilly road. The university was perched atop of a hill offering reflection panoramic view of the beauty of sea and land and also served as the island's main tourist attraction. This scenery and levied students resident permits made AUC a natural source of revenue for the island state.

There were not many attractions to see except the hot springs and lovely flowers mingled with warm and kind residents. 400 American and Canadian students attend the medical school and these created a lively social atmosphere while attending the school.

The people were friendly and I had lots of friends amongst Montserratians. Huge tourist ships dock at the harbour twice weekly. Tourism was full bloom when I arrived in Montserrat.

At the university campus I was roomed a fellow classmate, Robert Lowry, an Afro-America from Brooklyn, New York. Even though I spent only a few days with him before moving out, I found Robert Lowry to understand and a kind person.

Came January 7th, 1987, I got up very early, prayed and went to be officially inducted or registered as member of the class of 1987 through 1992 which ceremony took place at 8.30 AM.

Classes started the same day and our class of fifty students was among the largest to enroll at the university. Some who had done Dentistry; others were secretaries and research assistances before deciding to read for a medical degree as career. Most of the entrants had degrees in biology, chemistry and mathematics. A few were transfer students from other Caribbean medical colleges.

Every thing including my classes went on well until med semester when my asthma flared. I reacted severely to the pollen and humidity and was hospitalized on several occasions. This ill heath of mine made the school officials concern as to whether my health would allow me complete the semester or even continue attending or the program at the university.

I insisted to be allowed to continue and made it clear the asthma normally goes away in a week until the next pollen season a year later. I literally forced myself to attend classes under heavy medication of Salbutamol, and prednisolone.

I went into serious asthma attack while taking the final exam of the first semester at AUC. Hence I had to repeat the semester. I moved from the dormitory believing that I might be allergic to some perfume Lowry uses or pain on the wails.

I had a room next door to school and my landlord was none other than the university Gardner, William Ryan. This kind man checks me at night to see if my asthma did not flare. The attacks abated with falling levels of pollen. Fate had to have it that I will complete medical school but the experience that followed was not one I would even wish for my ardent enemy.

Fatou Koma was sent to be with me nine months after my restarting of medical school. Wife joined me at the middle of the third semester and it helped me relax while continuing the struggles. She arrived after the infamous surprise visit of Richard Smith on behalf of the Diocese, who had been against my attending AUC from the onset we brought up the idea as an alternative to solving my INS nightmare.

Like most, Richard Smith, fails know how much willpower God gave me and my determination to get through medical school with or without his involvement. Hence, when Richard insinuated that I failed to let my friends at Diocese know of my marriage.

I got angry because I did write to the Bishop and Hugh about it while in Guinea Conakry to let them know God's gift to me in Guinea. Richard harped on it and made me look the person I was never meant to be as he failed to see the link and possibility of poor mail service in Africa.

I was operating on assumption that the Diocese knew through letters I sent them before leaving for the Caribbean. My wife's joining me finally gave Richard Smith ammunition to detach me from the Diocese and the Ad Hoc Ceesay Committee disregarding the effect my asthma had on me in my first semester at the island.

When Richard was through he persuaded all, except one angel, Mrs. Lois R. Leonard, went along with him and discontinued their sponsorship of my medical education at the American University of the Caribbean School of Medicine.

Fatou's arrival to Montserrat coincided with my having lost all means of support but true love being what it will always be, Fatou refused to return and leave me under such predicaments. Simply, she weathered the storm with me without ever regretting it or demeaning me.

She at one time volunteered to write to the Bishop and send photocopies of her arrival time in Montserrat to clarify the matter for them but I refused on the grounds that some of them have known about it for I wrote to them about our marriage before leaving Guinea. I assured the Committee that as long as I am on thee right, God would see me through this ordeal, even though it might or was going to be of the greatest uphill battle for me.

God relieves of us of all burdens if we believe in Him and the types of Richard Smith and company. I told her we must be kind to our selves and fellow humans. We must never fail to help the needy, as did our parents, parents' parents for generations of life.

Later that year, by December 6th, 1987, we received the following letter from my father in-law, Alhaj Ousman Koma. He wrote to us while visiting a friend, Alhaj Ebrahima Conteh in Monrovia, Liberia.

Wife and I were very surprised and at the same delighted when we read the letter. We had prayed long for her father to come to terms with our marriage.

We needed his blessing for the anything to work out for the future of our family and children. So his reconciling sealed the marriage forever in the African traditional way.

Even though the letter was no monetary source for us it lightened the shock and confusion the Richard Smith Caper brought onto our lives. Please understand that both fatou and I wholeheartedly forgive Richard Smith for being the devil's advocate in my life. Without further ado here is the panacea.

C/O Alhaj Ebrahima conteh
99 Saikou Ture Avenue

P. O. Box 154
Monrovia, Liberia
West Africa
December 6th, 1987

Dear Alhasan,
"Ah salaam aleikum. Wa rahmatullah wa barakatu."
I receieved your letter of September 1, 1987, only a few days ago. I am no longer in Kindia but in Monrovia, Liberia.
The several letters and money you sent I deliberately refused to receive. You know that I was greatly annoyed at Fatou Koma foe leaving the husband I had given her.
However, time, your assurances in the letters just received and the fact the rest of my family agreed to the marriage between you and Fatou Koma have brought me to accept the marriage as one favoured by God.
I, therefore, now give you all my blessings. I shall pray for your well-being and total success. As I say this I want Fatou Koma know that you are the last man I will ever give her to marry.
So you must remain together until the time Allah calls you to your final destination. It means much to me to hear that Islam is at the center of your lives and that you are keeping the salat as prescribed by Allah in the holly quruan and practiced by the holy prophet Mohamed sallaho alahi wasalam.
Once you have both Islam and education you have been greatly favoured by Allah, so never relent in your quest for piety and knowledge.

You must continue to write and by Allah's grace I will reply your letters. With prayers that Allah's peace and blessings be upon you both. I am closing now
Faithful Yours
Alhaj Ousman Koma
Your father in-law.
Fatou and I were in cloud nine and more than delighted and relieve knowing that my father in-law had seen the light at the end of the tunnel. Hence we sent him the following reply the next mail day in Montserrat.

School of Medicine
AUC, Plymouth
West Indies
December 18, 1987

Dear Alhaj Ousman Koma,

Fatou and I were delighted and relieved by your recent letter dated December 6, 1987, which reached us today. We are indeed touched by your final acceptance of our holy union in marriage. It is a profound holy anointment from God and you, our father.
We are all in good health and spirit. God has atlas given peace to our marriage and minds for knowing that all of you loved us. May Almighty God and His prophet Mohamed grant to all of us good health and longevity.
Be rest assured that only death will separate Fatou and I. Also I will do all I can to help the rest of the family where possible.

Our regards and best wishes to all and remember us to others members of the family. Looking forward to hearing from you soon. Please have the people at your mosque pray for us. Wasallam
Your Son-in-law
Alhasan S. Ceesay

This letter and what it meant rejuvenated my wife and me. At last everyone on both sides of the families is now for our marriage. God had finally sealed us forever. We thanked God and slept in each other's arms until morning.

I continued to fight to complete my medical education. My landlord, William Ryan, turned out to be a humane person and indeed a caring landlord. Wife and I at times went without food for days and it was only the landlord who would once on a while bring food to us to feed our dwindling bodies.

The University cared the least whether we went hungry and only catered for its tuition fees believing that money was being sent to me from Diocese of Michigan.

Wife and I collected berries, any edible leaf on the island, fruits, and pears for meals. She would rather starve with me than use the little money we had to fly back to Guinea. She said, "When I married you I did so not only for the good times but also the bad ones. God is only testing us.

Let us put our hands up to Him. He does answer prayers." Indeed we prayed and I worked harder on two fronts, the school and meeting the bills. My experience is that when it rains for me it pours cats and dogs ceaselessly for a very long period at a time. If you think life was bad enough as it is, wait you read about what happened to tiny island of

Montserrat on September 16th, 1989. We just could not believe the challenge that followed that treacherous day when Hurricane Hugo hit the Island with vengeance.

THE YOUNGER CEESAY KUNDA GENERATION

Chapter 31

HURRICANE HUGO: SEPTEMBER 16, 1989
THE DAY HELL BROKE LOOSE.

For readers who do not know, a hurricane is a tropical cyclone with winds of 74 miles per hour or greater and are usually accompanied by torrential rain, thunder and lightening, never heard or seen, that some times move into temperate latitudes such as the Caribbean zones.

A year prior to hurricane Hugo neighbouring Jamaican was devastated by hurricane Gilbert. Most Montserrantian never expected or experienced winds stronger than 60 miles per hour and only reads or hear about the terrible thing Gilbert did to Jamaica.

This was all rudely changed by 11.45 p.m. on Saturday September 16th, 1989. This day gave Montserrat and its neighbouring islands a rude awakening and a taste of her first hurricane in fifty years. The first was in 1660, the second in 1928 and now hurricane Hugo in 1989.

This wild bestial wind of September 16, 1989 blew mad all night with a fury that destroyed all of Monsterrat to pieces. Ninety percent of the homes had their roofs blow away with the high tide that swept the Island.

Things were smashed or smithereens while the thunder and lightening blazed with vengeance. One could at one time hear the cows, sheep and other domesticated animals frenziedly and frantically running to their doom as the wind and rain built up vehemently.

Mine and wife's life became threatened and at serious risk when a flying galvanized sheet left us at the mercy of wind and rain and flying tree trunks with galvanized sheets from nearby buildings. As matters got out of hand we knelt and fervently prayed for our lives and survival of everyone on the path of this monstrous wind.

The hurricane must have poured at least 5 to 15 inches of rain on the island in less than ten minutes on top of the destructive bellows of wind. It was until Sunday, September 17, 1989, that the wind slowed down to forty miles per hour.

And by 1.00 P.M. people were able to or dared to venture out and survey the damage left behind by hurricane Hugo. Only thirteen elderly people became casualties of the hurricane and the whole nation lay in twisted rubbles.

All I saw near my place were metal and concrete inter-twined and blown to some far away location or ditches. Fallen trees, tables, telephone poles, galvanized sheets and all of these in a meshwork of cables and parts of roofs from buildings blocked roads to what was left of the university campus. Upon daring to venture to the campus I saw a small Hiroshima of Japan.

Everything just looked like after the dropping of the Atomic Bomb. Thank God no student died or got injured. The students held on well but were very frightened. There was no pandemonium. It was as if everyone was partly spellbound or sedated for the scenery was too calm and orderly.

Some demanded immediate evacuation while others just wondered about in a daze. The few who were in control of themselves helped gather the remaining food supplies and water. Everyone stayed in the first floors of the dormitories since the roofs of all second floors were no longer there or safe shelter for anyone nor were the waterlogged rooms habitable.

Monday saw a lot of student meetings and the Dean came in to alley our fears and to let us know that efforts were being made to get in touch with the outside world.

Yes, Montserrat was completely isolated from mankind during the first two days of the aftermath of hurricane Hugo. By Tuesday, September 18, 1989, most of the students had enough of the encounter to their necks.

All they kept asking was when will they be able to leave Montserrat. With this, rumours ran wild on the grounds of the ruined campus. The once showcase of Montserrat was now reduced to rubbles and twisted galvanized sheets all over the places.

It was not until Wednesday September 19, 1989, that we had a glimpse of the outside world in the form of a British Frigate, HMS Alacrity, which docked at harbourless Montserat.

One of her helicopters flew over to survey the island and then headed to Antigua perhaps in consultation with the British and American Embrasures and consulates. Later that day more planes flew over us but none dropped anything or came down.

The helicopter landed men from the Frigate and these went to work, setting up communication centers and helping the government and the governor of Montserrat.

Everyone tried to recover as much as possible of his or her retrievable belongings. The British sailors helped to clear the feeder roads and the ship served as lifeline to the rest of the world. At the campus we cleared the tennis court and made a helicopter-landing path.

It worked, for in one overpass flight of the helicopter the pilot saw the big cross with a circle around it. He circled the campus twice and flew back to the ship. After a long half an hour later he came directly and hovered for a while before heading to the temporal landing ground the students had prepared.

The huge helicopter landed smoothly and frightened and eager students swamped the pilot. Being an experience fellow he asked his co-pilot to take off and leave him on the ground with the students. The rush tampered immediately as the metal bird too off and hovered over campus.

All of us wanted to touch the gentleman and thank him for bringing hope to our hearts. He spent roughly twenty minutes with the students discussed with the staff and likewise the student government before being flown back to the ship where he relayed our messages to the American Consulate in Antigua.

That very day, the American vice councilor, Steve Vanhuness, reported to the campus. Yes, and yes again, America does take care of its own in time of crisis like this one. Steve spoke with Dr. Paul Tien, president and owner of the university, and with the student government and then left for his base in Antigua.

The campus settled while diplomatic maneuvers took place between Antigua and Washington, D.C. The general student body was expecting a word or two from the consulate but no matter how uneasy life was for them they must wait for Washington's directives on how to relief or evacuate them from the Island.

Meanwhile several lists of students by name, nationality and home addresses were constantly being compiled and prepared for possible evacuation. The Consular returned the next day with word from the state department that a plane was on the way to take only American and Canadian students to the United States at a cost of $178 per student.

By Friday, September 23, 1989, most of the students were ferried to Antigua by a British Coats Guard ship that brought supplies to Montserrat. Only the staff, a few students, my wife Fatou Koma and I were left on Campus.

The American Consulate refused to evacuate Fatou and I because we were not American or Canadian according to Mr. Steve Vagueness, vice-consular at the U.S. Consulate in Antigua.

I broke down and tried to contact the Gambia High Commission in London on several times but was unable to get through for scarcity of International lines at the time.

I tried the next day but could not get anywhere with the telephones, which sapped the little money left in my account. This left Fatou and I in more financial precariousness. At this time I started worrying about Fatou and wanted help to return her home until life returns to normal.

It was just plain risky for her to remain on the island. People believing that the university would never open its doors again came looting at night. At one time I had to stand my grounds from rouges wanting to break in the makeshift room Fatou and I used while trying to sort things out.

It was pathetic and shame how adversity reduces some men to less than animals. At this stage I never cared what the Gambia may or may not do to me all I wanted was and safe place for the lady who gave so much of herself to me.

And now not only mine but her life is at risk from attack by night hooligans. A sympathetic, Mr. K. Cotter and all at the Command Centre need be praised for their hard work and kindness. They were very helpful and sympathetic about my plight.

For the first time and in mall my travels I felt like an orphan stranded and marooned in a tiny island in the middle of the Atlantic Ocean.

It felt scary but as usual, I left my fate in God's hands and at the same time prayed for His forgiveness, mercy and guidance over Fatou Koma and this nightmare.

Fatou Koma-Ceesay turned to be much stronger and steadfast than I credited her. It was during one these depressed moments that Professor Steve Deschner and his wife Derby came to my help.

I had already had a difficult night with looters who thought that the school would not open for years. On hindsight, it was a very tough night that Fatou and I had prepared our minds for death on a desolate Island.

It was difficult trying to remain sane in situations like this and at the same time protect my wife from molestation and fortune hunters of hurricane Hugo. Dr. Deschner spoke to me and offered to talk to one Miss Gayle Baumgardner at the Condominiums with regards to her sheltering my wife and I until a more safe state or place could be found for us. Meanwhile one of the last American students to leave the island, Dean Mcfinning offered his car for me to sell and use the money to buy air ticket for my wife to fly to Gambia or Guinea Conakry.

A word or act of encouragement during difficult times or failures is worth more than a dictionary of praises after a success.

Miss Gayle Baumgardner, a former Peace Corps volunteer, now resident in Montserrat, turned out to be another of those rare breed of kindness. Upon being told of our predicament at the campus by Dr. Deschner, she accepted to lodge us at the Shamrock villa and out of her kind-heartedness she loaned me money to buy air ticket for Fatou Koma-Ceesay to fly to the Gambia until the improvement of the situation.

I would reimburse her by working for her and helping her clean the mesh hurricane Hugo left behind at the condominium complexes. We were overwhelmed by her generousness and noble act for a humane cause.

My wife and I shall ever be obliged and most grateful to her. I am personally profoundly grateful to Miss Gale Baumgardner. A friend in need is a friend indeed. Gayle's participation was a touch of an angel's hand from heaven.

With this understanding reached. Drs Deschner and Ronda Cooper helped me transport my books, and little belongings left with us to the condominium. Drs. Deschner and Cooper continued to show great interest in us and we are indebted to both for time and help they gave us.

On hindsight, everyone on the Island agreed that it was wicked to leave us stranded on the island while other students were taken out to America. Gayle and I went to town and bought Fatou her ticket to freedom.

Fatou Koma, who lightens my spirit, had to leave for the Gambia after two weeks of stay at the condominiums with me. So we flew to Barbados to the British High Commission for her to secure a transit visa via London on her way to the Gambia. This done we headed for Barbados International Airport.

There, Fatou began to shed tears uncontrollably. I tried to square up my shoulders, stepped back a little and in a voice choked with love and emotion said, I wished I were going with you to Africa. My eyes were full of mist and deep down I was crying and yet praising God for saving our lives and for relieving my wife from the difficulties that lay ahead in the coming days at Montserrat.

Very soon the PA announced the boarding for BA flight to Heathrow, London. Fatou Koma was jus able to hug me and say, "Good luck and good bye Dr. Ceesay." And she disappeared into the boarding queues for British Airways flight 259 heading for Heathrow, London.

My studied composure cracked as I watched the plane disappear into the clouds with my heart and the only woman I loved. Fatou Koma brings joy to me like a child's first exposure to magic. When I hear her speak it is always positive and she speaks with candour and humour.

Fatou is a delight to be with. It is feeling I never felt until I came across her. Oh, no, no do not rashly conclude my feeling for to be that of an infatuation love. No that fades while ours sprouts daily and full of joy.

Fatou Koma is love and gift from God to me. You can laugh at me if you wish but this how I feel about her and she feels the same or more about me. Now that my Fatou Koma-Ceesay was gone I embarked on bracing myself for the task of getting out of Montserrat and completing my pre-clinic courses. I was in Montesrrat the next day and in solitude lonelier than the grave.

A word or two about Miss Gayle Baumgardner would now befit the saga of my current life after hurricane Hugo. Gayle had, according to friends, devoted all her life to teaching and sharing her day with others. She is nicknamed the mother Theresa of Montserrat.

Like a missionary she was literally known by almost everyone and was always helping the needy. Gayle was a giving heart that yearns and beckons people to allow her hem lighten their burdens just as inscribed at Liberty Island.

Gayle seems to say, "Come to with your laden hearts. I shall do my best to lighten your load." Miss Baumgardner was unique, for at the condominiums she was duped, "Primary Manager" for she knew everything about the place and how to get problems solved quickly better than the then designated manager of a place. All one had to do was to ask Gayle about something relating to the condominium and the answer would spew out as if its from a well organized computer.

Gayle knows were to find things better than any on the grounds. Rain or dry this heart of gold is on the move helping others. When asked, Gayle where next? She would calmly and with a broad smile, reply, "I was just going to visit an old friend and help restore so and so thing for him or her."

Gayle works from dawn to dusk with a capacity unique only to Gayle Baumgardner. Having worked with her and as well as observed her, I at times wished I had a way of keeping her rested just for twenty four hours a week. But rest makes her miserable as she once told me.

I do not want that to happen to her for boredom would mean suicide for her. It will be too anguishing an experience for this princess of Montserrat. Gayle Baumgardner was, a jack-of-all-trades, teacher, carpenter, a junk sales person, and above all, a devoted philanthropist.

My Miss Gayle Baumgardner like mother Theresa was a living example of sharing and caring in the literal sense of the word. This angel was happiest when helping others and restless if not engaged in some form of work.

She was true and trues the most holy workaholic. I hope this short synopsis gave a bird's eye view of the lady of Montserrat. Meanwhile the Deschners, Derby and Steve, became interested in helping me go to the USA as we became more and more acquainted with each other. Dr. Ronda Cooper arrange my meeting with the Skeletal staff who were about to depart for America to join the rest of the students at the Wayland Baptist University in Plainview, Texas, left on the Island.

They tried all they could to travel with me but again visa and money problem blocked that effort in my behalf. Hence it was agreed that I stay with Gayle Baumgardner and my exam papers would be sent periodically to an official to proctor while I take the exam.

Time came when the Deschners and other teachers had to leave. We had developed strong bonds and they too will soon be away from me. I thank God for making them care and they became the lifeline between the University in Texas and I in hurricane ravaged Montserrat.

They made certain that all the agreed arrangements concerning my exams were carried out in time by the administration of the medical school. The Deschners also solicited funds for me while in America so that I can complete payment of my fees to the American University of the Caribbean.

It is said that our genetic endowment may well limit our heights and intelligence which we can attain, but it is our environment and experiences, which determines to what extent our potential can be reached or realized.

Hence, their agreeing to keep the channels of communication open while at Texas was indeed a benevolent act for which I was most grateful to this very day. This gracious couple, despite delays and unforeseen complications, left their doors and hearts open to me.

They relayed requests and messages to the Dean and professors while AUC piggy bags at Wayland Baptist University. Fatou and I certainly look forward to the day we can gather all these immaculate wingless lovely angels at our villages and the banks of the River Gambia where my villagers will be able to serenade and thank them for helping me fulfill my dream of providing needed medical aid to the villager.

t was during this sad and lonely time that another blow was dealt to me. News reached me from the defunct Ceesay Committee at Diocese of Michigan that my angel, Mrs. Patricia Koblyski had died. Pat, as everyone calls her, was the Refugee coordinator for the Diocese of Michigan in Detroit, and the first person I spoke to upon arriving at the Diocese center.

She devoted her life to helping people and became my best friend and confidant. She along with Lois R. Leonard fought very hard for me during our discussions and had always come up with brilliant ideas on how to go about bringing a solution to my crisis.

She brought lots of positive help to me and I will never forget the kindness and love she showed me before her cancer took her away from me. I knew chemotherapy was not a miracle cure but that she would succumb so early took us all by surprise.

I cried for more than four days, being unable to stop my tears welling whenever I think about Pat Koblyski and kindness she represented to me. The feeling still persist in my heart.

Could you imagine she cried along with me on the first day I met her and told her about my experience with INS. I sent the following letter to Bishop McGehee and Diocesan Newspaper, The Record.

C/O Miss Gayle Baumgardner
The Condominiums
Plymouth, Montserrat
West Indies

IN LOVING MEMORY OF MRS. PATRICIA KOBLYSKI, DIOCESE OF MICHIGAN

Dear Editor,

I wish through your paper to express sympathy and sincere condolence to Mr. Bob Koblyski, his family and the Diocese of Michigan for the untimely lost of our dear friend and sister Mrs. Patricia Koblyski. The departure of some leaves us bewildered, shocked and flushed. We ask why at this time dear God?
Mrs. Patricia Koblyski is now gleefully resting in the right hands of our maker. We will miss her. For me, a part of me went along with her. She was a good friend and a true Christian heart that was dedicated to all of us God's children.
 Four years ago she cried with me and at that same time helped to wipe my tears. She gave hope of freedom and assistance to me and to entire villagers several thousand miles away. Patricia Koblyski knew none of them but like the rest of you she more than any was dedicated in seeing that we all breathe the air in peace and walk together side by side in

freedom on mother earth. Pat, thanks a million for having lived a full Christian life and for all of us. Our profound gratitude and indebt ness goes to you for being our Good Samaritan.

The only befitting legacy I have for you and my villagers is returning to serve rural Gambia and especially the villager you fought for during these last minutes of a full Christian and a wonderful life of giving to others. We will never, never forget you and May your soul rest in eternal peace by the right hand side of the Almighty God. Amen!!

Your everlasting Friend

Alhasan S. Ceesay

With Fatou Koma-Ceesay back in the Gambia I continued my scourged or blighted life at the condominiums. I stayed in Montserrat like an orphan working all day and studying up to 1.30 A.M every night for four good months before being join the rest of the students at the Wayland Baptist University in Plainview, Texas.

In that interim I chanced to make a lot of friends at the condominiums. Most rewarding of all was the bond that developed between Rudolf and Sophie Kurt; retired German couples who had come to make this nation island their home away from home. The rumor about a marooned American University of the Caribbean's student on the island needing urgent help spread in town and around the business community like a wild fire making me even more embarrassed to go to town.

So on December 19, 1989, I decided to take a break from my studies and be with Rudolf and his wife Sophie Kurt for a chat before they retire for the night. I will come back to this day later.

Dr. Ceesay anbd Kula Samba, Olivet College
Olivet, Michigan, USA 1970 to 1971

Chapter 32

THE SEARCH FOR A SPONSOR

The death of Mrs. Patricia Koblyski left me devastated and concerned. She meant a lot to me and her sincerity and determination to free me was unsurpassed by any other member of the Ceesay Support Committee.

Her death was indeed a tragic loss to my villagers and I. We pray and mourn her passing. Mrs. Lois R. Leonard's statement summed up my feeling about Patricia A. Koblyski when she wrote, "It still seems terribly strange to go in that building (meaning the Diocese) and not see Pat Koblyski."

I missed her very much. Her death ushered in pain and a sense of great loss for me. May she rest in peace with God in Heaven. Patricia Koblyski was one of those who fought vehemently against the intentions of Richard Smith effort to stop my going to the Caribbean.

Instead, Richard wanted me to do nursing because we fail to see eye to eye on most points he raised during our meetings. It was as though he felt a black should not challenge ideas he tabled. This became great snarl between us with Lois enjoy the tug of war going on between Richard and I.

Still determined to stop my getting help from the Diocese managed to get himself selected to pay a surprise visit to AUC medical school in Plymouth, Montserrat, West Indies. He was eager come and check on my performance and to use any negative aspect of it to derail me.

He now had the opportunity because some of the staff like David Breidenbach was not happy with me. This was Richard's chance to drown me into oblivion to the bottom of the Atlantic Ocean. Hence on December 1, 1987, I received a departmental notice from Dr. G. F. Breidenbach, assistant dean of the school telling me that Richard would be on campus shortly.

The memo ushered an ominous sign of anxiety akin to surveying the forest before walking among the trees. It exacerbated the paroxysm that caused a retrogressive dream for me. It brought all the arguments we had fresh in my mind. It was a Delphien memo that foretold a bleak future for medical education and aspirations.

The memo simply read, "A Mr. Richard Smith, who apparently is one of your sponsors, will be on Montserrat and AUC on December 11, 1987. He will be meeting me 9.00 A>M. Please let me know where you will be contacted between 9.30 and 11.30 A. M on that day.

I met Breidenbach the same afternoon to let him know where I would be on said day of Richards visit to the campus. I was not happy meeting the man who fought against my coming to AUC for he had expressed such opinion too many times during our debate about alternative route to relieve of my torturous INS experience.

Richard cared little about time it would take for my INS Appeal Board appeal to come through. Age and time were not going to wait for me. Richard Smith did not care about stressed my life went through in the past fours of exile in skid row America.

He might have construed a drug rehabilitation center to be a palace for an African like me. He did not care about the rebound effects of being constantly turned down by the INS would have on me nor what it meant living with addicts and former convicts at Ledyard.

All Richard Smith cared was to reverse the decision, which sent me to Montserrat in the first place. This being his primary intention, chagrined Richard Smith showed up on campus on December 4, 1987. I had gone to town to mail letters that day.

He was only able to meet my ach enemy Breidenbach and some staff to reward him with false ammunition and negative information he wishes to take back to maligned me to what was remaining of the Ceesay Support Committee. Richard Smith, though a newcomer to the committee want to run the show and got angry with me when he found me nut manipulability.

He disliked the Diocese sponsoring me and fought it very subtle ways at time trying to illicit hot tempers from me.

After meeting the staff at the American University of the Caribbean Richard Smith went on a tour of the Islands or what I apply duped "Island hopping." We finally met at 7.45 pm in a very hostile encounter and animated indeed, which was punctuated with angry argumentative discussions between us.

At the end I assured him that he was no God and did not live my life nor do I wish him such an experience in his lifetime. I made it clear that I was not going to worship him or any other human being for that matter in other to get to where I want.

I left him fuming at his hotel and had a word with Breidenbach for untrue statement he spewed to Richard Smith. David denied most of it but I know better for everything happened in my absence and I now did not care what Richard plans. I made up my mind to transfer to next-door medical school at Ross University if the AUC yielded to Richard Smith's dark plans.

He went back to Detroit, Michigan armed to destroy me. I wonder if he were not originally deep from the South? I learnt on the next day of his return he conveyed an emergency meeting of the Ceesay support Committee and gave them such scorching and negative report about me that the committee or what was left of it blindly swallowed his version wholeheartedly and felt obliged to cease raising money for my studies at American University of the Caribbean school of medicine.

He did his best and not being present to defend myself, he left my integrity standing on slippery ground, which lead to a surge of anger against me. He even told them that I do not attend classes where as the only class I missed was when I had asthma and had to go to hospital three days. Breidenbach took that as my not wanting to attend his classes. All the remaining members, most of who were new members I never met, of then Ceesay support committee under Richard's wings, except Lois R. Leonard and those unable to attend that meeting felt that they no longer could solicited money for a cause that seemed to have some doubts or shadows in it being successful.

Mrs. Lois Leonard felt that or explained her reasons for dissenting with the decision of the committee as follows, "My reasons for voting against the rest of the committee was that I felt that we had made a promise and we were not keeping it.
We promised to send you enough for five semesters. And we stopped sending it before the time was completed." I finally heard from the committee current coordinator and one whom I have high regards, Rev. Hugh C. White. It said:

Diocese of Michigan
4800 Woodward Avenue
Detroit, Michigan 48201
December 28, 1988

Dear Alhasan

You are an important person to the many friends you made here in the Diocese area. The realization of this makes what I am about to say difficult. From our vantage point following Richard Smith's trip to see you in Montserrat, and following two meetings of the committee earlier this month we have concluded that we must suspend any further financial help for the reasons that we cannot continue to raise funds for your medical school education at AUC.
By authorization of your support committee, and with the concurrence of Bishop McGehee, we have deposited to your account at Barclays Bank in Monttserrat, a check for $4121.00, which represented the balance of the funds.

You may use these funds towards your fourth semester at the school or you may use them for whatever purpose you see fit for your future interest. Please know that this decision was difficult for us to take.

Also know that we have some understanding of the pressure and stress you have been under in attempting to make way through medical school. If any additional funds are obtained for you in the immediate weeks ahead, we will forward them to you personally.

Such additional funds are not likely to be in any significant amounts. The one dissenter on the committee to the action outlined in this letter was Lois Leonard. She hoped that we would make an effort to raise the necessary funds for the balance of your studies.

It was the judgment of the committee that such an effort would not be credible or successful in the face of your situation and record. We hope you will let us know how you made out in the light of the action, which we have taken. We live in remembrance and respect of you.

Faithfully,

(The Rev.) Hugh C. white

This note brought melancholy, darkness and grief to me and I grew more depressed and frustrated with life. I made several attempts to put forth my side of the story. It fell on deaf ears and failed to reunite me with the Ceesay Support committee.

Close sources told me that negative report given by Richard Smith made it very difficult to convince or convene a meeting even if Hugh White were willing to try to call one after his convention project was

over. Under the circumstances I will not secure a visa to the USA to rally the committee into some sensible direction. Richard Smith had fired the first short in this war and I shall return mine with having the doctor of medicine degree confirmed on me. I manage to talk to Bishop McGehee by telephone but found his head buried in sand like an Ostrich. He was eager to get to the Lambert Conference in England than deal with my case.
He did ask Hugh White to look into the affair and in reply to my inquiry Hugh White wrote but I never receive his letter. However, I received the following separate surprise not from the administrative assistance to the Bishop.

Diocese of Michigan
4800 Woodward Avenue
August 12, 1988
 Dr. Alhasan Kunsa Ceesay: Badibou Folklore

Dear Ceesay,

This will acknowledge receipt of your note dated July 27, 1988 to Bishop McGehee requesting more funding for your studies. The Bishop is vacationing I England and will return to the office September 6, 1988, at which time he will receive your correspondence.
In the meantime, I refer you to previous letters written this summer concerning your finances. The most recent of which is the letter dated July 28, 19888 from Hugh White informing you that the Episcopal Diocese of Michigan does not have the ability to raise any more funds for your continued

support. Hope you are able to re-think your situation and work towards another goal that will not only give you satisfaction, but also help others in need. You have come too far and your spirit is too great to give up completely.
I urge you to find some one there who will be able to assist you in the getting on with your life.
You do remain in the thoughts and prayers of the people of Diocese of Michigan. Peace.

Mrs. Sheila Gardner
Administrative Assistance
To the Bishop

The raw truth was that, for many of my friendsinterested in my struggles, their participation ended with my decision not to wait for the ruling of the INS Appeal Board. I have always believed that God's ways were the best solutions.
The waxing and waning of interest plus the fact that distance makes the heart fonder helped Richard Smith in landing his final knock out blows to my cause at this crucial moment in my life.
I certainly forgive him and hope that the outcome, as it is today, will let him know he was no God and faith and hard work can indeed overcome the most difficult challenge one may be faced with in a given moment in time
The core outcome of all these were that I found myself totally marooned, like Robinson Crusoe, in tiny Montserrat which only God and very few people or organizations to turn to for help. I again refused to allow this hillock God placed on my way to stop my journey.

I had faith in God, hard work and the goodness of man. I swallowed my pride and made a lasting ditch attempt, after offering prayers, for God to be on my side, to contact the committee. I knew a lot of them cared and that time might turn the tide to my favour.

I could not nor would I accept that my good friends and foot solders at the Diocese of Michigan would throw me to the wolves as easily as they it occurred. There were friends and good Christians who struggled and fought along my side all those trying years to help me realize my goal.

What has Richard Smith, my Brutus told the Committee? Why would they not have patients knowing that we are not far from the end of the road? And the triumph of giving and receiving would have taken happen for the villagers. I dispatched the following.

School of Medicine

A PHOTO DIARY

Dr. Alhasan Sisawo Ceesay, MD

Dr. Alhasan Ceesay and wife Fatou Koma-Ceesay

Mr. Sisawo Ceesay, Father

Mrs. Famatanding Tarawaleh, Mum holding baby

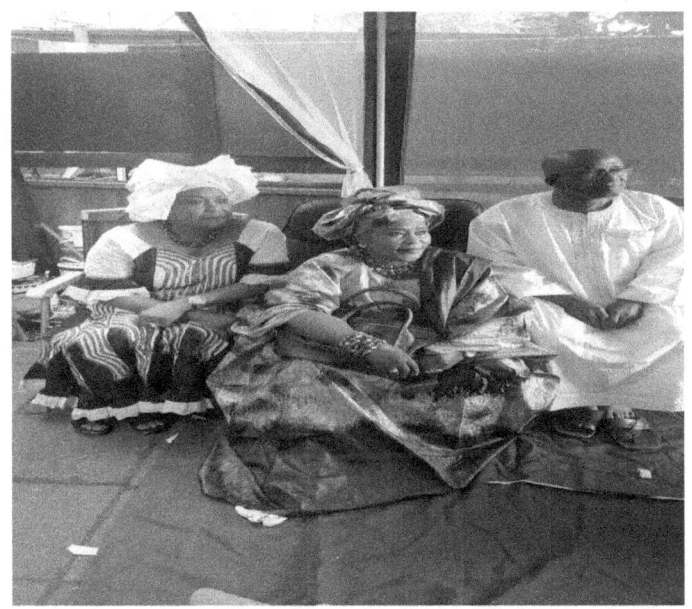
L-R: Sukai Bouvier, Sali Darbo and Kebba Dampha

Mrs Binta Ceesay, my daughter

Dudou Ceesay, brother in green with family

Mrs Fatou Koma- Ceesay: rose that never wither

Dr. Alhasan Ceesay warm friend handshake with friend Abdinnisir Hassan

Mahmud Adam Abdinnisir Hassan True friends.

Miss Famatanding Ceesay, Daughter

Miss Binta Ceesay, Daughter

Miss Roheyata Ceesay, daughter

Dr. Alhasan Sisawo Ceesay graduating fro the
American Universirt of the Caribbean Schoool of
Medicine, 1992

L-R: Dr. Alhasan Ceesay, Prof. Sulayman S. Nyang, Mr. Cloyd Ramsey, and Prof. Francis Conti

Soft spoken kindhearted Faisal Alin

Yusu Mohamed Ali, alias 'Open Ali'; an angel without wings

Dr. Alhasan Ceesay Holding Africa

Ebrahima Bojang, a real generous Gambian angel and custodian of our culture.

Dudou Ceesay, brother with raised hand, at the annual Njawara Seyareh

American University
Of the Caribbean
Plymouth, Montserrat
West Indies

Dear Support Committee,

The suspension of your aid for my studies at the above university was brought to my attention by your December 28, 1987 and July 28, 1988 letters, which were duly received. They are humbling notes by special friends of good will. Suffice it to say the loss of confidence of such special friends is indeed agonizing albeit challenging.
For me it was God's dictum and in humanistic terms a simple misfortune and coup de grace of a permanent festering sore. It marks another sad pivotal stage in my life and experience. I owe to all of you profound gratitude and highest regards for the noble deed.
The money sent has been paid to the school to fulfill the intention of the Church and Christ-like donors. Please tell your envoy, Richard Smith, that the shouts and inanimate discussions and anger de displayed when we met were all a burst of caring and his desire for me to get something good out of the venture.
I thank him but sadden that he took back wrong information and impression to the support Committee. Hence, the untimely decision has not only compromised and compounded my problems but made it very complicated. God's will has it that we are healed by our struggles and made stronger by faith in Him and our sufferings will be painless.

I will believe that God love all of us and be assured that I will not let you down. All of you sought to be Christ like and have opened your arms and hearts to me. We are all God's children and I have no better friends than you. I will surely continue the struggle to the end.

Thanks for letting me touch the core of your hearts. May God continue to be our guide in today's light and tomorrow's darkness. Again. All of you have my admiration and respect. My family is greatly indebted to you. I will do all I can to bring joy to my country and your hearts. I will look for solutions and do ask for your sincere prayers. Thanks a million and keep in touch. Goodbye for now.
Yours Sincerely
Alhasan S. Ceesay

This letter and many more fell on deaf ears. Some wrote to say how unduly influenced the committee was by Richard Smith's negative report and others expressed the feeling that the Church has disappointed me.

Needless to say my goal suffered further delays under the circumstances as I worried more about my dwindling finances and the state of my family in the Gambia. However, I never lost faith or direction towards my goal.

I sent appeal letters to anyone, except the Diocese of Michigan, that I thought would reciprocate kindly upon hearing my plight. Among these was Dr. Nelson Herron, a friend and former colleague at Alpena Community College in Michigan. He wasted no time in recruiting interested friends like Ms. Deirdre O'Leary, of Dublin, Ireland.

They sent me $400 and contacted the Medical Missionaries of May in Drogfield, Ireland seeking assistance for me. The Mission responded favourably as can be seen in the following letter to Ms. O'Leary.

Dear Deirdre,

In reference to our telephone call of last evening, I am happy on behalf of Medical Missionaries of May (M.M.M.) to enclose a check for IR500.00 towards Alhasan Ceesay's final year medical fees. I hope and pray that he will be successful in his exams.
May his years as a doctor in his country of the Gambia be fruitful and rewarding for him and his people. Thanks for your concern for him and his many difficulties and wishing you all the very best. With kindness regards and with every good wish.
Yours Sincerely
Sr. Rosemarry Mohan, MMM
Central Business administration
God has His own ways of solving the impossible moments, which are incomprehensible to man. **Help in small amounts continued to reach me from Mrs. Lois R. Leonard, Judge & Mrs. Viola S. Glennie, Dr. Charles T. Egli, Mr. Cloyd Ramsey, Mr. & Mrs. Bill Johnson of Birmingham, Michigan and many more who wish to remain anonymous donors.**
Despite all these inputs my financial obligation to the Medical School could not be met because of an increase in tuition fees. The donations amounted to drop in the bucket with regards to what I owed the medical school, rent, and student permit fees to the

government of Montserrat. I tittered upon the brink of starvation. I got my meals by picking fruit and berries from nearby hills. My over abundant pride made it impossible for me to beg for food from the street or from the students.

The weight of the burden became unbearable to make breakdown and lost my guard when I revealed my state one of the very reliable group of students. Rodney G. Carter, being one of them, was moved to tears and offered me whatever food was left over in his refrigerator and pantry.

We became great friends and he has since become one of my advocates and had spoken to lots of people in Alabama in an effort to raise more funds for my studies at the American University of the Caribbean Aside from this, he helped me type all my correspondence to various organizations, individuals, Embassies around the world and part of manuscript when he was not studying.

My deepest appreciation goes to this kind human being with great concern for needy people. My spirit never waned. Only my body started to shrivel and to give up for lack of rest and food.

I lost tremendous weight and looked like a living ghost among the students. I became a feather of less than forty kilograms that avoided strong winds and walked near walls during storms to avoid being swept away into the Ocean.

Things got worse when money stopped trickling down. I no longer could pay for rent, light bills or buy gas to cook with. William Ryan, my landlord turned out to be a kind and exceptional being, felt sorry that I had to undergo such brutal hardship away from home.

He empathized with me know all that had transpired in my case since the suspension of my grant by my Detroit sponsors. Willie Ryan assured me that I could stay as long as I needed and pay him whenever I have money or working at one of the hospital somewhere.

In addition to this benevolent act he would once on a while bring food to me when it seem to him that I have not had food for days. Mr. Willie Ryan is my Montserrat just as Gayle Baumgartner was to me during hurricane Hugo.

He has always been generous and kind to me. I look forward to the day I can reciprocate to him and his family for kindness rendered me. Not many in Montserrat bestrode such generosity to me.

In my experience, when it rains, that is when I get woes, it pours and does so with vengeance and incessantly. My life looked like an endless struck or string of bad news upon bad news.

Coming to think about it, who would have expected the Ceesay Support Committee to be so easily bamboozled by some one seemingly from the South, who in the first place was not in support of my leaving the USA for the Caribbean.

With these roadblocks the Registrar, Mrs. Mary Rose Tuit (bless her heart) assisted me by releasing the following letter to potential contributors or donors to help alleviate my financial debts at the America University of the Caribbean.

America University of the Caribbean
School of Medicine
Plymouth, Montserrat
West Indies

TO WHOM IT MAY CONCERN

Mr. Alhasan S. Ceesay, student number 24026, is a student at the American university of the Caribbean School of Medicine, situated in Momtserrat West Indies. The school is listed in the Directory of the World Health Organizations (WHO).
This student is in need of financial assistance to enable him complete his forth and fifth semesters at the School. The tuition fees for a semester now is $4600.00 Any courtesies extended to him will be greatly appreciated by the administration of this Institution.
Respectfully
Mrs. Mary Rose Tuit
Registrar
The school failing to receive any payment in my behalf made the administration and Finance office pursue me with constant reminders that my tuition payment deadline had long passed.
Finally, on October 12, 1988, I was asked to see the registrar no later than 4.00 P. M. that day. I went with full knowledge of what was about to befall me. I was told that the school had waited patiently and long enough and that no substantial payments were made in my behalf.
In view of this I was advised and instructed to take a leave of absence from the university and try to raise the money for the rest of my studies at the medical school.
With a leaden heart, I spoke to the Dean about my problems and other friendly faculty and I was advised no differently. I should have known that the Registrar was just an escape goat in the whole affair.

Anyhow, I thought it senseless to have to stop schooling in the middle of the semester. If allowed to complete the term I would only have to attend the next semester to complete my basic sciences.
I went home and thought through about it and then Concluded that perhaps explaining my situation to Dr. Paul Tien, owner and president of the university, in a desperate last minute ditch might lead to some type of reprieve if not a deferment payments or give a new schedule of payments. The hopelessness of the situation was such that I *wrote the following with my tears to Dr. Tien.*

American University of the Caribbean
School of Medicine
Plymouth, Montserrat
West Indies

Dear Dr. Tien,

Most likely my situation has been brought to your attention. I will be most grateful if you would kindly grant me audience to explain the cause of the delay in my payments.
Briefly, I lost my original sponsors in early part of the year but was able to recently get the Catholic Mission in New York to take over sponsorship the rest of my studies at the America University of the Caribbean. This has just been recently approved and they promised to send an initial payment of $4500.00 within the next fortnight for me to pay some of my outstanding Bills at the school.

Also, I have just received my application forms from the World Health Organization that has been completed and sent to Geneva. The fellowship will cover the entire cost at this school and clinical rotations.

Meanwhile, most of the embassies I contacted have promised to help me upon consultation with their home based offices. In view of these developments I am kindly pleading that you give me 45 days extension on my payments.

Again, I sincerely regret the delay and do promised to continue to make certain that such delays never happen again. Greetings and I am waiting anxiously waiting and looking forward to your kind considerations in this matter.

Sincerely

Alhasan S. Ceesay (4026)

Dr. Paul Tien was a forthright man and he granted me the audience I requested. We met and discussed my case thoroughly and I left that meeting with the impression that he would let me finish the current semester but may not be allowed to register for the next semester if no money appeared.

Two weeks later the Catholic Mission's promise failed to materialize because someone told them of the difficulties I had with previous sponsors from Michigan.

Whoever spoke to the Catholic Mission got to Dr. Tien for I shortly there after received the following thunderbolt memo from him in a memorandum directed to, copied to the registrar and the staff. It simply said, "We inform you that you will have to leave the school if all outstanding payments to the American University School are not paid by

November 18, 1988." By now I have weathered many thunder storms in my life but I have to admit this was the mother of them all and this bombshell did more than ruffle my feathers. My plight magnified many fold.

If I leave where would I head? I was not able to return to USA nor was it possible for me to return to the Gambia at the time. It was too close to my asylum fight that they would not be willing to look the other way. Montserrat was not a place to be stranded for help was certainly not going to come from a small poor island nation like it.

My having told school officials the risk I would be at if were not allowed to finish my education until the promises show up made them worry more for fear that I may after all not be able to get help with the payments needed to clear the outstanding bills. The school was not going to continue with the build up of unpaid bills surrounded by uncertainty that help may not surface sooner.

My fighting spirit was rekindled and I fought back with the only means at my disposal, my mind, pen and paper. I wrote endless letters to America, Britain, France, Canada, Russia, Saudi Arabia, United Emirates, Japan and numerous other countries embassies appealing for assistance to complete my medical training.

I emphasized the need to help me out of my precarious state my standing was at AUC in Montserrat. The saying that, "A drowning man will hang onto any straw for dear life." Was very true in my case. I would write to any name or organization suggested to me.

For some reason I was confident that Britain, Canada, France USA or Japan would come to my rescue. Why? I guess it was just a hunch and out of admiration for these countries and their stand against injustice and currently having done a lot for people in Africa.

Initial responses from the British, American, and Canadian Embassies suggested that I write to their counter part embassies based in the Gambia for these administers assistance program available to the Gambian national.

It dashed all my hope of getting help as long as it had to involve Gambia or emissaries located in the Gambia. If the Gambia were able to influence the state department as the ambassador did in my asylum case, what would it not do with people next door and in the Gambia?

Nonetheless, the embassies wished me good luck in my search for financial relief and continuance of my medical education. The replies were copied to their respective offices in the Gambia.

The Japanese embassy said it was unable to help at that moment.Meanwhile the medical school campus reeled with the news of my financial plight and the termination of my schooling until when I can pay up all outstanding bills to the American University of the Caribbean.

The students rallied and collected donations in my behalf without my knowing for fear that I will feel obliged to them or feel pity for myself. I will never ever forget their kindness, especially; Robert G. Carter, Luis Shone, Mohamed Saleh, and Nahil who spear headed the whole affair in my behalf with tact and respect.

With the donation I bought food and reduced a portion of the outstanding bills. It neither dented the amount I owed the school nor gave me leeway to continue my schooling for that semester. I continued to be embattled by unforeseen events while time flies. I kept on pleading for help worldwide.

Finally I met the Dean and accepted to take a leave of absence effective from October 12, 1988 to January 1989 with hope that enough money would be raised to allow me to register for the upcoming semester. January 1989 has now become the new deadline but I cannot attend classes until then and only if all outstanding bills were paid by registration day.

Worse, I have to repeat the fourth semester all over as it was going to be erased from the record that I attended it. None of the exams I took during the said forth semester were acceptable for recording because of none payment of tuition fees.

I left the Dean's office with tears welling uncontrollably down my cheeks. What a life! I said to myself. I thank God for the challenge and asked for His guidance. The students felt very sorry and sad for me and feared the worst.

There were those who seriously believed that I might end up taking my life because of the effect of series of disappointments from organization, churches and governments.

Hence the students made certain that someone was around me most of the time chatting or bringing notes for me to copy and read ahead of the coming semester.

They reassured me that some have written to their parents requesting money earmarked for me to lighten my burden. Yes, the human heart is good for all these acts of kindness were done without my knowing them taking place on my behalf.

They certainly did their utmost in trying to enlighten and lighten my spirit. The propensity to sudden roadblocks, some how, seem to be the ordain way for me.

Nonetheless friends like Mr. & Mrs. Bill Johnson of Birmingham, Michigan, Lois R. Leonard, Ferry Burns, Cloyd Ramsey and Nelson Herron among others became very special as they brought cheers to my life and accorded me all the moral and financial support they could give at the time.

Here are the synapses of the angels who made life bearable foe me the time. Jerry Burns and I met through a mutual friend and had since then built up a very unique friendship.

He is a nurse and former Peace Corp who served in Niger during the John F. Kennedy era. He fell in love with Niger and her people who inundated with kindness.

He liked their culture and systems, their good nature and hard working of the Niger Fulas. He developed strong bond with the Niger people. Never did two have similar philosophies, religious tolerance, and political views than he and I.

We are just like twins living in distant lands both with nursing backgrounds and are committed to being our brother/sister's keeper. We always had lively and cheerful meetings in which we discuss trends and shifts of values, global politics, governments, schools and at times about as flimsy as the decadence one sees at certain parts of Detroit' Cass corridor. He helped relentlessly to lighten my plight and we remain in contact to today.

Mr. & Mrs. William (Bill) J. Johnson came to my sphere through their son Bill Johnson, jr. who was at the time a class mate of mine at Wayne State University in Detroit.

There an unbelievable bond of friendship developed between Bill jr. and I. Biochemistry graduate level was not a forum where most make friends. But for Bill jr. and I it started here and never faded.

My forty-third-birth day was just two weeks and because of it Bill calls me the grand daddy of the class.

I was the oldest and poorest in that class and very soon our classmates relaxed about my age. The Johnson's were very kind and friendly people and cared a lot about plight of others. Bill Jr. was intelligent, gentle, compassionate and alert to current affairs.

Come my birthday he crowned the occasion with a special gift. He met me at school and in his modest and gentle way quietly and simply said, "Please accept this little token to remember your day with." I was happy and grateful for we had only casually known each other less than a month and here was Bill sharing my day as he showers it with kindness. The moment and graciousness of the act remained indelibly etched in my mind to today.

Bill works part time for a mining company and anted school on part time bases. Our conversations ranged from the spiraling downward education, politics, the developing world of Africa, people's basic needs and how to meet these to bring relief to recipients. We believing improving the lives of others, in due course, improve our own. Upon learning about my difficulties at the American university of the Caribbean Bill Johnson, Jr rallied to assist me in my endeavors.

His parents generously donated one thousand dollars in addition to the two advanced donations of five hundred dollars Bill jar sent me. The Johnson's continued to touch my heart with tender hearts of generosity and sharing I will never forget.

I visited the family few days before heading for Montserrat during which time they spoiled with gifts and dinner fit for a king. They tried to stuff me so as to put some pad of fat on my skeletal frame.

It goes without doubts that I engorged myself to the ears and yet remained the featherweight I came in with.

Most of the discussion centred on my plight with the Gambia, my determination to over come it and return as positive contributor to the Gambia. They told of having wonderful time and had lots of friends during their diplomatic tenure in Africa. It is William J. Johnson's believe that the third world needed more aid from America then been forthcoming in recent times.

I left them with full appreciation of the humane concerns for other and the wish to help the developing world. Bill Jr's father Mr. William J. Johnson was U.S. Ambassador to Kenya during the Kennedy presidency.

He too fell in love with Africa. He and lovely wife Majorette Johnson made many return trips to Kenya and other neighboring African states. Hence, I was family from day one of our meeting to new.
Despite the fact that I have been away from the U>S>A. for years we still write to each other and they continued helping me find solutions to the seemingly endless financial woes that beset my life and educational pursuits.
Hence, when AUC threatened to end my schooling, it was through kind contributions of the Johnsons that helped pay an outstanding bill of three thousand dollars to the American University of the Caribbean school of Medicine. This came in at the nick of time or at very critical moment for me in my adventure to gain medical education and return to serve the Gambia.
AUC was taken by surprise in manner I cleared all outstanding bills in time to reregister for the forth semester I lost during the financial fiasco of 1988/89 academic year for the basic medical sciences courses.
Both AUC and I send a thank you note to the William Johnson and family for magnanimity and kindness shown by their helping out at the school. Praises be God's for letting such kind people come to my rescue at the nick of time when everything looked hopelessly bleak.
Germane to my survival were insistence that failure be not the last chapter in the saga of my experience and that the Gambia be the benefactor in all these mesh, which will remain in my mind for some time. The most rewarding element was the steadfastness with which my friends backed my seemingly never-

ending stride towards the Doctor of Medicine degree (MD). Amongst these were long time friend and colleague at Alpena Community College (1967 – 69) in Michigan. Nelson Herron, who became unique friend since we met at Alpena.

Upon hearing about decision of AUC regarding my medical training, Nelson Herron, out of kindness and concern for me, voluntarily lent me another $4600.00 to reduce the huge bill I then owe the school and to advance towards my registration fees. Without these inputs from the Johnsons and Nelson Herron my medical education/training at AUC would have come to an abrupt nose dive for oblivion or a catastrophic end as envisioned by Richard Smith and his followers.

No matter how brilliant one is, going through uphill challenges the way I had was, to say the least, frustrating, challenging, and worse way to have to go through competitive medical school in such a fashion.

I was never sure if my registration would be completed, cancelled or where the next penny was going to come from to help me finish my schooling. By this time my pride gave way and I turned into a beggar as I had very little choice or control over events that kept unfolding in my path.

Like a mule leaden with bags of salt, I struggled under the yoke of poverty being buoyed only by constant surge of inextinguishable ambition to forge ahead for the Gambia and my fellow men.

To this were the phenomenal encouragements I received from Americans. Channing Poiock said, "The only good luck many great men ever had was being born with the ability and determination to overcome bad luck." My life at this stage had blossomed to one percent inspiration and ninety-nine percent perspirations. Things were not relenting and I could not help my wife or parents back in the Gambia.

Remember, our cultural norms and obligations made it obvious that a forty plus male should be able to care not only for himself but also for his aged parent and others, rather than being stuck in class at a desolate impoverish island like Montserrat in the West Indies.

Bellow is samples of requests and replies that trickled by after a lengthy wait and hope of getting help.

World Health Organization
CH1211, Geneve 27, Suise
March 29, 1088

Dear Mr. Ceesay,

In reply to your letter of March 8,1988, we would inform that WHO fellowships can only be awarded at the request of the candidates' national Health Authority.

We would advise you, therefore, to write to the Gambia Ministry of Health asking to be nominated for such a fellowship. You will receive the relevant application forms from the Ministry if they are willing to sponsor your candidature.

Yours Sincerely
Mrs. B. J. Amara
Fellowship Division of
Health Manpower development

This was sent after I told them my predicament with the Gambia. The Canadian version ran thus

Bureau Des Conseillers Technique
De La Cooperation Canadiene
P. 3373, Dakar, Senegal
December 5, 1988

Dear Sir,

This is to acknowledge receipt of your letter of September 21, regarding a scholarship from the Canadian International Development Agency. The number of scholarships available is extremely limited and all applications are coordinated through the Ministry of Education of the Gambia, North American scholarships.
Thus we suggest that you contact the Ministry in Banjul for information on current scholarship programs. Thank you for your interest in studies in Canada.
Yours sincerely
Alime touzim
Coordinator Des bourses ACDI
The only reply that shaded light of hope was from the British High Commission in Banjul, the Gambia of all places. Upon getting my letter the staff of the Commission got in touch with the Gambian authorities and after softening things, sent me the following response.

British High Commission
P.O. Box 507, Banjul
The Gambia, West Africa

November 29, 1988

Dear Mr. Ceesay,

The High commission has asked me to thank you for your letter of September 22, 1988, which did not arrive here until November 17, 1988. We were sorry to hear your financial predicaments. But unfortunately we are unable to help you as scholarships scheme is run as government to government basis only.
In other words, you would need to receive official backing from the government of the Gambia before we may consider sponsoring you. However we have spoken to the Ministry of Health. I do hope that you were able to find a sponsor in time.
Yours Sincerely
Paul Chart
These and many more like in kind from world embassies and countries left one thing clear to me that destiny is not a matter of chance it is a unique question of one's choice.
And medicine is my committed choice for which I am willing to continue the struggle to the day I get the MD degree and eventual return to serve the Gambia as a dedicated physician.
I have always been convinced that all good things start in difficulty before becoming easy and rewarding. I again, in desperation, lunched another barrage of appeals and even contacted Mr. Paul Chart at the British High Commission in Banjul as if though his last letter of November 29, 1988 never reached me.

Paul replied reiterating reasons in this previous letter and made it clear that the High Commission will not sponsor me. He concluded by saying, "However, I have taken the liberty of mentioning your predicament to Dr. Hatib Njie, Director of Medical services at the Department of Health in Banjul, in hope that he may be able to suggest a solution to your problems."

Here you have it. The Pandora's box opened by Paul Chart's discussion of the matter with the Director was the following:

Medical and Health Department
Medical Headquarters
Banjul, The Gambia
February 21, 1989

Reference MED/109

RE: application for sponsorship

Dear Mr. Ceesay

I write to inform you that Permanent Secretary Management Office is the person in charge of training at home and abroad.
You may therefore apply directly to him for sponsorship. Send your application to him as quickly as possible.
Yours Sincerely,
Signed for Director
Medical services
The Gambia

At this juncture small opportunities like this one were not left alone or unexplored. I at the back of my mind was expecting nothing to come out from the Gambia.

However I wasted no time and prepared an application with the following letters of support from various staff and current Dean of Medicine at the American University of the Caribbean School of Medicine in Montserrat, West Indies.

Here are a few of the letters sent along with my application.

American University of the Caribbean
P.O. Box 400
Plymouth, Montserrat
West Indies

March 23, 1989

TO WHOM IT MAY CONCERN

Mr. Alhasan Ceesay has requested that I write a letter in support of his request for financial aid in completing his medical training. I have known Mr. Ceesay for several years as his professor in Physiology and as the Dean of the Medical sciences. Mr. Ceesay is a very personable and articulate man who interacts well with both the faculty and his classmates.

He is a hard working student who is totally dedicated to becoming a physician and practicing medicine in the Gambia. Thus far Mr. Ceesay has had to endure major financial problems in his pursuit of a medical degree.

I feel Mr. Ceesay is very deserving of financial support for the remainder of his training and will become a compassionate, competent and caring physician for his people.
Sincerely
Robert J. Chetok, PhD
Prof. Of Physiology
Dean of Medical Sciences

Another letter was from. Dr. D. E. Vonwomer, my professor of Pathology and retired former Dean of the College of Medicine, AUC.

American University of the Caribbean
P. O. Box 400
Plymouth, Montserrat
West Indies
March 25, 1989

TO WHOM IT MAY CONCERN

Mr. Alhasan Ceesay has asked me for a letter supporting his application for financial support for the remainder of his medical schooling. Mr. Ceesay is a hard working student and who spends many hours preparing him to become a physician. He is highly motivated and spends most of the hours of his day studying so be might become a physician to serve the people of the Gambia.
Mr. Ceesay is extremely consciencious, very diligent in his work, and is also very pleasant cooperative young man. He is well liked by his fellow students and his professors and gets along well with all. This young man has a very critical financial problem.

He needs financial support to continue the last half of his medical school curriculum. I hope it is possible for someone to assist this dedicated man so he will be able to return to his country and practice medicine.
Sincerely
D. E. Vanwormer, MD
Professor of Pathology
Advisor.
The final addendum from the American University of the Caribbean to be sent to the Gambia was a note from the Registrar of the university, Mrs. Mary R. Tuit, Who sent the following.

American University of the Caribbean
School of Medicine
Plymouth, Montserrat
West Indies

RE: Application for financial Assistance

Mr. Ceesay is 5th semester student at the American university of the Caribbean School of Medicine. He will finish basic sciences in August 1989. Mr. Ceesay is expected to take up clinical assignments at the East borne District General Hospital, England coming September 1989.
The administration of the school will be grateful if you will facilitate financially his continuance of his studies. Any further courtesies extended to him will be greatly appreciated. Clinical in England will cost another $6450 per semester. See enclosed breakdown of payments.

Respectfully
Mary R. Tuit
Registrar

These and lot more from my professors at the university were packaged and sent registered mail to the Permanent Secretary, Personnel Management, Banjul, the Gambia, as advised by the Director of Health's letter of February 12, 1989.
The school staffs were relieved and confident the financial burden would soon become history and be off my shoulders since to their expectation the letters of support were going to be the barometer of my progress and for the scholarship committee in the Gambia to look at in making final decision on my appeal.
Knowing what I knew and have gone through from the hands of the Gambia government, I just prayed for the reversal of tides in my favour so that I can move forward with my objective of serving the Gambians.
My fears and expectations were brought to light three months later when I received the following reply from an official in behalf of the Permanent Secretary, Personnel Management Office. Here is the full text of that heart-wrenching missive in reply to my request for financial assistance at a crucial stage of my medical training.

Personnel Management Office
The Quadrangle, Banjul
The Gambia
West Africa
June 13, 1989

EST/X811E/TEMP/C82

REQUEST FOR SPONSORSHIP TO UNDERTAKE A MEDICAL DEGREE: MR. ALHASAN S. CEESAY

I wish to acknowledge receipt of your letter dated March 28, 1989, in which you requested this office to seek assistance on your behalf from the British government in the form of scholarship award, so as to enable you to complete your medical degree at the American University of the Caribbean School of Medicine.
In this regard I am directed to inform you that our 1989/90 overseas Development Training Program has been finalized and it is therefore too late to make any provisions for you in the aforementioned program.
Sorry for our inability to be of much help to you in this circumstances.
Sincerely,
L.T. Jorbateh
For Permanent Secretary

If I had not applied prior to writing then doubts wound continue to linger between the Gambia Ministry of Health and I. I had prior to applying for financial assistance asked the Director if the said Overseas Development Program was then still available.
I was told by the Director to send my application quickly for he had had a word with the Permanent Secretary of the Personnel Management Office. Anyhow, if adversity reveals genius now was the time for something to happen for me.

I had already been assigned to a hospital for my clinical training and now the last straw of hope and source of financial relief I expected slipped by in thin air. Like before, I accepted my fate and said, "God I know you care and love me and you will help me solve this difficult hillock.
No one can stand the assault of sustained challenges. I will endure as ordained by your wish." Louisa May Alcott said, "Far away there in the sunshine are my highest aspirations. I may not reach them, but I can look up and see their beauty, believe in them and try to follow where they lead."
Is it not true that obstacles are those frightful things we see when we take our eyes off our goals? No hillock or crisis like this development will ruffle my feathers.
I continued to swim towards my ship, instead of waiting for it to come to me. I braced up again and wrote several letters and asked friends to write in my behalf to any organization or government they think would come to my assistance for the medical degree meant a lot not only for me but the villager whom I intend to provide modern affordable medicines.
In this desperate state of my life, Jacob Riis' statement said it best for me. He said, "When nothing seem to help, I go and look at the stonecutter hammering away at his rock perchance a hundred times without as much a crack showing in it.
Yet, at the hundred and first blow it will split into two, and I know it was not that blow that did it, but all that had gone before." I am another stonecutter, mine comprises of humans, the most harden element on earth, so to speak, that I will be

relentless with my unyielding rock, the MD degree, for my people, until I receive the right to practice in Gambia and Africa. Each day is a specific thrill that leads to that exhilarating moment of victory for Gambia and mankind.

It is a hard march toward the day I will be able to serve the Gambia as a physician. I feel favoured, if not blessed, having Mrs. Lois R. Leonard on my side. I became her potage when she came to discover my strength, perseverance, and endurance to face very difficult challenges.

She was the only member of the remaining Ceesay Support Committee that did not throw the towel at my face, present at the backstabbing meeting held while my friends Richard castigated me. Lois shared my agonies and ecstasy as events unfolded during my stay in Montserrat, West Indies.

She and a few others were source of relief and blessings to me. Lois Leonard would once on a while send me fifty dollars to put food into my dying body held by skeletal frame that refuses to be dismembered by starvation.

Upon hearing about my assignment do clinical rotation at Eat Borne she rallied friends and collected seven thousand dollars to help me start my clinical clerkship. Unfortunately the money had to be applied to clear unpaid past bills I owe the school.

The university would not let me move without the remaining financial bill being cleared. This development adversely affected my classes for that semester. However, I remained obliged to Lois Leonard even though she was no longer able to help since she had exhausted all resources and contacts available to her, which she lamented. On hindsight had the Gambia not fought back my clinical clerkship would not have been delayed or postponed to September 1990 the very least cost went higher as tuition was increase to $4600 a semester.

Henry Forth said, "Failure is the opportunity to begin again more intelligently." So like Abraham Lincoln who said, "I will do the best I know how, the very best I can, and I mean to keep on doing it to the end.

If the end brings me out all right, what is said against me will not amount to anything. If the end brings me out wrong, then ten angels swearing I was right would make no difference."

Chapter 33

WELCOME TO UNITED STATE TEXAS

Let our narration detour in time to bring other events I passed through before the above developments. The kaleidoscope, which followed hurricane Hugo, only multiplied the whirlwinds of worries that were running through my head. I had just finished three courses and had taken the last of nine exams I was assigned and needed $18,000 us dollars to enable me start the clinical phase after my last semester at the Texas Campus.

A void followed despite a series of telephone call to would be sympathetic persons in the USA and Canada. I waited for days and weeks and nothing seem to materialize to allow me start the clinical clerkship after Texas. On December 19, 1989, Rudolf Kurt and his wife Sophie Kurt invited me for a chat and lunch with them.

This day was another pivotal one in the saga of my life. After lunch and a detailed history of my case, these aged German couple, turned events around for a good start in my career. As reneged will have it, one thing lead to another until when, to my delightful surprise, Rudolf and Wife Sophie Kurt, revealed that they have agreed to lend me $6000.00 (six thousand dollars!) to help me start my clinical studies in England.

Rudolf went cross and brought a checkbook and made two separate checks of three thousand dollars each to the American University of the Caribbean. One was to be applied toward completing the outstanding tuition bills and the other to be used directly towards my clinical training in the United Kingdom. I, in utter disbelieve shrouded with gratitude, hugged and thanked them several times and promised them that they will never regret helping me.

I was released to go and I ran from the condominium to the American University of the Caribbean financial officer, Mr. Soong, supervising the renovation of the campus. I made the payments to the University's account at the Barclays Bank down town Plymouth and he issued receipts to that effect and cleared my outstanding bills with the university.

Mr. Soong then called Texas to AUC allow me join the students at Wayland Baptist University where AUC is piggy bagging the after effect of hurricane Hugo, in Plainview. The following letter and events after them signaled some relief in my blighted life. Some earlier appeals for sponsorship yielded enough to allow me start arranging for a visa to travel to the United States to complete my basic medical sciences.

Two days after I made those payments and for some reason the owner and president of the American University, Dr. Paul Tien, showed up on campus with engineers to estimate the cost of rebuilding the university. I wasted no time bringing my newfound luck to light and went to meet him as soon as friends told me of his being in the Island.

I requested that he add his weight to my attempt to secure a visa from the American Consulate at Antigua for me to travel to Texas and join the rest of the students at the campus of Wayland Baptist

University in Plainview. He was very happy to oblige. When he finished he school my hands and said, "Ceesay, you are a good fighter. You have my respect and good luck in your clinical training." This was what he told the US emissary:

American University of the Caribbean
School of Medicine
P.O. Box 400
Plymouth, Montserrat
December 20, 1989

Consulate
Visa Section
U. S. Embassy
Antigua, West Indies

Dear Sir,

This is to inform you that I support the request for a visa application made by Alhasan S. Ceesay. Mr. Ceesay is a student of the American University of the Caribbean. He wishes to enter the United States in other to take the last classes of the basic sciences before proceeding to England for his clinical experience.
Upon completing his residency program, he will return to practice medicine in the Gambia. All assistance to him to enable him complete his studies would be most welcomed. Thank you for your help in this matter.
Sincerely
Dr. Paul Tien
American Univ. of the Caribbean

The following day I bravely held onto my letters and flew to Antigua and reported at the visa section of the U. S. Embassy 8.00 A.M the next morning.
I was among first to be interviewed and I imaged smiling gleefully for a visa had been granted and affixed on my passport.
I can now join my colleagues four months after hurricane Hugo and very laborious work at the condominiums. I boarded TWA and headed once more for the United States of America.
This time I landed in Miami International Airport in Florida and took a shuttle flight to Lubbock airport in Texas. I was expecting to meet Dr. Steve Deschner at this Airport but he failed to turn up because of changes in his scheduled lectures and that of my flight.
This posed no difficulty for me, having been in America as long as I did. I just went to the bus stand and took the one marked Plainview. I arrived at the Wayland Baptist University in Plainview, where the American university of the Caribbean had temporally relocated after hurricane Hugo. I lodged with a student until the next day when I completed the formalities of registering for my last basic medical science courses.
The office used money lent to me by the Kurts of Montserrat to cover areas I thought have been taken care off. The officer insisted that the previous semester was not fully covered even though I showed that three thousand us dollars was paid in Montserrat.
This stalemate put me back into square one and only worst I had no one to turn to in Texas except the Almighty God. I still feel cheated by AUC for

having to find that my payments were not regularized to erase the outstanding bill on record. The financial nightmare of my life surfaced at a very difficult transition time for me. Again, I accepted that one must whittle today for a rewarding tomorrow.

All that mattered was for work and struggle to go on, the curse endured, hope still lives and that my dream shall never die. I am part of all that I have endured and met. I will strive to seek, to find and never yield to challenge.

I made a concerted effort to visit churches and tell whomever I meet on the way what my plight was and that I desperately needed a loan to help me finish my medical education. It was during one of these trips that I came across an angel from the blue, in the body of Rev. Mark D. Meyer.

He was then in charge of St. Mark's Episcopal Church on 710 Joliet Street, Plainview, Texas. I found him at the entrance of St. Mark's Church just about to leave to minister to an old man, a member of the Parish who was under the weather.

One look at my faced made him decide to listen to my narrative and about the urgency of it. He expressed dismay at the fact that I was left stranded for four months in tiny Montserrat hopelessly destroyed by hurricane Hugo.

He could not believe the heartlessness of not being evacuated along with the American students. The American University of the Caribbean just abandoned me to find my way out of Montserrat while the American Consulate flew American and Canadian students back to America.

The end result of the short conversation was an extensive interview about my goal and utilization of my training was an invitation with his Sunday service group on the following Sunday.

He revealed, during our meeting, that he too was a medical aspirant but changed his vocation to the Priesthood before getting too far into the art of Medicine He also said his father was a doctor and a member of the board of the American Medical association.

My eyes opened widely hearing that I now have someone interested in me whose father's recommendation to any medical school would give weight for consideration by admission committees. I therein and then prayed silently for God's help so that this angel of His would heed my plight. Rev. Mark D. Meyer turned a God sent relief to my challenge.

He spoke to his congregation and came to Wayland Baptist University and made a down payment of $4200 (four thousand two hundred us dollars) in my name as a loan. He contributed one thousand and the rest came from Church funds. Another member of the church, Mr. John Morse gave $500 as a personal gift to me.

Rev. Mark D. Meyer's efforts did not end here for as the year waned and my financial blight remained unbearable, he asked me to stay with him at his residence on 1409 Garland Street, Plainview, Texas. I stayed there with him until it was time for me to proceed to do my clinical clerkship in England.

Through him I made a lot of friends in Plainview among who were Dr. Thomas Allen of Grace Presbyterian Church, Dr. Hoyt Huff of First Christian Church, Dr. & Mrs. Douglas E. Kopp and (The Rt. Rev) Bishop Sam B. Hulsey, Bishop of the Episcopal Diocese of North West Texas at Lubbock, just to name a few of Christ's modern day disciples who came to my aid while I was in dire financial state in the last leg f my basic medical sciences.

In response to the overwhelming generosity and Christian stand these people took in my affairs I wrote the following note of appreciation for the uniqueness of their gesture towards me and for enabling me move forward in my aspiration to serve the Gambia as a physician.

In the mean time various small gifts kept pouring in to keep me happy. Many invited me to their homes to meet with their families or have some meal with them whenever convenient. Plainview was my Texas and rev. Meyer my redeemer from earthly hell.

We refer to each other as brother in Christ and humanity.

He solicited help for me from groups like the Domestic and Foreign missionary Society of the Protestant Episcopal Church in the United States and numerous other church organizations in the USA and England.

Between us we used to write more than twenty-five letters a day appealing for help to enable me meet my goal for the Gambian villagers. Rev. Mark D. Meyer and I have same objective in life, i.e. to seek piety, by having strong faith in God, to gain knowledge to better serve our fellow human being

by providing hope and relief to those we may come across in this life and finally to live a simple human trail of love and commitment to peace and good will to all on earth.
It entailed a life of sacrifice, devotion to our faith and commitment to move forward despite deterring challenges and roadblocks we may come across.
Rev. Mark used to jokingly say to me, "Ceesay if all Muslims were like you then the whole world would been one big Christian brotherhood."
This told more about our sense of oneness that a dictionary could define in a billion words closeness of two earthly creatures of God. Here is the letter I mentioned earlier on.

American University
C/O Wayland Baptist University
Plainview, Texas, USA

Dear editor and Friends,

Sometimes god has a way of stepping into our lives when we least expected it. Such was the state which Rev. Mark D. Meyer and I. He steeped forward at a critical time of my plights and was kind and generous also helpful to my mission to serve the Gambia as a physician.
Without further adieu, I humbly and most gratefully acknowledge the loan he got for me from his kind congregation and other interested persons in Plainview.
Your kindness has touched me deeply and made me more determined to succeed and return to my country, the Gambia, in due course. Rev. Mark D.

Meyer and I have become good friends and brothers in Christ. I am most grateful to all of you for this continued contribution to the Gambian people. Please convey our profound gratitude for this unique assistance to not only members of your church but to all those who one way or the other, in various gestures of generous acts, have helped to make my path a little bit easier to walk on.

You are very special to me and in the hearts of my villagers.

I will certainly return to provide much needed modern medical service to the villages in the Gambia. We are indebted to all of you. Please come visit us. The villagers are itching to meet you and serenade you for kindness and your willingness to share generously with us so as to bring hope and relief to people in rural Gambia. Finally, God bless you and be rest assured that I will keep you informed of my progress wherever I am.

Please continue to pray for my success and eventual return to serve my people in the smiling cost of the Gambia, West Africa. Cheers and regards to all

Your friend

Alhasan S. Ceesay

Gambian/AUC student

This letter ushered in more friends from far and wide of Texas. I had people asking me to meet with them as far away as Huston, Dallas and other heartland cities in Texas.

It was also while at Garland Street that our discussions vied onto my idea of a village clinic in the future with which to fulfill my dream of bringing modern medicine to the forgotten and neglected villager's health care needs.

Again, we went into full gear and wrote to hundreds of charity groups asking for ideas and assistance on how to get started on what would later be the present Manding Medical Centre at Njawara village, The Gambia, West Africa.

Most of the replies stress that only local organizations were eligible for possible funding and that most were already too committed to take on any other aspirants like my clinic.

These negative replies had a little dampening effect on our drive but we pushed on as hard as can be to raise funds for the future Manding Medical Centre. We did developed friendship with architectural group, L. James Robinson and Associates, located at 205 West 4th Street, Plainview, Texas, 790723, headed by Mr. L. James Robinson.

This friendly rapport led to the first architectural plan of Manding Medical Centre. We only altered few parts to suit the Gambian environment and the board and any who saw it had unanimously adopted the plan.

The above made a unique hospital plan that would when completed will stand the test of time and will serve its intended purpose. Time flew fast and soon came the most difficult event between two that have become one in spirit.

My basic medical courses ended in July 1990 and arrangements were afoot for me to proceed to either Kinston Hospital, Kingston upon -Thames, or Essex County Hospital, Colchester, England by September 1990 to do my clinical clerkship.

The last week was very intense for both of us. Leaving for good or for a long time was unbearable. Rev. Mark D. Meyer had, like Mr. L.A. Bouvier, become the ideal friend and an honest person to turn to. We are totally devoted folks to our believes and causes and we care a lot about plight of the downtrodden of life.

Meanwhile, the American University of the Caribbean sent the following letter to Mrs. Mickey, Program Coordinator, Kingston Hospital informing her about my plans to do my clinical clerkship at their hospital.

American University of the Caribbean
School of Medicine
P. O. Box 400
Plymouth, Montserrat
West Indies July 14, 1990

Mrs. Mickey,
Program Coordinator
Kingston Hospital
Gals worthy Road
Kingston Upon Thames
Surry KT2 7BE
England, Uk

Dear Mrs. Mickey,

This letter is being sent on behalf of Alhasan Ceesay, a student of the American university of the Caribbean School of Medicine. Mr. Ceesay is a citizen of the Gambia and in other to obtain his visa to come to England the British Consulate requested a letter be sent from you stating that he has been accepted into your clinical program.

I have spoken with Dr. Youel in this regards and he has informed me that he will be assigning Mr. Ceesay to your program to begin on September 3, 1990. I have sent the student a letter to this effect to take to the consulate's office.
However, they also require a letter directly from the hospital. As the US visa will be expiring in July, at which time he will need to relocate to England, will you please send a letter as soon as possible to the British Consulate-General, Suit 2250, Dresser Tower, 601 Jefferson, Huston, Texas 77002, attention, Mrs. H. M. Tanks, British vice Consul. We appreciate your assistance in this matter. May I also request that you send a copy of the letter for me to place it in Mr. Ceesay's file. Thank you.
Sincerely
Jackie R. Allen
Secretary to Liaison Official
Another letter dated September 1990 was sent to Essex County after an unforeseen delay in hearing from the British High Commission in Huston, Texas. It read,

American University of the Caribbean
School of Medicine, P. O. Box 400
Plymouth, Montserrat
September 6th 1990

Dear Dr. Peter R. Wilson,

Alhasan Ceesay has been assigned to begin clinical clerkship at Essex County Hospital, Colchester on October 8, 1990. This is to certify that Mr. Ceesay is academically qualified and administratively approved

to begin the clinical clerkship program at the American university of the Caribbean School of Medicine as a third year medical student in September 1990.
Signed: David Bruce Youel, M.D
Robert Chertok, PhD
Dean of Clinical Sciences, Dean of Medical Science

Dr. Alhasan Kunsa Ceesay: Badibou Folklore

I took this last with me to Huston and after a lengthy interview disproving allegation I choused England to emigrate instead of just doing my clinical. I made it very clear that had that been my intention I will not select UK being already on American soil.
The officer after few minutes of reflection concord and offered me student visa to attend Essex County Hospital's clinical program in Colchester, Essex, England in October 1990.

Chapter 34

ENGLAND AT LAST: CLINICAL TRAINING
1990

I flew to the British Consulate at Huston, Texas to be interviewed for a visa to enter the United Kingdom to do my clinical clerkship at the Essex County Hospital in Colchester by October 8, 1990. No, my financial curse never left me.
It was a dragon that would show its head again and again while I was in England. Rev. Mark D. Meyer went with me up to Lubbock airport on the day of my travels to the UK.
At Lubbock airport, we prayed and hugged each other, with eyes full of tears, several times before we could say our final goodbyes. I left Huston with a student visa and boarded BA flight 0224 on the September 12, 1990 heading for Heathrow International Airport, London, England.
I landed at Heathrow on Wednesday September 12, 1990. My impression of England and her people never disappointed me.
The people were friendly but much more business like. The immigration Officer received my document and placed a call to Essex County hospital to verify status as student with them. This done a leave to remain in the U.K was stamped onto my passport and allowed to proceed to my final destination, Colchester.
Arrangements were made for me to stay at a hotel call the George located at the High street down town Colchester, Essex County. The hotel staff was very kind and helpful as they brought food from

nearby restaurant because the hotel kitchen had closed for the night when I arrived at o1.35 a.m. The following day, at about 8.30 Am. I reported to Dr. Peter R. Wilson's office, clinical program director for the American university of the Caribbean, at Essex county Hospital in Colchester. I later on that day met Mrs. Penny West, a very kind lady, the program administrator for further briefing of our program and what was expected of us while in England.

There I met two other Americans ladies and two gentlemen students from previous classes at the American university of the Caribbean School of Medicine, who also came to do their clinical clerkship at Essex county Hospital.

I was moved from the hotel to flat 2 Kensington Court, 47 Roman Road, Colchester administered by the Pullars estate agents. We went through one week of orientation and familiarizing ourselves where about the shops and postal services, bus stations for the National Express services and many other things of interest in the city.

We were then issued schedules and units and department/ assignment to begin our clinical training. I was only able to pay for the first semester of the training because promises to help me finish failed to materialize. This led Rev. Mark D. Meyer to lend me another $2000 (two thousand us dollars) on March 6, 1990 and again another personal loan of $900 (nine hundred us dollars) later.

These monies were deposited to the university in my name but the cost per semester was $4600 leaving me $1700 short of meeting my financial obligation to the school for the second semester at the clinics.

It was during those frustrating moments that I decided to bite the bullet and called a long time Gambian friend of mine, Dr. Ebrahima Malick Samba, to come to my rescue. This he did by promptly calling his bank in London and authorizing them to send me three thousand seven hundred pounds sterling loan to help me complete the semester.

I received it with gratitude and humility. Praises be God's for only through Him have miracles been happening for me. Two weeks later the same bank sent another equal amount allotment from Dr. Samba.

In my acknowledgement letter I thanked Dr. Samba for the two disbursements and told him that the University had already debited them to my accounts to clear the outstanding bills. Later that week the bank called and wrote to say they made a mistake by sending me the second allotment from Dr. Samba's account and that I should return the money forthwith.

At the time all monies sent to me had already been applied toward my fees at the American university of the Caribbean. Dr. Ebrahima Malick Samba kindly intervened and blamed the bank for the mistake and let me now owe him Four thousand four hundred pounds sterling instead of the original approved three thousand seven hundred pound sterling.

No other Gambian would have acquiescence other than this angel friend of mine. He proved to be true and true real friend in need and in good times. I will reimburse him all monies I owe him whenever my earnings improve.

This saga allowed me to sail on through until November 11, 1991. The bubble busted again. AUC threatened to throw me out of the program upon my failure to meet payment of the balance of my areas with the school.
This treat lead Dr. Peter R. Wilson, Program Director for AUC at Essex County Hospital to intervene with the following letter to Dr. Bruce Youel, Dean of Clinical sciences for the American university of the Caribbean.

Colchester and North Essex
Postgraduate Center
Essex County Hospital
Colchester, Essex CO3 3NB

Dr. Bruce Yuoel
Dean of Clinical Sciences
American University of the Caribbean
April 24, 1991

Dear Dr. Youel

RE: Alhasan Ceesay

As Director of the AUC students in Colchester I take exceptions to the highhanded and unreasonable attitude in regards to this trainee doctor who has hitherto given you no cause for anxiety in respect of his funding and through no fault of his own has found himself in dire financial distress because his government has in some way delayed funding.
I am making every effort on his behalf to find someone to help him financially by contacting the

Gambia High Commission etc and I expect you to allow him adequate time to sort out his finances. I shall continue to provide him with clinical training here and I expect you to honour that and I shall be in touch with you before the end of May to see if we can reach suitable compromise.

I would like you to decided whether you can offer any financial help yourself and when and what scholarship you are prepared to offer him.

Yours Sincerely
Dr. Peter R. Wilson
AUC Program Director
Colchester General Hospital

Dr. Peter Wilson not only looked for more sources of help to alleviate my situation but he generously donated one thousand pounds sterling from his bank for me to pay AUC and the rent at 47 Roman Road in Colchester.

Among other letters seeking financial help for me was one sent to the student adviser, Mr. Peter Bird, of the African Education Trust on 38 King Street, London on March 20, 1991.

Dr. Peter R. Wilson
Program Director for AUC
Essex County Hospital
Colchester, Essex CO3 3NB

Mr. Peter Bird
Advisor
African Education Trust
38 King Street
London
March 20, 1991

Dear Sir,

RE: Alhasan S. Ceesay

I enclosed confidential letter of recommendation for the above student for you consideration. Please do not hesitate to contact me if you feel I can be of any further assistance.
Yours faithfully
Dr. Peter R. Wilson
AUC Program Director

CONFIDENCIAL LETTER OF RECOMMENDATION FOR MR. ALHASAN S. CEESAY

Alhasan is an extremely consciencious and competent man, determined against all odds to complete a Doctorate course in medicine, so that he can return to use his knowledge to serve his people. I have no doubts about his sincerity of his purpose nor of his dedication and hard work and various scholarships he had earned en route.
He managed to be one of few rural students without financial backing from his family or government to receive secondary education and gained one of the extremely rare university entrances and took a masters of science degree before embarking on his medical studies.
Enrolled after years of hard work in the USA trying to save enough money during his undergraduate career in science in the states, he joined the American University of the Caribbean as a matured student for his clinical training and funded himself

through the first five semesters of this course. He applied to come to England as do many students from this university in order to gain his clinical experience in an English hospital and was assured by the Gambia high Commission that he had been warded a Commonwealth Foundation training scholarship for the remainder of his clinical training. Only after beginning his training in the UK did he discovered that the Commonwealth foundation Training body were unable to fulfill their apparent promise to the Gambia High Commission and since then he has been desperately borrowing money from those who sponsored him during his training hitherto and has written many letters since then begging for help from the Gambia Ministry of Health and Education Department.
He has been unable to any more than token financial help. Anything you can do to help now will enable this very consciencious man to complete his course. It would be tragedy if he were not able do so. He has, to my knowledge, many letters of support to back mine; which he will also be submitting to you. I have no doubt.
Peter R. Wilson
Program Director
Severals Hospital
Colchester, Essex

On February 22, 1991 the Bishop of Colchester, The Rt. Rev Michael E. Vikers, sent the following appeal in my behalf to Hon. Bakary Darboe, Vice president and Minister of Education, Banjul, The Gambia, West Africa. It read:

Dear Vice President/Minister of Education

RE: Mr. Alhasan S. Ceesay

I understand from Mr. Ceesay, with whom I have been speaking this morning, that he was on the telephone to you either yesterday or the day before, about the financial crisis, which threatens to place the completion of his studies in jeopardy and end the possibility of his returning as a trained physician to the Gambia.

I have been drawn into Mr. Ceesay's situation over the last four months, partly through a colleague in the United States who was able to give some assistance and encouragement during an earlier stage of his studies.

I can vouch for the critical nature of his present situation and I am sure that you will wish to do anything that you can to assist him. His university has recently told him that, unless he is able to pay the tuition fees due, $5200 (five thousand two hundred us dollars) by the 5th of April, 1991 he will be placed on a financial leave of absence during which time he will not be permitted to continue classes. With best wishes

Yours sincerely

Bishop Michael E. Vickers

Some help surfaced but not from the Gambia government. A Liza Gilbert replied to one of several appeals both Dr. Peter r. Wilson and I sent to The Africa Education Grant Advisory Service in London and gave the following good news for decades.

Assistant student Advisor
African Education Grant
38 king street
London
May 23, 1991

Mr. a. s. Ceesay
Flat 2, Kensington Court
47 Roman Road
Colchester, Essex CO1 1UR

Our ref: EG91/0123

Dear Mr. Ceesay

Further to your case I am pleased to inform you that the Education Committee of the family welfare association has kindly agreed to make you an award to assist you in your present difficulties. A cheque in enclosed made payable to your place of study as previously explained.
I would be grateful if you could acknowledge receipt of this check. It you take the enclosed cheque to the finance off ice of your college they will be able to administer it for you and will either draw up a further cheque or pay the grant in cash.
Enclosed is two thousand six hundred pounds sterling for fees. The committee has asked that if the ministry in Gambia do eventually pay the fees, they could be re-embossed but do not expect repayment otherwise. With best wishes for the future.
Yours Sincerely
Liza Gilbert
Assistant student Advisor

Prior to the above letter I had applied to dr. Peter r. Wilson to contact the Postgraduate Committee in my behalf for possible assistance with an emergency loan of six thousand five hundred pounds sterling to enable me pay the rest of the remaining two and half semesters of my clinical training.

Rev. Mark Meyer and Mrs. Lois R. Leonard also made efforts to collect money for me. Mark sent $500 on 28/10/91 followed by another $2600 on 25/11/91 and finally $900 on the 27/3/92.

All these monies went into payment of tuition fees and rent. To add fuel to fire, the university increased its tuition fees up 6% throwing students like me into more financial crisis than can be imagined.

Dr. Peter R. Wilson was also successful with his appeal from the Postgraduate Committee to which amount he added his own one thousand pounds sterling as a loan to me. He informed me of the grant from the Postgraduate Committee thus;

Colchester and North East Essex
Postgraduate Medical Center
Essex County Hospital
Colchester, CO3 3NB
May 10, 1991

Ref: PRW/PAH

Mr. Alhasan Ceesay
Flat 2, Kensington Court
47 Roman Road
Colchester, Essex

Dear Alhasan,

I am able to give you good news. The Medical advisory Committee of the hospital agreed to my recommendation that you should be offered immediately a loan, interest free, of six thousand five hundred pounds sterling to enable you to complete your studies in medicine and take your degree as you had hoped to do.

The M.A. C. recognize that you have studied conscientiously and I do not believe you would have receive this offer unless several of the tutors with whom you have had contacts had not spoken up enthusiastically in your support on knowledge of your conduct.

The M. A. C. recognize that you are in no position to guarantee repayment of this loan and in any case do not expect you to begin repayment until June 1994 when they hope you will be in a position to do so. I would strongly recommend that you advise your friends that you would have completed your studies and then give them priority in repayment. At least two of the consultants in this district know the Gambia intimately and are aware of the effort you have made in your efforts so far to get in your course and training and all wish you well in fulfilling your ambition to become a doctor and serve your people as I am sure you will be able to do.

We shall expect you to complete your clinical training including the electives in the near future. Please come and see me.

Your Sincerely
Dr. Peter R. Wilson
AUC Program director

This was a historic relief anointed by the Gods on mount Olympus. It marked a pivotal point in my quest for the elusive medical degree for the Gambia. Needless to say I was flabbergasted, more than delighted and terribly relieved that the tuition fee problem has now been laid to rest forever.

Wife and I prayed for all, especially for Dr. peter R. Wilson and M.A.C.

We felt eternally indebted and profoundly grateful for their generosity, understanding and stand to see me get the medical training I want to serve my people with in the future.

I sent the following note of thanks and appreciation for the good will to the Postgraduate Committee at Essex County Hospital in Colchester.

Flat 2, Kensington Court
47 Roman Road
Colchester, Essex CO1 1UR
May 20, 1991

Mr. Kitchen, chairman
Medical Advisory Committee
Postgraduate Medical Center
Essex county Hospital
Colchester, Essex CO3 3NB

Dear Committee,

RE: In Appreciation/grant

This is to acknowledge receipt of the six thousand five hundred pounds sterling loan you approved to help me complete my clinical training here at Essex

County hospital in Colchester. Thank you is awfully inadequate and words cannot aptly convey to you the gratitude and appreciation Gambia and I have for the help you so kindly rendered us. We are profoundly grateful got this kindness and generous contribution in our behalf.

Rest assured that the fruits of this benevolence would be fully shared with the sick and needy villagers. This humane gesture now makes that venue more certain.

Finally the six thousand five hundred pounds sterling loan will be repaid in full and in time. I will return to serve the Gambia, especially villagers. I will keep in touch with most of you, especially the M.A.C. Again, God bless and a million thanks for being so helpful to us. I remain ever so grateful to all of you. Cheers and regards.

Your Sincerely

Alhasan S. Ceesay

Gambian Medical Student

I met Dr. Peter R. Wilson the next morning and we had a cordial and memorable chat that day. He was very relieved that I could now work toward serving my nation and fulfilling my dream fro my people who are desperately in need of medical care.

I gave him a note of thanks for him and his staff who worked acidulously to help me resolve my financial woes.

I felt happy with Mrs. Penny West, Mrs. Hornby and all those who assisted to bring hope to my venture. It simply said:

Flat 2, Kensington Court
47 Roman Road
Colchester, Essex CO1 1UR
May 20, 1991

Dear Dr. Wilson,

Thank you for your May 10, 1991 letter informing me of the six thousand five hundred pounds sterling loan the Medical Advisory Committee approved in my behalf through your relentless kind initiative efforts. I am most grateful to you and the committee for this humane gesture as such critical state of my medical education.
It is very kind and generous and the Gambia and I remain touched by it. You have again extended your healing hands to touch us in the Gambia. Wife and I remain profoundly grateful and feel privileged having you on our side and as a friend.
Secondly, we thank you the trip to Hartfield House and the dinner with the Rotary Club. It was our first time out of Colchester and we really fully appreciated the gesture.
Hartfield House is an appreciable history of English Monarchy. The loan will be fully repaid within the stated time. Finally, kindly convey sincere thanks to the Committee, Mrs. Penny West and Mrs. Horny and all the staff for their love and kindness showed us. It was an admirable ceaseless effort from all of you that brought light at the end of the tunnel for the Gambia and I.
Wife and I are deeply touched. I will be at your office for us to plan the rest of my medical training. Cheers and regards. God bless you, my friend.

Yours Sincerely
Alhasan S. Ceesay
Gambian Medical Student
This phase of my life in Colchester will be incomplete without mentioning of few other angels wife and I met. Our first friendly contact, aside hospital staff, was an unusually easy going old lady, Mrs. Maureen P. Smith, who lived across our building on Roman Road.
She was the first neighbour who came to visit with us and we hitherto formed the warmest long lasting bond of friendship with her. We tease her as UK's deputy ambassador for Africa and Japan. Why? Shed had friends from all over the world but more so of Japanese and she spends nearly all her holidays in Japan. We loved her for breaking the social ice for us and through her we met lots of other good people in Roman Road.
I first met nurse Lorna V. Robinson while at my surgical rotation at the Colchester General Hospital. She had just returned from vacationing in the smiling coast, the Gambia. She came to see me at the surgical ward the moment she was told of a Gambian student doing his clinical training at the hospital.
The meeting was brief but I found her friendly and we decided to meet my wife at the end of the day. The meeting will not be until the birth of our first daughter, Famatanding Ceesay, on the 17/9/91 that Lorna and husband turned up at the Colchester Maternity Hospital to congratulate us.

Lorna Robinson took the most important photograph; baby Famatanding Ceesay, in the history of my family. Meanwhile she and wife got on as if they had known each other for centuries. They became sisters since that meeting.

The two visited each other frequently and we maintained links with Lorna Robinson. Last but the least was friendship we built with the Gassons of the Causeway, Boxford in Colchester. We met this lovely family through my contact with one of their sons, Daryl Gasson, who was then working at the Colchester General Hospital.

He was interested in the Gambia and hence invited to meet with the rest of the Gassons at Boxford. At Boxford the Gassons were more than delighted to meet wife and I. Everyone wanted to pick baby Famatanding and we had exhilarating and memorable two days with this family before returning to down town Colchester.

We really cherished friendships we built with countless families in the Colchester area and did tried to keep up with all after leaving friendly Colchester in 1992.

As time passed we lost contacts with some friends but Lorna Robinson became our extended family in the UK. She visits us while in the Gambia during her summer holidays. My daughter, Famatanding Ceesay, calls her "Auntie Lorna." We always look forward to her next visit to the Gambia.

Her personal contribution to my family is immense and we remain grateful to her untold number of kind gestures to the family. Being interested in helping others and having observed my work with the villagers, this lady took interest in it and agreed to help me get drugs, equipment, and to sensitize would be interested sponsors of a village health organization, when she returns to Colchester. She did as promised and had for years sent numerous packages of materials donated to Manding Medical Centre at Njawara village.

She visited Njawara, my home village, in 1995 and saw how much need there was for the contribution to help provide much needed medical service to the villages.

She was swamped at the village by throngs of villagers wishing to thank her for being kind to them and for helping in their medical care needs. Moved by this show of gratitude from villagers Lorna Robinson braced to do even more and today there is the usual, "Gambit Night" or Gambia Bazaar fund raising activity every weekend at Colchester.

Through her efforts we today have the Colchester friends of Manding Charitable Trust, which is and extended arm of Manding Medical Centre and serves as our liaison for the UK and the European Community countries.

The Charity was formed through her relentless efforts help of a solicitor, the Charity Commission has registered the friends of Manding as a charity in England and Wales since August 21, 2001 to further the objectives of Manding Medical Centre at Njawara in the Gambia, West Africa.

As far back as June 6, 1993 Lorna Robinson released the following flyer on behalf of Manding Medical Centre. The appeal read thus:

82 Finchingfield Way
Black Heath

Colchester, Essex CO2 OOAU
England
6/06/93

Dear Friends,

Dr. Alhasan Kunsa Ceesay: Badibou Folklore

I am writing on behalf of Dr. Alhasan Ceesay of the Manding Medical Centre at Njawara village in the North Bank Division of the Gambia, West Africa. My husband and I are helping Dr. Ceesay and the villagers establish a hospital that is surely needed as the nearest hospital is some 70 miles away strewed with bad roads, and no ambulances or proper transport for the ill villagers.
It will provide valuable medical, surgical, obstetrics, gynaecology, Paediatrics and other ancillary medical services. We hence write to you to join us as a partner in this humanitarian venture. #50 will buy a tone of cement and we need about 480 tones to build the center.
Any help in the form of money, equipment, contacts etc will be more than welcomed. We want to contribute in a positive way by providing medical aid and facilities to the villages, which will generate interest with greater participation, form a healthy agricultural society that may lead to improved nutritional and economic gain.
Finally, your help in bringing this gift to the villagers will be more than welcomed and deeply appreciated. Please help us catch dream for the villager.

Also feel free to contact me should you or any need further information on the above project at Njawara in the Gambia. Regards
Yours Sincerely
Lorna V. Robinson

These and many more Colchester human angels were picked on the way as the years unfold. It has been my home way from home and a support line, if not lifeline for Manding Medical Centre at Njawara village, the Gambia, West Africa. God bless all.

Dudou Ceesay at Njawara Seyare, the Gambia 2016

Chapter 35

THE MD DEGREE, 1992: HOME SWEET HOME

If there remain any out there who happens to be skeptic or cynical disbeliever in the existence of a curse or anything like it, be warned not to become a convert by the following events that are about to unfold right before you in these pages.

These events herein cannot just happen or come out of the blue by themselves after all my life had gone through these twenty-five years. Every major step of my life had met with stiff resistance compounded by painful, wretched, ill fated, contemptible, if not unsatisfactory, bitter experiences.

It is unbelievably hard to contemplate the challenges and inhuman roadblocks I had to face in my life. Hence dear reader, I suggest that you take a seat and prepare to be mesmerized.

My life seem to follow the path of a sailor who, no, not that of the ancient Mariner and his Albatross, nor would Barron Murchison's adventure match it or be more thrilling in nature, finds himself sailing uncharted waters of life without a compass.

Yes, I am sailing through this life as if though no other hell surpasses this very one I am traveling. Let me tell you what happened few years ago, in 1989, when I was in Montserrat.

While there hurricane Hugo decided to sweep by the Island nation hitting it with such ferrous vengeance that the roofs of buildings, including one we took shelter at, were blown away to the Caribbean Sea leaving only the sky to be our mantle.

It poured torrential waves of rain bringing water up to our necks. The razor sharp wind blowing at 175 to almost 300 miles per hour speeds nearly took me to sea like a kite. Wife and I held onto a pillar all night with micelles flying from all directions pass us. Each of those heavy poles, corrugated sheets or doors hitting us would spell our doom.

Wife and I prayed and readied us for our survival and all those on the path of this devil hurricane with such ferocity and evil wind cum rain-washing away life. We were lucky to survive that night but lost most of our belongings, including house we took shelter at.

Why I survive if I were not to face another holocaust of a greater magnitude? Do not worry this was just the top of the iceberg. I hope I have wet your appetite and that you are braced or ready for what good old Montserrat would spew at me after graduation ceremonies.

Like any aspirant completing medical school, I was excited and looked forward to a rewarding life of devotion to helping likewise bringing hope and relief to the sick and needy for the Gambia.

I had looked forward to the good life and leaving behind most of, if not all my woes and financial troubles and follow a new path of devotion to God and service to my fellow man.

Life is full of choices and I made mine to do medicine. All I ever yearned for was the simple contribution of what my skills and strength can for others.

My heart yeaned for relief, but do you think the elements would let me have a little peace with which to appreciate family and the beauty of life?

Having completed my clinical training at Colchester General Hospital and having met all the requirements for graduation, I bid farewell to my Colchester friends and headed for Montserrat on March 21, 1992.

Check-in time was scheduled for 7.40 a.m. at Gatwick North Terminal, London. You guess it right, the car we were traveling with lost a wheel six miles to Gatwick and the spare had busted in two places the night before.

Luckily an observant traffic police officer noticed us and decided to come and find out what was going on or what we were up to and how he could help us. Being an unusually kind and nice Bobbie he decided to call a repair crew to come to our rescue.

What an omen for traveler! I made it to Gatwick North Terminal at the last announcement for boarding British Airways to Antigua, West Indies. The departure for the flight was 9:45 Am.

Everyone at the BA checking-in counter rushed to help me get on board the plane, delaying the take off time another twenty minutes. Some of the passengers thought I was some diplomat or VIP, to cause the pilot to want to wait for my joining the flight. This brought me publicity and attention I did not bargain for on board.

Finally, BA flight for Antigua managed to take off and away we went into soon blue skies with jet engines purring like a tamed cat sleeping on a couch. The initial first four hours of flight were perfectly calm but not for long afterwards. The plane started to experience all of sudden bad weather and steeply went into turbulent weather.

Luckily the captain was an exceptionally good, good experienced and adept enough pilot to get us through very serious thunderstorm and lightening. It was a frightening fifteen minutes before we were clear above most of the heavy clouds and on course to Antigua.

We were relieved for no one sustained any injuries and the rest of the flight was bearably comfortable. We finally landed in Antigua around 3.45 P.M. an hour late but safe and sound. I had no problem at Antigua International arrival terminal.

I even recognized some of the old hand at the terminal. Hence after hour's airport formalities we boarded Liat 596 flight heading for Montserrat, now my favourite island nation in the West Indies. The flight took only fifteen minutes over the Caribbean Sea and we were at Montserrat Airport.

I took a taxi to Plymouth, capital city of the island and very soon was reunited with my former landlord, Willy Ryan and other friends. This was March 25, 1992 three solid years after hurricane Hugo and one could still see the scars of the then mighty Hugo.

My landlord's house and many others were still in disrepair and only few strong buildings were worth to dwell. Hotels and Condominiums were in full gear and I was to stay at the residence of Miss Gayle Baumgartner until after the graduation ceremonies scheduled for the 28th of March 1992.

This was an unbelievable big day I had worked very hard for and nothing was going to spoil it for me. I planned to savour every minute of it as historical for the Gambia and my family.

Sadly neither my wife nor any friend of notary could make it to my graduation because of the cost of transportation and lodging them in broken down Montserrat.

I was to secure a visa and head for the US to do my internship and residency programs after receiving the MD. degree from the American University of the Caribbean at Montserrat, West Indies. What happened or followed next is worse than my other recent bad experiences.

It was like a dream, but let us for the meantime continues on about graduating. Every graduating student was happy when March 28, 1992 dawned. It was a day we all had dreamt of in our ambitious push to better our lives and those whom we touch on our path.

As for me, I was ecstatic and more than thankful that God had let me see the day I will finally receive the Doctor of Medicine degree. However mixed feelings emanated because not one of my friends showed up, despite having promised to do so, and worse of all my return to America was uncertain. Being on the Island brought back all those bleak and difficult day seven months of starvation and solitude I had to endure in Montserrat before being able to join the students at Wayland Baptist University, Plainview, Texas.

We were on the graduation procession three days after my landing in Momtserrat. There was a big fanfare and neon signs congratulating and wishing every graduate well and a mélange of blooming verities of roses in full glory and splendor. There were blooming verities of roses everywhere the eye can see on campus.

Like all graduations, whether in Plymouth, Montserrat or any institute of learning, long speeches mark the occasion. In Monserrat, it always shows the Governor at his best political cum academic jargon.

This was normally followed by advises of a few other dignitaries in attendance. We took the Hippocratic Oath with all its solemnity and I again thanked God for the favour He has done by allowing me see the day of my graduation from medical school and I renewed my covenant to return to serve the Gambia no matter how difficult it might be getting to my objective of providing modern medical aid for the rural Gambian villagers. Very soon we dispersed and parents and friends of graduates wished us well and retired to their hotels. We had a graduation party that lasted through the wee hours of the night for some but I had to leave around 11:00 Pm. because I missed my wife and family back in the Gambia. Gayle Baumgartner was away in America and the room I currently occupy was already booked but another guest arriving on the March 29, 1992.

It meant that I had to find a place as quickly as I can before the arrival of the people whose room I was at. I needed few more days to seek a visa from the US Consulate in Barbados before I can proceed to do my internship and residency program in medicine in America, or so I thought until when I got to Barbados, West Indies.

My former Landlord, Willy Ryan, tried to buoy me up by being overly kind and even helped me look for vacancy for me to stay until I sort things out from Barbados and could fly to the USA to start my medical program as hoped or worse head for the Gambia. I left my luggage with Willie Ryan and flew to Barbados the next day to seek for a visa to enter the United States for the sole purposes of doing my internship and residency program in medicine before returning to the Gambia.

At Barbados I met an almost impossible visa consular officer who insisted that I return to the Gambia and seek a visa from the American Embassy in Banjul, the Gambia.

I pleaded with her that I had at the time spent all my money and by so doing it would cost more to travel to the Gambia and I would lose my chance for doing the promised internship and residency program and other consideration that were taking place at teaching hospitals in my behalf in America. She called one of these hospitals in the US and was told that unless I am able to visit with the institute no further action in my behalf would be considered. Despite the fact that it was now made clear to her that my going to Africa would mean losing the chance of further training in medicine in a US setting earmarked for me.

The officer rejected my visa application request to travel to America. Unless I am able visit with the teaching hospital in America my dream of being an American trained physician is abruptly brought to rest.

No, her reason for rejecting my request to travel to the USA was not based on my having previously asked for political asylum in America. My voluntary departure from America in December 1987, removed that record from the books and immigration data, and hand had nothing to do with subsequent entries. On hindsight, I was even able to renter in 1982 and 1989 after hurricane Hugo to join the AUC students at the Wayland Baptist University campus in Plainview, Texas. Previous visa counsellors would have not let me in had the asylum request been a deterrent.

I thanked her after several attempts to reason things with her and thanked God before returning with a laden heart to Montserrat. At which place I contacted Rev. Mark D. Meyer in Nebraska. He and other American friends along with Congressman Doug Bereuter of Nebraska agreed to intervene in my behalf by writing to the Ambassador, G. Philip Hughes requesting favourable review and reconsideration of my visa application.

All my friends agreed with me that travelling to the Gambia to seek a US visa was an unnecessary expense and time consuming drill or venture in my own history with the Gambia I could afford at the time. My brother and friend in Christ, Rev. Mark D. Meyer sent the following communiqué to the Immigration officer at Barbados.

St. Mark's Episcopal Church
1714 Grant Street
P. O. Box 72
Blair, Nebraska, USA
April 22, 1992

To: The United States Immigration Officer
From: Rev. Mark D. Meyer

Dear Sir/Madam,

I write on behalf of Dr. Alhasan S. Ceesay and appeal to you to please award him a visa to enter the United States in order to finish his internship. Alhasan came to my office in January of 1990, when I was a priest at St. Mark's Episcopal Church in Plainview, Texas.
The campus of the American University of the Caribbean had been offered some vacant classroom and dormitory space at Wayland Baptist University in Plainview. Alhasan had then used up all his funds in coming to Plainview from Montserrat, and I was able to help him with room and board to finish his classroom training.
At the end of that time he was able to get the United Nations Scholarship for clinical training in England. He was forced to spend to spend four months in Plainview trying to get a visa into England to do that clinical training. During that time, he stayed with me in a spare bedroom and I get to know him very well.
He is a devoted man and passionately believed he has a mission and duty to serve his people in the Gambia. I am so convinced of that fact that I have spent over $10,000 (ten thousand dollars) of my own money to help with tuition, plane fares, and phone calls to the Gambia government and the like. My father congregation in Plainview added their own funds, as did the Roman Catholic Archdiocese of Lubbock, Texas. I understand your concern. I know how many foreign medical students end up staying in the United States.

My father is a former president of the Illinois State Medical Society and was at one time on the AMA Education Committee, and I heard a great deal about foreign medical graduates, believe me I also read the recent Newsweek article on the subject. I know the problem.

Alhasan Ceesay is not part of that problem. As a priest, I believe I have some degree of discernment of a person's devotion and I have rarely seen devotion and conviction to a cause as to his commitment to serve the villagers in the Gambia who are so medically under-served.

He has suffered a lot for that end and I stake much of my life savings on it, and countless prayers gone to his way in these past years. Please believe Alhasan Ceesay when he says that his desire is to return to the Gambia and serve his villagers.

He is telling the truth. His time is short to take the necessary licensing exams in the United States. He needs a visa if he is to do internship here. I have little money of my own to send him for plane fares to Barbados or the United States and he has absolutely none of his own and is living from hand to mouth. His future is very much in your hands. Please do not hesitate to call: home 403-553-2412, Church 403-462-2057. Thank you

Sincerely

The Rev. Mark D. Meyer

Mark further wrote to his congressman, Honourable Doug Berreuter, who in turn sent the following appeal on my behalf to the US Ambassador G. Philip Hughes in Barbados, West Indies. It read,

Congress of the United States
House of Representatives
Washington, D.C. 20515
April 2, 1992

The honourable G. Philip Hughes
Ambassador
U.S. embassy
Barbados, (PPT. Miami, Florida 34054)

Dear Mr. Ambassador,

This is a request for your service in behalf of my constituent, the reverend Mar. D. Meyer who has befriended Alhasan Ceesay, a young man from the Gambia. Alhasan Ceesay is a graduate of the American university of the Caribbean in Montserrat, West Indies. He is training to be a doctor and has completed his clinical work at Colchester General Hospital in England.

Alhasan must now do a year's internship here in the United States to complete his licensing training before returning to the work in the Gambia villages. I have been advised that his request for a visa was denied.

Therefore, I am now asking that his request be given reconsideration. What he needs at the time is visitor's visa with prospective student designation so that the internship can be completed.

He will return to his country to practice medicine with his own people. We need to be able to assist him in this direction. Should you need to contact this young man he is Alhasan S. Ceesay, C/O Gayle

Baumgartner, P. O. Box. 27, Plymouth, Montserrat, West Indies. I call your kind attention to this request for its most sincere and any help accorded him will be sincerely appreciated. Best wishes.
Doug Berreuter
Member of Congress

Along with this were letters from Lois Leonard, and numerous others, which I packaged with the following, appeal, requesting to be allowed to enter the United States of America.

P.O. Box 27
Plymouth
Montserrat
West Indies

The Counselor
Visa Section
U. S. embassy
Barbados
West Indies

Dear Sir/Madam,

I am a Gambian self-sponsored student from Njawara village. I initially did my undergraduate and graduate studies in the U.S. A. 1967 –1973 before attending the American university of the Caribbean school of Medicine in Montsetrrat, West Indies. All my previous schooling and recently earned M.D. degree came through the kindness and help of American friends and hard work on my part.

I am committed to my people in the villages and do seek your kind considerations to issue me a B2 prospective student visa for me to go and complete my training, i.e. do my internship and residency program in medicine, so that I can be proficient physician serving the Gambia.

Please take my word of honour that I will return to the villages as soon as I complete my residency program in internal medicine. This is my objective in life and I will not fail my people for there is an overwhelming need of proper modern medical service in rural Gambia.

I will contribute towards that end in due course. In brief, the villagers and I appeal for your understanding of our situation and real need for this assistance. We thank you for taking time to reconsider our request and do look forward to seeing you in the Gambia some day.

Again, my obligation to the Gambia is supreme and I will return to serve people as soon as I finish the next phase of my medical training. Go bless and thanks a million for your considerations in this matter.

Yours Sincerely
Dr. Alhasan S. Ceesay
AUC/Gambian Student

It would not be until April 22, 1992 before a sinister reply came from the U. S. ambassador in Barbados addressed to congressman Doug Berreuter of Nebraska, USA. The fight to and from Barbados had already dented the little money I had left with me.

And the silence was like lead over my shoulders for every passing moment spells a tragic loss and waste of time. Most inhabitants of the island were foraging for food and might or would not just be able to add mine atop of theirs. That stab at the back letter in a memoranda form reads:

Office of the Ambassador
U. S. embassy
Barbados, West Indies
April 22, 1992

To: the Hounorable Doug Berreuter
House of representatives
2348 Rayburn House
 Office building
Washington, D. C.

Dear Mr. Berreuter,

 Thank you for your letter of April 2, 1992, concerning the non-immigrant visa application of Dr. Alhasan S. Ceesay, your constituent Rev. mark Meyer contacted you on behalf of his friend. Dr. Ceesay applied for a non-immigrant visa on March 31, 1992 and was found ineligible for the visa under section 214 (B) of the Immigration and Nationality Act.
This section of the law requires that all applicants for non-immigrant visa be able to determine to the satisfaction of the consular officer that they have social, economic or family ties that would compel

them to return to their home after a temporary stay in the United States. The officer who interviewed Dr. Ceesay was not convinced that Dr. Ceesay has sufficiently strong ties to the Gambia to compel him to return there after a medical internship in the United States.

Dr. Ceesay has just finished two years of clinical training in England and was refused a non-immigrant visa in London under the same section of the law when he applied there before applying to Bridge town. Dr. Ceesay may reapply for the visa and a different officer will review his case. His application will be given every consideration under United States Immigration law.

Please do not hesitate to contact me again if I can be of further assistance in this or any matter.

Sincerely

G. Philip Hughes

Ambassador

This reply to congressman Berreuter reached me very late and as such left me dumfounded and angry at the unnecessary cost the strictness and red tape placed on my visa request by the Immigration officer at Barbados.

It would not be until August 1992 before the way was cleared for me to fly back to the UK and eventually the Gambia. Before then I lived on one can of sardine, which lasts three days before I dare open another.

And I stayed at a partly destroyed house with no running water or good toilet. Half of the building was without roofing, as it was among the casualties of hurricane Hugo in 1989. I plaid hide and sick with rats, which wanted some of food and crumbs, I managed to bring from town. I have to stay awake almost all night for fear of being swept away into the Atlantic Ocean. My former landlord once on a while would bring some fruits or yams for me to boil for food to keep me bone and skin together. Simply, I lived by the skin of my teeth with no hope of help coming from any angle for me.

My U. S. friends were discouraged and I became embarrassed to ask more than I have already done. Mrs. Lois Leonard and Rev. Mark D. Meyer kept plugging in as much as they could humanly afford. It reached a point I could not walk to town because of lack of energy.

I would stop every fifty meters to rest and did the same on my return from town, a distance of three miles from my shanty. In fact I duped this half-roofed and blown windowless house, as Hotel Gambia and entered in my diary the snakes, various lizards and Iguanas that crises cross my bed room at night or come to take shade during the day.

That I did not loose my mind or get bitten by some unknown wild rodent was pure luck. The nightmare ended abruptly when Rudolf and Sophie Kurt, stepped in the second time and help me with an airfare back to the Gambia.

I could not believe it when I boarded Liat flight 596 heading for Antigua and later BA flight to Heathrow International Airport, London. These few words or phrases sounded musical to my ears. They spell freedom from being marooned and from the inhuman conditions I found myself after graduating from medical school.

In the back of my mind was the Gambia political chasm but life I endured had made me inert to fear of dying any longer. Normally, elation follows events like graduation, wedding or the arrival of the first and subsequent babies, but in my own case hell lost its head and metered the worst punishment it could throw onto a living being.

I never at any moment wished for death and had strong believe that God, who had this test for me, will pull me out safely when His time comes. I was vigilant in my prayers and seek that the Almighty come to my salvation sooner. I hope you have seen why it was necessary for me to prepare you for the curse I faced in Montserrat.

It looked unreal but I had endured worse than I am able to say to you. So faith, or devotion to God and kind people got me out of that mesh, just as happened when I was at the Mariner's Inn in Detroit, Michigan, USA.

There too it was very challenging if not difficult and crazy living among former drug addicts, alcoholics, felons, gun turting teenagers and the downtrodden of Cass Corridor in Detroit.

At Heathrow I met a very kind Immigration Officer who was very sympathetic to me. The haggard sight and story he heard almost moved him to tears. He verified my passport and allowed me to proceed and actually my skeletal state and euphoria was so high that it was bound to carry anyone one I came across. I did not at this time cared whether or what the Gambia might say or do to me. All I wanted to close that history and chapter of my life by either resting eternally with my maker or serving the Gambia.

The officer and I joked and laughed through the time I was before him. It was big and stark difference between my experiences with my good U.S. visa officer at Bridge Town, Barbados, West Indies.

I contacted the Gambia Embassy and had the voice of a long time friend, Mr. Bai Ousman Secka, and he came to my rescue and lodged me for forty-eight hours I had before my next flight to the Gambia via Paris, France.

Secka took me to stay with him at 35 The Avenue, Kilburn, London NW6 7NR. Here all my hidden fears were wiped out for I met with lots of Gambians who assured me that tranquility and civility had returned to my beloved home, the Gambia.

There were no more witch hunting and that the Senegalese troops have disband and gone home for good. With my confidence rejuvenated about the Gambia, I was happy lad that boarded Air Sabina flight from Heathrow, via Brussels and to one of the best homes on earth, the smiling coast of the Gambia.

Flying over Senegal gave me so much lift and euphoria that made me very eager to meet my family. By the way my father died while I was in Montserrat. I had lost one of the dearest and best of all fathers. Mother on the other was very poorly health wise.

My arrival's dramatic effect on her gained extensive recovery even though her failing heart would not bounce to health. She was in her nineties and very frail. Legend and luck had it that I landed in the Gambia August 9, 1992 not the least scared of anything going wrong. I was shocked by the dry state of affairs, especially the weather and dust that seem to envelope everything it comes across. I later learnt it was the Desert that is causing such havoc. I encountered no problems at the Airport or with the security and two of best friends Latif Sanyand and Kering Marenah were there to pick me up from the Airport.

This gave me confidence that the political problems were then over for my friends and perhaps me. All said and done my return surprised many except my sister Binta Ceesay who was expecting me more than a month ago. She joked saying, "I dreamt of meeting you at Njawara.

I was certain of your return in one piece." That is my lovely sister Binta Ceesay for you. She loves to lighten people's hearts. Everyone was eager to find out what happened to me and how everyone copped during the challenges.

The next day it was agreed that that I stay at uncle Sherif A. Sey's place at Fagi Kunda until we know the direction and development that may follow my return. I stayed at uncle Sey's for six months. While at Fagi Kunda alhaj Kebba Sanneh and his wife, Matida Sanneh, surpassed all friends in making sure that my resettlement was bearable.

I met the rest of my family, relatives and friends at different villages in the Badibous. I visited relatives at Njaba Kunda, mother's home village, Saba and finally Njawara, my home village.

I found Njawara turned into a ghost town. All the familiar shops and businesses were either closed or moved to either Banjul or Farafenye and other new trading centers which surfaced after independence.

The village was dead and in need of a socio-economic spark to rejuvenate it back to her golden good old days. I felt at lost and sad being in Njawara with out my father and to see my home village as dead as I found her.

Most of the youth moved to where they can get jobs or hoped to pick up one. Some became teachers while others tried their luck at other vocations. The population of a once thriving three thousand or more inhabitants has now dwindled to no more than 800 residents.

The cattle and sheep looked hungrier than I ever known and again the dust seems relentless. Even the old colonial roads were abandoned for new dirty potholed once leading to dying hamlets. Despite these horrors, I was very pleased being home once more in my life.

For once there were familiar cheers and laughter I can relate to and not feel alienated. My elder brother, Dudou Ceesay and I had a long chat about everything ranging from the last days of dad to current state of affairs of the family and our younger siblings who relocated to the Kombo area by the Gambia's Atlantic coast.

I was taken back and pretty ashamed of the way our compound had ran down through the years. It shadows our pride and for what resources existed if everyone cooperated. I was relived about how much he knew about my sufferings persistent determination to bring joy not only to the family but also to all those we can charitably touch. My poverty stricken life made me very depressed but I bounced back quickly and started implementing one my promises I made to myself and for my people.

I returned to Banjul to recuperate and plan my future in the Gambia. My wife was at her home in Kindia, Guinea Conakry, at this juncture and was aware of my return but we had agreed to test the waters first before calling her to the Gambia and having to let her loose again.

It would be December before I ventured to the villages. This time, I went there with a mission in mind for them. I started at my village and later many others. My message was simply to start doing something that will not only unite us but would be beneficial to generations to come.

I made it very clear that the going would be worst than climbing a slippery mountain with bare hands and very little food to take along, but the summit holds a great reward for all concerned. I suggested need to create some form of self-help village health organization to cater for our sick and needy.

Even though I made sure it was known that projects like these take time and hard work and perseverance fro all of us and worse some of us may not live long to reap its fruits. Even where that happens or turns out to be our fate we should be happy that we stood and did something for the next generation Gambians.

The villagers were more than enthused and right away. Torro Bahen village, donated land between Torro and Njawara for the prospective medical center project. This then was christened as Manding Medical Centre, to be located at Njawara, Lower Badibou, North Bank Division, the Gambia, West Africa. I followed this with monthly health field trips at which nearly 1500 sick villages attend the secessions.

We had our meeting at health centers were with help of volunteer doctors we treat the sick, give health education, talk about sexually transmitted diseases, Aids and guidance for family planning along with antenatal and postnatal advises to would be mother and mothers.

I did this until September 1993 before taking up a job as a house officer at the Royal Victoria hospital (RVH) Banjul, the only referral hospital in the Gambia at the time. The RVH currently caters for 350 patients. I was delighted resuming duty at the RVH as one of the physicians serving my motherland.

Ninety percent of the nursing staff was new to me as most of my classmate and those that followed had either gone to higher paying jobs or retired and opened their own mini-pharmacies.

Colonial discipline I left in our nursing day had gone with its master and now the changes make one wonder whether that noble commitment we had in becoming nurses had not melted away because of salary interests and the political era.

Time has certainly changed. My wife and daughter rejoined me in the Gambia by May 1993 for the first time since they left me in London. We moved to a new rental apartment in Bundung Mauritania, a suburb of Sere Kunda.

I had to change my monthly trips to the villages to a bimonthly field trips because of my job commitment at the Royal Victoria Hospital and because the cost to me. My salary at the RVH was an insulting meager D1567 (One thousand five hundred and sixty seven dalasis) on integrated grade 8 scales.

Whatever that meant, it was not sufficient to keep a dog alive more over the extended family that doctors encounter in the Gambia. I enjoyed my work at the RVH despite the rankles and insults that followed. I plan my travels to these field trips for the benefit of al Gambians.

Meanwhile, I was able to register the organization Manding Medical Centre and called attention of the International charities to the establishment of the center at Njawara village, the Gambia and our need for assistance to fulfill our dream of providing modern medical aid to the villagers.

Manding Medical Centre is now a registered charity in England and Wales at Colchester, Essex County, UK under the name of "Friends of Manding Charitable Trust" with charity number 1088136 effective since August 21, 2001.

Also Alpena City in Michigan, USA, under leadership of Dr. Avery Aten have spearheaded and established the Alpena Friends of Manding Charitable Trust, Michigan, USA since May 2005 after the Alpena Community College's leadership class' visit of the center in same year.

Chapter 36

MEDICAL OFFICER: RVH THE GAMBIA

There was no fanfare welcoming me back to the Royal Victoria Hospital (RVH) were I started putting into gear my medical dreams and ambition of providing much needed quality medical service to the villager.

I resigned from the Medical and Health Services, while a Dresser Dispenser, in 1967 to travel to the United States and study for a medical degree with which to serve the Gambia and man.

My re-entry to the Medical and Health Services, per say RVH, coincided with turbulence at the helm of the RVH. Dr. Hassan Jange had just tendered his resignation as chief executive of the hospital and the new tsar was one Dr. Ogbaselasse, a WHO technical assistance to the Gambia for many years.

My employment was left to him and like all new brooms dr. Ogba Selaisse swept well and clean. He left no stones untouched regarding my qualifications and background. Dr. Ogba Selaisse contacted my university and requested my transcripts sent directly to him.

It took two months of investigation before he called me in for an interview. At the interview he made it clear that he could only start me as a House Officer for one year and that I most do a three months rotation in Pediatrics, surgery, medicine and Obstetrics and Gynecology under consultant supervision.

My monthly salary was fixed at grade 8 levels with a starting point of an insulting meager, if not measly D1567 per month on the integrated scale. This amounts to $156.70 us dollars or poultry seventy-five pounds sterling a month.

My colleagues started at grade 9 upward but Chief Executive Ogba Selaissse deemed it proper to set mine at grade 8 integrated scaling. Family and loyal friends begged me to take the offer for the time being and so this salary disparity continued on from September 1993 to October 1998.

I agreed to the rotation schedule but had to point out the fact that there existed a limited number of consultants at the RVH units that I am supposed to do my internship. Ogba was not happy with my observations.

All doctors of my level were sent to teaching hospital in Ghana, Nigeria or Sera Leone but I was made to do my internship at the RVH with scant consultants to supervise me. Ogba left my file pending because of I knew I was not treated right to start with.

I had to take the bull by the horns when my starting date dragged on and on beyond two calendar months by appealing the case directly to the Permanent Secretary and Minister of Health for a ruling on the matter.

In the interim the America University of the Caribbean faxed the following to Dr. Ogba Selaisse, Chef Executive of the Royal Victoria Hospital.

Dr. G. Ogbaselasse
Chief Executive, RVH
Banjul, The Gambia

Dr. Alhasan S. Ceesay is a graduate of the American university of the Caribbean School of Medicine. Most of our graduates practice medicine in the United States. Our graduates must earn the Education Commission for Foreign Medical Graduates (ECFMG) certification.

To earn ECFMG certification the graduate must pass step 1 and 2 of the United States Medical Licensing examination (USMLE) and an English language proficiency test.

Most states in addition would require additional postgraduate training in specific area (residency) for an unrestricted License. I hope this information is beneficial to you

Sincerely

Robert J. Chertok, PhD

Dean of Medical Sciences

This information help to speed up the processing for it was also copied to the Ministry of Health. Hence an angry chief executive called me the following Monday and asked start rotations under watchful eyes of Dr. Ayo Palmer, head of the Pediatrics unit.

Ogba added a stern warning to me while I was just on my way out of his office. He in an angry tone said, "You most not forget the protocol in the medical field. I am the head of this hospital and not some politician beyond the RVH fence."

With my letter in hand, I smiled at it all and asked if he dare make such remarks before the very politicians who have been his umbrella in the Gambia. We eventually developed mutual respect for each other but never turned to be, as the saying goes, one's beer drinking friends.

Ogba never liked his authority challenged and was one that had very little trust for power zealous folks. Hence my presence some time ruffles his feathers because of question I asked and seeking intervention where I felt some foot-dragging was going on in the matter.

Another branch assisting the chief executive was the Medical Advisory Committee (MAC). This comprised of heads of units of the hospital and it helped in the maintaining of proficiency, ethics, and standard of medical practice in the units. I met with the MAC after chief executive Ogbaselaissse sent the following letter to me.

Hospital Management Board
Royal Victoria Hospital
Banjul, The Gambia
May 11, 1993

Ref: RVH/21/vol.v

Dr. A. S. Ceesay
5B Ingram Street
Banjul, The Gambia

I am pleased to inform you that the Hospital Management Board has, in principle, approved your appointment as House Officer in the Royal Victoria Hospital.

Please note that your appointment is subject to successful internship with the Hospital Advisory Committee (MAC) and the appointment Committee.

You are advised to report to Dr. Oldfield, Chairman
of MAC for further information and action.
Sincerely
Dr. C. Ogbaselaisse
Chief Executive, RVH
Cc: Permanent Secretary, MOH
Chairman: HMB, Chairman: MAC
File & R/file

Dr. Oldfield, Chairman of MAC sent this follow up
after the committee reviewed my file forwarded to it
by the CEO of the hospital.

Hospital Management Board
Royal Victoria Hospital
Banjul, The Gambia
June 15, 1993

Ref: RVH21/vol.v

Dr. A. S. Ceesay
5B Ingram Street
Banjul, The Gambia

Dear Dr. Ceesay,

RE: Provisional Registration with the Medical and
Dental Council

Further to my letter Ref:RVH21/vol.v May 10, 1993
the Medical Advisory Committee has scrutinized
your application for internship. You are required to
be provisionally registered with the Medical and
Dental Council.

Your internship will commence as soon as you present a certificate of provisional registration.
Sincerely
Dr. F. S. J. Oldfield
Ag. Chief executive
Cc: file & R/file
Chairman: MAC

A memo was released to the various heads of units, Registrars Gambia Medical and Dental Council (GMDC) and copied to me.

Hospital Management Board
RVH, Banjul
The Gambia
September 9, 1993

Ref: RVH21/vol.v

Registrar
GMDC
PMB 137
Banjul,
The Gambia

Sir,

The above doctor will do a supervised rotating house job three months each in Pediatrics, surgery, medicine, Obstetrics, and Gynaecology.
Grateful if Council can consider him for provisional registration.

Your Faithfully
Dr. G. Ogbaselaisse, FROG
Chief Executive
Cc: Permanent Secretary, MOH
Chairman, HMB
Dr. Alhasan Ceesay, File & R/file

The Gambia Medical and Dental Council is an autonomous body of doctors who by act of Parliament is authorized to verify qualifications of new doctors wishing to practice in the Gambia. The Accreditation Committee of the GMDC interviewed me and the following was sent in response to the chief executive's September 9, 1993 request.

The Gambia Medical and Dental Council
Kanifing
P. O. Box 137
Banjul, The Gambia
October 5, 1993

The Chief Executive
Hospital Management Board
Royal Victoria hospital
Banjul, The Gambia

Dear Sir,

Ref: Provisional registration for Dr. Alhasan Ceesay

Reference is invited to your letter RVH21/vol.v on the above subject.

The provisional registration is granted on the terms of your letter.
Dr. Alhasan Ceesay had been requested to formally apply for provisional registration. This does not preclude his commencing the rotation house jobs.
Yours Faithfully
Mr. Mbye Faal (MBBS FROG, FWACS)
Registrar

My official appointment to the Medical and Health services of the Gambia would not surface until October 26, 1993, almost five months from the first day I applied for a job at the RVH. It takes less than a week to process application from other doctors but for me it dragged on endlessly for five solid months.
Here is the full text of my reunification with the Royal Victoria Hospital visa avis the Medical and Health Services of the Gambia. It is a dream come true indeed.

Hospital Management Board
Royal Victoria Hospital
Banjul, The Gambia
October 26, 1993

Ref: RVH/Board/3/vol.11

Dr. Alhasan S. Ceesay
Bundung, Serekunda
The Gambia, West Africa

Dear Dr. Ceesay,

APPOINTMENT

I am pleased to offer temporal appointment as House Officer with effect from the first of September 1993 for a period of one (1) year. Your Salary will be at the rate of D18, 768.00 (Eighteen thousand seven hundred and sixty-eight dalasis) per annum (i.e. D1564 per month) of the integrated pay scale.

You will be required to conform to the General orders regulations, Financial Instructions and Public Service Commission regulations in so far as they are applicable to you. You will be entitled to 22 working days leave for every completed twelve months of service.

Please indicate in writing whether you will accept this appointment on the above terms. This appointment is terminable either by the Hospital Management Board or you upon giving a written notice of one month or payment of a month's salary in lieu of written notice.

Yours Sincerely

Dr. G. Ogbasesailesse

Chief Executive, RVH

Cc: Permanent Secretary MOH
    Permanent Secretary PMO
    Chairman: HMB
    Accountant General
    Auditor General
    Principal Accountant
    Personal file & R/file

As indicated earlier on in the chapter I reluctantly accepted the above insult duped as appointment because of pressure from family, close friends and my love for the Gambia. The salary would not feed a rat much more help me get a compound to raise a family. Having made up my mind to serve my people I worked long and hard hours.
I persevered more than any of my colleagues at the RVH; this earned me coveted respect within the administration and the staff. If nothing else. The MAC continued managing my Internship and sent the following:

Medical advisory Committee
Royal Victoria Hospital
Banjul, The Gambia

Ref: HLS/MAC/1.94

Dr. Alhasan Ceesay

RE: Posting to Surgical Unit

As part of your rotation of duties in fulfillment of registration for full professional registration, you are being posted to the surgical unit for six months with effect from August 1, 1994. You will of course be assessed in the usual manner.
Sincerely
Dr. F. S. J. Oldfield
Chairman: MAC
Cc: Consultant Surgeon I/C
Consultant Obstetrics & Gynecology
Chief Executive, File

The Chief Executive wrote:

Hospital Management Board
Royal Victoria Hospital
Banjul, The Gambia
August 1, 1993

Dear Sir,

Re: Dr. Alhasan S. Ceesay
Further to our discussion (Ogba/AgbakwuruI on the above this is to confirm that Dr. A. Ceesay would be deployed to the surgical unit under your supervision for his house job with effect from 1/8/94 for a period of six months.
You are kindly requested to submit progress report to this office at the end of three months.
Yours Sincerely
Dr. G. Ogbaselaisse, FROG
Chief Executive, RVH
Cc: Dr. Azadeh, OBS & Gyne unit
Dr. Alhasan Ceesay, File & R/file

Dr. Agbakwuru left for Nigeria and was replaced by Dr. U. Jones who at the end of my surgical rotation sent the following report about my performance in the unit.

Hospital Management Board
Department of Surgery
Royal Victoria Hospital
Banjul, The Gambia

The Chairman
Medical Advisory Committee
Royal Victoria Hospital
Banjul, The Gambia
June 14, 1995

RE: Surgical Internship
Dr. Alhasan S. Ceesay

I write to affirm that Dr. Ceesay completed an internship in the General surgery between August 19994 and February 1995. He was punctual to duty and his performance was satisfactory.
He was a good colleague to have in this unit, with good relations with the staff and patients alike. His standard was satisfactory.
Sincerely
Dr. U. O. E. Jones
Head of Unit
Cc: Chief Executive, RVH
File, & R/file
Dr. G. Ogbaselasse resigned his CEO post early 1996 and was replaced by Ansuman Dampha, as Chief Executive of the RVH. Mr. Dampha got on my case immediately in an attempt or effort to restore the long and dragging affair about my being fully registered with the GMDC. He contacted the registrar Mr. Mbye Faal as follows.

Hospital Management Board
Royal Victoria Hospital
Banjul, The Gambia
May 3, 1996

Ref: HMB/PF

Dr. Mbye Faal, Registrar
Gambia Medical and Dental Council
2 Radio Gambia Road
PMB 137
Banjul, The Gambia

Dear Sir,

RE: Application for full Registration

I forward herewith for your consideration application from Dr. Alhasan Ceesay for full registration with the Gambia Medical and Dental Council (GMDC). Supporting documents are also attached.
Yours Faithfully
Ousman Dampha
Chief Executive, RVH
Cc: Dr. Alhasan Ceesay
File & R/file

Dr. Mbye Faal, Registrar for the GMDC insisted on having more appraisal report sent before he would proceed. He did not like the format of the ones presented in my behalf. In a nutshell this was one of many ways this Registrar would forestall my registration for years to come.
Nonetheless we persevered and sent him different forms designed by his office.

Hospital Management Board
RVH, Banjul

The Gambia
June 11, 1996

Ref: RVH/21/vol.v

The Registrar Gambia Medical and Dental Council

RE: Submission of application report on Dr. Alhasan Ceesay's rotation

Please you will find copies of appraisal report from various heads of units of the Royal Victoria Hospital about Dr. Alhasan ceesay's performance during his rotation at these units. We forward these for consideration by you for full registration with the GMDC.
Yours Faithfully
Ousman Dampha
Chief Executive, RVH
Cc: Dr. Alhasan Ceesay
File & R/file

The delays went on until September 1996 when I decided that enough was enough and I wrote the following reminder to Dr. Mbye Faal alias Jack Faal and copied it to various officials including the Director of Health Services.

Royal Victoria Hospital
Banjul, The Gambia
September 5, 1996

Dr. Mbye Faal, Registrar
GMDC, PMB 137
Kanifing, The Gambia

RE: reminder regarding my application for professional registration with the GMDC

Dear Dr. Mbye Faal,

This is to remind and call attention that my application remains pending despite my having completed the assigned rotations and having submitted all relevant documentation for you to kindly consider a year ago.
I would be most grateful if you would kindly deliberate on my application for professional registration. Anxiously awaiting your kind consideration. I now have waited for more than a year. Thanks
Your Sincerely
Dr. Alhasan S. Ceesay, MD
Cc: Chief Executive RVH
Director of Health Services

Two weeks later Mr. Ousman Dampha, CEO of the RVH following reminder to the GMDC's registrar with his own. Mr. Mbye Faal's refusal to act on my application was frustrating both the administration and me.
The Chief Executive of RVH again sent the Council a reminder but instead he was replied by a Mrs. M.C. Jallow on behalf of the Director of Medical and Health Services.

Republic of the Gambia
Ministry of Health

The quadrangle
Banjul, The Gambia
September 16, 1996

HP/89/01/(77)

The Chief Executive
RVH, Banjul
The Gambia

RE: Reminder regarding my application for Professional Registration

Please find attached a photocopy reminder of an application for professional registration from Dr. Alhasan S. Ceesay, MD for your attention.
Kindly take appropriate action on this application as soon as possible.
Yours Faithfully
Mrs. M. C. Jallow
For Director of Health Services

Again the CEO of hospital sent another reminder to Mr. Mbye Faal, alias Jack Faal, in other to seek appropriate action from Council on my behalf.

Hospital management Board
RVH, Independence Drive,
Banjul, The Gambia
September 8, 1996

Ref: RVH/21/vol.1

The Registrar
GMDC, Kanifing
PMB 137
The Gambia

RE: Reminder for the professional Registration of Dr. Alhasan Ceesay

I wrote series of letters with regards to the registration of DR. Alhasan Ceesay with photocopies of all relevant documents and appraisals reports from the various units in the Royal Victoria Hospital (RVH) but still no action has been taken.
The Hospital Management Board would like your office to kindly take the appropriate action as soon as possible.
Yours Faithfully
Ousman Dampha
Chief Executive, RVH

Cc: Director of Medical Services
Management Advisory committee
Hospital Administration
Chairman, HMB
Dr. Alhasan Ceesay

The CEO received, as usual, no response from Mr. Mbye Fall, alias Jack Faal, Registrar. It was now clear to me that my case was being bandied and deliberately left pending by none other than

Mr. Mbye Faal, alias Jack Faal. The delay and refusal to give any tangible reasons for the GMDC's indecision about my case left no doubts in my mind that Mr. Mbye Faal, alias Jack Faal would play God with me until when it suits him or until he discovers that he was far from being a deity and that he cannot break my spirit, will, and determination to serve the Gambia.

Nonetheless he was reminded about the need to act urgently on my request by Ousman Dampha, CEO at the Royal Victoria Hospital, Banjul.

RVH, Banjul
The Gambia
October 17, 1996

The Registrar
GMDC, PMB 137
Kanifing, The Gambia

RE: Registration of Dr. Alhasan Ceesay

I am sending a reminder for the registration of Dr. Alhasan Ceesay. If you can remember some time ago the Hospital Management Board had written to your office with copies of internship appraisal from unit heads to back up Dr. Ceesay's registration, which were submitted to your office. Thank you for your usual cooperation.

Yours Faithfully
Ousmab Dampha
Chief Executive, RVH
cc: Management Adviser
Hospital Administrator

Chairman: HMB
Dr. Alhasan Ceesay
File & R/file

Dr. Faal, alias Jack Faal, disregarded his previous appraisal forms and made new ones himself and asked that evaluations be submitted again on my behalf. This was done, with everyone wondering if I had wronged the Registrar inadvertently.
I told all concerned that I have no personal knowledge of having offended or said anything that should ruffle his feathers or turn him so callus towards me.
I made it very clear that I shall continue to pursue what were my due, if not my rights, to whatever reasonable ends it may lead. There were lots of sympathizers and people who believed that the Registrar was wrong in dragging my registration for as long as he did.
The new forms, I duped Mbye Faal registration forms, were dully signed and sent to Dr. Mbye faal along with a letter from Chief Executive Ousman Dampha, Ref: RVH/21/vol.v, dated November 8, 1996 in which he categorically stated, "Here are enclosed copies of comments for the full registration of Dr. Alhasan Ceesay.
I do support the recommendation from the heads of units." Well dear reader, I hope you can make sense out of the above nightmarish jigsaw or puzzle. Mr. Mbye Faal continued to wield his seal of power over poor fledgling medical doctor Alhasan Ceesay.
He refusal to act while hiding behind elusive authority is laid bare by the above sequence of event and exchange or the one way traffic of support

correspondence from the Royal Victoria staff and its Chief Executive. It was slap on the face of the system and very discouraging as I later found out that all Banjul born returning doctors from Russia were sent to teaching hospital in Nigeria or Ghana and even Sera Leone while I was be subjected to the whims and caprices of the registrar of the GMDC. Mr. Mbye may become the tsar of doctoring in the Gambia but with such exercise of power as he has taken in my case it was certain he would not be in the post forever and not for longer than he has. He will either retire or be forced out by lawful means in due course.

If I were in his shoe, I would write a letter of support for him and plead with the visa consular to reconsider issuing B2 prospective student status to allow my doing the internship and residency program as was scheduled.

No instead I was used to be pon for power tug of war that I had nothing to do. I doubt if he ever saw it that I was a Gambian like him needing his guidance. Why on earth was this man putting me through the grill and unnecessary roadblocks on my way?

Did he fail to realize that God is the only ultimate and ever lasting power in this life and after it? My measly salary of D1564, in other words an equivalence of seventy-five pounds sterling per month, was woefully inadequate and not able to sustain my family's need.

I have three daughters in school and poverty is depriving them the normal things and privileges their peer children are enjoying. Hence, I decided to try the big guns to bring relief to my situation and my family to allow me provides better footing for my children, if not my sanity. Here is a drowning man trying to cling onto straw floating towards him.

Bundung Mauritania
Serekunda
The Gambia
December 16, 1996

The Chief Executive
Royal Victoria Hospital
Banjul, The Gambia

Dear Chief Executive,

I would like to call attention that my House Officer job started September 9, 1993 and end September 1994. However, I have since the completion of my house rotations been left on grade 8, receiving D1564 per month of the integrated pay scale.
The only other emoluments include transport fee or allowance of D150 per month and D100 per month call allowance.
On the other hand my colleagues are paid a total of D5246.67 per month as follows.

Salary	D1979.00 per month
Responsibility allowance	D1250.00 per month
On call allowance	D100.00 per month
Car allowance	D400.00 per month

Residential allowance   D200.00 per month
None Practice allowance   D416.00 per month

Total payment per month to my colleagues equals D5246.76 (five thousand two hundred and forty-six Dalasis and 67 Butus per month). While I earn a mare total of D2750.00 per month.

I am hereby submitting this claim covering a period of two years, i.e. from 1994 t0 1996 inclusive at which time I have been kept at grade 8 scale of D1564 per month.

Hence the difference in wages and allowances is D2492.67 per month which multiplied by 24 months will amount to D59, 624.04 C fifty-nine thousand six hundred and twenty-four Dalasis and 4 Butus) due me to date. Again, banking on your good judgment and sense of fair play I look forward to a speedy, likewise a positive resolution of the above request.

Thank you for being kind and for reviewing the above matter. I anxiously await your response.

Yours Sincerely

Dr. Alhasan S. Ceesay, MD

Cc: permanent secretary, MOH
Director of Health Services
Chairman, HMB
Accountant General
Auditor General
Secretary Public Service Commission
Management adviser

I was not sure what got to Chief Executive Mr. Ousman dampha of the RVH but his letter to me was no longer someone I had hoped would stand his grounds and do what was dully right for the Gambia.
Here, in his cold feet, is what he thought was appropriate to get my case off his back. I duped it my 1996 Christmas card.

Hospital Management Board
Royal Victoria Hospital
Banjul, The Gambia
December 24, 1996

Ref: HMB/PF/091

Dr. Alhasan S. Ceesay
House Officer
Thro, Head of Medical Unit
RVH, Banjul, The Gambia

Dear Dr. Ceesay,

I refer to your letter dated December 16, 1996 relating to the above-mentioned subject and to inform you with regret, that the Hospital Management Board cannot entertain your claim in view of the fact that you are still a House Officer on grade 8. I am to inform you further that until such time that you obtained full registration with the Gambia Medical and Dental Council and promoted to the post of Medical Officer grade 9, you will

continue to receive your present salary and allowances.
Yours Faithfully
Ousman Dampha
Cc: Permanent Secretary, MOH
Permanent Secretary, PMO
Director of Health Services
Accountant General
Auditor General
Secretary, PSC
Management Adviser, HMB
Hospital Administrator
Personal file & R/file

Here is another in the saga to laugh, cry or wonder about. I would be until March 1997 when the Registrar of the GMDC, Mr. Mbye Faal, ventured to break his traditional silence in my case by finally breaking the lull from his end and throwing out the following insult, as usual of his attitude towards my registration request.
It is a shame that such cruel raw power would be exercised for no earthly dignified reasons. So here ifs the fabricated vomit he sent to the chief executive, RVH.

The Gambia Medical and Dental Council
PMB 137
Banjul, The Gambia
March 4, 1997

Mr. Ousman Dampha
Chief Executive
Royal Victoria Hospital

Banjul, The Gambia

Dear Sir,

RE: Registration of Dr. Alhasan Ceesay

Reference is invited to your letter Ref. RVH/21/vol.v of November 8, 1996 on the above subject. I am to draw your attention that the recommendations from the Heads of Units that have your support were incomplete in all cases as indicated on the certificate that are now being returned.
The certificates from Obstetrics & gynecology units, please note that there is no entry in the Registry of the Medical and Dental Practitioners in the name of Dr. B.S. Camara, consequently this individual cannot sign a pre-registration certificate.
Enclosed are new forms of certificate completion of apprenticeship, which you can now use in place of the old ones, which are no longer valid.
Yours faithfully
Kinay Drammeh
Administrative Secretary
As you by now noticed nothing new comes from Mbye Faal, alias Jack Faal. He is not the leader who encourages his juniors nor does he really care how much my innocent children and Gambia were affected by his foot dragging callous act.
Let me magnify this statement by just saying that a happy doctor is great asset to his patients as he or she would be able to give more of their time to the practice of medicine than groping for crumbs to

keep their families fed. No wonder, most of our professionals, especially doctors are staying abroad. At times one tends to believe that self-interest kept them away from the downtrodden poor of their countries.

I now can see why some choose to stay rather than go through this shameless and doggy dog treatment day after day, In August 1997 we received another joke from the Administrative Secretary, GMDC, adding insult to injury. Notice that this one-man show tends to show its toothless dragonhead with definite loss of memory.

The Secretary's last letter was four months ago to a matter as urgent as had been my case. Again, I vowed to keep fighting for my rights no matter how long or how much foot dragging Mr. Faal may choose to do regarding my registration.

Let me remind him that the darkest tunnel has light at the end of it. I just wished him well and he can continue enjoying his folly. I will serve God and work for the Gambia. My family and country are my concern, not personalities.

The Gambia Medical Dental Council
PMB 137, Banjul, The Gambia
August 25, 1997

The acting Chief Executive
Royal Victoria Hospital
Banjul, The Gambia

Dear Sir,

RE: Registration of Dr. Alhasan Ceesay

Thank you for your letter Ref: HMB/PF/091 Dated June 1997.
Please note that section 2b of the certificate of Apprenticeship in Internal medicine reads, Save with the limits herein specified, work under supervision."
The Accreditation and Registration Committee (ARC) accordingly recommend that Dr. Alhasan Ceesay do extra four (4) calendar months at the RVH department of Internal Medicine with the current head of the said department.
Following the satisfactory completion of the full registration status may be granted to Dr. Ceesay. Kindly let us know the name of the current head of Internal Medicine, so as to address a letter directly to him.
Yours faithfully
Kinay Drammeh
Administrative Secretary
This sort of reply not only delayed my registration but tantamount to a stab on the backs of the head of units at the RVH, the MAC and the administration of the hospital. Hence, the current head of unit at the Internal Medicine department RVH was urged by well-intentioned members of the staff, to write letting the Registrar reconsider this unnecessary request imposed on me.
It would now be complete three years since completing my apprenticeship and he still continues to spew out poison and disgust onto my face. Anyhow, here is the letter from then head of Internal Medicine at the RVH.

Department of internal medicine
Royal Victoria hospital
Banjul, the Gambia
September 22, 1997

The Registrar
Gambia Medical and Dental council
Kanifding, The Gambia

Dear Registrar,

We are in receipt of your letter dated August 25, 1997 concerning Dr. Alhasan S. Ceesay's need to do another extra 4 months internship at the Department of internal medicine. Having worked with Dr. Ceesay since May 1996 to the present time, September 22, 1997.
I came to know him and his abilities as a doctor. He is capable and a very confident doctor. I find him proficient and a hard worker. I hence, recommend him to you for your kind consideration and for full registration.
I here by enclosed a completed form from May 1996, the time I met him at the Medical unit to September 22, 1997.
Thank you very much for any assistance given in behalf of this dedicated and capable Gambian doctor. Regards
Yours Sincerely
Dr. Jimenez Osvaldo
Consultant
Head of Medical Unit
Cc; Chief Executive, RVH
Chairman HMB

File & R/file

Again, this was met with the usual silence or refusal to respond to letters concerning me. At this juncture of my Another Chief Executive, Dr. Mariatou Jallow, came to the helm of the RVH. I was urged to do the 4 extra months on internship at the department of internal medicine as recommended by the registrar to get him off my back and bring this ugly chapter of my life to close.

We all held our breath and plied through the bitter four months of anguish and callous injustice to my children and family. So I did the rotation with malice but with much more zeal to work harder for the good of my patients and the Gambia.

I worked long hours and at times volunteered to take emergency night calls for a sick colleague or to make life easier for one that had an unexpected urgent need to take care of important family business in the interior or as far as in neighboring Senegal.

The four months Apprenticeship that were supposed to be trying flew past so quickly by the time anyone noticed. We again filled evaluation appraisal form or certificate of completion of Apprenticeship form, as the registrar Mbye Faal calls his new invention.

I stopped anyone urging me or volunteering to have a face-to-face chat with the registrar in other to soften him. I felt that no human being of good intent would treat a beast or a dog in manner I already endured from the hands of this person that calls himself a Gambian. No, no! I will not demean myself for such a person.

He does not deserve the blessing of anyone trying to reason with him. Let him keep at his high pedestal and I will be with the common man who appreciates being human. Let me assure him that he has only waxwings and they do melt at unexpected heights and temperature making the fall very sudden and devastating if the person survives the encounter. I am certain he will come down to us earthlings one fine day.

I use to tell my wife and family when their spirits seem to broken because of this senseless saga, to humbly submit to the Almighty God's will for me. The new Chief Executive, Dr. Mariatou Jallow, passed the completed appraisal forms from the heads of unit at the department Internal Medicine RVH, to the Registrar, as requested, on January 6, 1998.

You bet your bottom dollar the registrar did not care to reply up to today. Dr. Jallow sent the appraisal with the following covering letter.

Hospital Management Board
Royal Victoria Hospital
Banjul, The Gambia
January 6, 1998

Ref: HMB/PF/(091)

Att: kinnay Drammeh, Administrative secretary

The Registrar
Gambia Medical and Dental Council
2 Radio Gambia Road
Mile 7, Bakau, The Gambia

RE: registration of Dr. Alhasan Ceesay

Thank you for your letter dated August 25, 1997 in connection with the above caption. Please find attached certificate of completion of apprenticeship in the medical unit covering period August to December (4 months).
Dr. Ceesay is currently still in the Medical Unit. The head of Medical unit is Dr. Jimenez Osvaldo.
Yours Sincerely
Dr. Mariatou Jallow
Chief Executive
It was not until November, 1999, five grueling years after completing my Internship, that a newly appointed revamped and dynamic Hospital Management board, lead by Mr. Kenneth Njie, that light started to shine at the end of the tunnel for me. These Gambian angels, being convinced that I was not properly treated during the past five years, decided to put their feet down and did the correct thing by promoting me to the post of Medical Officer to stop the starvation and pain inflicted upon my family by this long drawn inhumane saga Mbye Faal's refusal to register me imposed.
Words are aptly inadequate with which to thank and register profound gratitude to them for brining this phase of the saga to an end.
Deep appreciation and sincere thanks to the new Hospital Management Board members and especially the Chairman, Mr. Kenneth Njie, the Director of Health Services, the Chief Executive, RVH, and last but not the least Dr. Alieu Gaye, an admirable and respectable man with whom I have worked with at the medical unit on and off for three

years. Though younger than me he had always shown courtesy, willingness to encourage his colleagues and is pleasant to team up with. Alieu, a million thanks for the interest you have in the Gambia and service you are so diligently rendering the Gambian people.

I wished I were endowed with youthful energy you devote to the Gambia. Yes, Alieu, any time you appear in the wards, it brings a spark of joy to my heart for I know you will give the day all you know and to the best of your abilities with due respect and concern for the patients.

Thank you for weathering so much for our people. Be happy that many noticed and are very grateful for your relentless service to our people. My dear reader, the coveted letter from the management board is thus reproduced for your perusal.

I hope, like me, you will be able to let a sigh of relief at the pinnacle of hell the above experience dragged my life.

Hospital Management Board
Royal Victoria Hospital
Banjul, The Gambia
November 22, 1999

Ref: HMB/PF/091/(41)

Dr. Alhasan Ceesay
Medical Officer
Thro Head of Medical Unit
Royal Victoria Hospital
The Gambia

Dear Sir,

RE: Appointment as MEDICAL OFFICER

I am directed by the Hospital Management Board to inform you that approval has affirm in appointing you as Medical Officer, grade 9.1, with effect from October 1, 1999.
You will be paid allowances commensurate to your grade in addition to your salary as Medical Officer accordingly. By copy of this letter, I am informing the Principal accountant accordingly.
Congratulations.
Yours Sincerely
Mrs. Corea
For Chief Executive
Cc: Permanent Secretary, MOH
Permanent Secretary, PMO
Accountant General
Auditor General
Chairman, HMB
Principal Accountant, RVH
File & R/file

It was a courageous act for which history will crown them as one of the highest dedicated board that ever served the RVH. Their stand to right wrong is an admirable yearning in many hearts and it dwarfs the high pedestal our registrar assumes his post. Needless to say everyone concerned was happy about this outcome and asked me to extend personal gratitude to the board and the entire administration at RVH for having the foresight, decency and moral courage to stand up and do justice to the Gambia and me in the face of the past ceaseless wrong that the refusal to register me inflicted upon me since the completion of my Internship five years ago at the RVH.

The appointment letter did not address the sticky point or business of compensating me for the five years in which I worked underpaid compared to my colleagues.

I will pursue that avenue but for meantime let the elation ride its course until when things are sorted out. I thanked God many times more than I ever did and now worked even hard for my people. My new income went into clearing old debts incurred over the years to pay for school fees and other necessities to allow my daughters attend school.

I was not able to buy a compound or a car to take my children to school. God has His mysterious ways of solving seemingly incomprehensible problems to human minds. At this juncture matters had gone too long and it would be foolish of me if I did not get my redress.

Now I decided to take the bull by horns by taking my case to the nation's second highest authority, vice president and Secretary of State for Health, Social welfare and Women affairs, H.E. Isatou Njie-Saidy.

Doctors do not like being involved with politics but there comes a time and experience in one's life one must take a stand for what is just and rightfully ours. I went before these officials because of sincere conviction they only they can move the registrar into recognizing that he has dragged my case unnecessarily for too long a time.

Having gone through all the expected authorities of the RVH, I sent the following appeal requesting arbitration to resolve my Professional registration saga with the GMDC.
Some friends were hesitant about the move believing that drawing politicians into the scenery might just be another cause to make the registrar feel big and further prolong my agony by stifling intervention any kind in the case.
I told them that it was Parliament that enacted such power as the registrar wheel and it may just be their onus to step into the arena to make sure that coming Gambian doctors would not have to undergo such experiences as I endured from the registrar's delaying tactics.
Armed with confidence of being on the right I told my wife and friends to believe in one God and His name was not "Almighty GMDC Registrar" Here is one of several appeals I made to higher ups.

Department of Medicine
Royal Victoria Hospital
Banjul, The Gambia
February 23, 1998

H. E. Isatou Njie-Saidy
Secretary of State for
Health, Social Welfare
& Women Affairs
The quadrangle
Banjul, The Gambia

Dear Vice President and Secretary of State,

RE: Request consideration of resolving Professional registration raw.

I write calling attention to a dilemma regarding my professional registration with the Gambia Medical and Dental Council that has been unsolved for the past four years.
I took up service with the Royal Victoria Hospital in September 1993 as House Officer and was asked to do three months Internship rotation in Pediatrics, Medicine, Surgery, gynecology and Obstetrics as stipulated by the enclosures in this letter.
My registration has been, since hitherto hindered by sequence of unnecessary delays and foot-dragging by the registrar Mbye Faal. My colleagues receive a salary of D5246.67 while I remained on a salary of D2750 since 1994, under grade 8 integrated scales. Various chief executives of the RVH sent a series of reminders to the Gambia Medical and Dental Council (GMDC) registrar but I am yet to be registered despite having completed my rotation and dully recommended by heads of units at the Royal Victoria hospital since 1994.
The last reminder was sent the GMDC registrar on January 8, 1998. To that reminder the administrative Secretary told us that I would not be registered unless a head of unit at the gynecology department, who signed one of the certificates, registers with the Gambia Medical and Dental Council.
Now Dr. Jimenez Osvaldo is the current head of unit at the department of Medicine and the only one authorized to sign such evaluations.

He has done so as per enclosed. Let me reiterate that both the chairman of the board and chief executives have done all they could within their jurisdiction to resolve my case.

Hence, banking on your good judgment and sense of fair play and as a Gambian, I am appealing for redress of my case to allow me to be registered and as well be compensated for the four years I have been left on grade 8 at not fault of mine.

Thank you very much for your kindness as well as for taking time to resolve my case. I am anxiously awaiting your reply.

Yours Sincerely

Dr. Alhasan Ceesay

Cc: Permanent Secretary, MOH
Permanent Secretary, PMO
Director of Health Services
Secretary General. PSC
Chairman, HMB
Chief Executive, RVH
Chairman, MAC
Registrar, GMDC

A meeting with Vice President H.E. Isatou Njie-Saidy was arranged for me to discuss my problems her for she double as the Secretary of Health of the Nation.

Sure enough she was the right authority to turn to for arbitrate the case when everyone else was unable to move Mbye Fall to unravel the dilemma. The Vice President listened to my woes for a good ten minutes and then told me that although she empathized with my unfortunate case, she was not familiar with the Medical and Dental Council's yard stick for registering doctors.

This discovery came to me as a surprise I expect persons appointed to head the health of the nation should be verse in how people are allowed or disallowed from practicing medicine in the Gambia. She did promise me to have a staff look into the affair.

She suggested my petitioning the president's Office to help since the Council was under that sector. This to me seemed like throw the buck to another person to do one's dirty job.

I thanked her for giving me audience and with laden heart I promised to press forward with the idea of meeting with H. E. President Jammeh to have my case solved.

I wrote to the president but protocol has it that as a civil servant, I need to bring my case before the Secretary General, president's office. I passed through the Secretary of State for presidential affairs who redirected me to the Secretary General's Office were the matter should be handled.

There I met, Mr. Tamsir Mbye, a colleague when we were students in America. Seeing him calmed me down and gave me confidence that perhaps the matter will soon be resolve.

Tamsir and got to business after a short reminiscence of the good old days in Washington, D.C. with this light or welcome atmosphere I thought things might not be as horrible as I had braced myself.

I gave him a complete rundown or trend of the case and he, in the normal politician's way, promised to do all he could to solve it to satisfaction of all concerned with the case. Being an in-law to the registrar Tamsir Mbye assured me that there was no need to speak with the president about my case or fiasco he just heard and that he would do all he could to resolve sooner than later. I left his office naively happy because I believed Tamsir Mbye does know how much I struggled in America to get my schooling done.

He used to visit with me at my flat. So there was doubt in my mind that someone like him would take my cause with alacrity and seriousness to bring it amicable resolution.

That much confidence and relaxation about him knowing was a costly mistake because Tamsir Mbye was about to go to China or some place with the president and the juniors he delegated my case only cared to talk to the registrar and communicated what they got from that office back to me.

I have no doubts that H. E. president Jammeh never heard a word about my plight with the GMDC. A letter was written to me purporting to represent the president's views as stated in the following below. Mr. Tamsir Mbye came back and took a retirement leave and so I was not able to meet with him because he traveled out of the Gambia.

First let me give you the reply that came from the state house. Brace yourselves.

Republic of the Gambia
Department of State for
Health, Social welfare &
Women Affairs
State House, Banjul
The Gambia
May 3, 1998

Ref: AD 543/01/(172)

Dear Sir,

RE: request for consideration of resolving Professional Registration raw

I am directed to acknowledge on behalf of Her Excellency the Vice President and Secretary of State for health, Social welfare and women's Affairs receipt of your letter of February 23, 1998 relating to the above mention subject.
Such matters fall under the purview of the Gambia Medical and Dental Council. However, this office will approach the registrar of that body with a view to resolving this long drawn issue. Thank you.
Yours sincerely
Sukai Bojang
For Permanent Secretary
Two weeks later I heard from the Secretary General's Office as indicated below. Both letters threw mud at my face for they strengthened the noose the registrar had around my neck.
Both offices totally relied on wrong information supplied by the registrar instead of even checking with people on the ground and in the know about my case at the RVH.
To put it mildly they agreed with everything the registrar spewed. Whatever dossier the registrar may have on me was nothing other than his inventions or inventive creation. I would like to make it clear that this was just round one in a boxing bout between the GMDC registrar and I.

In the next round I will meet with H.E. President Jammeh and lay my complain before him.
I will demand for just resolution and compensation for the four years I was under paid because of the aforesaid saga.
The appropriate person(s) will make the compensation when God's time comes. I was certain that someone out there cares and knows about my pains and deprivation this registration nightmare has done to my family and Children.

The Republic of the Gambia
Office of the President
State House, The Gambia
May 17, 1999

Ref:OP277/14/01/1V(8-JP1)

Dr. Alhasan S. Ceesay
Department of Medicine
Royal Victoria Hospital
Independence Drive
Banjul, The Gambia

RE: Request for consideration and arbitration to resolve Professional Registration raw.

I am directed to acknowledge receipt on behalf of His Excellency The president of the Republic, your letter of July 8, 1998 in which you sought intervention and redress with regards to your bid to registrar with the General Medical and dental council.

Regrettably, this office is constrained by its inability, in the fact of the council's decisive position, to interfere in the registration process.
Yours Faithfully
Joseph P. Jassey, Capt. (RTD)
For Secretary General

These two heart wrenching letters left me much more ready to fight my case to the courts. The weak gives up easily but determined one does continue and become heroes.

I am not giving up because of this first volley of blows in the fight. This fight will go on to the final minutes no mater how long it takes to resolve. The truth will make up for the pain my life endured and mistakes made in dealing with it.

God will have me have the last laugh in this kaleidoscope. I am by the above poised to struggle against injustice and misuse of power in office. Both fiend and foe warned me to accept that this was a fate accomplish for me from God and that any further act will only continue the agony my life has endured since my return to the Gambia.

I laughed at such suggestions and asked the person if he or she were present when God was planning my life or would they have stopped knowing that they right?

I made it clear that this rift has to be dealt with squarely and there will be no cowardly surrender by me. Letting matters end now would only set a very bad precedence for future doctors or civil servants as it will allow monsters to gnaw innocent souls like me that may come their way.

No, no chance for that to happen in this case and this will be the last time a registrar of the Gambia Medical and Dental Council would toy with a Gambian doctor's bid for registration at will as if the registrar were dealing with powerless little children. Some prayed for my success while others left bewildered at my determination.

Of course my integrity, professional right were at stake plus my children's future relied heavily on the outcome of the stalemate. I am not in any going to give up my entire life's investment lying down for all the wrong reason of the registrar.

I know the truth is on my side and in the long run it will be so apparent that even Mbye Faal or some God fearing person will bring this Alice in wonderland Gambia tale to an abrupt and amicable end.

Meanwhile, I continued my daily work schedule at the Royal Victoria Hospital and the bimonthly health education activities I started in the provinces. This and my family became the only relief to me. All my plans of buying a compound and a car to take the children to school went over the window because my measly salary hardly feeds us to the end of the month.

My wife, who deserves the highest commendation through out the saga, never for one moment broke down. She had been fully supportive through out this ordeal and has helped me a lot with the children by selling tie-dye materials.

My friend, the going is rough if not very turbulent at present but its true that "laughs best he who laughs last."

The struggle continues until the dawn of justice for all future doctors wishing to register with the Gambia Medical and Dental Council. Roadblocks, roadblocks everywhere when will these treacherous immoral obstacles be removed out of my way? I will hop, skip and jump over every one of them if need be to bring medical service to villagers.

Till then, meet you at the next appeal round of this elusive Jarkcle and Hyde saga of an entrant doctor. By now you have heard me mentioned monthly health field trips to the provinces and I hinted at some point the formation of a village health organization at Njawara called Manding Medical Centre.

The next few pages will be devoted to the interesting part of my life instead of boring saga with the Gambia Medical and Dental Council (GMDC). First let us take a break and contemplate on how I chased elusive time since birth to now.

The Mbalows a happy and cohesive family

Chapter 37

CHASING TIME TO CATCH A DREAM

It is said that time and tides never wait for any one. For me I have been chasing elusive time from the day I came to planet Earth. It has been from time immemorial a challenge of my life. The chase stared at birth when I stopped breathing in the first hour of my life.

In those precious minutes and hence hours to follow time left me behind and I was declared none existent and was to be buried first thing in the morning. Alas! I woke up before dawn and I have been chasing time since February 14th, 1942 to the present time.

My peers in other villages started schooling at the age of 5 years and I started primary school when I was 12 years old. I enrolled at college at the age of 22 years. And I graduated from medical school at age 50.

There has always been this huge gap between time and when things happen for me. Time, where are you? Folks once on a while tease me for being the father of classes I attend. I wish there was a way I can reverse or stop time so that all delays in my life would level up with elapsed time.

All my peers have grown gray or have complete white hairs or totally bald but I look like some 28 year old lad and as fit as a 16 years old athletic kid, even though I never ceased chasing after time. Time for that precious priceless record of history has not arrived for me.

Imagine at my raw age of 68 I am still struggling to get my postgraduate courses for the MRCP level in medicine while my comrades have retired long time ago. William Shakespeare said of time thus: "Come what comes May. Time and the hour runs through the roughest day."

For me it kept flying and irreversibly so. Friends console me by telling me; "Your time will come." In desperation I ask when? Time cares less for it will tick with or without us. Hence, it is my duty to catch up and do so well and early to live footprints on the sand of time worth following when my time comes.

Navigating through the valleys and gorges strewn at us on life's path is a nightmare. I came to England for two reasons; they are to do the MRCP degree and to bring international awareness to my self-help village health NGO, Manding Medical Centre at Njawara in the Gambia, and return to my homeland in the shortest possible time.

This time would not allow as I unknowingly fell into the deepest darkest gorge of visa and job problems. The Home Office's refusal to change my status to that of student left me in limbo and a destitute. Returning home without at least completing the plab exam would be disastrous as experience had taught me while doing my internship in the Gambia.

This made it difficult to pass my exams because of being torn between hunger and struggling to find help to send money to feed my equally beleaguered wife and children back in the Gambia. I became catechetic and weak that even the archangels of death and hell would feel sad and sorry upon meeting me.

It got so bad that I collapsed at the Central Library in Manchester by because of hypoglycemia. Again time and tide refuse to wait for poor Dr. Alhasan S. Ceesay. All my compatriots got through the PLAB because most of them had monetary help enabling them to pay for expensive PLAB review courses. For me I had to feed from the surface of my teeth while I chase time to take my exams under very difficult circumstances that would drown most people.

Time was far ahead of me and I needed to catch up before my dream becomes too late for the Gambia and me. Let me reiterate that the greatest of all faults is to be conscious of none. Hence, time would have not slipped from my fingers had I taken a moment or two to seek for a student visa while at the British Embassy in Gambia.

Anyhow hindsight is always too wise as I later learnt from bitter experience. Despite this long and hard experience, I never gave up and things happened at a surprising and lightening speed for the arrival of a new dawn in my life and goal for the Gambia.

I passed the PLAB exam and started winding down and preparing for my return to the Gambia, the smiling coast of Africa.

These were not only ten painful and trying years but also the most challenging years of my life on planet earth I will never forget nor will I ever wish the worst of my enemies to endure such torturous experience.

Thank God to good Brits and Yankee friends and my steely will that I was able to sail through for my villagers and country. I remain deeply grateful and eternally indebted to all who stood by me from the year 2000 to the present.

Dr. Alhasan Ceesay and daughters, Gambia 1995

Chapter 38

CREATION OF MANDING MEDICAL CENTRE NJAWARA, NBR THE GAMBIA

When God wants to destroy someone, He first made him an unusual dreamer. So Gandhi had his dream of people solving social deference none violently and Martin Luther king, jr. held onto his admirable dream of children of Jews and Gentile, black and whites holding hands and living in harmony spearheading peaceful cause for mankind. There are the Albert Schweitzer's and mother Theresa's of the world dreamers who spent their lives believing in their dreams for mankind.

My dream, since 1956, was the simple goal of providing medical aid to those far and in remote villages.

The villager, who is forced to walk miles on end to seek medical aid for his already dying child, wife or friend, deserves a better health system.

Something I saw in 1956 left an indelible mark in my mind and I have since then asked and prayed that God help me bring part if not full solution to the kind of tragedy that was passing right before me. I was hopelessly unable to give relief except to comfort those involved.

In 1956, while on my way to Saba village, I met an anxious father carrying his son and his almost dead pregnant wife on the back of donkey heading for the health center at Kerewan village, another three or more miles from where I met him. The child was vomiting yellow stuff, he was sweaty, his eyes were reverted backwards and the pregnant lady groaning every time the mule moves. There was some greenish fluid dripping off her lapper. She could barely hold the ropes controlling the donkey. I went to Kerewan later that evening and asked about the status of that family, only to be told that the boy passed away half a mile to the dispensary and the lady was referred to the central hospital in Banjul but the family had no money to pay for her transportation nor was the River ambulance available as it was undergoing maintenance at the Dockyard.

To cut a long story short, both child and mother died because of lack of medical facilities or modern medical aid to the villager. One or all of those lives could have been saved and remain beneficial to the country than the fate that befell them.

I prayed and grieved with the family for months and redoubled my efforts at school in other to solve such development in future. I committed myself to medicine from that day on and never regretted making such a challenging decision in my life. Hence, when on the day I was taking the Hippocratic Oath, I not only swore to uphold all therein but to make sure that God help me not to ever deviate from my commitment and promise to be part of the solution in the health services of the Gambia, to foster health education for the villager, and to complement the existing medical facilities in the Gambia as well as ease the shortage of medical service personnel.

To many, except the dreamer, such Erewhons leads to failure as they turn to be white elephants. Some friends tease me by flatly promising to rise from their graves on the opening day of such an Alice in wonderland project. Let me make it crystal clear that I had no elusions about what was needed, or to be done and that the building of the hospital would indeed be a lifetime challenge I am fully ready to grapple with.

There would be a lot of well-wishers but very few will ever want to join until the opening day ceremonies. So first things first, I met an attorney friend Mr. Ousainou Darboe, a villager like me, on September 24, 1992, and pleaded for his assistance with the legal aspects of setting up a charitable foundation, Manding Medical center at Njawara village in the provinces for the sole purpose of providing much needed medical aid to the villager. He was very obliging and requested no payment in return for his services.

In the mean time I got a board of governors elected while he prepared the memorandum and articles of association of Manding Medical Centre at Njawara village. Also, I met with the Lower Badibou district chief, Kitabou Singateh, who by the way was my primary school class mate at Kinte Kunda from 1953 to 1957, the District Authority, Commissioner and the kerewan Area Council.

All of whom were more than delighted and did all they could under the law to help me set up a grassroots local advisory committee, which was headed by the commissioner, to assist the board and also let the villagers feel being part of the ongoing project.

At my home village, Njawara, a group organized itself and formed a pioneering committee to formally ask the Alkalo (village head/mayor) and the people of Toro Bahen village to donate the earmarked land between it and Njawara for the sole purpose of establishing the Manding Medical Centre on it. The land issue was partially cleared by the first week of the appeal.

October 1992, Alkalo Alh. Omar Koi Bah of Toro Bahen, along with alhaj. Musa (Njabi) Bah and Sirimang Bah called my brother, Doudu Ceesay, the elders of Toro Bahen and I to officially inform us that the earmarked land of two plots have been donated to me for the sole purpose of erecting a medical center and hospital facility for the villagers of the region and Gambia.

We thanked him for his foresight and kindness towards future generations. I went back to my lawyer, Ousainu Darbor who by then had finished all work needed for the registration of Manding Medical Centre.

We are forever indebted to Alkalo Omar Koi, residents Arfang Bah, Musa (Nyambi) Bah and Sirimang Bah, and the people of Toro village. Lastly but not the least our venerable able lawyer Mr. Ousainou Darboe, without whose kindness and legal mind the registration of Manding Medical Centre would have taken longer that it did assisted me.

I also express profound gratitude to the Hon. Chief of Lower Badibou district, Kitabou Singateh, the commissioner, and the local district authority for their understanding and willingness to contribute positively towards our goal and growth.

I submitted the registration application material to the Attorney General's Chambers at the Justice Department, Banjul, on October 22, 1992 and Manding Medical Centre was officially registered as an incorporated charitable organization under the companies Act, 1959 by the 27th of October 1992. Manding Medical Centre' certificate of incorporation is number: 224/1992.

With the completion of the paper work and registration of the center, I embarked on a blitz of letter writing informing philanthropists and organizations world wide about Manding Medical Centre and the need for assistance or donations of medications, equipments, medical videos with which to teach our cadre and villagers to become health worker or evangelist, or nurses and to help us build the center.

To complete the establishment process, after the land was officially ours, I wrote to the following letter to the Ministry of Health informing them of the formation of Manding Medical Centre, a self – help health organization at Njawara, Lower Badibou, North Bank Division, The Gambia. Our temporal address was at 5B Ingram Street in Banjul, capital of the Gambia.

Manding Medical Centre
5B Ingram Street
Banjul, The Gambia
March 2, 1993

Permanent Secretary
Ministry of Health
The Quadrangle
Banjul, The Gambia
West Africa

Dear Permanent Secretary

Re: Application for the establishment of a Medical Centre at Njawara in the North Bank.
We are pleased to bring to attention the setting up of a self-help Health organization in the North Bank Division at Njawara village. The directorates and members of the organization would be more than grateful if the Ministry of Health would allow us establish Manding Medical Centre at Njawara village, Lower Badibou District of the Gambia. Manding Medical Centre, when fully operational, will provide medical, surgical, gynecological and obstetrics.
Pediatrics and other facilities to the villagers. It will also help ease the shortage of medical facilities in that region. Manding Medical Centre will have health education secessions in the villages as an effort to enlighten our youths.
Again, thank you for taking time to consider our application and we certainly look forward to a positive recognition of the need for such a center in the rural sector of the Gambia. We can be reach at your convenience. Regards
Yours sincerely
Dr. Alhasan S. Ceesay, MD
Director/Coordinator
Meanwhile the villagers grew more enthused and throngs of them attended our monthly health field trips or clinics. The attendance grew so large that we ended up listing the villages to attend in turn of nine villages per trip. This usually totals to a bit above 1,000 patients at a given visit.

I normally go on weekends with three doctors and at times four volunteer doctors along with Nurses aid Mrs. Mbee Sonko and Ida Njie to assist us do the job. The field trips/clinics start with an announcement by Radio Gambia giving the names of villages expected to attend and at which village health center.

The clinic day starts with an early morning breakfast by the team and then a ride to the village health center where we would find the villagers and their sick ones assembled. Every occasion starts with the offering of prayers and then the various village heads, in attendance help us in organizing the flow of people wanting to be see by one of our team doctors.

In most cases the day goes trouble free but at certain localities the political tension does make it very difficult to have such large groups of people without little arguments. Thanks to the Commissioner (s) for deploying the police or making them available to quell trouble and help us maintain order during these clinics.

Commissioner Lamin Koma can tell you how rough things can be at some of these clinic centers. He was trapped in one of these bad moments of people rushing to be in the front line of the queue to see one our doctors. The Ministry of Health finally sent us the following affirmative reply as thus: -

Ministry of Health & Social services
The Quadrangle
Banjul, The Gambia

Ref.P510/289/01(95)

Dr. Alhasan Ceesay
Manding Medical Centre
5B Ingram Street
Banjul, The Gambia

RE: Application to establish a Medical Centre at Njawara

I acknowledge receipt of your letter of the 2nd March 1993 on the above-mentioned subject. I wish to inform you that this Ministry has no objection to your application to establish Manding Medical Centre at Njawara.
This initiative is in line with our national health policies and we would render our support in our joint efforts to improve the health of the people.
Signed: N. Ceesay
For Permanent Secretary
After several more field trips it was suggested we apply for a None Governmental Organization (NGO) status. It was believed that if we become and NGO, help would come our way quicker.
I went to work on this suggestion and arranged for Tango Secretariat Centre to send one of the United Nations voluntary program officers to come and evaluate our performance relative to the objectives of Manding Medical Centre.
This was accepted and a field trip was set up for September 12 to 22, 1995. Radio Gambia made the announcement well ahead of the time for our arrival and the following was the outcome of that august gathering of September 21 &22, 1995.

Chapter 39

TANGO SECRETARIAT TRIP REPORT ON MANDING MEDICAL CENTRE SEPTEMBER 21 – 22, 1995

A field trip to Kerewan at the North Bank Division was organized by the Manding Medical Centre Executive Director Dr. Alhasan S. Ceesay in conjunction with Tango Secretariat Centre to see the organization's activities and meet the members before recommending the organization as a member of Tango.

On September 21, 1995, two meetings were organized in two big centers where members gather to air their views and experience from the organization. Alkalos, chiefs, imams, women, men and youths attended these meetings.

The key leadership from five villages in their speeches showed interest and support for the project and organization. Alkalo of Toro Bahen Omar Koi and chiefs donated the land for the constructing of Manding Medical Centre, the hospital and its ancillaries.

The two meeting were highly attended and successful. The Tango (UNV) program officer Mr. Muloshi on behalf of Tango gave a keynote speech on Tango's operations and activities as an umbrella organization and urged members to work hand in hand with the organization in their efforts to develop their villages and North Bank area.

The three meetings with the commissioner during the field trip on our courtesy call were successful and encouraged the executive Director of Manding

Medical Centre, Dr. Alhasan Ceesay, to cooperate with the strict, especially the commissioner who is one of the advisors in the local committee. The commissioner thanked Tango for making the purpose of the mission clear to him and promised that he will try by all means to cooperate with Tango in the area of Technical advice and institution capacity building.

Clinic day was organized on September 22, 1995 at Njawara and 150 people attended and got treatments.

RECOMMENDATION

Looking at the caliber of leadership and development activities compared to some NGO tango members in comparison to Manding Medical Centre, the organization need consideration since they have already activities with a promising future. Looking at the composition of the Board, they have people with a great vision.

They have strong membership and backup at the grassroots levels. The organization has chosen to do what is right at the right time and their concentration in one area is vital and a good starting point.

Any success achieved by any organization depended on good leadership and discipline. Manding Medical Centre has quality leadership and deserves NGO status.

Signed: M. Muloshi
UNV Program Officer

We were delighted by the recommendation made by the United Nations voluntary Program Officer in the Gambia. We redoubled our efforts to contact organizations seeking help worldwide.

In between letters and monthly field trips to different select health centers we were blessed with visits from interested friends and groups or representatives of similar organizations in the globe. I had several telephone calls to Dr. Edward Brown, an official of the World Bank in Washington, D. C. responsible of the bank's health affairs at the time. He was very receptive and had several added discussions with Dentist Melvin George, then Director of Medical and Health Service for the Gambia, on how the bank could help in the financing of the building of Manding Medical Centre.

These talks went on well and Dr. Edward brown gave me his promise and personal commitment to helping the project and that we have to start in a small scale and the building will have to be done in several well planned phases.

Dr. Sidi C. Jammeh, a former Armitage School colleague, promised to help me keep the momentum at the bank alive by consulting and constantly reminding Dr. Brown of the need to help us with the project.

Among our guest were a couple from Colchester, Essex, UK, Lorna V. Robinson and husband Keith Robinson were very impressed by our project and enthusiasm of the ordinary villagers about Manding Medical Centre.

They fell in love with the idea and objectives of the self-help health organization and promised to help as much as they could. We had by this time submitted application for NGO status and ACCNO Secretary replied thus:

ACCNO Secretariat
Dept. of Community Development
13 Mariner Parade
Babjul, The Gambia
September 12, 1994

Ref.CD/ACCNO/Vol3/(183)

Dr. Alhasan S. Ceesay
Director/Coordinator
Manding Medical Centre
P. O. Box 640
Banjul, The Gambia

Dear Sir,

RE: application for an NGO status within the ACCNO framework

Please find enclosed a self-explanatory letter from the Ministry for local government and lands concerning the approval of your application for NGO status.
ACCCNO Secretariat congratulates your organization for successfully completing the registration process and wishes you a fruitful relationship in the field of development.

Thank you for your cooperation
Yours Faithfully
Musu Ngujo
For: ACCNO desk Officer
Cc: file & R/File
Replies from our worldwide appeal letters did not pour in money nor did they materialized beyond promises to help in due course. Hence, I decided to open up a pharmacy at my expense at my residence in the Bundung area of Serekunda using the proceeds from its sales to finance the health field trips and activities of the organization.

This meant spending an extra three to fours at the pharmacy daily after eight hours at the RVH before rejoining my family. All drugs used for the treatment of patients at our field trip clinics were purchased from sales I made at the Bundung Pharmacy.

A local agency, known as IBAS, lent me D8000, interest free, which was used in buying drugs and paying for transportation for the project's activities. The loan was completely repaid well ahead of the allowed sixteen months period given by IBAS. We are obliged and grateful to Aja Ndey Oley Jobe and management of IBAS for their kindness to assist us at the time.

Just when things were about to be financially complete for us to start the first phase of building the various sections of the hospital, came the unexpected coup d'etat of July 22, 1994. The reaction from would be our donors and supporters or sponsors were swift and equally unexpected. All those who were considering giving the project a chance sited likelihood of sudden national unrest and instability as reasons for their withdrawal of promised aid and participation while some suggested my waiting until after the transition phase of the coup d'etat before they would reconsider reopening our files with them.

Again it resorted to case of the chicken the egg, which came first as no one, knew when the transition will end and we kept our fingers crossed hoping that daylight will be ours in not far distance.

It was a severe blow to our hope and for getting the type of interest and support that was engendered for Manding Medical Centre would be difficult to match after such crisis that occurred in the Gambia.

Many were acting in conjunction with their governments, which were not sure of what the future under military rule would be for the Gambia. All prospective and possible international sources earmarked for Manding Medical Centre were either frozen or evaporated into thin air with the coup leaving me floating in the middle of the ocean of despair without a life jacket except God's merciful hands.

I knew the villagers would grow restless if nothing happens in the direction of building the center.

I called an emergency general meeting with members from most of the villages and told them of the new challenge and development and this information not only fell on deaf ears but left their spirits dampened.

Interest waxed and waned at some quarters but I kept on trying my best not to be despondent like the others have shown. I kept the organization alive under very limited funds raised from the pharmacy at Bundung until my trip to the UK in January 2000. Before leaving the Gambia, the Commissioner for north Bank Division and chairman of the local advisory committee for Manding Medical Centre, Mr. Lamin Koma, gave me the following letter to assist me in my fund raising drive while in England and possible other European countries. It read thus:

The Commissioner
Kerewan Village
North Bank Division
The Gambia, West Africa
June 15, 1998

TO WHOM IT MAY CONCERN

I hereby write to testify and confirm that Manding Medical Centre is a self-help health project situated at Njawara village, North Bank Division.
As the Commissioner of this division I was elected as the Chairman of the local advisory Committee of the Manding Medical Centre.
As I am concerned, I am aware of this self-help project since it took off the ground, by the able hands of Dr. Alhasan S. Ceesay, a born citizen of Njawara village.
The purpose of the establishing of such a medical centre is to provide medical attention/care to all Gambians irrespective of religion, tribe, nationality or gender and age within the country and sub-region.
It is in these regards that this office writes to seek for your assistance in providing support in cash/kind to make this medical center a reality. I look forward to your continued support and cooperation.

Signed: V. Baldeh
For Commissioner
North Bank Division

The new millennium started with good omen for Manding Medical Centre. I have been invited to go to Europe and America on a found raising trip for the center but could not because of my commitment with the Royal Victoria Hospital (RVH).

I needed a longer vacation period to be able to travel and keep my job at the sane time. Above all my family needed the monetary support, which would fade away if I lost the post at the RVH. Hence, to my delight and greatest timely occurrence I heard from my long-standing friend in Colchester, Mrs. Lorna V. Robinson, inviting my wife and I to come to the UK to attend the wedding of their younger daughter on January 9th, 2000. Coincidentally, I had just started my annual leave, which was to finish on the 26th of January 2000. The excitement mounted when we received a fax from the visa officer at the British High Commission in the Gambia requesting that we report to the visa processing office with our passports on Tuesday 8.30 am January 4th, 2000 for processing of our visas for our pending travels to the UK.

This took me by surprise because of the casual way we had discussed the possibility of such a trip. So when we got the telephone call followed by the said fax from the visa section I was caught off guard and had to rush through all the preparations for my wife and I to travel to UK without a second thought on whether adequate arrangements were being made for my eventual pursuit of a postgraduate degree (MRCP) in internal medicine.

Hind side has it that I needed to discuss this aspect with the visa councilor and request for eventual student visa status or leave to remain until my completion of the post graduate degree I wanted to pursue. God's ways and timing are best for every occasion.

I was yearning to get a way out of the financial limbo the center ran into since the change of government in the Gambia. Now that opportunity was suddenly thrown on my laps by Lorna Robinson's open-ended invitation for my wife and to attend their daughter's wedding ceremony in the UK.

Interested donors started being weary about Military rule and possible restlessness that may ensue. Hence, Manding Medical Centre literally lost all it's prospective over seases support as well as sponsors most of who had cold feet after the July coup d'etat of 2004.

I ended up running the center from my meager salary of D1500 or seventy-five pounds sterling per month and of literally hard labour with long hours at a time. The other source was from what little I could make from sales at the Bundung pharmacy.

To cut a long story short we were granted visas to travel to the UK. We left the Gambia on the 6th of January 2000 on a new footing and challenge to bring back some life into Manding Medical center while in England. I got on the ball as soon as the wedding ceremony was over.

I obtained a three–year study leave from the Management Board of the Royal Victoria Hospital in Banjul. This gave me all the time I needed to try to rekindle interest in the center and thereby inject into Manding Medical center cash flow it needed to help us meet or our targeted goal and objective for the farming community in the North Bank Division of the Gambia. It was more like a miracle entering this new concrete and direct ways.

Help from my host Lorna Robinson of Colchester, Essex, UK further anointed my hands. Lorna and I wrote several letters to various places, including celebrities and organizations, most of who replied in the negative because of perception they had about the political climate in Gambia since the coup d'etat of July 22nd 1994.

Nonetheless some hinted being interested at a later date, meaning when the solders return to camp. A few donated small amounts plus hospital items. By now it became clear that we have to counter the perception most, on this side of the isles feel or had about the Gambia at the time.

This dreadful start did not alarm me much for I am fully aware of the wrong information about the average African in the village, who like most is just a descent human being trying to earn an honest living for himself, family and community.

Villagers are least interested in all the political gimmickry shrouding and clothing their lives. I do not at all blame the rest of world for getting sick and tired of helping and not seeing any tangible good come out of it and worse some African politicians and regimes show no interest in helping move the African people onto better and modern rewarding modalities of life.

They offer more lip service than opening avenues for progress. How many knew that the Ethiopian starvation was politically orchestrated by the then Mangestu regime? Genocide regime and the heartlessness of some African politicians made me feel sick. To remove any possible skeptics regarding Manding Medical Centre and its objectives we decided to have it registered as a charitable organization in the UK under the name of Colchester Friends of Manding charitable trust.

The Robinson knew a solicitor who would be so kind to help us with the legal aspect of the registration process with UK charity Commission. They spoke to Mr. Bruce Ballard of the Birkett long Solicitors to come to our aid.

This kind gentleman, like my lawyer friend, Mr. Ousainou Darboe, gladly agreed to help and sent us a draft of the Trust deed. After a series of changes were made on the draft he forwarded our request to be registered in the UK as a charitable organization helping its twin partner or parent group, Manding Medical Centre at Njawara village in the Gambia, West Africa. Meanwhile, we concentrated our activities through media campaign effort to call attention to existence of Friends of Manding and their desire in building a hospital for Manding Medical Centre at Njawara, the Gambia.

Again we ran into a very gentle heart in the person of Miss Helen Anderson of Colchester who was the Community website editor for Essex County. She went head over heels regarding the idea of helping others so far away when approached by Lorna Robinson.

Helen thought the idea wonderful and at the same time helped us have our own website and also had an article published by the Evening Gazette which had a large reader circulation. In the same vein I got the interest of Dr. Linda Mahon-Daly, Dr. Peter Wilson, Dr. Laurel Spooner, Dr. Richard Spooner, Dr. Philip Murray, Dr. Barbara Murray, Dr. Fredric Payne, who by the way was our Medical superintendent under who I worked at the RVH during the later part of colonial Gambia, along with many surgeries in the Colchester area.

These were my Good Samaritans of the day who worked acidulously to make Manding Medical Centre become a reality for the villagers in the Gambia.

Dr. Linda Mahon-Daly helped distribute letters about Manding Medical Centre to nearly all her colleagues in the Colchester Borough and so did Dr. Laurel Spooner. Bless their hearts for kindness and job well done.

The news article published by the Evening Gazette brought us another very helpful and kind person, Mr. Malkait singh who is an ophthalmologist and had made several trips to the Gambia before knowing about the Friends of Manding.

He was delighted to join Neville Thompson, Connie Thompson, Lorna Robinson, Keith Robinson, Loenard Thompson, Mark Naylor, Barbara Philips and others as pioneering members of Friends of Manding. Mr. Malkait Singh and I grew to be very good friends and he had since given me lots of personal monetary help to cater for my exams and family back in the Gambia.

I am very grateful for interest and kindness, and concern he showed about my family. A few months after the formation of Friends of Manding, Dr. Laurel Spooner spent a week in the Gambia vacationing and doing some fact finding about the center. During which time she visited Manding Medical Centre at Njawara in the North Bank Division. The villagers were happy to meet her and thanked her about good work being done in Colchester regarding Manding Medical Centre. Everyone was happy about the news that people in the UK were poised to assist Manding Medical Centre go forward in its drive to provide medical aid to villagers.

A meeting of member of the Friends of Manding was scheduled for the first week of February 2001. Mean while our solicitor continued pressing for registration of Friends of Manding, which is the arm and Manding Medical Centre's Colchester branch support group, as charity in the UK.

Dr. Laurel Spooner suggested we start with small-scale form of the center and then gradually expand as funds become available. This consideration would be studied in full and deliberated upon by the committee during the forth-coming February meeting.

Chapter 40
WHAT IS MANDING MEDICAL CENTRE?

Manding Medical Centre is a self-help village health organization founded by Dr. Alhasan S. Ceesay, located at Njawara village in the North Bank Region of the Gambia, West Africa.
Its objective is to provide medical service to the villagers by providing efficient and affordable medical aid to all people in and around the Gambia, especially the rural sector. We are dedicated to relieving suffering and ensure effective treatment for villagers and all attending Manding Medical Centre at Njawara, NBR.

ESTABLISHED:

The Manding Medical Centre is founded by Dr. Alhasan Sisawo Ceesay, a native of Njawara village in 1992, because of sheer shortage of medical service to the region and the preponderance of premature deaths by children from Malaria, malnutrition, diarrhea, and worm infestations. T hese childhood maladies account for almost 25% of Gambian children's death before the ripeful age of five years. The Gambia Ministry of Health officially recognized the Centre in 1995 and prior to which it became a None Governmental Organization (NGO) on September 12th, 1994.
In addition, the Manding Medical Centre now has Friends of Manding Charitable Trust, Colchester, Essex, UK as its arm and liaison in the UK and the European Union countries. The Friends of Manding is a registered charity in England and Wales.

Its registration number is 1088136 since August 21, 2001. In similar development and purpose, Dr. Avery Aten heads the Friends of Manding Alpena Charitable Trust, Alpena, Michigan, UAS since May 2005.

MISSION STATEMENT:

Suffering in another human being is a call to the rest of us to stand in fellowship. It requires us to be there and it is a mystery, which demands the spirit of caring, sharing and our presence.
Our duty as healthcare professionals is providing medical care, which is a fundamental right of all human beings. This village health organization is dedicated to providing medical aid to the rural sector and farming community in the Gambia.
It will compliment the health service in the Gambia in addition it will promote preventive medicine in the hinterland of the Gambia.

MEMBERSHIP

:Well over twenty thousand villagers, comprising of farmers, village heads, and chiefs, the Kerewan Area Council, Commissioners and local District Authority are now fully active enthusiastic members of Manding Medical Centre.
All are welcomed to join the endeavors of the center. People from the rest of the globe are more than welcomed to participate or share with us Your dream in bring much needed medical service to people in desperate state because of lack of medical facilities.

ACTIVITIES

Manding Medical Centre tries to alleviate some of the above mentioned health problems and situations by having bimonthly health field trips/clinics to villages teaching them about health, preventive medicine and hygiene that would help reduce the number infected and the vectors responsible for these diseases.

We encourage antenatal and postnatal attendance of clinics by mothers and we treat the sick amongst them with minimum charge to not so elderly and pregnant young ladies. The service is free to children, the very elderly, and the indigent needing emergency treatment.

The rest pay amounts well below tat in private practice. Money accrued is subsequently used to buy drugs with which to treat the patients and for other projects of the center.

When in cession the center treats well more than 1000 patients per field trip to the villages. We provide free information and advisory service on aids and sexually transmitted diseases (stds) to the young, all patients, their relatives and friends.

We also plan to have a Nursing School in due course to augment not only staff but also the government health centers when the need arises.

IMMEDIATE GOAL AND APPEAL

The villagers are very enthused about the center and Toro Bahen village, next to Njawara village, has donated two plots of land for the building of the center and its ancillary units, which is now leased to manding medical center for ninety-nine years. More than 2000 children die tragically from malaria and other childhood ailments stated above for shortage of health services.

We are eager to start building the children' and maternity wings of the proposed Gambia General Hospital at Manding Medical Centre and do need raise the required 900,000 pounds sterling to accomplish our goal.

Ten bags of cement cost thirty pounds sterling or $60 (sixty us dollars). Also we would be most grateful if we could be assisted with medicines and equipment to facilitate our work. Hence we implore you to kindly support our yearning to build the children' and maternity wings of Manding Medical Centre.

We are dedicated to providing medical aid to the villager, especially children. We are investors in people and you are invited to join the endeavors of Manding Medical Centre at Njawara village, the Gambia, West Africa. Help us make a difference and beacon of hope for the villagers.

Please give generously. Today's hope can be tomorrow's reality. We want to contribute positively towards the health services of the Gambia, and with this center in place it will create greater health awareness and privation by the villagers.

Cash contributions of any amount should be sent in the name of Manding Medical Centre, to the Friends of Manding charitable Trust, 82 Finchingfield Way, Blackheath, Colchester, Essex, CO2 OAU, and England.

It is vital to be certain that Dr. Alhasan S. Ceesay is informed of your contribution via email thus:

alhasanceesay@hotmail.co. UK. Your kindness and humane consideration to help save lives will always be deeply appreciated and grateful for by the villagers, the Gambia and I.

OVERSEASES LINKS

The Friends of Manding in Colchester, Essex County, UK, is a local group comprising of residents, doctors, and nurses who regularly visited the Gambia and are in support of Manding Medical Centre.
Manding medical center through the auspices of the Friends of Manding recently received recognition and registration by the UK Charity Commission. They serve as support and our liaison in the Europe Union.
The Friends of Manding in behalf of Manding Medical Centre at Njawara has been entered in the central Register of charities with effect from August 21, 2001; the registration number is 1088136 for England and Wales.
Also, a similar charitable trust, the Alpena Friends of Manding Charitable Trust of Michigan, USA, has been established in Alpena, Michigan in June 2006. It's headed by Dr. Avery Aten a resident physician chairman of the Women and newborn of the Alpena region Community Health along with the medical community of Alpena.

Chapter 41
MANDING MEDICAL CENTRE MILESTONES

Manding Medical Centre has been in my mind's drawing board since the early 1950s but it took off in earnest when I returned to the Gambia, after graduating from medical school in 1992. The Centre is registered as a charity with the Attorney general's Office, Department of Justice, Banjul, The Gambia, since 1993.

The Gambia Ministry of Health also recognized it in the same year. Toro Bahen village, Lower Badibou, NBD, Gambia, donated two huge plots of land for the location of the center in 1993. Our none governmental (NGO) status was approved in 1994. On September 21, 1995 Tango Secretariat sent a United Nations voluntary program Officer, Mr. Muloshi on field trip to evaluate the organizational and extent of support for Manding Medical Centre at Njawara village.

Mr. Muloshi's recommendation after two days field trip to the region stated thus; "Looking at the caliber of leadership and development activities to some NGO Tango members in comparison to Manding Medical Centre, the organization need consideration since they have already activities with a promising future. Looking at composition of the Board, they have people with a vision.

They have strong membership and backup at grass root levels. The organization has chosen to what is right at the right time and their concentration in one area is vital and good starting point. Any success achieved by any group or organization depends on good leadership and discipline.

Manding Medical Centre has high quality leadership and deserves NGO status". It was not until my travels to the UK in 2000 that the Friends of Manding Charitable Trust was formed and registered as charity in England and Wales by the UK Charity Commission.

Friends of Manding is the extended arm of Manding Medical Centre at Njawara, The Gambia. They serve as our liaison in the UK and the European Union. Please browse on our website thus: friendsofmanggambimed.btck.co.uk, to learn more or for further information about our work and organization. We are still on fund raising activities to earn enough to enable us build the children' and maternity units of the hospital at Manding Medical Centre at Njawara.

In May 2005, 11 American students and their instructor Mr. Thomas Ray visited Manding Medical Centre at Njawara. Additionally, input from has now resulted in Alpena City, Michigan, USA, twining by proclamation with Njawara and Kinte kunda villages in Gambia respectively on the 5th of December 2005.

In June 2006, Dr. Avery Aten, Chairman of the Women and Newborn of Alpena Region Health Community along with the medical community of Alpena commenced processing application for a charitable Trust to be named Alpena friends of Manding Charitable Trust, Michigan, USA.

This will soon be finalized and up and running to help Dr. Alhasan Ceesay in the provision of medicine and educational assistance to schools in the Lower Badibou district, the Gambia, West Africa.

In August 2008, Dr. Alhasan Ceesay and the Badibou Cultural Dance Troupe will visit Alpena and other cities in Michigan for fund raising drive to enable the building of the Manding Medical Centre children and maternity units at Njawara village. Dr. Richard Bates, an Obynge, and a number of medical professionals involved in obstetrics and gynecology at Alpena, Michigan joined Manding Medical Centre's crusade on 17/08/07.

Dr. Ceesay with daughters, Bundung Serekunda

Chapter 42
TEMPLATE FOR REGIONAL DEVELOPMENT

Manding Medical Centre became a template for districts elsewhere and villagers to nurture, develop further and handover to the next generation. This None Governmental Health Organization epitomizes a developmental watchtower for the region. Manding medical center at Njawara village is now a pulsating source of hope, jobs, training and superb medical service to the region.

Every one knows that government alone does not move things fast enough. Society must be radical and pragmatic to pitch into its development.

We know all too well that the developed world got where its because private efforts were self prophetic and projects like Manding Medical Centre goes long ways to initiate and stimulate community to work together for a positive agenda for its people. Manding Medical Centre is a positive good that help our regions to cross the road.

We thank every one for making it possible that our center became a platform and guide in rejuvenating our regions. We now provide medical service to all Gambians and none Gambians domiciled in the Gambia. We will create more jobs as need arises. This was the reason why I gave my life's comfort for reward that will benefit most needy villagers.

It came through determination and kindness of many people worldwide. There are some things only governments can do but together communities through collective initiatives can achieve at least fifty percent of their developmental needs in addition to government effort.

Chapter 43
APPEAL TO INTERNATIONAL COMMUNITY

Dear Readers,

The above information about Manding Medical Centre is included in this work only hoping that it will help spread the word more extensively and draw awareness to a greater community of people and readers of my work.

It is my believe that lots of good people out there may want to participate or give to the cause and goal of the enter should they be aware of its existents for the villagers.

Hence, I am appealing for help and participatory support from all able to extend their hearts to make this much needed medical endeavor to come to fruition for the rural sector of the Gambia. Who knows you might even end up coming to bask in our beautiful seasides and relish Gambian generosity.

Music for me is reaching out to help others and my patients are yearning for your kind participation and donation in cash/kind. Thanks a million for considering our appeal. God blesses your heart(s). I write with believe that by it money can be generated to provide a much needed medical service to the rural sector.

Writing about the Manding Medical Centre may course some Good Samaritan and any wanting to leave foot prints on the sand of time for a good cause to come to our assistance to help us meet the goals of the center at Njawara village, the Gambia, West Africa.

My head, heart and soul are devoted to my family, the Gambia and Manding Medical Centre. It is not a God given calling but a mere conviction that our rural folks deserve better health service than currently available and hence human calling to want to contribute positively to bring resolution of some of our rural health service inadequacies.

I never had an angel come down to me nor have I ever heard the voices of God saying, "Ceesay, you must do so and so" as many mocked Manding Medical Centre emanated from sheer conviction that it is a dutiful way of doing the right thing for curbing premature deaths of children before reaching 5 years of life from malaria, water born diseases, and warm infestations; and in the same vein providing both pre and postnatal care to the pregnant.

Hence, portions of proceeds of sales in all my work go to help meet the center's operational costs and in providing scholarship to indigent indigenous rural candidates due course return to serve rural Gambia wishing to read for a medical degree or agriculture and Medicine.

Chapter 44
AMERICAN GUESTS VISIT MANDING MEDICAL CENTRE, NJAWARA, THE GAMBIA

The telephone call of the 5/01/05 and following fours later from Mr. Thomas P. Ray (Tom) opened the Pandora's box that became harbingers to a remarkable trip to Manding Medical Centre at Njawara village in the Gambia West Africa by the Alpena Community College's Leadership class headed by none other than Mr. Thomas P. Ray. I contacted Mr. Ray as soon as it was brought to my attention that some ACC students were contemplating visiting Manding Medical Centre at Njawara in May 2005.

My message sent on the 6/01/05 to Mr. Thomas Ray ran thus: An old friend, Mr. Mathew Dunnkel, staff of Alpena Community College, had a long chat with me last night and he brought to my attention of a possibility that the leadership class plants to travel to the Gambia as guest of the Manding Medical Centre at Njawara.

I am more than willing to and happy to pave the way for those that would venture the trip. I do need an e-mail or fax from you indicating desire to go to the Gambia on a mission for Manding Medical Centre.

I will speak to both the district authority and the schools about your most welcomed trip to the Gambia. Manding Medical Centre is a self-help village health organization I setup in Njawara upon returning to the Gambia in 1992. We provide medical service to villagers.

Torro Bahen in Lower Badibou District has donated Land for location of the medical center and its ancillaries. We only have a corrugated shed as a clinic at present. We are now on the verge of building the first phase, being the children and Maternity units of the center, and do need monetary assistance.

I am delighted to know of your intentions. Please contact me, as soon as get this I want to speak with the class. Mr. Thomas P. Ray replied the next day 7/01/05 thus, "I was thrilled when Mathew discussed the possibility of a trip to the Gambia for our leadership students.

I will meet with whole class next week to discuss the possibility. As I am sure you are aware of the cost of airfares from Alpena to the Gambia is high. So I will need to be certain the students are committed to raising the money needed before we begin making plans.

I have traveled to many locations, but never to Africa. So I am also very excited about the prospects for myself. Afterwards I met with the students on Tuesday the following week. I will e-mail you with further information. I wish to commend you for your personal achievements.

I plan to purchase a copy of your recent book to share with my students and for my personal reading. Thank you for your help and enthusiasm."

I replied advising that he bargain for insured group tickets. And on the 12/01/05 Thomas Ray emailed that he had spoken to the students who had agreed to take on a service trip as part of the course. They would only be able to travel in a group and stay from 10 to 14 day at Njawara in May 2005.

Thomas wanted to know if there was an existing program at Njawara that would be able to accommodate the students. He further assured me that the students would be comfortable in a dormitory housing or make shit dormitories. In addition I let Ray know on the 14/01/05 that I have spoken to the Commissioner, north Bank Division and the local District Authority in the lower Badibou District regarding their pending trip to Njawara as guest of Manding Medical Centre and the region.

I assured him these authorities would be more than happy to have his class visit with them. I requested that he e-mail me stating specifically y what they would want to do while in the Gambia. I suggested that they could help teach in some schools. I assured them that even though business and some residents have moved out of Njawara there is still some activity at the village.

Thomas replied sending the following on 15/01/05, "Thank you for the great news. I am very excited about the prospect and have begun search for group airfares with special student rates. I will inform the students on Tuesday and contact you immediately afterwards via email.

I have a few questions. What costs do we need to expect in the Gambia and in your village? How will we travel from Banjul to the village? We need to be certain we have both for ourselves and for the foundation from which we hope to receive grants. When I write the other email, are there tasks other than tutoring that I should include?

Are there other ways we can help while we are there? I am more excited about the prospect of this service trip everyday and the students are quite enthused. In another email dated 15/02/05.
Thomas Ray wrote, "The students in the leadership class are so committed to this project that they voted to contribute their own money toward the travel to Njawara in May.
I have begun drafting the letter to the commissioner many times, but I have some questions. Am I asking the commissioner to help organize local housing for us? Do I want his permission to visit Njawara/ Should I tell him what we would like to do there? What subjects might they tutor? Are there any construction projects for the center or the village with which we could help?
I would also like to know if there are any material supplies we could bring with us to donate to the center or the village? One possible way for us to save money would be to fly into Dakar Senegal and travel from there overland to Njawara."
All the above concerns and questions were answered but a small hiccup in fundraising occurred leaving a distinct possibility that the students will not be able to raise enough to make the trip. The reason for the reduction of those coming being that the majority of sources for funding the trip fell through.
This left all of us jittery but Thomas Ray and his leadership class were in no mood to change their plans to travel to the Gambia in May 2005. On the same day 15/02/05 I received another email from Jay Walterriet, Director of Public Information for Alpena Community College.

It stated that he was asked to contact me for more photos of myself and those of the clinic at Njawara. He wanted more information regarding the leadership-planned trip to the Gambia. I was told that the local television station would like to do a segment on the leadership class and their trip.

As part of the segment photos I sent as much relevant photos as I had at the time to enable the reporter to do his TV-segment on the planned leadership trip to Njawara the Gambia.

Mr. Ray on the 17/02/05 emailed thanking me for providing the photos and also assured me that the Alpena Community College students have received good deal of interest from the local media regarding the Leadership trip and both he and Penney Boldrey were trying to provide all of the information they could.

My email was given to reporters who might want to contact me for more information. The entire twenty students could not enlist for the final take off to Africa. Hence, Thomas P. Ray and 11 students took on the venture of their lives to the Gambia as guest of Manding Medical Centre at Njawara village. On 17/02/05 Thomas P. Ray, instructor of the leadership class, sent me the following email copy of the final letter he sent to the commissioner and the local district authority at the Lower Badibou District spelling out their intentions and wish while guest of Manding Medical Centre for a two weeks duration. Here is the letter.

Thomas P. Ray
Alpena Community College
666 Johnson Street

Alpena, Michigan 49707
17 February 2005

The commissioner,
North Bank Division
Kerewan Headquarters
Lower Badibou
The Gambia, West Africa
17/02/05

Dear Commissioner,

I am pleased to inform you that our plans to visit Njawara on behalf of the Manding Medical Centre. I am the Advisor and instructor for a group of college students from Alpena Community College in Michigan in the USA.
We plan to visit Njawara in May and hope you will help us find lodgings with the local families during our two weeks stay. Our plan as of now is to fly out of the US on May 6th to Banjul via London and return on May 19th 2005.
During our stay in the Gambia, our hope is to provide any assistance we can to the community on behalf of Manding Medical Centre. We would like to visit the schools in Njawara and tutor the children and share stories and activities with them.
I also hope that we will have the opportunity to visit the important centers of the community and learn as much as we can in our short stay about the people and life at Njawara and Gambia.
I have communicated our plans with Dr. Alhasan S. Ceesay, who has kindly extended the invitation to us on behalf of Manding Medical Centre.

Sincerely
Thomas P. Ray
English Instructor
The Regional Commissioner and the district authority of Lower Badibou in the Gambia acknowledged this letter. Now being certain of the trip I set to inform my Board members about the trip even though it was widely known affair leaving everyone expectant.

The certainty of the trip was concretized by Thomas's March 10, 2005 email. It simply updated me on the progress made regarding the trip and that the students have raised half the amount of money needed to travel to the Gambia.

He further reaffirmed the fact that everyone concerned is working hard on the remaining sum. They arranged inoculations and are preparing to apply for visas to the Gambia.

Ray said they were all enthused and have used my address in Gambia for the visa information requirements. Again, I was delighted for things were now heading the right direction for the historic and unique trip to Njawara.

I am now certain that more doors boost ours and the centre's goal for the Gambia will be opened by this simple friendly act of the Alpena Community College. Here is finally my dispatch to board members of manding Medical Centre at Njawara village.

Manding Medical Centre
United Kingdom Contact
245 Great Western Street
Manchester, M14 4LQ

England
25/03/05

Dear Board Member,

I am pleased to bring to your attention about American guests to Manding Medical Centre at Njawara. Mr. Thomas P. Ray along with 11 Alpena Community College students will be visiting the Gambia as our guest in May2005.
They will be leaving the USA for the Gambia on May 6th, 2005 and depart for the United States on the 19th, May 2005. I would be most grateful if you give some of your time to meet them and make their visit memorable.
There are many benefits to be accrued for the center and the Gambia. I am at present arranging the form of placement and possible scholarships in various fields of study at my previous colleges in Michigan USA.
I have been in constant contact with Commissioner Batala Juwara at Kerewan and I would like all of you to brain storm and make this an ongoing link between us and Alpena Community College and other Michigan cities I am now in negotiation with. Alpena city has developed interest in our project.
I am also happy to report that my former college, Alpena Community College, has awarded me, "Distinguished 2005 graduate."
Find enclosed correspondence from Mr. Thomas Ray, in behalf of the leadership class of Alpena Community College to the Commissioner Batala juwara and Sefo fafanding Kinteh.

I look forward to your understanding and participation to help open up the Pandora's box of goodwill for the Gambia. This is a onetime opportunity for the Gambia that would make out two people linked for good goals and noble cause for generations to come. My regards and keep in touch.
Yours Sincerely
Dr. Alhasan s. Ceesay, MD
Founder/coordinator
Cc; Ousainou Darboe
Fafa Mbye
Dr. Dawda Ceesay
Dr. Ayo Palmer
Mr. Saim Kinteh
Mr. Sambou Kinteh
Mr. Mustapha Njie
Elh. Maja Sonko
Dodou Ceesay
Siswao Ceesay
Mbee Sonko

On April 7, 2005 Thomas Ray updated me stating that the visa applications were going well and that most of the students have received their visas. In addition let me privilege readers to some of the emails to me about the pending trip by students and what it would mean to them.
Alison Jane Smolinski said, "Hello Dr. Ceesay. I am really excited about the service trip, only a couple more weeks. Right now we are trying to prepare for the trip, just getting the basic necessities and what we should be packing.

I just read about you are trying to build a bakery at Njawara. Even though our resources are limited, is there any or something we could do to help out? I thought we could help in some way. I also want to say thank you for the wonderful experience you giving to us.

I realize it will be truly an eye opener. I feel as if I could be able to repay you for these two weeks that you about to give us. Thank you Dr. Ceesay."

Another email from Brittany Posthumous simply said, "I am one of the students from Alpena Community College that will be coming this May 2005 to help.

After learning all the things that you have done I must say you are an inspiration and the world can use more people who care as much as you do. I can't wait to come to Njawara. I am very excited to be able too help and thank you for the invitation."

Lastly, Ms. Grace Schmitz sent in the following before leaving for the Gambia. "I am a member of the Alpena Community that will be assisting you this May at Njawara.

I am greatly looking forward to my visit to the Gambia. Thank you so much for the invitation."

The Friends of Manding, a charitable Trust at Colchester, had the following in its website about the pending trip to Njawara, the Gambia.

It read, "News flash 12 Americans visiting: A class of 11 students and their instructor Mr. Thomas P. Ray from Alpena Community College, Alpena, Michigan will be visiting the Gambia as guest of Manding Medical Centre from the 6th of May to the 19th of May 2005.

They will be visiting communities and tutor at local schools. Alpena has developed interest in project Manding Medical Centre at Njawara. We are negotiating are negotiating to have this exchange as an going affair between Alpena and Njawara."

As time drew near to the flight to Gambia Thomas Ray contacted the Commissioner on several occasions to clear last possible huddles that may surface.

Nonetheless preparations went smoothly and Mr. Thomas P. Ray and his Alpena Community College leadership class left America on May 10th, 2005 via Madrid and then Dakar, Senegal before embarking at Banjul, the Gambia.

As fate would have the team instead hired a bus from Dakar to Hamdali village in the North Bank, which was nearer to Njawara village. I later learnt that they were given a VIP escort from Hamdali via Kerewan to their final destination Njawara village. As expected, I called the mayor/village Alkalo of Njawara, Aja Hadi Panneh and enquired about tour American visitors.

She told me they were fine and housed at the semi motel used for foreign guest at Njawara village. Mr. Thomas Ray and I spoke at length with Sefo fafanding Kinteh who reassured me that everything possible will be done to help make, "Our guests comfortable and like wise a memorable visit in due course."

I spoke briefly to the Commissioner the next day to get feed back from him. He was elated and concord that good can emanate from such interaction between diverse people.

The two weeks flew fast for the students most of whom did not want to leave at the time for kindness rendered them by the villagers. It is said that good thing do not last long and this was the experience of the students who went to Njawara in May 2005. Here are the reactions of the American students after their trip to Njawara, the Gambia.

The Alpena Community College started sending report and appraisals of their experience as guest of Manding Medical Centre at Njawara. Alison Jane Smolinski was first to submit a commentary.

She wrote, "Hello Dr. Ceesay, the trip to Njawara was incredible! I did not want to leave. It was an experience of a lifetime that I will never forget. Everyone in the village was very kind and helpful. I have never met such kind people in my entire life. I found the villagers doing everything possible to make their lives better.

I realized that many people work together to get a job done or finished. This is absolutely wonderful. Everyone was helpful in the village. The people of Njawara gave us such wonderful hospitality. The food and shelter was more than we deserved.

Also your wife, Mrs. Fatou Koma-Ceesay, was all too good to us. We had a remarkable time with her at Bundung/Serekunda.

Her cooking was excellent. And the gifts she gave all of us, we did not deserve. Your family is wonderful and was too kind to us. I would like to thank you for the incredible experience you have given me. I could not asked for anything more. I immensely enjoyed myself. I want to go back one day. I also want you to know I will do my best to help in whatever way I can.

I realize that actions are louder than words and hope I can prove that to everyone. Thank you." Another missive came from Grace Schiimtz. It read, "I really enjoyed my time at Njawara. The people treated us very well and it was a pleasure to spend two weeks with them.

Your wife is a wonderful person and was very hospitable to us. I will always be grateful to her kind treatment. I hope to make another visit to Njawara in the future. It is a wonderful place. It was an eye-opening experience. The people were absolutely marvelous.

They treated us as their own family and welcomed us with open hands. I had no idea that they would be that hospitable. I really miss walking to the river and spending time with the children. It was my first experience in Gambia and hopefully it will not be my last. I hope I can return their kindness.

Would love to see how the kids have grown." The last but not the least came from Mr. Thomas P. Ray, English instructor and leadership advisor at the Alpena Community College, Alpena, Michigan, USA.

It read: "I want to thank you for the opportunity you provided my students on this trip to Njawara, Gambia. The entire experience was enjoyable and valuable as a means of teaching my students something about the responsibility that comes with the privileges they enjoy here.

Everyone was kind to us on the trip and the students came away with many great souvenirs and memories. I have many digital photos and am working on producing a CD of them to send out.

I also plan to type up a version of my journal for posting on the Internet and I will send parts of that to you. I plan to call the village this weekend to extend my appreciation to everyone. Do you know anything about the proposed potential sister city relationship between Alpena and Njawara?
I would like to start making some local contacts here to help that process. I am also hopeful that future trips will be possible for my student." As you know very well man proposes but God disposes things. Thomas Ray took over the running of the Department and with that came a hand full of challenging responsibilities.
He was not able to provide CD until the 11th of October 2005 after several reminders from me and those visiting my website:
www.friendsofmandinggambimed.btck.co.uk or www.publishkunsa.com) Finally, Mr. Thomas P. Ray contacted me on 4/11/05 to let me know he had the college mailing office send the CD and other materials registered delivery to me.
Then he made a donation of $1000 (One thousand us dollars) in the name of Friends of Manding, a charitable trust at Colchester Essex County that organizes fundraising for Manding Medical Centre at Njawara village.
With regards to the state of the sister city status in the pipeline, I was the proponent of it. It was one of my goals for inviting the Americans to my village in the Gambia. I just believed that unveiling the false masks and stigmata others had about Africa would create harmony in its unique way.

People need to accept difference in the cultures. I transmitted all reactions presented by our American visitors to the Commissioner, the chief and village heads especially Aja Hadi Panneh of Njawara village. Sadly, Mr. Ray left Alpena Community College for another lucrative post in one of the universities in New York.

I am still trying to trace but was not making head way at the time this book was being printed. Friends and his former students are trying to trace him out and hope to do so in due course.

Mr. L. A. Bouvier, centre/arrow and friends

Chapter 45
DISTINGUISHED 2005 GRADUATE WARD

I attended Alpena Community College (ACC) in Michigan from September 1967 to December 1969. My contacts with friends at Alpena never waned. Hence, the wheels of profound recognition by the institute started rolling when Mathew Dunckle called me to let me know he read my book, "The legend against all odds."
He was very impressed and intrigued by my experience and fortitude since my leaving Alpena Community College in 1969. I met Mathew Dunckel when he was twelve years old. His father Dr. Elbridge Dunckle was my academic advisor while I was at the Alpena Community College.
I will without any hesitation or reservation still recommend Dr. Dunckel for academic advisor to any foreign student attending the college.
It was during one of our telephone conversation (02/0i/05) that Mathew Duckel told me of the possibility of Alpena Community College recommending me for the Distinguished 2005 Graduate Award offered annually by the college to outstanding Alumni.
Alpena Community College recognizes its graduates annually for their academic and their career accomplishment for their communities. It simply recognizes the aspirations of Alumni for their people.
The Pandora's box was opened by an innocuous telephone conversation in recognizing my aspiration and goal for providing medical aid to Gambian villagers.

Mathew asked me to fax him any and all possible documentation about work and me I do in the Gambia. He would then speak to the relevant authorities regarding my being nominated for the Distinguished 2005 Graduate of Alpena Community College coming May 5th, 2005 spring/summer commencement.

Mathew did just as promised. In a nutshell, here is the letter from Mrs. Penny Boldrey, Executive Director Alpena Community College Foundation. It read:

Alpena Community College
666 Johnson Street
Alpena, Michigan 49707
January 6, 2005

Alhasan S. Ceesay, MD
245 Great Western Street
Moss Side
Manchester, M14 4LQ
England

Dear Dr. Ceesay,

Mathew Dunckel shared the information that you recently provided to him regarding your professional achievements since your early years at Alpena Community College.

I am extremely pleased to share with you that your many outstanding accomplishments have earned you the distinction of Distinguished Graduate of Alpena Community College (ACC) for 2005. We commend you for your humanitarian efforts in founding and developing the Manding Medical Centre in the Gambia, West Africa.

I am anxious to read your book, "The legend against all odds" once Mathew has finished with it. Without a doubt, you serve as an example of how a solid educational foundation from Alpena Community College can launch a lifetime of achievements.

You will be honoured at our spring commencement Exercises on Thursday May 5, 2005, which begins at 7 pm in the Park Arena at Alpena Community College.

We invite you to join us on that evening. However, we certainly understand that making a trip to the United States, on so short a notice, may not be feasible. During the commencement program, I will share a synopsis of your extraordinary career that has earned you the honour of Distinguished Graduate.

If you are able to join us, you will be invited to join me at the podium to receive your award and to address the audience if you wish. Would you be willing to provide us with the following: (1) a copy of your professional resume, (2) a paragraph on your memories of Alpena Community College and how your experience helped you achieve your goals and (3) a professional photo for use in our alumni newsletter as well as an ad that will appear in Alpena News.

Please feel free to call me or e-mail me with any additional questions you may have. Again, congratulations! We look forward to hearing from you in the future.
Sincerely
Penny Boldrey
Executive Director
My response to this honour and invitation to my second home America was swift and obvious as penned below. I emailed Penny forth with as my heart was overwhelmed with joy for being recognized by my Alma Mata Alpena community College. It simply read:

245 Great Western Street
Manchester, M14 4LQ
England
13/01/05

Mrs. Penny Boldrey
Executive Director
Alpena Community College
Foundation
666 Johnson Street
Alpena, Michigan 49707

Dear Penny Boldrey,
I am overwhelmed and do not know where to begin this note of thanks to Alpena Community College. In my mind it is the American people who deserve such honour and distinction for I am only recipient of the goodness of the Americans.

I am humbled and further rejuvenated by the thought and recognition of my goals and work for the Gambia. I remember in the 60s when people used to tell me, "You will end up just like all foreign student who came to America.
They end up getting trapped by the greener pasture syndrome of America." To such challenges my response had always been, I for one will disappoint a lot of you for I will never rest until I bring to my people the American know how and willingness to share with others.
This stance has never changed and will not ever change because the only I can, in small measure compared to what you did for us poor ones, pay back is to able to show what the USA is all about and her stand for the little guy anywhere on this planet.
I will look into my schedule to see if I can afford to be in Alpena May 2005. I will let you know by the end of February 2005. Meanwhile I am faxing a resume and will try to send my photos via email or surface mail.
Where it is not possible for me to attend in May 2005, would it be okay for my first American family friend, Mrs. Rita Riggs, to represent me at the ACC spring commencement? She was the first people in Alpena that opened their homes to me.
She and her family will certainly appreciate recognition of their help to this simple Gambian. None toeless rest assured that I have not yet slammed the door to my seeing Alpena once more. Timing and visa problems might make it unattainable.

Again, please accept profound gratitude to all of you and to Alpena Community College. God blesses you and rain peace on earth in 2005. Cheers and regards.
Sincerely
Dr. Alhasan S. Ceesay, MD
Mrs. Penny Boldrey wasted no time in replying thus:
Alpena Community College
Alpena, Michigan 49707
13/01/05

Hi Dr. Ceesay,

Yes, I did receive your curriculum vitae and thank you for forwarding that to me. We are extremely proud of you and your accomplishments. Once I get my hand on your book, I will pay special notice to the ACC chapter. The best part of my job is the opportunity to meet former alumni and learn of the impact ACC had in their lives.
Please believe me that we understand if you are unable to join us at commencement on May 5, 2005. Indeed we would be pleased to have Rita Riggs accept this honour on your behalf.
Rita is a remarkable and kind woman. My husband speaks fondly of her and has stayed in close contact with her. I look forward to getting to know you better through our correspondence. And meet you in person someday. Regards

Mrs. Penny Boldrey
Executive Director
 As tine drew near to May commencement and at the end it was not possible for me to travel and

attend the ceremony in person. So Mrs. Rita Riggs and her family stepped in for me. Her elder son Robert Riggs was designated to receive the award in my behalf as representative of the Rita who was in her 80s at the time.

I emailed the following remarks to be read by Robert Riggs at the time the award is given. It is titled:

A FUTURE FOR ALL

Mr. president, staff, graduates, Ladies and gentlemen. I am deeply moved and humbled being chosen Alpena Community College's Distinguished Alumni for 2005. This recognition belongs to America.

Without the good will and foresight of the staff, students and the community of Alpena in 1967, I might never have had the chance to earn education with which to help my people move forward in life, Hence, allow me reiterate profound gratitude to Alpena Community College, my fellow student, people of Alpena and America at large.

My life after Alpena Community College has been full of trials and tribulations detailed in my first book, "The legend against all odds". One relief in it is the robust blessing and peace of mind I have knowing that I am right in what I am doing for my people.

There are those who claim heaven in being rich but for me it is reaching out to help others that matter in life. Upon graduating from medical school, I returned to the Gambia and setup a self-help village health organization (Manding Medical Centre) at

Njawara in an effort to provide a much-needed medical service to the rural sector. I am happy to report that membership has grown beyond twenty thousand villagers.

Please join me to catch a dream for my villagers. Manding Medical Centre will help portray the America we all dream and yearn to be part. We are on the verge of building the children and maternity units and do need monetary, equipment and medicines assistance in our drive to provide this unique service to villagers.

To the graduates, I would like to remind you that, the great tide of history flows and as if flows it carries to the shores of reality what binds us as one human race.

Be aware of the extent, depth and gravity of the challenges ahead as you set out to transform, reconstruct and integrate America into a global icon. Sincere congratulations for your march towards success and fulfillment. Alpena Community College has given you the first footprints.

Walk your way with head held high and determination to succeed in the world. Confucius said, "Our greatest glory is never failing, but in rising every time we fail" Stockpiles of Atomic bombs or weapons of mass destruction and dictators do not measure greatness.

I believe strongly and sincerely that with deep-rooted wisdom and dignity, innate respect for human rights and lives, the intense humanity will make us more cherished and better leaders.

This will make us able to contribute towards the future and progress of mankind.

I am happy for you and hope that you will fly the American flag for it is the great American constitution. Finally, I would like to pay tribute to pas and present staff, students and Alpena community for having given me the opportunity to forge for my people.

Allow me make special mention and express thanks to the remarkable and noble friends I met in Alpena. Sincere thanks from my family, villagers and I to Howard and Rita Riggs, Judge Philip and Viola Glennie, Mr. Henry Valli, Dr. Eldridge Dunckel, Dr. Strom, Bill and Magnet cruise, Dr. Charles T. Egli, Mr. Cloyd and Norata Ramsey and the Medical Arts Clinic, the Jesse Baser Foundation and all who helped make my sojourn to Alpena a remarkable success.

If I have a million friends, I would like many more to be like you. I hope you will believe in, as well as join me, in my dream of providing modern medical aid to the Gambian villagers. Thanks a million and bless America.

DR. Alhasan S. Ceesay, MD

Mrs. Penny Boldrey called to let me know she confirmed the details with Robert Riggs, who was selected by the family to deliver the speech. She assured me that Bob was all set with my remarks and had been practicing many times.

Rita and Donna will also attend with other friends. To make it official she sent this note to Robert Riggs (Bob).

Alpena Community college
666 Johnson Street
Alpena, Michigan 49707
April 21, 2005

Robert Riggs
312 Liberty Street
Alpena, Michigan 49707

Dear bob,

Dr. Alhasan Ceesay has informed me that you will be representing him at our commencement ceremony and accepting the distinguished Graduate award on his behalf. Our spring commencement exercises will be held on Thursday, May 5, at 7 pm. There will be VIP seating near the front left section of the Park arena for you and your family.
During the commencement program, I will share a brief synopsis of Dr. Ceesay's career. I will invite you to join me at the podium to receive Dr. Ceesay's Distinguished Graduate Award.
Following the presentation, you will have the opportunity to share Dr. Ceesay's remarks. I shared with Dr. Ceesay that his comments must be kept brief (2-3 minutes) because our program consists of many individuals who will also be addressing the graduating class.
After the ceremony we would like to take some photographs, so if you could remain near your seats, I will come to you. A reception at the Jesse Besser Museum follows commencement and you are also invited to join.

Enclosed you will find a copy of Dr. Ceesay's remarks. I look forward to hearing from you. Please call me to confirm your participation.
Sincerely
Penny Boldrey
Executive Director.

Two weeks prior to the ceremony I received an email from Karen Eller, administrative assistant in the president's ACC office of public information, letting me know that she intend to write about me in the College's newspaper, the Lumberjack Link issue of the spring/summer Alumni news letter publication.

Penny Boldrey also informed me that Kerrie Miller, news writer for the Alpena News would like to feature me in the local paper. I immediately emailed the following to Kerrie Miller at the Alpena news.

Hi Kerrie,

I just received Penny's email with the good news that you want to feature me in the Alpena news. For me this would be a dream come true. Yes! By all means go ahead and feel free to contact me should you want more information about work or me I am doing in the Gambia.

I am a simple person that loves helping others get on with life the best way they can during their short sojourn on mother earth. I strongly believed that those of us privileged to learn from America have responsibility to share American goodwill with our people.

That would be the only way our people can experience the real America that stands for the downtrodden and the innovative.

I still feel very happy when I come across an American. If your paper is able to help me get Manding Medical Centre at Njawara out of its current limbo, then you would have participated in the most noble and worthy cause that will outlive us and will be a spring board of hope and medical service for generations we can ever dream of.

We are still on fundraising stage to build the first phase, the children and maternity units, which according to estimates will cost around £250,000 or about $500,000 I committed a portion of proceeds of my books, "The legend against all odds, Medicine for the villager and When hearts melt in love" to the Manding Medical Centre but they are not selling enough to get things in fast gear.

I need help to bring relief to my villagers. Well, this is enough introductions until I hear from you. God bless you and thanks a million for being kind towards us.

Sincerely

Dr. Alhasan S. Ceesay, MD

Kerri replied requesting a synopsis of how I found out about Alpena in the 60s. So I sent her the following summary. I came to Alpena City by simply going to the then American consulate in Banjul, the Gambia and asked for a catalogue with information on American colleges.

As a beggar normally has no choice, I started from the top alphabets. Well, Alpena Community College was there and was the first that accepted my application among the schools that replied to my desire to pursue further education in America. This part is well documented in chapter in my book, "The legend against all odds" highlighting my experience at ACC from 1967 t0 1969. I was born and bread in abject poverty and I am only fighting for my villagers to have a chance to proper medical care nothing more and nothing less.

I hope you will help me get your readers interested in Manding Medical Centre and its objective for the villagers. Thank you for taking upon the task of writing about my work and me in the Gambia. Manding Medical center is at present in limbo and we yearn for a boost or a short in the ram to get things moving faster. Please visit our wed site: www.friendsofmandinggambimed.btck.co.uk or www.publishkunsa.com

Signed: Dr. Alhasan S. Ceesay

I will reproduce both articles by Karen Eller of the Alpena Community College News letter, the Lumberjack Link and that by Kerrie Miller of the Alpena News respectively. For now let us head to spring commencement podium to hear or listen to what Mrs. Penny Boldrey had in mind about this simple village doctor.

Robert Riggs and family attended the ceremony in time but is now Penny's turn to deliver her remarks about my achievements from the day of Alpena Community College to the present. It is simple and movingly states: "Good evening and congratulations graduates!

The Alpena Community College Foundation created the Distinguished Graduate award not only to recognize, but to honour our graduates who have gone on to contribute to society through successful careers. Our recipient tonight serves as an example of how a solid education foundation from ACC can launch a lifetime achievements I am pleased to share with you that our 2005 Distinguished Graduate is Dr. Alhasan S. Ceesay from the Gambia, West Africa. Dr. Ceesay received his Associates of Arts Degree in 1969, exactly two years after leaving the Gambia.

He credits many individuals, and the generosity of others, as the driving force behind his success. Following his graduation from ACC, Dr. Ceesay transferred to Olivet College, on full-tuition scholarship provided to him by the Besser Foundation. In 1971, he earned a Bachelor of Arts Degree in Biology from Olivet, and in 1973 completed his Master of Science degree from Michigan Technological University at Houghton, Michigan, USA.

Dr. Ceesay taught biology for several years in the Gambia before entering University of Liberia Medical School in 1979 and years later completed his medical education at the American University of the Caribbean at Plymouth, Montserrat, West Indies where he was awarded his Doctor of Medicine Degree in 1992.

Dr. Ceesay again returned to the Gambia and provided free medical assistance to the villagers for an entire year before he took a position as House Officer at the Royal Victoria Hospital, Banjul, the Gambia, and was eventually promoted to the post of Medical Officer in 1999.

He is the proud founder of the Manding Medical Centre; a self-help village health organization located in the Gambia, which has provided much, needed medical care to over 8000 villagers.

In his autobiography, "The legend against all odds", Dr. Ceesay shares his struggles to survive in his quest for an education. All the proceeds from his book go to supporting the Manding Medical Centre. Dr. Ceesay and his wife have three beautiful daughters, ages 14, 11, and 7.

In my correspondence with Dr. Ceesay over the past few months, he shared his profound gratitude for his American education. He said, "In my mind, it is the American who deserved such honour and distinction, for I am the recipient of the goodness of the American."

Due to travel difficulties, Dr. Ceesay is unable to be here tonight to accept this ward. However he has asked his first American family, the Howard Riggs family to represent him. At this time I will ask Robert Riggs (Bob) to join me at the podium to accept the ward for Dr. Ceesay.

Indeed, it is truly an honour to recognize Dr. Ceesay for his many accomplishments and humanitarian efforts. We congratulate him on earning the Distinction of Distinguished Graduate of Alpena Community College.

-Penny Boldrey-

I am told that Robert Riggs eloquently delivered my remarks aimed at the ACC graduates and residents of Alpena City. It was most welcomed as was later reported by those who emailed me after the ceremony.

This distinguished Graduate award came thirty-six years after I left Alpena, Michigan. Mathew Dunckel sent me the following comments about the events of the award. It read: "Alhasan, your address was given at the commencement.

It was the portion of the evening that was enjoyed by most. Partly because it was delivered well and partly because of my father was mentioned. I think what you said was inspirational for our students and brought home the need for them to think internationally.

Tom Ray is making final preparation to depart for the Gambia with the leadership class early next week. What a great adventure for the students. I am looking forward to hearing about it on their return. Thank you for helping make it possible.

Your Friend

Matt.

A month later I emailed penny Boldrey the following, "I received both the award and enclosures. Accept my deepest appreciation for the kind words spoken about me in your presentation speech during the spring graduation ceremony. Thank you very much for your kindness."

Thereafter, I suggested we pursue the possibility of twining Alpena with two villages in the Gambia.

Dear Reader, I hope your patience is not running out as you are eagerly looking forward to the publication from the Alumni and friends of Alpena Community College.

Karen Eller wrote to let me know that she was assigned to write an article about me for the local paper announcing my receiving the Distinguished Graduate 2005 award.

She reported having read my book, "The legend against all odds" to garner more information about me to help her on the matter at hand. She let me know that she found my story very interesting and she intend to do a good job of bringing me to public attention in the article. Here then, without further ado is Karen Eller's promised article about me. This idea unfolded, exploded and led to the chapter on sister city proclamation.

THE LUMBERJACK LINK: ALPENA, MICHIGAN
DR. CEESAY NAMED DISTINGUISHED GRADUATE

Dr. Alhasan sisawo Ceesay of the Gambia, West Africa, was recognized with the Distinguished Graduate Award at the ACC spring commencement ceremony in May 5, 2005. On hand to receive the ward for Dr. Ceesay was members of the Howard Riggs family, his first host family when he came to Alpena in 1967.

According to Dr. Ceesay, "The Riggs were the ideal American, an average working class who readily shared the little bit God gave them with others less fortunate." Dr. Ceesay earned his Associate of Arts degree from ACC in 1969 and went to Olivet College to earn his Bachelor's degree in Biology with help of a full-tuition scholarship from the Besser Foundation.

He earned his Masters degree in biological sciences from Michigan Technological University in 1973. In 1979, Dr. Ceesay returned to Africa and entered the University of Liberia Medical School in Monrovia. Because of political unrest in the Gambia in 1981, Dr. Ceesay escaped to the United States in the hope of completing his life long dream, "to provide much needed medical relief to the villager who is forced to work miles on end to seek medical aid for his already dying child, wife or friend."

During the time he was seeking political asylum in the United States, Dr. Ceesay, never gave up his quest for education, and he continued under very strenuous conditions to take classes at Michigan State University and Wayne State University.

He was finally accepted at the American university of the Caribbean School of Medicine in the West Indies, and he began the final segment of his journey to becoming a doctor.

In 1992, after 25 years of educational struggles, Dr. Ceesay was awarded his Doctor of Medicine Degree from the American University of the Caribbean. He returned to the Gambia where he provided free medical assistance to the villagers for an entire year before taking a position at the Royal Victoria Hospital, Banjul, the Gambia, West Africa. Dr. Ceesay founded the Manding Medical Centre in 1993.

This self-help village health organization provides much needed medical aid to the villagers of the Gambia. His autobiography: "The legend against all odds". Chronicles his struggles to survive in his quest for Western education.

Proceeds of his book go to support Manding Medical Centre at Njawara village and provide scholarships in medicine and agriculture for indigent rural candidates in the Gambia. To learn more about Dr. Ceesay's ambitions, you can e-mail him at: alhasanceesay@hotmail.com.

Dr. Ceesay was honoured to receive this distinction from ACC and would like to "express thanks to the remarkable and noble friends" he met in Alpena. He credits the goodwill and foresight of the staff and students at ACC for giving him the chance to earn an education and help move his people forward in life.

--Karen Eller--

I thanked Karen Eller for work well done for the revealing commendable article. Here now is that featured by the Alpena News written by staff Kerrie Miller. Enjoy Miller's version about me and my goal.

ALPENA NEWS, MICHIGAN, USA 2005
A LONG ROAD FROM GAMBIA TO ALPENA

When he was 14, Dr. Alhasan S. Ceesay saw a family tragedy unfold that would change his life forever. As he was walking to school, he saw a woman, pregnancy full-term, who was obviously ill. Her husband was carrying their young son who was nearly comatose from illness.

Ceesay later found out the pregnant woman's baby died in her uterus and she died from toxins built up in her body as a result. The young boy also died three quarters of a mile before his family was able to reach the Health Centre at Kerewan village. "That day I said, "If God will help me none will ever have to go through that again."

That picture is what made up my mind for me'" Ceesay said. Ceesay, a native of Njawara, the Gambia, is a graduate of Alpena Community College, class of 1969.

He earned his Associates of arts degree from ACC before attending Olivet College, Michigan Technological University and Howard University, earning his doctor of medicine degree from the American University of the Caribbean in 1992.

But how does a young man from a village in the Gambia get to Alpena to attend its community college? In an e-mail message, he stated that after reaching the American Consulate, and asking for a listing of American Colleges, Alpena Community College was at the top of the alphabetical list.

And ACC was the first to respond to his application. Once here, life was not without challenges. In a telephone conversation, he said it was first time he had left his country, and when he got here no one spoke his language.

"But I do not give up", he said. Another goal Ceesay never gave upon was making it possible for the village families, such as those like the one who affected him as deeply as a young man, to have access to health care services.

With the creation of the Manding Medical Centre, which has helped over 8000 patients free of charge, he is doing that though progress has been slow in coming to the center. Ceesay said officially he employed by the central government and is only able to help the villagers on the weekends.

He is able to man the center along with the help of three or more doctors who volunteer their time. Ceesay say the center sees no fewer than 500 patients and as many as 1500 patient in a weekend. He said currently the center is in limbo and is a little more that a shed.

He has been working on fundraising to get the first phase the children and maternity units built. It is expected to cost approximately $500,000. Members of the ACC Leadership class are currently conducting fund-raising to go to the Gambia and help with the children and volunteering at the center. The trip will last two weeks. Ceesay is the author of a book chronicling his life's experiences called "The legend against all odds" (available at Amazon.com) and he has committed all proceeds from its sale to the center.

He said he is never regretted the decision he made to become a doctor. "Sometimes I feel like I have oil on my feet and I am climbing a very steep hill." Ceesay said. "I have always believed I will reach my goal… you have to be crazy like me and you have to ignore lots of things that take you away from your goals."

A typical day in Ceesay's life begins at 5 am with prayer, before boarding public transportation to the hospital where he works, 7miles from his home. From 7 ---11 a.m. he does morning ward rounds, followed by clinics, then evening round.

Days can last up to 10 0r 11 pm before he heads back home. "In between, I try to please my wife and children. It is a very simple life really." He said. He and his wife have three daughters, the oldest of which has dreams of attending Alpena High School and ACC before going onto medical school like her father.

Ceesay's long-term goal revolves around the Mading Medical Centre at Njawara village, which he hopes will continue to grow for generations helping mare patients. "I plan to stay at the center until the day they bury me. That and having my children educated, That is it." He said.

--Kerrie Miller--

Kerrie dispatched a copy of the above as soon as it got out of the printers of Alpena News.

And in return I sent her the following appreciation note of the good work she did. Kerrie, I just received the copy of the article in the Alpena News featuring me. It was a job well done. I hope it help move my dream of providing medical aid to villagers a notch higher for Manding Medical Centre and the Gambia villagers.

The Gambia and I are most grateful for enlightening your readers about us and our need for a medical facility. Extend our thanks and deep appreciation to the staff and management of Alpena News.

We shall effeminately be in Gambia in due course. We look forward to your crew attending the ground-breaking ceremonies in Gambia soon. I have started a collection of documentations about me to be placed in Dr. Alhasan S. Ceesay's Archives.

Kerrie replied stating that they missed me at the ceremony but she look forward to attending the grand opening of the center.

Penny Boldrey simply said, "I will certainly make sure you receive a copy of our alumni newsletter once its completed. Indeed, we are very proud of your accomplishments and humanitarian efforts."

Chapter 46
TWINED ALPENA-NJAWARA KINTE KUNDA

Having been now recognized as Distinguished 2005 Graduate by Alpena Community College I made a proposal for a sister-city or twining relationship status between Alpena City and select villages in the Gambia, West Africa.
I, you guessed right, contacted Mathew (Matt) Dunckel as a soundboard or trial balloon for the above idea. Mathew replied that it was sound idea and suggested my contacting the Alpena City Council members on the subject as soon as possible. He gave their web of the council members.
In addition he supplied names of Councilman Dave Karschnik and Councilwoman Carol Shafto for me to initiate direct contact with the Alpena City Council.
Mathew told me that the Mayor was John Gimlet and the City Manager was Alan Bakalarski. Armed with this vital information I made my first push for the twining through Mrs. Penny Boldrey, Executive Director at the Alpena Community College, Alpena, Michigan.
I had doubts that getting her interested in this unique wish of the villagers she would do all she could within her power to not only contact the right people in authority to make it eventually happen but would open up more doors for my villagers and our health project at Njawara.
Mrs. Penny Boldrey upon hearing from me linked with Councilwoman Carol Shafto on June 14, 2005 thus: "Hi Carol, from one Distinguished graduate to

another…..I received the enclosed message from our 2005 Distinguished graduate, Dr. Alhasan Ceesay. I am wondering if perhaps you can help me with his inquiry regarding the possibility of twining between Alpena City and two villages in the Gambia, West Africa."

Mrs. Penny in-turn informed me that she had contacted a good friend Carol Shafto, who is a member of the Alpena City Council and also an Alpena Community College Distinguished 2003 Graduate recipient, regarding my request for twining between the above communities. She enclosed Councilwoman Shafto' response to the twining idea with Gambian villages.

My reaction was swift and I contacted Councilwoman Shafto thus: "Hello Councilwoman Carol. Mrs. Penny Boldrey sent me correspondence she had with you regarding a proposal I made to the Alpena City. My initial email kick starting a twining proposal between the city of Alpena, Njawara and Kinte Kunda villages in the Gambia, West Africa, was sent to Mayor John F. Gimlet, Dave R. Karsctunick, Mike Polluch, Sam Eller and Carol Shato. It read:

I am pleased to write and inform you that I am deputized by village heads of Njawara and Kinte Kunda to contact you and initiate a twining/sister city status proposal between Alpena and the above two villages.

Njawara is my home village and Kinte Kunda is where I attended school in the early fifties. Thomas Ray and the leadership class students visited both places during their two weeks stay in the Gambia. They met the chief of the District Sefo Fafanding

Kinte at Kinte Kunda. Kinte Kunda village has been the seat of many chiefs of the region and Fafanding is the most recent of several from this village. Njawara is historically a trading center connecting Gambia and northern Senegal.

Today she has become a tourist Mecca and destination. One can easily log onto information about Njawara on the Internet It boasts of lot female education oriented projects. In addition it has an agricultural training center.

The contact was made on behalf of the heads of two villages and the district authority in the North Bank Division of the Gambia. This twining would be a very rewarding interaction and educational for both your and the villagers.

The people are eager to make worthwhile friendship with America. The chiefs and village heads have urged me to initiate their wish for the twining between them and Alpena City or any city willing to go into such relationship with the villagers. You can link with Thomas Ray and his students for feed back on their personal experience as guests of Manding Medical Centre at Njawara village, the Gambia. The villagers and I would be most grateful if given the chance to link up with Alpena City."

Councilwoman, Carol Shafto sent in this hiccup: Dr. Ceesay, I cannot proceed with any more discussion with the City council of Alpena until I am much clearer about what a Twining proposal entails. Could you describe to me what you have in mind? Although we may be supportive of your work at Njawara and Kitne Kunda in the Gambia, we cannot really act on your request until we know what we are agreeing to. Could you send me a brief

outline of what you are seeking from the City of Alpena? I will be happy to act as a liaison between you and the City, but cannot do so until I have a clear idea of what I am advocating for.
Thank you most sincerely." –Carol- On July 13, 2005 I sent the following required clarification to Councilwoman Carol Shafto. "Hello Carol, I am glad to hear from you.
To be simplistically clear, twining means a sisterhood relationship between Alpena and the villages for mutual rewards of those involved. Hence, it is a friendship like affair where people from Alpena can be part of and like wise the villagers involved but at no cost to either party. For example Councilwoman Carol Shafto choose to spend two weeks in the Gambia helping reorganize or create a more functional administrative system or even learn from the villagers.
In brief it is a two-way international relationship. Call it cultural bonanza where cultural dance troupes from the Gambian villages can be coming to entertain Alpena and other cities during the summers.
This will help raise funds for the city, the villages, likewise our health project Manding Medical Centre at Njawara. It will provide much awareness and understanding of the two people merged in friendship. It is like adopting each other and opening up rewarding human adventures at no cost involved. In a nutshell, it means ratified friendship between Alpena and the two above villages.
I hope this makes it palatable for Alpena to want to be part of such endearing relationship. I thank you in behalf of the Kerewan local authority, the

villagers and the Commissioner for North Bank Division, the Gambia. God bless all of you." –Dr. Alhasan S. Ceesay- Needless to say Councilwoman Carol Shafto was very pleased with the above clarification and appealed to Alpena City Council to consider the idea of twining on behalf of the Gambian villages.

Hence, Carol on the 13/7/05 sent me this email after reviewing the above message of clarification of what it means to twin with an African village. It said, "Hello Dr. Ceesay, I have forwarded your information to the Mayor and City Manager and offered to be the liaison if the City should consent to comply with this request. I will keep you posted with any development." –Carol-

I updated the Commissioner and all concern at the Lower Badibou district authority along with the two villages heads involved in the sister-city state regarding progress of my initiative with Alpena City few weeks after

hearing from councilwoman Carol Shafto he Commissioner and local authority sent the below covering letter in support of my push a twining relationship with Alpena City in Michigan, USA..

Njawara/Kinte Kunda
Lower Badibou District
North Bank Division
The Gambia, West Africa
E-mail: njawaranato@yahoo.co.uk
November 5, 2005

Dr. Alhasan S. Ceesay
Manchester, M14 4LQ
England

Subject: Twining of Njawara, Kinte Kunda & Alpena City, Michigan, USA

Dear Dr. Ceesay,

Your first letter dated September 23, 2005 has been received and the cont of which is understood, both the Commissioner, the Chief and the Alkalolu (village heads/ mayors) of Njawara and Kinte Kunda are very pleased and much interested in having Njawara, Kinte Kunda and Alpena City twined.
The Communities of both villages met and discussed the issue and they are very much happy about the lofty ideas. Njwarara and Kinte Kunda are located in the North Bank of the Gambia. They are just about 90 kilometers away from Banjul, the capital of the Gambia.
Kinte Kunda is just two kilometers away from our administrative headquarters, Kerewan where both the Commissioner and Area Council stay. Where as Njawara is located 9km kilometers away from Kerewan. Regards
Sincerely
Aja. Hadi Panneh (Alkalo)
Alh. Fafanding Kinte (Chief of Lower Badibou)
Cc: Batala Juwara (Commissioner, NBD)
I replied to the above with this short note dispatched immediately to the village Alkalolu, the

chief and Commissioner, North Bank Division at Kerewan village.

245 Great Western Street
Manchester, M14 4LQ
England
16/11/05

A BIG THANK YOU

Dear Commissioner, Chief/Alkalolu,

I am profoundly grateful to you. Sefo Fafanding, the local authority, Kerewan Are Council and especially Alkalo Arfang Bah of Torro Bahen, lastly but not the least a big thank you goes to the people of Badibou, Njawara and my sister Hadi Panneh alkalo of Njawara Village.
I am very happy for support and understanding given to Manding Medical Centre. I am pleased to inform you that I have initiated a twining process between Alpena and the villages of Njawara and Kinte Kunda.
I have forwarded your note of the 5/11/05 to the Alpena City Council. Copies were also sent to Mr. Thomas P. Ray at the College. Again, thanks you for making our American friends happy and welcomed to our beloved country. God bless all of you. I will continue working for our development.
Sincerely
Dr. Alhasan S. Ceesay, MD
Director/Founder/coordinator
Manding Medical Centre.

I forwarded the letter from the district to councilwoman Carol Shafto to reinforce my stance and wish of the villagers to be friends to Alpena City. I urged her to kindly take action on behalf of the villagers.

Mrs. Carol Shafto
Council Woman
Alpena city council
208 North First Avenue
Alpena, Michigan 49707

Dear Mrs. Carol Shafto,

The enclosed is reply to your last email dated 25/9/05 regarding the twining proposal made to the Alpena City council earlier on by me on behalf of Njawara and Kinte Kunda villages in the Gambia, West Africa, respectively.
The enthusiasm about having this relationship with Alpena is immeasurable. The villagers are looking forward to a warm and fruitful relationship between the two people. They all pray that you would be as eager to consummate it as they have already done in their wishes and hearts.
Finally, may friendship and human kindness be an everlasting link between all humans. God bless you and we look forward for a positive reply soon. My personal regards and thanks to the City Council and all of Alpena.
Yours Sincerely
Dr. Alhasan S. Ceesay, MD

On September 21, 2005 I sent a reminder to Carol Shafto regard the lofty idea of twining Alpena with Njawara and Kinte Kunda villages in the Gambia. I enquired if Mayor Gimlet had taken any action at the time. I assured her that all hopes of bring this entity into reality wholly and solely relied on her good work.

We bank on her efforts. The next day God smiled onto our dream to befriend America.

Councilwoman Carol Shafto sent me the following reply to my inquiries about the status of my dream for America and the Gambia.

It rang in the most melodious and cherished news I ever had for a long, long time after my being admitted into medical school and upon treating my first patient in the villages.

Here is Carol Shafto's historical e-mail. "Good morning Dr. Ceesay. I appreciate your persistence in accomplishing this goal. Without that it surely would have failed. I do apologize for this delay. I have just returned this week from a wonderful month long tour of the UK and Ireland.

My last communication, before I left, with the City Manager was that this was a good idea, will be good for public relations, and that we should go forward with the proposal. The Mayor is also in favour. So there is absolutely nothing standing in the way of this happening.

I am willing to do the work of it, but I honestly have no idea what to do. Do you know procedures or paperwork or any such thing from your end? Is it as simple as a proclamation? I would like to have more information about your village, your people, and why you are interested in twining with Alpena.

What connection there is with the city? I would then put together a presentation for the City Council and ask them to decide that we are sister-cities (the term used here, although I know the UK and Europe use "twining") with the villages of Njawara and Kinte Kunda.

We could erect a sign at the City entrance, etc. If you have any idea or directions for me, please let me know. Also any information you can provide on your village would be helpful. I will continue to work with you on this until it is accomplished. Your friend in Alpena" –Carol Shafto—

I followed this letter with an addendum to what already were at hand with the councilwoman's desk. Being the architect of this friendly union much was expected of me.

And so I never relented supplying as much information as many times as I can afford. My phone bill sprouted to a warping six hundred plus. Most important addendum was the one below.

SYNOPSIS OF NJAWARA AND KINTE KUNDA VILLAGES

Njawara is a 350 years old market village situated on the bank of the Miniminiyang bolong, a creek of the River Gambia, in the Lower Badibou District of the North Bank Division of the Gambia.

Njawara has a population of a thousand residents and is 95 kilometers from Banjul, Gambia's capital city. The village lies close to the fringes of Senegalese border and has been the trade hub or link between Gambia and Senegal during the colonial era.

Njawara was established and founded by the Panneh family of the Wolof tribe and initially called "Mpanneh Village" the elderly still refer to it as Mpaneeh. Among the residents of now Njawara are Mandinkas, Fulas, Serere, Jolas, Koyaginkas, and Bambara tribes' men.

All of who are farmers, with a few serving as petty traders, growing Peanuts, rice, coos, millet and a variety of vegetables. The nearest government administrative post is nine kilometers away at Kerewan village. Njawara lacked modern luxuries of electricity, proper telephone, sewer system, pave roads but water is now pumped from a nearby borehole.

The village has a thriving school and a dynamic citizenry working hard to improve their lot and the future of the younger generation. Kinte Kunda village has been the political base of Lower Badibou District for decades.

It has provided us with several chiefs in the past and sefo Fafanding Kinte is the most resent contribution. Kinte Kunda village comprises of mostly Mandinka tribes men and women. It is the home of venerable late Sefo Njanko Kinte who, in the 30s ruled the district with an iron fist.

It was he who imposed one of his brothers, Almami Kinte, to take over the administration or village headship of Njawara (Mpanneh). Nonetheless he was a respected chief. Kinte Kunda was the first village that had a school in the entire Lower Badibou district and I am told that the chief insisted that the school be built in his home village leaving a row that lasted through his rein.

Kinte Kunda has now smaller population than Njawara and the current appointed chief of the district, Sefo Fafanding Kinte resides there. Residents of Kinte Kunda are all farmers eager to improve their lives and those of their children. They are friendly, peaceful, charming descent hard working people who contributed a lot to growth of the Lower Badibou District in the North Bank Division.

Today Kinte Kunda is highlighted by the movie Roots of Kunta Kinte' ancestral home. The villagers and I are interested in the twining with Alpena, Michigan in an effort to open up the Pandora's box of friendship, goodwill and more understanding of people and cultures that would allow us relate in this shrinking globe we all share.

There is a lot we can do for each other once the ugly veil of ignorance, misunderstandings and fear is removed. And this can be done only through learning and interacting with one another. I am sure the students, who went to the villages, can tell how much warmth and friendship they received from the villagers they met at the Lower Badibuo District, the Gambia.

Exchange visits and whole host of beneficial programs to both parties can be organized within the framework of this twining. Once again, I personally appeal to the Mayor and Alpena City Council to give this desire of the villagers a chance of fruition for Alpena City and the above villages in the Gambia. DR. ALHASAN S. CEESAY, MD

In sort while, I received the following reply from Councilwoman Mrs. Carol Shafto of Alpena City Council letting me know the final details, date of the proclamation for the sister-city relation between our villages and Alpena, Michigan. Without further ado I present the message as sent on November 17, 2005.
"Good morning Dr. Ceesay.
After many months of communication with you, I can finally announce a DATE for our twining/sister-city Relation! The Alpena City Council will adopt a resolution to establish a Sister-city Program with Njawara/Kinte Kunda villages on December 5, 2005.
I am going to be personally preparing the resolution Since it will be a part of permanent record for both the villagers and the City of Alpena. I would like to be sure all of the information is accurate. Penny Boldrey suggested that I email the text to you after completing it.
If you are willing, you could read it for any factual errors or omissions before I send it on to the City. If you are willing I will send it via email when it is ready some time next week.
Finally, I have invited several people to the City Council meeting to provide testimony and support for this proposal. Both Penny Boldrey and Thomas P. Ray will be there.
Also they are inviting some of the students who went to the villages to also be present and speak to the issue. So it would be a very nice presentation and will be more than just a formality.
Also if you would like, I can arrange to have a tape of the meeting sent to you. Our meetings are videotaped and played for the public on the public

access television channel several times a week between meetings. I can make a copy of the tape of the meeting and have it sent to you or to the village officials or both if you would like.

Also, the resolution will have an official seal of the City of Alpena and the signature of the Mayor. I will have as many copies as you need made and will laminate them so they will be preserved. I will send you those to you and whomever you designate. I will get several if necessary.

I am so pleased to finally be able to bring this completion. I know it must have been frustrating to you to have to have this take so long and to have us seen to be so unresponsive.

I hope this totally enthusiastic ending make up for all of that! Your Friend in Alpena" –Carol Shafto--- On the day of ratification or passing of the resolution for the sister-city status/relationship between Alpena City and Njawara/ Kinte Kunda villages several speakers were heard.

These included, among many others, Penny Boldrey, Mr. Thomas Ray, two student representatives of the leadership class that visited Njawara in May 2005 and Dr. Avery Aten. This was buffered by a loop of fifty photo slides of the villages taken by the students while in the Gambia.

At the end of the presentation Mayor John F. gimlet read into the record the above proclamation and vote was tabled to pass it. The sister-city proclamation between Alpena City with Njawara and Kinte Kunda villages, Lower Badibou District, the Gambia was moved by Councilwoman Carol Shafto, Seconded by Councilman Karscnick, that the proclamation to establish a sister City program was carried by unanimous vote. A copy of the sister-city Resolution passed by Alpena City Council on December 5, 2005 is reproved for your pleasure to read.

PROCLAMATION TO ESTABLISH A "SISTER-CITY" PROGRAM WITH NJAWARA AND KINTE KUNDA LOWER BADIBOU DISTRICT, THE GAMBIA, WEST AFRICA

WHEREAS, the City of Alpena recognizes and supports the concept of global cooperation and community, and

WHEREAS, the villages of Njawara and Kinte Kunda through their leaders and Dr. Alhasan S. Ceesay, have reached out their hand in friendship and goodwill, and

WHEREAS, relationships were established by students and faculty of Alpena Community College when they were warmly welcomed to the villages for a service project earlier this year, and

WHEREAS, mutual understanding of our diversities as well as our similarities and the cultural exchanges that will result, will be beneficial to the citizens of both areas, and

WHEREAS, true global community is often established one person at a time, and one city and village at a time, leading to beneficial relations and programs for all,

NOW, THEREFORE, I John F. Gilmet, by virtue of the authority vested in me as Mayor, DO HEREBY PROCLAMIM a sister-city program with the villages of

    NJAWARA AND KINTE KUNDA
    LOWER BADIBOU DISTRICT
    THE GAMBIA, WSET AFRICA

And urge all area citizens to extend the hand of friendship and an embrace of genuine fraternity to their friends in NJAWARA/KINTE KUNDA and pledge support and loyalty as these communities of two great nations join together as "Sister-Cities" Signed at Alpena, Michigan, United States of America on this 5th day of December 2005. Councilwoman Mrs. Carol Shafto read my reply into the record for Council and Alpena City residents. It states:
ALPENA, THANKS FOR TWINING WITH US

Lord Mayor John F. gimlet, Alpena City Council and resident of Alpena, please allow me convey heartfelt thanks as well as greetings from the Commissioner, NBD, Kerewan Area Council, the chief of Lower Badibou, the Alkalos (village heads) of Njawara and Kinte Kunda.
I am today full of joy and gratitude for twining resolution ratified by the Alpena City Council. I am speechless as one of my dreams for the villager and America has now materialized in this twining resolution passed by Alpena.
We are two good people now merged in goodwill for humanity and friendship. This coming together will achieve a lot for both of us.

There is a lot for us to gain as well as learn from each other and generations to come will thank us for having taken the first footsteps of bringing people of diverse cultures and understandings together. Enclosed is message from the Gambia in response to the most welcomed news in your last email. This is the top of the iceberg for there is lot more benefits in this act.

In addition, as long as I live Alpena and the Gambia will not only benefit from this unique venture but will smile yearly for having dreamt along with me. Let me, in passing; mention with thanks the first harbingers of this day.

They are Mr. Thomas P. Ray and his leadership class of students from Alpena Community College, who visited Njawara village in May 2005. Thomas Ray and the students laid the marvelous foundation we today concretize.

Mrs. Penny Boldrey and Mathew Dunckel deserve our appreciation for remaining interested and in constant contact with me. The Gambia, the Lower Badibou District Authority, village heads and villagers remain eternally grateful for giving us the chance of twining with you.

Huge thanks to Alpena City, the Mayor of Alpena, John F. Gilmet, and Alpena City Council for work well done. Councilwoman Mrs. Carol Shafto who relentlessly steered the twining proposal to completion also deserves our profound gratitude. The villagers and I are eternally indebted to all at Alpena.

In addition, we look forward to working hand in hand for the reward of all parties. Finally, I would like to pay tribute to past and present friends at

Alpena who helped me reach this pedestal. All of you helped make my sojourn to America a remarkable success. I would like many more of my friends to be like you at Alpena.

I hope you will believe, as well as join, in my dream of providing modern medical aid to the Gambian villagers. Thanks a million and God bless America!

Your Friend
Dr. Alhasan S. Ceesay, MD
Founder/Co-ordinator
Manding Medical Centre
Njawara, The Gambia

Two weeks later I received three copies of the "Sister-City" proclamation along with a videotape of the Alpena City Council meeting of December 5, 2005. Also enclosed were the Alpena News and a copy of the Alpena Public notices showing minutes of the City Council meeting, which carried ratification of the sister-city proclamation by a unanimous vote.

I must confess exhilaration in my heart for Alpena City Council having done so much for my villagers without reservation and accomplished with great speed.

I contacted the current US Ambassador in the Gambia, Ambassador Joseph D. Stafford alerting them on the arrival a package from Alpena City Council for them to kindly deputize in ceremony of handing the proclamation copy marking sister-city status between Alpena City, Njawara and Kinte Kunda villages in the Lower Badibou, District, North Bank Division.

Manding Medical Centre
UK Contact Address
245 Great Western Street
Manchester, M14 4LQ
E-mail: alhasanceesay@hotmail.com
October 10, 2005

Joseph D. Stafford
Ambassador
Embassy of the USA
Kairaba Avenue
P. M. Box 19
Banjul, the Gambia
West Africa

Dear Ambassador Stafford,

RE: Alpena, USA -Njawara-Kinte Kunda twining/Mamding Medical Centre

I am Dr. Alhasan S. Ceesay from Njawara village and currently on studies in the UK. This is to introduce the above self-help health organization at Njwawara as well as kindly request favour of your good office's service in behalf of Alpena City, Michigan and the villagers of Njawara and Kinte Kunda, the Gambia.
I pioneered the above center, after graduating as a doctor and upon returning to the Gambia in 1992. It became an NGO in 1994 after being fully registered by the Justice Department and recognized by the Ministry of Health in 1993. In addition, we are now a registered Charitable Trust, as Friends of Manding, in England and Wales by the Charity Commission

of the UK. Our charity number is 1088136 since August 21, 2001. One can learn more by browsing our web site thus: www.friendsofmandinggambimed.btck.co.uk or www.publishkunsa.com . It will show our home page, "Friends o Manding". Alternatively one can email me alhasanceesa@hotmail.com. The same home page will show.

I have also written two books and hefty portion of sales from these books is earmarked to help support Manding Medical Centre at Njawara and our goal of providing medical aid to the villager, especially children.

More information about my work and commitment to providing much needed medical service to the region in conjunction with the Gambia Ministry of health can be seen in our web site as above.

Finally, I am more than delighted to report that Alpena City in Michigan, USA has just ratified a Sister-City program with my home village Njawara and Kinte Kunda village respectively in the Lower Badibou District, North Bank Division, the Gambia. Hence, I have asked the Alpena City Mayor's Office to send five copies of the final proclamation declaring the Sister City status between Alpena and the above two villages in the Badibou to you for your office to kindly deliver the documents to the Commissioner North Bank Division at Kerewan. Thank you for taking time to assist us in the above matter. Please feel free to contact me any time convenient to you.

Best washes for good health and achievement in the coming year. Regards to your family.
Yours Sincerely
Dr. Alhasan S. Ceesay
Founder/Coordinator
Manding Medical Centre
Njawara, NBD, The Gambia

I followed this letter with two telephone calls to the United States Embassy in the Gambia to verify receipt of the package sent from Alpena to Ambassador Joseph D. Stafford.

The secretary told it normally takes a month or more before none official mail arrives at their desk. I was assured that the office would do as requested whenever the package reaches the Embassy.

I called Sefo Fafanding Kinte and Alkalo Hadi Panneh and told them to be checking with either Ambassador Joseph Stafford directly or one of the officers in the know for their copies of the Sister city proclamation of which the villagers are unsung heroes for having received the Alpena Community College students who visited Njawara in May 2005 with open hearts, hospitality, generosity and warmth.

It was not until Thursday, February 16, 2006 that Ambassador Joseph D. Stafford and team where able to deliver, in person amid tumultuous reception and celebration, the sister-city proclamation between Alpena City, Njawara and Kinte Kunda villages in the North Bank of the Gambia.

I made it clear that the brief ceremony at Njawara on the 16/02/06 marked the end of phase one of the sister city relationship between Alpena,

Michigan, and us. I suggested the following four areas for food for thought by all concern. They are:

EDUCATION

This already started in earnest as some in Alpena express desire to sponsor worthy candidates at the Njawara Primary School for an experimental period of one year. Higher levels such as College, nurse training or other relevant skill areas will in due course be included.

HEALTH

A lot is planed for health oriented programs and Manding Medical Centre will be enhanced to a much functional status. Already Dr. Avery Aten and other colleagues in Alpena Health care delivery are working on program to assist us in our services and health care delivery. There will be training programs for health personnel etc.

TOURISM

With building of a 66 bed ultra-modern hotel I have in mind and finding ways to create tourist attraction to the region will in due course make Badibou the Tourist Mecca of the North Bank Division.

CULTURAL EXCHANGES

Exchanges entailing having cultural dance troupes from the Lower Badibou District travel to Alpena, Michigan and other American cities during summers to display our artistic fabric of entertainment, history, and arts. These are a few ideas in the pipeline. Feel free to add yours to enrich the program. This is by no means binding or final but seeking more suggestions on how to benefit both parties in this unique twining program just approved by Alpena City.

Let me make it crystal clear that there is no financial commitment from Alpena City. However, the cultural show can net us or raisa lot of money upon performing in America. I thanked the Commissioner, NBD, Sefo Lower Badibou, Kerewan Area Council and the district authority for having worked so hard with me to provide this excellent opportunity to our people.

I promise more was on the pipeline. Three weeks later I received from Councilwoman Mrs. Carol Shafto announcing good news of her efforts.

"Dr. Ceesay, we have sent five copies of the proclamation to the American Embassy in the Gambia, which you provided the address.

I also have three copies of the proclamation for you as well as a copy of the tape of the meeting, a copy of the Newspaper where the action appeared, and a copy of the newspaper with the official minutes of the meeting. I will get these out today.

It was a most wonderful evening, as you will see on the tape. Five people, your friends old and new, spoke in favour of the proclamation. This included Dr. Avery Aten who I have now spoken t with and who is very enthusiastic about working with you by phone he said. But you will be able to see him and hear what he had to say during City Council meeting of December 5, 2005.

Also peaking were two students who have visited the Gambia, Thomas P. Ray, Penny Boldrey, and me of course. I read your wonderful letter for the record. We also had a loop of over fifty slides showing on screen during the presentation.
It was the nicest Sister-city ceremony we have ever had-by far! Usually we just read the proclamation and that is it. I think this ends my part in all of this – except for one thing my son and I were going to "adopt" a family through Save the Children.
This involves sending a letter each month and with an amount of money. We would be happy to adopt some children from your village instead if there is an easy way to do this.
We would need a name and address and what form we could make our donation in (money order?). We are not really wealthy but could send $20 - $25 a month for at least a year to a deserving child.
Of course, we would hope that they might send a note now and then but this all up to you. I hope you are pleased with all that has happened.
I remain your friend
Carol Shafto.
In reply I sent my friend Carol Shafto the following:

Manchester, UK
November 20, 2005

Hello Carol,

Now I am able to respond to your email. First, please accept our eternal indebt ness for having worked so hard to bring the twining into reality. Only God can reward your efforts.

Please kindly extend our heartfelt gratitude to the Mayor and your fellow councilors at Alpena City. Kindly send me the Mayor's telephone. I need to convey our appreciation to him.

I had a long chat with the villager and they were in cloud nine about the approval of the sister city program. I will be forwarding the names of deserving school children you might want to sponsor/adopt.

I will call you before forwarding the names, about it when I get the list that the parents and headmaster promised to send me. Again, thanks a million and God blesses you and yours. Best wishes for good health and successful 2006. I look forward to our traveling to the Gambia soon. Regards

Your Friend

Dr. Alhasan S. Ceesay, MD

In the interim Mrs. Penny Boldrey was also busy doing a story for the Alpena Community College Alumni News. In addition Carol Shafto had a feature about the approved sister-city program done by a local newspaper.

She was very happy about it as the below email from her shows. "Good Morning Alhasan Ceesay, "Our Story" is headline, above the fold, in the Alpena News today! It is wonderful publicity for your project. I will send you copies but you can read it on-line today only at http://www.thealpenanews.com. It reads, "Alpena's sister city ACC graduate initiates partnership with the Gambian villages." And there is a wonderful colour picture of one of the ACC students with village children. I hope you enjoyed the story and you are pleased with my efforts for publicity.

The news reporter, Sue Lutuszek, will do a follow up story about people "adopting children for education purposes", like I am doing with my son. It is a good day for celebration checks the Web Site.
Your Friend
Carol Shafto

The first hatchling of this merging of diverse hearts is as follows.

Njawara Basic School
Lower Badibou District
North Bank Division
The Gambia, West Africa
January19, 2006

Dear Sir/Madam

RE: To whom it may concern

These students are promising student whose parents are not able to fully support their educational needs. As a result, we would be very grateful if a concern person(s) can assist the students and their parents in taking care of some of the financial difficulties they are encountering to earn an education.
These include school fees, uniforms, books, bills and other school needs. Thank you and in anticipation, I remain
Yours Faithfully
Lamin K. Juwara
Principal

The initial list of needy students was sent to Councilwoman Carol Shalto on 23/02/06 for what is now dubbed Manding medical center scholarship grants. The fax read:

Manchester, UK
23/02/06

Hi Carol,

Hope you are okay and back at work. I hereby forward a list of school children from Njawara Basic School needing sponsorship. Feel free to contact those you think would like to participate in sponsoring a child for this educational project. The first three candidates in the list are earmarked for you and your son(s).
See name 1 – 3 in the accompanying list. Send all monies via Western Union in the name of Aja. Hadi Panneh, Alkalo/village head of Njawara, to any Gambian bank that Western Union deals with in the Gambia.
Then email me stating the amount(s), date sent, and for who. I will follow up by contacting Hadi Panneh, the Principal of Njawara Basic School about and the child's parents about it. I will also let the chief of the district know about such benevolent acts from America to the Gambia.
This ascertains prompt disbursement. In addition, I will have Aja Hadi Panneh (Alkalo), the parents, the Headmaster and where possible the recipient student(s) to write acknowledging the amounts received.

Please feel free to contact me if you have any questions or ideas to promote the above noble educational commitment. Once again, thanks and we remain grateful for your stand.
Your Friend
Dr. Alhasan S. Ceesay, MD
Thing went well until advent of catastrophic economic melt down of 2008. This not only derailed our planed visit to Alpena and marjor Michigan cities but it pulled the rug off under my feet.
In the interealm I wrote several books in an attempt to bounce back and resuscitate the Sister-Cityhood formed between Gambian villages of Njawara and Kinte Kunda with Alpena.
Below is letter I emailed to the Mayor, City Council and all concerned at Alpena, Michigan, USA.

284 Great Western Street
Manchester, M1 4LP
England

Date: 15/10/12

The Editor
Alpena News
Alpena, Michigan 49707
Cc: mayor & Alpena City Council, Dr. Avery Aten,
Mrs. Penny Boldrey, ACC

Dear Editor,

RE: RESUSCITATION OF A DREAM,

It has been years since the inception of a sister-city relationship between the villages of Njawara, kinte Kunda, and Alpena city was established. Please allow me use your good paper to update as well as breath life into the dormant state of affairs. First let me in behalf of the villagers, the lower Badibou district authority, the Kerewan Area Council and I express sincere apologies for the unfortunate turn of event due to the unexpected economic down turn that rocked the developed world shortly thereafter.
It derailed our planned visit of 2008. These years (2007 -2012) were marked by catastrophic economic enthrals that sent most dreams to the drawing board.Yes,
Alpena and the villages did then what was most gracious and admirable by proclamation of a sister-city relation entered into with Njawara and Kinte Kunda villages in the Lower Badibou district of the Gambia, West Africa.
Things may have gone dormant since then but I remained more committed than ever to the cause and we intend to honour all we said in letter read by Council woman, now mayor Carol Shafto during the December 2005 proclamation ceremony by Alpena city Council.
I would like you try and imagine difficulty villagers found themselves, during these economic down turn, not knowing where the next meal for

their children would come from as they try to make ends meet under the cruel clutches of poverty, drought, and the sharp talons of AK47 governance. This left me being the lone crusader with pockets full of holes.

Sources I relied upon to bring the dancers dwindled and faded faster than expected as the economic down turn took it toll world wide. Worst Gambian politics made it very difficult for me to weed out excess baggage that wanted to travel with me.

Those of you familiar with African politics would understand my dilemma and accept that it is ill wind that blows no one any good.

Hence, I had to walk gingerly on very sharp political blades and at the same time face disappointed faces from friends like you who worked so hard to create venues for my dancers in the hope of raising some money for the building of the maternity and children's wards at Manding medical Centre at Njawara village.

On top of this night mare I lost, Mrs. Lorna Robinson in March 2009, who had been my rock of Gibraltar in the United Kingdom. This was followed by an unexpected immigration/visa nightmare that made life unbearable for me. Hence the villagers' inability to contribute financially on top of my stranded state in the UK made matters worst for our initiative.

The additional request of a P1-visa by the USA further delayed fulfilment of our travels to Michigan. I had to take the bull by the horns and took to writing in the hope that the books will raise enough to enable us fulfil Manding Medical Centre's goal of providing medical aid/service to children and villagers. Poor sales hampered that drive despite my having written eleven books; some of which are: (1) The legend against all odds, (2) Medicine for the villager, (3) When hearts melt in love, (4) Country for president, tribe, and Party.

The above are published by Publish America, Frederic, Maryland and can be purchased from amazon.com. The following, see attached, are published by Lulu.com: (a) The three princess of Baibou Manding (b) Njawara Bantaba, (c) The legend of Saaba Minyang Baa (d) Forever etched in my heart (e) Our guilty pleasures (f) Thick wallet and gorgeous, (g) Your kiss melts my heart, (h) White Dove of Jahali konko (I) Come Dine at Njawara (j) Soul Sister,(K) The Silent warrior, and lastly (L) The Dugula Spy.

With this much one would say I was busy but I am worried for time and tides waits for no man and I am yet to get a third of what I aim at for the villagers.

I will continue to do all I can but sadly my efforts are yet to yield enough to put any thing on the ground. Hence this letter aside up dating friends and council is to map the way forward for the sister-City hood we enacted in 2005.

THE WAY FORWARD

Now that you have a snippet bird's eye view of the cause of the silence and inactivity of the sister-city hood program between Alpena, Njawara, and kinte Kunda villages in Gambia I submit the following means of resuscitating an honourable and good footing for friendship and the inspiration of generations to come. I will, at my expense, head a small delegation of five exclusive of dancers, to Alpena in May 2013.

The trip would strictly be business were we intend to have meaningful meetings and discursions with Mayors & Alpena City Council, Chamber of Commerce, Alpena Community College, High Schools, Farmers, and iron out the out standing business about the P1-visa for the dancers.

The delegation will comprises of Sefo Fafanding Kinte, Chief of Lower Badibou District, Dr. Alhasan Ceesay,

Mr. Kemo S. Kinteh, Coordintor of Njawara, Kinteh kunda and Alpena sister-city affairs in Gambia, and Miss Famatanding Ceesay and Binta Ceesay.

It's our hope that the sparks of friendship kindled in 2005 never fade in your kind hearts for humanity. Our trip is for the reinvigoration of the entered sister-city relationship. Together we can do lot for our communities.

Visit my new web site friendsofmandinggambimed.btck.co.uk. (Just type URL on toolbar; no google or www/http://) Best wishes and regards from the villagers and I

Yours Sincerely

Dr. Alhasan S. Ceesay: (e-mail: alhasanceesay@hotmail.com, tel. 44+7556092403.)

Founder & Coordinator

Manding Medical Centre

Njawara Village, NBR,
The Gambia, West Africa.

I had no dout in my mind that the good people of Alpena had no intention of giving up on my project. However the economics of the day made it hard for politicians to talk of doling money to foreign projects or paying expensive airtickets for travel to America.

Unlike the villagers I knew good heart of my second home (Alpena) and was certain that they would never disapoint cause like we started in 2005.The bellow tentative good news was sent by the Clerk of Alpena City, Michigan, USA.

3:30 PM

Reply ▼

To: Alhasan Ceesay

Hello Alhasan,

I have received your e-mail and forwarded on to Matt Waligora (our new mayor) and Greg Sundin (our Interim City Manager).

Sorry to hear of all the hardships you have been experiencing. Let me know if you need anything else.

Karen Herbert

Chapter 47
GRAND PA BAJOJA CEESAYON TRADITION

Children and elders look forward to the old wise sage's stories and lectures. Hence, we gathered beneath the shades of the spreading Mango tree to listen to the wise of the wisest at the village talk to us about marriage, christening, even circumcision, about leadership, and a whole host of compendium on Mandinka culture as practiced in the Gambia. Everyone listens, learns, and try to understand the importance of the message.

He started, after offering prayer for the gathering, saying that it becomes his duty to speak to us about tradition. The shifting sands of time may make his thoughts to appear a sphinx arising from the ashes of the old ways.

He said, "It's my pleasure to do my best bit at it," evoking broad smiles from the audience for we knew something interesting was about unfolding to us. He started the discussion by simply letting us know that every living thing one-way or the other procreates.

He said only man, through moral and judgmental powers enacted an elaborate form. The form being marriage following certain prescribed norms by society.

In general, nearly all humans practice marriage by the union or wedding of adult male and female into sanctioned and sanctified couples. There are monogamous, polygamous and even group marriages in some societies.

He emphasized that theses relationships between men and women are a blessing from God who chooses continuance of his wonderful creation in this fashion. The old sage stressed that the marriage was knoll and void and meaningless without blessing of the involved parents of both to be couples and priest of their faith.

He said, being unmarried at certain adult age, unless sickness and natural deformities prevails, was a taboo and culprits will and are severely chastised by their communities.

He told us that marriages were the couples are spoken for before they were born was in line. "How wise man?" Enquired his listeners eager for a much more concise and concrete reason for such unfair sealing of unborn lives, especially in today's generation and life styles.

He replied by telling us that such marriages were outcome desire on the part of the deciding parents not only to perpetuate long-standing friendships between proponents but also to reduce the possibilities of going for unwanted clowns.

This was followed by thunderous roar of loud laughter for it delighted the listeners.

Usually parents of both sides had or most likely experienced such offers to them or want to maintain loyal connection through to the next generation. There is no trade value in these arrangements made out of pure good and rewarding intention for the future couples and their parents.

Above all he emphasized, the proposals are not binding to the involved children to be couples. A well-meaning explanation is give to them when in their early adolescence as well as their twentieth year. If the would be couple express no doubt or have reasonable objections that would be the last chance before the intention of the involved parents is announced to the village and surrounding hamlets. Baring any objection the date of the marriage is set and the marriage is consummated at the Mosque on a chosen Friday afternoon.

He said there is no objection in marriages between tribes; in tribal and even Caucasian for they are God's children. What bad marriage is, being unfaithful, argumentative, unfulfilling partnerships, intolerance, and being lazy.

Time, tides and season waits for no man. Some marriages do come to an unfortunate end, called devoice. This tragedy happens when irreconcilable state persists between couples for long even after advisory intervention by parents, priest and community.

Devoice is granted to couples with understanding that children will not suffer its aftermath. Devoice are rare and far in between in rural areas as its outcome destroys and sets centuries of relationships between the parents of both parties in turmoil. Grand Pa counselled us to do all we could never to allow that to happen by first making certain our own side of the affair was immaculate and impeccable. He said the Pot cannot and should not call the Kettle black.

One cannot be demanding, deviant and intolerant and expect their partner to be overly receptive if not tolerant to them. The world is never always favouring to our way. No children like having their parents separated.

And the psychological effect on their lives cannot be measured and the pain and loneliness can only be told by those unfortunate to have devoiced parents. Living through such an experience is hellish indeed. In the event of death a husband, the wife, if she chooses, is normally adopted by the brothers of the deceased for her to stay along her children in the compound or village.

Most young ladies of child bearing age opts to move and marry to another man within the village or elsewhere, preferably not too far from the children of the previous marriage.

In most cases the children of devoice mothers stay at their father's home and are taken care of by the family of the previous deceased husband. Having said this much about marriage the sage turned onto the outcome of marriage, procreation and childbearing.

He said in a happy marriage between healthy couples children soon emanate. This brought in another roar of laughter while men peeked at the ladies pretending to be shy but most interested in this aspect of the lecture.

This was another occasion for paying homage to God, gratification, festivities and a host of pleasant responsibilities demanding more of us than we will ever imagine.

Parenthood teaches us different lessons of life, loving and caring way and managing of the upbringing of another tender human being is the most rewarding as well as challenging.

The changing phase of the newborn, toddler, teenager and eventually fully-grown adult/person is a marvel and unbeatable art only parents can experience. Grand Pa then rhetorically asked, what is the naming or usefulness of christening one's child? Few brave ones hazard an answer. Some said that we do so to give names and in illustrating one of the audience said, I am Jato, the strongest and king of the forest.

The old man laughed at the simplicity of the later answer and pointed to the next eager to cash into the discussion who, said I am Mansane Manneh and my father is well known warrior. At that juncture the old thanked them for their answers.

He accepted their version but added that there are a lot more to why we humans have this tradition in the animal kingdom. Christening, he began by saying that since mankind came up with the spoken word, he developed ability to communicate and differentiate things.

We all cannot be called Jato for it will be meaningless and confusing when one wants to call to a particular person in a group. Heads nodded in agreement with the sage. Hence, he gave a few tangible reasons why christening came to be a modus opera die in human societies.

Naming ceremonies serves as way of paying homage and expressing gratitude to God for letting us continue in this new comer and the other reason given for christening was to express joy that our loved one not only survived the challenges of pregnancy but scaled that risk in the last hour of child birth.

He said there was no greater sin than that of not appreciating, respecting, loving and protecting one's wife or mother. Mothers take risk and are the first in our coming to this world who risked their lives in other for us to join this earthly Garden of Eden. He jokingly asked if there was any father who went through the nine months pregnant. An old friend laughed and the wise sage retorted and said not you Mr. potbelly, drawing another laugher but more from the ladies who where delighted to note the impartiality of the sage.

Grand Pa admonished us to be always kind to both our parents, especially our mothers and wives. He then told us the third reason for christening, which was to provide a name for that innocent individual with which society will identify them.

A name can be colourful, historical and even off superstitious nature. It is a name for that individual and is echoed in his life unless changed or his or her death. Someone in the crowd asked what is in a name?

The old man replied they all sound sweet as a rose. The forth and last reason for christening was it gives the chance to couple or new parents an opportunity to share their joy and celebrate along with family, friends and the communities far and wide.

Christening brings people together and creates cohesion and bondage between villages. He warned us to note that no one is an island for we all need the other and it is always good to share our lives for what ever worth it may be.

We might just lift somebody's life by so doing. It will be good we open our hearts and share life than succumb to fear and innuendoes. Grand Pa concluded the christening subject by telling us that those were the times when women accept and appreciate gift, meaning babies, we gave them. It cements our loyalty to them.

A bust of laughter from the men's corner reverberated under the spreading Mango tree while the ladies applauded him. Among the last topics of the day the sage dwelt on relates with circumcision and why men do it.

He said in ancient days or times some disease occurred in the genitals of men and also it was noticed that some men experience serve pain when erective because of the foreskin tightening around the penis.

His blunt and frank talk about private parts of men was entertaining to the young ladies while embarrassing the old menopausal ones. All of which were drastically or dramatically eradicated when a wise butcher thought that removing a portion of the foreskin may just alleviate the agonies of these poor men.

The butcher tried it on few chronically affected men who after three months came with gifts to express gratitude for the blucher's coming to their rescue. Some even told of how they would not let their wives sleep the rest of the nights when they regained their manhood.

Again, laughter and peeking at some old men went on for a while before the sage proceeded with his lecture. He made it clear that such was not the case nor needed by women. He said it was mere stupidity that led to the current mutilation and circumcision of women.

This was not welcomed by the ladies and most elderly women protested for being castigated as stupid to recklessly cause harm to themselves in competition with men.

The old man pointed that pregnant women in ancient times might have had small pelvis for the exit of their babies to cause the village attendant to try to cut flesh out, similar to modern day's episiotomies, to widen the way to enable the baby's head pass through without much risk of death to mother and child.

This having brought relief to most ladies led to today's rampant female genital mutilation and an uncalled for circumcision. He said aside this error we must respect women even when we know it was a mistaken fashion.

Let us now devote the rest of the discussion on male circumcision. We have history telling us its origins as above but there are lot more Mandinka added aspects of male circumcisions.

We do it for the above reasons plus it is used to school or induct would be adult males into manhood and to prepare them for their responsibilities to themselves and community they came from. It engraves loyalty and team spirit in these men. It is a challenging 90 days crash course in sociology, responsibility and problem solving that would become memorable events in every male at the circumcision camp.

They are taught how to meet challenges of the seasons, fire, wind and storm, find solution and unselfishly relate these to the safety of all involved. Here African Pharmacopoeia becomes a miracle for as the green concoction prepared from leaves and tree barks are applied or plastered on to cut skin it stops bleeding instantly and allows rapid healing. No one ever suffers from tetanus infection.

Only a very few ever suffer from pneumonia for lying on cold floors. Local voodoo men and local herbalist handle the treatments of sick circumcised ones. Deaths from pneumonia or tetanus are far and rare in occurrence for herbalist had good medicines for it, which modern day African lost for lack of written recordings.

Today's so called civilized African allowed all these knowledge to disappear, in reliance on colourful pills and creams from lands beyond, right before their noses out of ignorance and the shunning of their traditions.

The old sage lamented about the error and Africans depending too much on the easy way out but failing to realize it might not be the best way out of having to use their brains to manufacture or modernize known local medicaments.

He worried that the young are drifting too fast towards colourful life while failing to know more about their own traditions and cultures. The end of the encampment moulds the boys into fully-grown mentally mature males according our world.

They return home ready to take reign from their parents, elders and become husbands as soon as possible. Yes the village is reborn again and certain of its continuity with its traditions upheld by incoming generation of adults.

The villagers and fathers of the newly returning adults gleefully server the occasion knowing that they too have done what was expected of them in the Mandinka context and will now continue to give guidance when and where needed but not enforcing it.

The handing over of Mandinka beliefs and customs from one generation to another along established customs or methods of procedure of the tribe is complete and the young now holds the baton. He said what he told us was based on style of the Mandinka traditions passed upon from centuries of creations.

With a stern face, literally pleading to us, admonished the gathering to be serious custodians of the Mandinka traditions and pass it on to our children so that they can disseminate it to their own. The sage then digressed and talks in great length about leadership as understood by Africans, especially the Mandinka.

Leadership starts with the head of house whole, heads of families, priests, village heads and chiefs, governors and the very head of state of the country. They all have one thing in common first they are voluntary servants of the people they govern or guide.

Secondly, their roles are akin to that of the umbrella, which when opened shades all and everything beneath it shades. It does not discriminate, that is engage in differentiation of tribe, advent colonialist, tribalism and foreigner phobia or encouragement of AK47 trigger-happy nuts and rebels.

Leaders must be humane, competent honest servants and not disguised mafia to their subjects. They should be kind, considerate as they themselves need love, and support until their time to die.

He reminded us that man has limited time on earth and should strife to leave footprints and examples that the next generation can follow and replicate for generations to come.

We wholeheartedly agreed with all he told and promised to be good leaders to family and state. In modern terms one can say comfortably those stockpiles of atomic bombs or weapons of mass destruction and dictators do not measure greatness. It is deep-rooted wisdom and dignity innate respect for human rights and lives, the intense humanity will make us more cherished and better leaders.

Africa would advance had the above stance been kept by our current leaders. It will make us able to contribute towards the future and progress of mankind.

The event of the day always end with a prayer and handshake with the old sage smiling up to his big ears. I would come last and say well done Grand Pa but you miss one point and he would smile knowing that I enjoyed the talk in good spirit.

Alpena Community College 2005 guest Students to Manding Medical Centre, njawarea taking need rest under the shade

Chapterv 48
RETURN OF AN AMBITIOUS VILLAGE SON

In the 50s, no one envisioned that a poor village boy, like me, would venture to leave his round hut home or village and fly thousands of miles across the vast Atlantic Ocean to the great apple city skyscraper New York, USA.
No, the big apple was never a day-to-day conversational topic among villagers. The talk of the village reverberated on the good or bad yield of the crops farmed for that season and who married whose daughter or the pending circumcision due in a couple of months time.
It was bad dream and foolhardy for any villager to think of such a perilous venture as was my plan. America, Europe or even famous Hong Kong became topics of conversation among a few due to the advent and arrival of radios and later television to our regions in the early 1960s.
There was no national radio in my country until 1963. We used to glue ourselves literally to Radio Senegal for International news and drama and theater entertainments. Television only surfaced in the Gambia in 1995.
There was only one government biweekly news bulletin, the Gambia News Bulletin, which served only government interest. It never said much about other places, not even America. Colonials kept us in the dark. Hence, it was suicidal thought to carry the idea of traveling to unknown continents.

It was recon as unfeasible because neither government nor family was in position to support such an ambitious mission. The challenging task or phenomena of carrying out a dream became my fate and I left the Gambia for New York in August 1967.

I was to engage in adventure that continued to today. Yes, dear reader, after many, many years of endless struggles and hard work I am now able to say I have the Golden Flees for the Gambia. In addition, I am finally on my way home, sweet home. I feel like I am heading for paradise.

Forgive me, for pinching myself to be certain that I lived to witness such a day in my life and to carry out this last leg of my sojourn. Allow me to be very elated and sentimental about today.

It is history in the making for me and I feel like being in cloud ninety-nine today. Dr. Alhasan Sisawo Ceesay of Njawara, Lower Badibou District, is finally heading back to the smiling coast of Africa. What a fit!! Preparing to return home carries enormous challenges and responsibilities.

Family and friends back in the Gambia were equally elated by the good news that I am finally returning for good after ten grueling years in the UK. Yes, I was returning to Njawara village and Manding Medical Centre for good.

However couched within this elation is a great expectation from all camps. Every one of them would want to know what have I brought from yonder land where milk pours out spontaneously from street pipes and money grows on trees waiting for able bodies to plug them off for keeps.

This golden mythical Europe and USA still exists in minds of yonder land. There would be speculations on the number of cars I brought with me, the quality of those cars, mobiles, yes, we too have been infected with the modern electronic bug and virus, televisions, cosmetics and clothing gifts etc, etc I am bringing along with me.

Was the rumored container mine and was it full of gifts for the villagers? Some even breathe a shy of relief hoping that I will employ their child or kin at the Manding Medical Centre.

There was rumour that I bought a small car for each of my daughters. The speculations, expectations and hope for salvation generated by the news of my pending return home became feverishly high that I felt inundated as to what to take besides personal necessities and the little humble possessions I had with me.

I know I cannot go home empty handed as during my student days. I am very happy to be heading home and I am determined to meet the challenges head on. As the saying goes, charity begins at home. Therefore, I bought dresses, shoes, Jewels, mobiles, and cosmetics for my wife and daughters.

I bought quality long Shari dresses for all eight brothers at a cost of an arm and a leg each. No, I did not forget my sisters, Binta Ceesay, Fatou Isata Ceesay, Jainaba Ceesay, Mariam Ceesay, Hawa Ceesay and Roheyata Corr-Sey.

No forgetting boys and daughters of my brothers. This is a family affair indeed. As for Njawara, Toro Bahen, and Kinte Kunda villages, I had a few hundred pounds for the elders to share appropriately among themselves or do whatever they wish with the gift. I bought sofas, office furniture and, computers for personal use. I got lots of pens and even watches to present to friends. Not all of the above dwarfed the magnanimous welcoming ceremony planned for my return. I fought cold feet when I went to tell my landlord my decision to go home to Gambia for good.

His face flushed with admiration mingled with misty eyes and expression of well wishes for my family and me. His last sentences were, "We are sorry that you are leaving the UK doctor. Do not worry, we will, by God's grace keep in touch. Bon voyage my friend."

I bagged all my humble possessions and gifts and then embarked on paying my last farewell visit to friends in Manchester, Colchester and London where I bought a one-way air ticket to paradise Banjul, the Gambia.

Friends in Manchester poured their hearts out in prayer and gave abundantly gift to take along to my family and friends. I remain grateful to each and every one of them. At Colchester, it was very moving. Mrs. Lorna V. Robinson and I have been friends since my medical student days in the 1990s when I was a trainee doctor at the Essex County and Colchester General hospitals, where she worked as a general nurse.

Lorna and I turn out to be good friends who worked tirelessly to bring Manding Medical Centre into fruition. She in the latter days of my sojourn to the United Kingdom stay was lifeline for both my family and I.

She and her husband Keith Robinson went to great lengths to ascertain that I was comfortable during my stay at their home in Colchester, Essex County. Recall that it was these kind angels who were instrumental in the setting up of the Colchester Friends of Manding Charitable Trust.

God blesses them and rain happiness in their golden hearts. Above all they opened up their hearts and pocket to support me and prevent from my starving to death while facing unfortunate circumstances that marred most of my stay in the UK.

They were magnificent and magnanimously generous to me and I remain eternally grateful to them for being so kind and considerate towards my family and I. George Eliot say it best about Lorna V. Robinson when he said, "Perhaps the most delightful friendships are those which there is much agreement, much disputation, and yes more personal liking."

Mrs. Lorna Robinson used to quote the great Albert Schweitzer's timeless saying to buoy me when my spirit gets low. It went like this, "Anyone who proposes to do good must not expect people to roll stones out of his way, must accept his lot calmly if they even roll a few more upon it."

There was mist in our eyes and uncontrollable drop of a tear or two dripping from our eyes down our cheeks as we bit the final goodbyes and urging each other to visit sooner than later. Other members of the Friends of Manding Charitable Trust were equally
touched but happy that I could finally go home and be with my wife and children who missed me more than can be imagined.

Those last moments remained eked in my brain because Mrs. Lorna Robinson's mould was a rare breed of good friends I ever had. One hardly comes across folks like her. They are few and swallowed by greater England.

Above all we are advancing in age. I look forward to not only seeing Keith and Lorna Robinson at the opening ceremony of Manding Medical Centre but to serenade them at Njawara village, the Gambia London, the world's historic nerve for power and regal pump beckoned as the train from Colchester snaked its way to this grand ancient city of Europe on the moat on the silver seas.

Here I met numerous Gambians who were helpful to me in my early days at the city. Among them was Aja jojo Cham-Ceesay. She is the adopted grand mother to nearly all Gambians in London and she doubles as the woman sage and matriarch of the London Gambian Community.

I lodged briefly at her flat in Mill Hill, London when I left Colchester in 2002. Again, the goodbyes and well wishes amidst misty eyes came from those present at the flat. Some even envied me for being able to disentangle myself from mythical greener pastures attraction and opportunities to go home and be with family and friends for good.

Yes, England is a big trap of mythical greener pasture that many find it difficult to part from once they found themselves entrenched in its net of false security and comfort. Going home made me feel like a hero serenaded by admirers.

I had mixed feelings of joy and sadness for I was leaving good friends. Most of who are or were getting old and we might never meet again in this life. Prayers and gifts rained in adding excess poundage to my luggage. Some walked with me to the ticket office, where I smilingly purchased a one-way ticket to paradise Gambia.

Other disbelievers walked with me to the bus heading to the Airport while others drove to see me off at terminal four at Heathrow Airport London. Soon our bus came to creaking stop and we disembarked, picked up our luggages and three of the fellows escorted and or walked with me into the terminal, as usual, full to the brim of travelers to the rest of the world.

I was eager to find my boarding queue and gleeful joined the good old Brit fashion, the long queue to the checking in counter. The flight to Banjul departs in three hours time. The boys hugged me and left and I looked at them until their disappearances in misty cloudy space of England.

Yes, it was pungent moment for me. Alas, I was alone in a crowded terminal and finding it hard to believe that I survived all the mayhem my life endured in these past ten years in Great Britain. The hall sounded like being among homing bees. However, soon it was my turn to hand in my tickets and have my luggage checked for the Sabena flight to Banjul, via Paris and Brussels enrooted to Africa. All said and done I had a big suitcase for which I paid a hefty sum of money for the 16kg beyond the allowed 50kg weight permitted for flights to Africa. It was worth it and leaving a few pounds sterling behind was a charitable act.

Checking in and tags all done we were asked to follow the line leading to the boarding lounge for our flight due to take off in an hour barring unforeseen delays.

On my way to the boarding station Lorna and Keith in misty tears and half Brits smiles but stiff lipped bade me farewell with hugs and wishes for safe flight back home.

They too have become part of me as I theirs. Lorna yelled I would come to visit soon. Huge the little girls for me and tell them auntie loves them. I remain eternally indebted and will carry this family's love with me till my last days in life.

Walking happily ten meters further down I came across another queue. This one dealt with departure formalities, where security, custom and immigration worked acidulously to clear the queue in time for boarding.

The security and customs searched my handbags and marked then ok for boarding. I met a very nice young fellow at the immigration post. He was all-smiles and upon seeing the last date of visa renewal looked at me and I told him my last renewal was in another expired passport already in the Gambia.

He looked at my face, as if saying, "Please go on. We have heard many twisted truths than this simple one".

He even jokingly asked if he was invited to my home in the Gambia. Guess what he was a regular visitor to Gambia and had spent nearly most of his holidays in the Gambia. Our brief chat let me know he knew the Gambia well. So I told him he is more than welcome to share bread with my family and I in the Gambia if he would not enter any unasked for recording. We shook hands and he stamped my passport. I gave him my card and he in turn gave me his e-mail address to link with him when in the Gambia. All is well that ends well.

He is proof that some youngsters are not bureaucratic and do have insight as to why people come to the UK. They know we come either to learn or make money to send to our beleaguered families back in Africa or other developing country I will certainly e-mail him an invitation to come to my home as soon as I am reposed.

Shortly after the last passenger got through boarding formalities a door was open to allow us start boarding our flight out of the UK. The big Sabena Air was flying via France, Belgium enrooted to Africa.

At the door of the big plane was a gorgeous lady who gave broad smiles and welcomed us onboard the flight destined to Rabat Morocco, Dakar, Banjul, Free Town and Conakry. I took my seat at a window in the non-smoking area. I pplied my seat belt before take off time.

The Airhostesses did their routine demonstration of usage of oxygen masks, safety gear under the seats and exit windows and what to do in serious air turbulent. Very soon the metal bird took off away from England's grey and almost cloudy skies heading to a much yearned brilliant bright and warm African blue skies.

Meals and refreshment followed but I could not eat much for eagerness to meet my family, especially the youngest of my daughter, Roheyata Ceesay, who I left at the tender age of two years. She looked grown and taller than me.

I can't wait to huge her and the other girls. A minute after take off I took a last pip at the UK bellow it and me cold cloudy weather I was happy to leave behind for good.

Three hours after the flight from Brussels the seat belt sign came on and I looked through my window. And "vous a la!" it was the Roget rocky mountain and Sahara Desert of Marrakech in Morocco. Yes, the heat bellow was harbingering to temperature of the desert bellow us.

We taxied and at last! I was once more on African soil not far from my own homeland, Gambia, the smiling coast of Africa. We viewed exquisitely beautiful embroidery and tapestry by none other than Arabian weavers.

I did not buy any but servo their beauty and intricacy of the display and carvings of both stone and wood. Forty-five minutes latter we were in our seats with seat belts fastened and ready for take off to the last leg of our flight to the Gambia.

The big jet engines rowed louder and louder until we swerved into the sky as if to challenge the African falcon or Eagle. Off we went far away from gray cloudy English weather into the blue skies over the mountains and desert sand leaving dust bellow. The desert became an empty void full of glistening sand dunes.

It was sand dunes until above 15, 000 feet before I lost sight of the desert amid clouds and longed for blue African skies. As I ruminated after take off, it became clear that things do not just happen, people make them happen and that the villagers would be more than happy I took this painful venture in their behalf.

With it also life taught me how to look after myself and that I can only give what I have and have learnt not to rest on my oars else I fall into very deep and turbulent sea of troubles.

The trip thought me to have to keep on running to remain with the best or be where I am. It sharpened my desire to learn and perform and work hard for what I believe possible even if at the time most may not want do or see things the way I saw or perceived.

I have learned to control my irritability and sensitive but remain very sensitive to the needs of others. This may be intriguing but this is the simple me appealing for you to join me to bring more medical aid to the villagers by making Manding Medical Centre at Njawara, in the North bank Region more viable and valuable to all living in the Gambia.

Ms Eliza Jones, Secretary Friends of Manding

Chapter 49

A PRIDE OF THE VILLAGER

Ideas are good but most be believed and allowed to grown into reality. Surely, God changes not the condition of a people until they seek to usher change. Today there is a tint of pride in our hearts and for which the glory belongs to God and every one who directly or other wise encouraged the fruition of Manding Medical Centre.

To my international friends, I find it hard to put into words or find one to thank you with for being with Manding Medical Centre. It shows that we have common desire to help others. Where there is unity of purpose there surely will be hope and chance to bring relief to others.

Today embellishes the magnanimity of your hearts. The Gambia remains eternally grateful. Who amongst us, except me, would have believed that what was once condemned as a white Elephant of a dream destined to doom or the least a catastrophic failure is now proudly flying the flagship of hope and medical service to the region while rewarding generations to come.

Friends in America and Europe use to ask, "Why are you hung up on a dream and the Gambia. Many of your peers have gone for the greener pasture and have secured comfortable lives for themselves and their families.

Here you are in utter destitute state with little or no one in Gambia caring". I patiently, replied that where my umbilical cord is buried is where my body rests eternally.

It is my feeling that just as each of us does have different ways of reaching and helping our homelands returning to serve the Gambia was my patriotic duty no other attraction can prevent me fulfilling. The provision of medical aid and service to the villager was not only a responsibility but for a charitable trust. My soul, head and heart, to paraphrase, are buried into the Gambian sand. Long lives Gambia! Yes, my critics were on the mark but failed to dissuade me for Manding Medical Centre was better and of bigger reward to the people than their scare mongering of it being a dream. Yes, I rather suffer the status of a temporal second-class human than yield my worth for a worthless end. Our countries need whatever skill or training we accrue from our travels overseas. To deprive them tantamount to a sacrilegious wasted life. Yes, there were times when I could not get a second-class stamp to put on an envelope without begging for it. Further more I slept in many rough places, including the cold and dangerous streets for a night at times more. Buoying me in this pit fall was knowledge that I was doing some thing right and needed by my villagers or the Gambia at large. The enduring of those dark and lean days is worth the means of it all. An old man once told me, "If you wish to find the true way, right action will lead you to it directly". We all took the right action for my critics showed me the other side of the coin and so what need to be done to achieve my goal. How great my foot soldiers were in making certain Manding Medical serves the villager for the Gambia. Today makes me close to thought that the villager has of me and I am with them in their reflection of me.

Chapter 50

AN ODE TO MY FAMILY

Family is nor oddment but one's dearest flesh and blood. This ode goes to my kith and kin of the Njawara Ceesay kunda dynasty. First praises be to the Almighty God for letting us descend to this Garden of Eden through Sisawo Ceesay and his brother Abdulie (Baba Salah) Ceesay.

Both were devoted, loving parents who taught us to seek knowledge, faith and be responsible participants in our communities wherever we may find ourselves.

Equal thanks goes to our mothers who stood by these men and helped them steer us in the right direction for a better tomorrow. Binta Ceesay is now the oldest matriarch of the family and our gratitude and appreciation goes to her for enduring all of us through decades.

She has always been a buffer and like our parents a very straightforward person who does not take sides when it comes to dealing with us her younger siblings.

Bravo to Binta Ceesay for being an envied bright example to the family. Dodou Ceesay is the oldest male child in the family. He having spent three quarters of his life within the Fula tribe tends to perceive life in that light.

He is my brother of the same father and mother. He is a very quite and shrewd fellow and well versed in the Quran. He too is moral support to all of us despite our philosophical divergences.

I am next oldest in the family in this Njawara Ceesay Kunda clan and there is enough about me in my books that can fill the back of a stamp. I just believed in reaching out to touch others and bring help, hope and relief to their lives.

Hence one of the reasons why I became a medical doctor and proprietor of a village self-help health NGO, Manding Medical Centre at Njawara village, North Bank Region, the Gambia, West Africa.

Omar Ceesay, the gentleman of the family, is next oldest and a headmaster at one of the Primary Schools in the Kombo enclave.

The guy is so nice and gentle that I used to tease him as Baba Sallah incarnated. His attitude is carbon copy of his father Abdulie Baba Sallah Ceesay. The mannerism, laughing, and humaneness are akin to none other than Babab Sallah Ceesay.

He is not the arbitrator but the easygoing fellow of the Njawara Ceesay Kunda dynasty. Ismaila Sisay, the genes of his mother persist in him. He is a nice fellow but of a no nonsense type among the clan. Thank God he is not violent but does not let anyone push him around.

He is forth in line when it comes to affairs of the clan. He is also a headmaster in the Kombo enclave. He like his father Baba Sallah Ceesay is skilful entrepreneur and at times too competitive. Our fifth in line male child of the Njawara Ceesay Kunda clan is none other than Ebou Ceesay.

Ebou is a technocrat and very gifted electronics. He once manned the Gambia's earth satellite for years before becoming Director of Operation at Gamtel House in Banjul, capital of the Gambia, West Africa. If there be any financial endowment or call luck in the family, it went to this fellow. We all praise him for help he quietly gives to the members of the clan at various times for various reasons. Ousman Ceesay, nick named "OS" is the youngest living male child of the clan.

He too is faring well but another carbon copy of the old man Baba Sallah Ceesay. He is easy going but not laidback fellow. He is a hard worker but not cut throat competitor.

No, no I am not forgetting our sisters. Jainaba Ceesay is next older lady to matriarch Binta Ceesay. Jainaba is one girl that epidermises and archetype of her mother. We have had our moments but still remain good friends and team members of the clan. Fatou Isata Ceesay is our last sister on Sisawo Ceesay's linage.

She is warm at heart and very easy to relate to, even though the Fula syndrome shrouds her. She participates fully in all activities of the Njawara Ceesay Kunda clan. Mariam Ceesay, is Huley Ndongo's elder daughter for Baba Sallah Ceesay. Mariam is an easygoing girl.

She has amiable attitude and personifies the old man Baba Sallah. She too is contributor to the clan. Last but not the least is Hawa Ceesay, the youngest girl of Huley Ndogo.

She is very intelligent and smooth operator. She has an exemplary character but fierce defender of her tuff. She too contributes to day-to-day function of the Njawara Ceesay Kunda Clan.

All said and done there is no way I will exchange any of the above for another kin. They are very kind, team like most of the time, and share lot of good qualities and examples to help propel the next generation of the Ceesay family at Njawara. We are not financially rich but have abundant love, care, and participatory zeal than most in the village. Bravo to Njawara Ceesay Kunda. May God grant us longevity and prosperity with peace in this life.

Alpena Community College students guest of Manding Medical Center at Njawara, Gambia, 2005

Chapter 51
ODES TO PRESIDENT NELSON MANDELA AND AFRICAN PATRIARCHS

Who but a patriot like President Nelson Mandela, the Madiba, can engender such unique international respect and admiration? Here is a simple man, teacher by profession, who strongly believed that God's children can exist in harmony in non-racial communities.

In his vein and for having spoken out for the natives of South Africa, he suffered twenty-seven years of incarceration in the most inhuman conditions of Robin Island in South Africa. Some of us would have succumbed to the weight and indignities imprisonment brings to one and strikes a deal to be free.

This chance he turned down several times unless the ugly serpentine head of racial segregation yields to human rights and full citizenry participation of every South African in the running of the affairs of his country.

He echoed the voices and feelings of decent people worldwide, and his refusal to pay lip service to his stand earned him much respect and admiration, which galvanized an avalanche of international protest and sanctions that almost crippled South Africa.

The same should be applied to all countries under military or dictatorship rule. What is good for the Gander is supposedly very good for the Goose. Democracy and human rights should have the same meaning worldwide and not cloaked with current double standard international interpretation couched under terms like the developing and developed countries guided by queasy rules. South Africa crumbled under pressure and finally did the right thing but unthinkable at the time.

The world in great awe stood still to watched a miracle unfold before it on that historic Sunday of February 11,Th 1990, marking the release of humble and simple teacher Nelson Mandela.

The world joined throngs of millions upon millions of South Africans to cheer and to let go a big shy of relief. For Nelson Mandela, it was the beginning of life all over and continuance of his commitment to human rights and the equality of God's children, for lack of better phraseology, the races of mankind.

The Madiba, Nelson Mandela saw human beings to be like him and not indignant varying hues as black-white, brown or tribalism injected in the minds of the weak, and selfish societies.

No wonder he worn resounding victory by landslide during the first multiracial election ever held in South African history. He set up an accommodating government and asked the people to reconcile and together forge a new future for South Africa. There evolved a democratic and peaceful transition to a multiracial South African governing body.

Will other African rulers follow his brilliant examples? That would be the day hell would turn into paradise and the Earth will stand still to salute mankind for finally making some sense in the way they govern.

The colonialist did their best to mesh up and left Africa but their replacements out surpassed colonialism by some of the most heinous physical and economic mayhem we see inflicted upon innocent people by outcast regimes that forcefully took over the governing of the peasants.

Today, in Britain, President Nelson Mandela and supporters celebrate the end of seven progressive and peaceful democratic years with a flawless transition of a democratically elected government under the stewardship of president

Tambo Mbeki. Today, there are only two former presidents of our time (President Jimmy Carter and Nelson Mandela) who travel the glob to bring help and relief to others.

Most former African presidents either died in office as an aftermath of a bloody coup d'etat or seek voluntary exile to some supper power state to chock on their spoils their stole from poor subjects they purportedly have been ruling democratically. With the exile of dictator president the UN and so-called supper powers gleefully praise themselves for having solved that country's nightmare.

For us Africans in the third world countries the replacement of heartless and corrupt politician by an undemocratic government rule of blood thirsty, merciless military juntas or rebels is more of adding an insult to injury than relief or kind and humane consideration of the people.

President Nelson Mandela is an enigma for all decent politicians to immolate, especially fledgling African governments. Nelson Mandela rekindles hope, joy and relief to our beleaguered hearts.

Allow me to digress to some stalwarts who began the race to self-rule in Africa.

Which generation of the forties can forget the grand contribution of the Pan African Movement and its struggles to topple colonialism and its empire mentality? African got sick and tired of colonial masters' policy of divide and rule with no development of the ruled at sight. Hence, Abdul Nasser's refusal to allow a foreign power to control the Suez Canal led aspiring politicians in sub-Saharan Africa to galvanize the people and ask for independence.

The seeds of the Pan African Movement in the bodies of Kwamin Nkrumah, Modibo Keita, Saikou Ture, Jombo Kenyata, Odinga Odinga, Ndambandi Sitoli, Julius Nyere, Patrice Lumba, Tafawa Balewa, Leopold Sidat senghore, Milton Magai, and Dawada/David Kairaba Jawara just to name a few became bees in the colonial bonnet.

Nkrumah led the communist path and lost the support entrusted him by Ghana and se went Modibo Keita of Mali. This should have woken the world to the fact that although Africa gave its back to colonialism she was in no way replacing it with communism.

Trigger happy inept military men fatally brought down Tafawa Balewa setting Nigeria into a helter-skelter path of ruin. The dust from that has just started settling.

Being Africa's most populous and one of the large countries Nigeria should set leadership examples and disallow further military rule. Hence, even though not of West Africa we cannot forget the likes of Patrice Lumumba of Congo who stood against the Belgian rule only to be brutally vanquished by Mabutou and his colonial proctors. Nor can we not salute our great man of Tanzania, former president Julius Nyerere.

He too lost the support of Tanzania because he went communist. Dawda Jawara was brought down by his complete reliance on the city machinery and tsars, which resulted in the founding father and farmers feeling betrayed and completely neglected and left hopeless in redressing their grievances and need by the Jawara regime.

Hence, no one came to its defense when the solders moved onto overthrow his regime. Gambian do not like military rule. We believe solders belong to their barracks and can be relied upon to defend the country and not turn over night half-baked political administrators or presidents.

To us juntas are pots calling the kettle black. Neither is the choice of the people, nor will we ever be free or progress under such stagnant situations. Good leaders and good governance are rare, few and far apart.

Who would be so heartless as not to recognize and sympathize with pain, humiliation and cruel rend the Jews met at the death gas chambers in Germany or the Palestinian youth meeting wanton, brutal and premature death for seeking the right to a piece of land to call home and dignity?

Oh my Lord why do thou watch men inflict such cruel ends to each other? Please rain peace into their hearts for them to be human again. Violence only breeds violence.

I wish there was a way to take the Olive leaf for them to make peace for themselves and for the shake of new generations of Jews and Arabs to come. It is wrong to use religion as a cloak to kill the innocent

We have seen amputation and wanton mutilations of people, women and children by rebels and yet so-called governments go to round table negotiation with leaders of such heinous devils and perpetrators of pain and suffering.

What can amputee child ever do with the stump of man's evil and wicked deeds left to remind him or her of mindless dark lowly creature of greed ravaging raving Africa? Let us live and let others to live this life freely as God would allow them on earth.

Did eons ago slave trade and today's go get rich quick Materialism left us disinterested and desensitized to the feeling and acceptance of our fellow human beings?

Has history of the world wars not taught us war has only losers and that carnage and spilling of blood is nothing but an indication of our weakness to confront the truth?

There are no victors after a war for both sides have by then lost someone dear to a family e.g. a father, businessman, husband, an uncle, a son or a friend, needless to say thousands if not millions of innocent women, the elderly and children die in the aftermath because of governments cowardly fearing to face the peace looking at it straight in the eye and stop both sides warring.

The truth is that no one wants to die, that is why we run to seek help as soon as something goes wrong with our health. We all in varying degrees feel hung pains and do need basic things like shelter and love or to be loved. Why then do we kill each other like rats for situations we can settle amicably if we allow truth to be our only yardstick?

If this is civilization then I rather be with the Neanderthals. A wise man once said, "When you come to the last page, close the book." Hence let us close the war-mongering book and rally for peace and coexistence in this unique planet of ours.

Oh, Mahatma Gandhi, Martin Luther King, Nelson Mandel and Jimmy Carter will you wake us so that we take courage to face the challenges that lies ahead not with nukes but hard work and erasing of ignorance and injustice from the surface of earth. Life is very short and we need bury our swords and nuclear arsenals and hold onto each other dearly for our children's sake and ours.

This is what the Mandelas and long ago heroes preached to us even though we continue to give deaf ears in the name of nationality and unfounded mythical power status. Does it have to be star wars or Armageddon to bring us to the simple reasonable realization we could benefit not only our generation but also future generations if work together as civilized human beings?

It is my believe that it is obligatory on us to leave better and inspiring foot prints for coming generation to follow and build upon. Let me bet if Martian were to land on earth and were to follow one of two directions i.e. one marked with blood and the other wheat and flowers they would all follow the later peaceful trail to happiness.

Hence, let us congregate for the sake of peace, progress and prosperity while shedding our hound like attitudes of wanton debasement of life.

We in the villages use to wonder why the worlds supper powers are so bent on giving charity from its hard-earn taxpayer's money as grants to inhuman governments.

We do not believe these donations to be of serious intent as donor should by now know that 99% of monies and good sent to these pilfers end up in private saving accounts in equally corrupt international banking services else where.

Stop sending aid in support of bad leaders and see in we will crumble. The thieves who have been misusing your generosity in the name of Africa or the third world will be on their knees asking for your handouts but not the farmer who never had help from such gestures of yours.

Do not let anyone convince you that we need dictators, rebels, or military juntas to govern us. We have been governing ourselves well before colonialism took root in our countries and are more capable now than ever.

Just keep your guns, dirty paws and forget the double standard interpretation of democracy and human rights for the third world countries and see if Africa and places like her will not shine better than the so-called developed world.

It is my fervent wish that the world powers will now cease supplying money and good to heinous governments and to direct their resources I creating environmentally friendly jobs for their own and in helping to educate and train the masses of the third world to allow a generation of enterprising people who can pass the baton of progress to others.

We beg and pray that no one trades or supplies weapons or facilitating it production or anything facilitating fertile grounds for rebel movements worldwide.

Help us build schools and universities along with the determined nature of the African to get reed of poverty to allow our people leap by lightening speed into the third millennium.

I hope the supper powers will heed to appeal like this and stop dolling money to murders and pilfers in the name of the helpless masses that indeed, remained helpless because your aid never reaches them.

Please wake up to these facts if you care about doing something worthwhile for the third world. Do not stain human decency by negotiating with human butchers like rebels and heads of military juntas. They are bandits and know no better than destruction of life and property.

The world yearns for character like nelson Mandela, simple, gentle and accessible to all. I believe, even in his final hour, he will be dancing to thank God for giving him the taste of life and the privilege to serve his fellow men.

So I speak for endless millions of peace lovers when I say thank you Madiba, Mr. President Mandela for bringing the sunny side of life and hope to us all. We will strive to work as one civilized human race under peaceful democratic rule.

Chapter 52
I REST MY CASE

Paul in a letter to Timothy 2 said, "I have fought a good fight, I have finished my course, and I have kept the faith." I hand this work for publication for you to be judge of the ravages of the years and how my life was that of extreme ups and downs.

In reality, I am very grateful to God even though my life met with various misfortunes, the most unbearable being the delay in my becoming a physician.

My life as witnessed in these pages was an assembly of trials and tribulation emanating from roadblocks placed on my path by inhuman laws and unfortunate dark circumstances.

Life has taught me to submit to divine decrees, whatever they may be from God. I feel on the whole overly rewarded and delivered even though I had no family here in England nor was I as lucky as others who can feel and experience the warmth of their wives and children on daily basis.

I succumbed to it as the way things were going to be for me and lived with this state of affairs while in Manchester, England. I experienced various turns of fate, enough for ten eliphant loads, while on the little moat of the silver sea called England.

With my travels I was able to see Europe, the Americas and have learnt a great deal from it as well as experienced numerous unforeseen adventures thrown on my path.

My life in England was pain; fear of deportation, hunger, extreme poverty due to joblessness, solitude and missing my wife and children I loved dearly.

I had a huge sense of duty in relation to the villagers and was not ready to fail them because of personal comfort or pleasures. Consequently Manding Medical Centre and benefits to be accrued from it became my most if not the only occupation and direction in life.

Here is Manding Medical Centre if managed well it will do justice to rural health service for the next generation of Gambians to build upon. The medical center is now a recognized charity in both the United Kingdom and America.

I am committed to serve the villagers so that life of the children and young people would be better than mine when I was young.

I hope Manding Medical Centre becomes a model testimony of the boy from Njawara village who doggedly struggled to become a doctor and despite various twists of life is able to provide medical aid and service to villagers in rural Gambia.

May be this will strengthen some other fellow to strive to do better than I did to bring health and happiness to the region. I hope my adventure persuades youngsters that man is capable of a lot more than he thinks he is capable of.

Our footprints must be inspirational to give heart to new coming Gambian generations. Twenty years ago none would dream of thinking me becoming an author or to challenge powers as I did in this little frame and life of mine.

I met a beautiful Maraka girl while I was in Monrovia, Liberia, West Africa. Fatou Koma is daughter of Elhaj Ansuman Koma and Jalian Ture of Kindia, Guinea Conakry.

Her positive attitudes towards me lead our meeting on weekends at cousin Sainabou Jobe's home. We started going out together and very soon I had the courage to ask her hand in marriage.

There was no bone of contention with regards for my love for her. She was the darling of my heart at first sight and I was not going to let a fly land on her from that day onwards.

We had a simple wedding because her father did not quite approve of me because of fear for his uneducated but very pretty daughter being dump at one stage of the marriage for another educated city girl.

I, in the long run, allied his fears and he ended up being one of my best friends and confidants I had up to the day he went to his maker. Fatou Koma-Ceesay and I are blessed with three beautiful daughters, princesses Famatanding Ceesay, Binta Ceesay and Roheyata Ceesay.

All of who, unlike me, had their schooling start at the age of five. The elder girl is aspiring to become a doctor and had been admitted to start her premed courses at Alpena Community College in Alpena, Michigan, USA.

Together Fatou Koma-Ceesay, the children and I went through all the tragedy of hunger, poverty and other sad experiences my sojourn in the quest of the Golden flees for the villager brought to us.

Fatou Koma-Ceesay initially hated Manding Medical Centre for she felt it consumed me and took me away from her and the children.

The call got me entangled in a web of unfortunate circumstances and laws. The marriage had at one point almost spiral to its end as wife' move became questionable. Nonetheless she remained a good mother and wife who took care of the girls in my absence. My mother in-law was battered by confusion and as to why Fatou stuck it out with me under such immense hardship.

Love is stronger glue! We loved each other and so we were able to stand by the other in good or bad times and my trip to England was the worse ever in our connubial life. It caused great turbulences in the marriage but I stuck with it for love's shake and the children who I love dearly.

Today, we are back together as family under the same roof while planning and supporting future of our darling girls. God bless Fatou Koma-Ceesay's heart and be reassured of endless love I have for her.

For now Dalliance said it best for me when he said, "Say of me what you will and the morrow will judge you, and your words shall be a witness before its judgment and a testimony before it justice. I came to say a word and I shall utter it. Should death take me ere I give voice; the morrow shall utter it.

That which alone I do today shall be proclaimed before the people in days to come." I wrote with the hope the life enshrined herein will serve not only as an inspiration to the despondent but a lesson never to allow this sort of experience it passed through this planet.

I wrote in the hope that life enshrined in my books will serve not only as an inspiration to the despondent and downtrodden but a lesson never to allow this sort of experience it passed through this planet. I wrote because I felt that my life has something worth revealing to the world to engender tolerance and understanding between people and their governments. I risked revealing today for all of us to learn from it and move to a better and rewarding future. Among the forces of life is one that stands a certain lofty peak a few is endowed with or able to explore its heights.

Ambition urges us to leave the lower surface of earth where the ordinary people live and ascend to heights that pierce the heavens. This mission has led to numerous Erie paths but for me this Pell-mell towards a better medical service for the neglected villager was a worthwhile adventure.

I am profoundly grateful and indebted to my wife Fatou Koma-Ceesay and our daughters, princesses Famatanding Ceesay, Binta Ceesay and Roheyata Ceesay for enduring all the pains that we went through in thick and thin times during my sojourn to America and England.

Also my deepest gratitude goes to cousin Yata Sey-Corr for helping keep my family hopeful. God bless her heart eternally. I forgive my own brothers and sisters who refused to cater for my family in my absence. Hello, hats off to Sey Kunda!

Chapter 53
MY ENDEARING LIFE AND FATE

For a while in my native innocence all I had was erudition and wit, which always misfired. Everything I touched came to nothing but failure, whatever I tried to achieve came crashing down on my head. At any given moment some mishap befalls me and nothing surprised me any more.
I took my current plight with stride and smiled as fate taunts me. I remain poor but my in extinguishable strong will enabled me face life squarely and took me through these dark days.
The twist of fate abated but my age had advanced beyond retrieval.
The above apocalyptic life is indeed trying moments for my family and I.
To view/purchase books: amazon.com Dr. Alhasan Ceesay books.
DR. ALHASAN SISAWO CEESAY, MD

Chapter 54

ABOUT THE AUTHOR

I was born in February at Njawara Village, Lower Badibou District in the North Bank of the Gambia. I am a scion of a Mandinka and Fulani tribe and am one of five siblings. I had my education at Kinte Kunda, then Armitage High School, ending up as a registered nurse at the Royal Victoria Hospital, Banjul, before embarking to the USA on my medical degree quest.

I graduated from the American University School of Medicine in Montserrat, West Indies, in 1992 and returned to the Gambia to start setting up a self-help village health NGO Manding Medical Centre. The Gambia Government and the Badibou local authority register NGO Manding Medical Centre. The centre has treated more than 90,000 patients free of charge.

I am married to Fatou Koma-Ceesay and we are blessed with three beautiful girls, Famatanding Ceesay, Binta Ceesay and Roheyata Ceesay. Unlike me, all of them started school early without the roadblocks I had to cross in my early years.

I am currently a medical officer at the Royal at the Royal Victoria Hospital on study leave. I write to raise funds for the building of a village hospital at Manding Medical Center, Njawara, The Gambia, West Africa.

Purchasing this book or donating cash or kind would boost our goal of providing medical aid to villagers, especially children who frequently die prematurely from malaria and childhood diseas due to lack of facilities and trained personnel. I hope that this work will inspire others to help bring much needy medical service to rural Gambia.

Alpena Community Guest students at site for Manding Medical Centre's children hospital, Gambia

Mission

Our objective is to improve the healthcare delivery to villagers, educating youths on STD and Drugs and quality of life for the people in rural Gambia. The Manding Medical Centre strives to accomplish this goal through primary health care and disease prevention, the promotion of health policy, health research and increased access to health care education for the people in the Gambia.

Have your manuscript become a book by submitting it for possible publication to acquisitions publishes Kunsa. Com
Please contact us to expose your work globally.

PUBLISH KUNSA.COM

GAMBIA HAS DECIDED TO BE FREE: PRESIDENT ADAMA BARO WHEELNG YAHYA JAMMEH TO EXILE IN GUINEA EQUITORIAL JANUARY 2017

www.ingramcontent.com/pod-product-compliance
Lightning Source LLC
Chambersburg PA
CBHW071229300426
44116CB00008B/971